Putnam Camp

Putnam Camp

Sigmund Freud, James Jackson Putnam,
and the Purpose of American Psychology

◆

GEORGE PROCHNIK

OTHER PRESS • NEW YORK

First photo insert:
Photos of Susan Blow, courtesy of Carondelet Historical Society.

Second photo insert:
Freud family at Jacob Freud's grave, courtesy of the Freud Museum, London.
View of the Allgemeines Krankenhaus (General Hospital), ca. 1895,
© Michael Huey and Christian Witt-Dörring Photo Archive.
Freud's study, courtesy of Susannah Stone.
Emperor Karl and Empress Zita at the funeral of Emperor Francis Joseph I,
November 1916; *Vera Sacrum* cover, January 1898, and *Cabaret Fledermaus*
program cover, 2nd issue, 1907, all © Michael Huey and Christian Witt-Dörring
Photo Archive.

Copyright © 2006 George Prochnik

Production Editor: Mira S. Park
Text design by Rachel Reiss

This book was set in 10.8 pt. New Caledonia by Alpha Graphics of Pittsfield, NH.

10 9 8 7 6 5 4 3 2 1

Library of Congress Cataloging-in-Publication Data

Prochnik, George.
    Putnam camp : Sigmund Freud, James Jackson Putnam and the purpose of
psychology / by George Prochnik.
      p. ; cm.
    ISBN 1-59051-182-4 (978-1-59051-182-4)
    1. Freud, Sigmund, 1856–1939—Friends and associates. 2. Putnam,
James Jackson, 1846–1918. 3. Psychoanalysis—History.
    [DNLM: 1. Freud, Sigmund, 1856–1939. 2. Putnam, James Jackson,
1846–1918. 3. Psychoanalysis—history. 4. Freudian Theory—history.
WM 11.1 P963m 2006] I. Title.
BF109.F74P76 2006
150.19'520922—dc22

                                                              2005034312

For my parents,
Marian and Martin Prochnik

Contents

Introduction

WOULD SIGMUND FREUD have been able to make sense of America today? Would James Jackson Putnam have been able to hold onto his unbounded idealistic faith in the inevitable progress of civilization had he been confronted with a typical night's roster of pop culture entertainment? Above all, do Freud and Putnam and the conversation they carried on hold lessons for us today, at a moment when self-reflection is often impugned as self-indulgence, a sign of weakness or, at the least, a practice meant to be confined to our houses of worship and private prayers?

The suburb of Washington DC in which I spent my wonder years could have been Disneyland for the psychoanalytically inclined. It wasn't only a matter of the pale, hollow-eyed father of my dear friend Francesca with his twitchy, penciled moustache, who lived down the street from us and was found to have been raping Francesca and her older sister for over a decade before a police car arrived to coast him silently away; or the stiff Vietnam vet dad who flushed into mulberry rages whenever he heard a helicopter overhead; or poor, lovely Mrs. Freid who cut my family's hair while her two blonde, cereal-commercial children played about her legs until she became convinced that a spy plane was watching her, relentlessly watching her, so that she had to fly away from everyone; or Mr. Fells, who played Uncle Sam every year in our Fourth of July parade because he looked the spitting image of the recruitment poster icon, and yet was finally driven out of town for squeezing babysitters and reveling in supermarket kleptomania at the local Safeway. Beyond these standouts, within a mile radius of our little brick tract house on its quarter acre moat, there were opportunistic pedophiles, a flasher who dressed in a bunny suit, one father murderer, drug abusers and vandals galore, animal torturers, arsonists, and wild-eyed emaciated Christian Scientists who refused to give money to UNICEF because the money kept communist children alive.

It would be comforting to think that incidences of mental malfeasance in my home suburb were disproportionate to the national mean. I am, alas, unconvinced that our little mall-bound settlement exceeded the volume of psychological stigmata of any American community priding itself as ours did on its safety, wholesomeness, and shopping. This raises the question of what does nourish mental well-being in our culture.

OVER TIME, I'VE wondered more about whether the lurid sexual, sadistic, and just plain crackpot behaviors festering behind the pasteboard doors of my suburb could in fact be fit into any classic psychoanalytic paradigm. Freud remarked in more than one place that repression was the core concept of psychoanalysis. Was repression truly a relevant idea in trying to comprehend this neighborhood? Somehow, the inhabitants of my suburb managed to be simultaneously repressed and all too virulently manifest. Not infrequently, people were repressed until the moment they crossed the linoleum threshold of their basements. Then all hell broke loose. As though our suburban homes were modeled on Freud's fanciful topography of the mind, with the basement playing Id, the living room, Ego, while the bedrooms were—what? Beyond the pleasure principle?

It's not, of course, the case that these kinds of questions bothered me in the years I was growing up. At the time, my concerns were largely, selfishly, confined to a riff on the gnostic doxology: How did I get here? What am I doing here? And, how the hell can I get far away?

My father's family had fled Austria in 1938. From a privileged world of comfortable apartments in the 3rd District, where family members worked as physicians, psychoanalysts, opera singers, cantors, and scientists, taking their pleasure in Vienna's palaces of culture, in Alpine summer chateaux, and inside Opel Olympias orbiting the Ringstrasse, my father found himself washed up in a Hell's Kitchen tenement and on the verge of starvation. The Jewish welfare society that kept his family from perishing encouraged them to move to Boston where there waited a subsidized apartment and an English language program that could help my grandfather train for his American medical license. In Vienna, he had been a prominent general practitioner with an illustrious clientele, including the high-ranking Nazi official who warned him that they were on the list to be transported within twenty-four hours. He was already in his sixties by the time he arrived in America, and though he managed to learn English well enough to rebuild a practice focused in gynecology and become a respected diagnostician—with a loyal share of female clientele soliciting from him something akin to psychological treatment—his practice never did well enough to enable the family to approach the lifestyle they'd enjoyed in Europe.

Still, my grandfather got his two sons into Boston Latin School and Harvard. It was while my father was in Cambridge studying geology that he met my mother, who was then teaching at the Shady Hill School, a progressive learning environment with a density of analyst offspring so great that one can only speculate how many teachers ended up prostrate on the couch themselves.

My mother's experience of America could not have been more antithetical to my father's. Born at Boston's renowned Lying-in Hospital ("where every day is labor day"), she was descended on her own mother's side from Cabots, Putnams, Lowells, Higginsons, Mathers, Cottons, Hutchinsons, and many of the other high-minded families that made up the insular, indeed ingrown, world of Boston's chosen families. Her father, a surgeon, was the first of a clan of impoverished Scottish immigrant tobacco farmers scattered across the Carolinas to break ranks and head north, in his case to Harvard Medical School. Once there, excepting his fondness for breakfasting on scrapple and grits, he washed away his southern heritage like so much red clay.

The home in which my mother grew up was a period piece of nineteenth-century Bostoniana, in which a Copley portrait of a bonneted great-aunt confronted a tropical watercolor of a dark native washing himself in a Samoan waterfall by LaFarge, and both were reflected in a centerpiece of antique silver service. My mother's reading rarely strayed into racier ground than the heretical speeches of Emerson, or the primeval metered yearnings of Longfellow's *Song of Hiawatha*. Even her speech patterns hearkened back to the conditions of an earlier era and no matter how often she was corrected by her impatient brood, she never stopped calling the refrigerator an "icebox" or our cavernous, fluorescent, airport-size supermarket, the "grocer's."

Indeed, my mother's New England upbringing with its tea parties, tobogganing and visiting cards may have been an even worse preparation for life in a late twentieth-century American suburb than was my father's upper middle-class Viennese Jewish life above the Belvedere Gardens. There was, anyway, little to choose between them for facilitating entry into the physical culture of consumerism, enraged driving, TV IVs, bong-athons, purple perversion, and purblind patriotism that dominated life in our subdivision.

BEHIND THE SCREEN of our home's picture window (identical to the blinded rectangles of other picture windows facing ours from across the street) were clustered, like stubborn prisoners, remnants of my parents' pre-suburban existence. The impressed articles consisted of a few pieces of heavy old dark furniture, three or four decent paintings from the Old World and the early modernist New, along with a handful of beautifully bound books. In the midst of this retinue, there was one object that held special fascination for me. Neatly framed on my sister's bedroom wall hung a scrawled letter from Sigmund Freud to my great-aunt, the pediatric psy-choanalyst Marian Putnam—"Aunt Molly" as she was known to us. The note was written in the early thirties, in an effort to arrange a meeting with Molly some time after she'd arrived in Vienna to begin her analysis with Helene Deutsch. Freud expresses a rather amused yen to learn about Molly's experience of the Austrian capital and regretfully informs her that he can enlighten her no further about his brief analysis of her father.

It's not immediately clear why Freud himself didn't analyze Molly. Her cabinmate on the Atlantic crossing and friend, Edith Jackson, had less apparent claim on Freud's attentions, and yet found her place on the couch at 19 Berggasse. Perhaps Molly turned down the opportunity because, with her habitual self-effacement, she resisted the idea of further imposing on the tired, sought-after old man. Or, perhaps, her hesitation was more com-plex, having to do with the long, charged friendship that her father, the pioneering neurologist/psychologist James Jackson Putnam, carried on with Freud, and with what she knew Putnam had told Freud concerning her-self. Or, just possibly, Aunt Molly's deferral before the prospect of a literal Freudian analysis had to do with thoughts she kept silent about regarding Freud himself. It's not unlikely that Freud himself balked at the thought of reawakening ghosts from the period when he was most messily in the fray of the battle to establish psychoanalysis.

Regardless, there on the quivery sheetrock wall of our ranchstyle home hung the handwriting of a twentieth-century giant—palpable evidence of a friendship which was the genie of much family lore. It joined the photographs carefully mounted in my grandmother's family album of James Jackson Putnam and Freud at the Weimar Congress in 1911 and the published trove of letters between Putnam and Freud that spanned from the time of their meeting in 1909 to Putnam's death in 1918.

There was oral testimony to this intimate relationship as well. I heard tales of Freud's visit to my great-grandfather's quirky Adirondack retreat, Putnam Camp, where I myself spent many summers growing up. The stories of Putnam Camp in the early years of the last century presented images of high-spirited eccentricity distinct from the weirdnesses of the suburbs. In costumed masques, intrepid mountain climbing expeditions, opera sing-alongs, and bonfire recitals of wilderness odes, turn-of-the-century Putnam Campers evinced a jolly communal creativity. I knew, as well, of other traces left by the Putnam-Freud friendship. Though I'd never seen the object itself, I was mesmerized, for example, by the legend of a metal porcupine that Putnam presented to Freud as a commemorative gift at the end of his American visit. I was proud that Freud kept the Putnam Camp memento of that prickly mammal on his desk until his dying day.

In my youth, these fragments of a story never struck me as puzzle pieces. The relics of the Putnam-Freud friendship functioned as stepping stones away from my home to a more meaningful world of study and professional service, in which unabashedly weighty ideas and idealistic ambitions had credibility. What I knew of the Putnam-Freud friendship suggested a dedicated exchange between two men of science, doctors of the mind, bent on harnessing the powers of current medical knowledge and imagination to comprehend human psychology so as to heal the troubled spirits who came to their offices as supplicants for an elusive solace.

It was my mother, Marian, named after Molly and Molly's mother Marian (and wimpled legions of Marians before her), who first talked to me about the relationship between her grandfather and Freud. She did so matter-of-factly. James Jackson Putnam was one of the most eminent psychologists in Boston; it was natural that Freud would seek him out when he was trying to win American acceptance for his theories. When I was a bit older, I began to read for myself about Putnam's unimpeachable reputation and the crucial role that stature permitted him to play in legitimating the psychoanalytic movement. If Putnam, whose pure-mindedness was above suspicion, could champion Freud, then surely, the rationale went, it could not be true that Freud was the pernicious, sex-crazed scandalmonger his adversaries in America and elsewhere accused him of being.

In 1909, my 63-year-old great-grandfather, blue-blood descendent of Puritans, Unitarians, and Transcendentalists, was arguably America's most respected neurologist and one of the country's foremost pioneers in the new Boston psychotherapeutic movement. A pillar of the New England professional and social elite, he'd married a Cabot and was close friends with the James and Emerson families. He'd also built a striking record of communal activism, both by working with established charities and by leading independent campaigns against the use of neurologically damaging substances in common building materials. Throughout his life, he was known by friends and detractors alike as a man of great integrity and ardent intellectual curiosity. By 1909, he should have been ready to rest on his laurels. But in fact, for years, despite the security of his personal reputation, Putnam had been frustrated with the clinical deficiencies of professional American psychology. Along with its inadequacy to patients' needs, the failure to deliver on the part of institutionalized practitioners also radically upped the competition from alternative mind-body-spirit movements like the Christian Scientists, Emmanuel Movement, and New Thought enthusiasts. Thus, even though Putnam was a respected figure near the end of his road, he was primed for revelation.

In the other corner waited the Mittel-European, cigar-chomping, Tarock-playing, antiquity-coveting, Faust-loving Jewish contender, Sigmund Freud. Where Putnam couldn't have been more ensconced within Boston society, Freud, as a first-generation Jewish emigrant from points east, wasn't accorded real respect by Vienna until the Austro-Hungarian Empire itself was a moribund affair. The success of Jews in the city's cultural life never translated into easy mobility in the bureaucratic institutional world of universities on which medical professionals depended for their standing.

Thus Freud was as much predisposed by social context to cultivate a psychology based on individualism, isolation, and the catastrophic conflict between inner drives and civilization as Putnam was conditioned to develop a theory of psychology grounded in communal responsibility and the potential for harmony among man's higher instincts, social progress, and the universe at large.

In 1909, Freud's overriding ambition was to turn his discoveries into an internationally recognized scientific discipline. America, though never exactly Freud's slice of *Sachertorte*, seemed to offer the best hopes for the transmission of his theories to the next generation. Sporadically throughout his career Freud was as concerned with the possibility of society's transformation as was Putnam, but from Freud's perspective there was no larger movement of civilized progress to glom onto; he himself would have to play the lonely role of visionary conqueror à la his lifelong heroes from Moses and Hannibal to Napoleon.

Ecce Putnam and Freud. They came from opposite worlds, cherished polarized ambitions, and promoted seemingly irreconcilable visions of human nature—and yet they struck up an unusually fruitful collaboration. The two met on Freud's one and only trip to the U.S., where he'd been invited to lecture at a small Massachusetts university. By the end of Freud's visit, Putnam's admiration was confirmed. He threw himself into the cause, doing everything in his considerable power to win over his American colleagues to the value of psychoanalysis. He wrote papers, lectured, debated Freud's U.S. opponents, practiced analysis on his patients, and did everything else possible for the last nine years of his life to make psychoanalysis take hold in the U.S. He and Freud became friends. By the time Putnam died in 1918, psychoanalysis had been launched in America. It was posed to begin an ascent that would continue uninterrupted for decades.

PART OF THE reason I liked this version of the story was because having, along with the Putnam-Cabot side, Viennese Jewish relatives myself who, if not always analysts, still spent the bulk of their time compulsively analyzing each other, it was comforting to imagine my opposing parts harmonized.

However, later on, as I became interested in actually reading the letters between Putnam and Freud, the simple outlines of their story tangled. It's true that Putnam came to be an important supporter of Freud, but throughout the years of their correspondence, the two men were engaged in a zealous intellectual debate that counterpointed the expression of their mutual good will. They were at odds over everything from the purpose of psychology and human potential to the nature of the Creator and ultimate meaning in the universe. It's a sort of duel in which Putnam swishes and swashes with an old-fashioned buckler and Freud fires a gun. Reading the letters, I found myself hopping to either side, enjoying the quixotic crash of Putnam's heavy blade, but getting a helpless kick out of squeezing the lighter, more deadly trigger of Freud's irony.

For much of their interaction, Putnam preached to convert Freud to his metaphysical vision of the universe. Freud, on the other hand, fought to justify his belief in a godless, scientific order of the world and to inspire Putnam's perfect faith in the ostensibly secular insights of psychoanalysis. In the midst of their intellectual arguments, both men also dropped their weapons to reveal disconcertingly intimate secrets of their home life. Why was it that Freud, who was notoriously opaque about the involutions of his domestic life, chose to share with Putnam his lack of sexual desire for his wife? Was it just a case of I'll-show-you mine if-you-show-me-yours since Putnam had first exposed his own dread of marital intercourse?

THESE WERE ONLY the explicit complicating factors of their friendship. Though I loved reading Freud and talking about his insights, it was impossible reading in greater depth not to feel, well, *horrified* by the manipulations, cruelties, and rampaging monomania of which he was capable. It seemed perfectly plausible that when Putnam got enthused about "Freudism," he was just plain snookered. If that were true, what became of Putnam's heroic championing of Freud?—not to mention my own Zeppelin stairway, if not to heaven, at least beyond the Beltway. Forget the question of whether or not he would have understood the place. Was Freud himself obliquely implicated in the psychology of that suburb?

As for Putnam himself, for all his undoubted uprightness, I found that he sustained a long, intense relationship with Susan Blow, a female ex-patient whom he kept mum about, despite the fact that she influenced much of what he wrote to Freud. Why the stealth? Putnam sounds at times almost saintly in his self-sacrificing will to do good. Wasn't that, in itself, suspect? We are trained nowadays to look for the big dark secret that the righteousness in a person's outward behavior is fabricated to mask. Clearly

Blow and Putnam carried on an exchange that was unconventionally intimate for a turn-of-the-century man and woman outside the bonds of marriage. Might that not have included the *coup de grâce* of physical consummation?

And then there was the whole matter of what it was that Putnam's impassioned philosophy actually consisted of. I felt bored into by Freud's own voice as I read the metaphysical essays of my great-grandfather and thought, *Lord, what I wouldn't give for a little spritz of Jewish irony in this desert of ethical earnestness!* And these reactions brought with them their own ecumenical measure of Freudian guilt.

Naturally, I wanted to know who won their debate—I suppose so that I could be on the winner's side. On the most basic level, Putnam's obscurity relative to Freud seems to answer the question. Freudian psychoanalysis, even when the object of attack rather than praise, is still a reference point. How many people have ever heard of Putnam's philosophically inclined psychology?

And yet, gradually, as I learned more, I began to wonder whether it was in truth an open-and-shut case of one lineage catapulting itself into the future while the other shriveled and died. Perhaps the ways in which Putnam's ideas have been carried forward through time are just disassociated from his name. Even where there's no direct influence, there are points of affinity between Putnam's theories and the work of a disparate array of thinkers that merit contemplation. These echoes indicate that whatever troubled Putnam in Freud's approach was no more fully resolved by Freud himself than it has been by the more authentically scientific varietals that have arisen in his wake, from cognitive therapy to the chemical protocols that HMOs favor most. Putnam, I came to believe, for all the fustian verbiage of his belief system, had put his finger on one of the great dangers of psychological treatment down to our own day.

The essence of Putnam's quarrel with Freud was that psychoanalysis could not stand alone. It was insufficient to denude the troubled patient of his or her delusions; he or she had to be given some higher motivation to live as well. Putnam argued that psychoanalysis had to be supplemented with philosophy and attentiveness to the complex needs of the human spirit. The psychologist was ethically bound to help patients discover their "best selves" and then use the innate impulses of that self to aim toward the ideals

of communal obligation and self-transcendence. If one concentrated exclusively on the self without a second therapeutic movement to connect
that self to others beyond the individual, how could one avoid eventual
absorption in the self—self-absorption?

Any number of popular psychology movements touch on aspects of
Putnam's thought. Martin Seligman's theories of "positive psychology" and
"flexible optimism," for example, echo a constant theme in Putnam's debate with Freud: the idea that just as important as the "demons" and negative influences Freud identifies in the unconscious are the deep-rooted
instincts to good that patients can benefit from heeding. Best-seller M. Scott
Peck's theory that this world is about "soul making"—a mental process
whereby we can guide our ego by aligning ourselves with God's greater
plan—offers another instance of an idea that could have come straight from
Putnam's work. James Fowler's notion of "stages of faith" through which
everyone can pass to universal self-transcendence mirrors Putnam's theories of graduated spiritual evolution along the road to sublimation. Even
Oprah seems at times to be exploring principles of psychological well-being
that share elements with Putnam's psycho-spiritual theories.

And yet, on the question of self-effacement and communal responsibility, advice from these figures usually tends to become fuzzier, more
mantric, or anyway contextualized by a goal of personal happiness that lies
exterior to Putnam's lexicon.

The era in which Freud met Putnam was an astonishingly exciting one
in America—one of those rare interludes in which the sense of human
possibility bursts spacious so swiftly that it seems for a time to escape boundaries altogether. It may not have been the Italian Renaissance, but it was
the period in which Mrs. Isabelle Stewart Gardner succeeded in re-creating
block by marble block a dazzling Italian renaissance palazzo on the improb-
able mushy ground of the fens bordering Boston's Back Bay. In the arts
and sciences America underwent a rich cross-pollination, while in politics
the Progressivists succeeded in galvanizing the sense of unbridled possibility into a concrete political platform that led to the implementation of
ambitious, reformist policy measures. This revitalization was driven by an
original fusion between spiritual philosophy and applied scientific practice.

Why, at this moment of brimming possibility, did America choose to
embrace Freud with a fervor he had never enjoyed in Europe? Ironically,
Freud's initial reception by Putnam and his colleagues may not have been

pointing the way to the future so much as closing a final chapter of the idealistic past. Freud himself never ceased to ponder uncomfortably on the ramifications of the muscular embrace America had ready for his theories. Karl's aphorism from the 1930s must have stuck in his craw, "I understand that psychoanalysis is a big hit in the United States. It figures: the Americans love everything they haven't got, especially antiques and the soul."

THE TENSION IN the relationship between Sigmund Freud and James Jackson Putnam is embedded in the name of the discipline to which they both devoted the better part of their lives. Freud insisted that the movement he founded was the culmination of psychology in the modern dictionary sense of the word, the apogee of scientific investigation into mind and behavior. Putnam, on the other hand, strove to marry the contemporary profession of psychology with its register of etymological significance. Thus, for him psychology was also, always, the study of *psyche*, an evolving theory of the soul. In the course of their conversation, each man sought to prove to the other that his own approach to psychological knowledge was the more accurate reflection of an objective, absolute truth. In this sense, they both straddled the millennial border with one foot in either century.

The chronicle of the friendship and debate between Freud and Putnam is psychological history of a particularly fraught strain as it is also, of necessity, the history of a moment when questions of what psychological health and illness consisted in, of how diseases of thought were bound with pathologies of the spirit and flesh, and of what all this meant for psychological treatment, were of the utmost urgency for many of the world's leading doctors, theologians, and philosophers. Even the more pessimistic like Freud nursed a romantic conviction that answers to these questions could swerve history toward utopia or hell. Among the more hopeful, like Putnam, a belief took hold that solutions to age-old problems of psychology and neurology were imminent and could engender an unprecedented harmony between the individual and society. The vision of cascading integration between brain, mind, body, soul, self, community, and the cosmos, signaled the advent of a new American dream, and of a fresh, non-doctrinaire faith in spiritual redemption.

ONE COMMON METAPHOR patients use when they speak of the effect of psychopharmaceuticals is that the drugs simply cut off the bottom register of their emotional capacity. As one friend on antidepressants put it, "the lower floors are just gone." This analogy conjures up the archetypal suburban basement. Yes, they were often frightening bizarre places, but they were also the location of the extremes of passion. Much of the psychological treatment strategy of our own day seems to be based simply on an ideal of compliance. Putnam unquestionably had ideas about how to cultivate a meaningful, good life while preserving the passions intact. Did psychoanalysis deepen or truncate the development of these insights?

In one of Putnam's most important papers, he invoked the biblical sentiment that "the people who do not see visions shall perish from the face of the earth." He argued that if it was within the analyst's power to help patients "sympathize with the strivings through which they seek to raise themselves to a better plane," the analyst could help them to achieve transcendence that strict Freudian analysis precludes.

Freud, on the other hand, was acutely aware of the dangers posed by "the people who see visions," the sorts of dangers that, among the noncompliant, are all too present in our own time. In one of his most revelatory letters to Putnam he wrote, "What I have seen of religious-ethical conversion has not been inviting." Invoking Jung's crisis, Freud talked about his disgust with "saintly converts." At some of Freud's s best moments, his conviction of all that *can't* be known trumped even his belief in his own theories.

These are antipodal positions that we jerk between today with a new breed of hysterical tremor. Yet all of us are in some way faced with the challenge of integrating the fundamental concerns of these two men. That is to say, how do we unite a critical understanding of our past and present behavior with a sense of social purpose for the future?

CHAPTER 1

The Utter Wilderness

*Of all the things that I have experienced in America, this is by
far the most amazing.*
                Sigmund Freud to his family, September 16, 1909

THE CARRIAGE WAS curious; the woods were impenetrable; the mountains were mammoth; the animals were novel, noisy, and persuasively wild. Freud, Ferenczi, and Jung, knocking knees in the vehicle provided them by their hotel in Lake Placid, peered into the tangle of glacial boulders and soaring timber as they bounced ever deeper into the Adirondacks.

History offers any number of poignant, unlikely conjunctions of person and place: Ovid weeping on a remote shore of the Black Sea in present-day Romania; Benjamin Franklin promenading through the Tuileries in his raccoon-tail cap; Eichmann seated patiently in suit and tie in his glass cage in Jerusalem. However, none of these exceeds in improbability the image of diminutive, soberly outfitted, 53-year-old Sigmund Freud rattling along in a two-horse buggy over a rutted dirt road into the heart of the American wilderness. How many cigars did he puff down to steel his nerves between Lake Placid and Keene Valley? Did he fret about whether he'd brought the right walking shoes? Wonder about how he would manage his rustic toiletries? Freud was openly anxious about the hair erupting across his face, no matter how dutifully he pruned himself. There were all sorts of Semitic stereotypes to worry about in comparing his hirsuteness with the prevailing state of Christian depilation. What in God's name was Freud thinking that wind-slashed mid-September morning as he made his way to my great-grandfather's Adirondack hideaway, Putnam Camp?

————

IN PORTRAITS FROM the era, Central European medical dignitaries all seem bent on butting everyone else out of the image with their own idiosyncratic renditions of "The Penetrating Glare." Freud himself, cigar cocked in his fingers like a pistol, often looks as though the photographer has just called him a name and Freud is about to shatter the bastard's lens by willpower alone. Unlike other members of his milieu, however, Ferenczi appears, in the main, hopelessly approachable. He was even more petite than Freud, not to mention pudgier and prone to wistful expressions of dreamy pleasure or pain. "Consciously I very often have *ideas of smallness*," he wrote in an early letter to Freud.

Ferenczi entered the expedition to America less in a missionary attitude than squire-style, to provide a measure of fawning support for the master on alien shores. He was often described as the most emotionally intuitive and sympathetic character among the early analysts. More than Freud, Jung, or Jones, Ferenczi worked to refine the practical methodology of analytic technique in the interest of actually trying to heal patients. This led him to push for an increasingly active role on the part of the analyst in the exchange with patients—a position the reverse of the worshipful passivity he evinced in his relationship with Freud. It was only at the end of his life that Ferenczi became skeptical enough to remark in his diary that, on account of their untruthfulness, "Freud no longer likes sick people."

Yet notwithstanding his nurturing sidekick role in 1909, during the North Country carriage ride, his nerves may have gotten the better of him. It was all somewhat savage and nauseating, wasn't it? As the journey stretched on—five hours to travel a mere twenty-five miles—Ferenczi's will to play Panza at the psychoanalytic round table began to peter out.

Jung's unstoppered relish for the whole scene could not have made things easier. As Ferenczi and Freud held on for dear life in a carriage shaking as though it were riding the belly of a dyspeptic divinity, Jung was eating up the view with the same gusto he'd displayed at the ramshackle hotel mid-journey, where they'd been plied by the natives with corn on the cob and brown bread with slabs of bacon. The message of all this was that the hour approached when Freud would need Ferenczi as never before. Freud already counted on him for "elevation of mood." Soon Ferenczi would prove himself capable of more noble repayment, as he wrote Freud, "I thank (I never get away from thanking) you."

His colleagues reinforced his suspicions. Jones observed to Freud that he found the American attitude appalling. "They want to hear of the 'latest' methods of treatment, with one eye dead on the Almighty Dollar, and think only of the credit, or 'kudos,' as they call it, it will bring them."

Nine months later, in response to one of a litany of nasty gripes from Freud about Putnam's colleague Morton Prince, Jung wrote Freud, "For some time now I have noticed the gentle zephyrs of prudery blowing across from America, for which Morton Prince seems to have a quite special organ. Everyone is terribly afraid for his practice, everyone is waiting to play a dirty trick on someone else."

Thus, from the outset, as would be the case for the remainder of his career, Freud's feelings about America were directly tied up with issues of money. And questions of money were associated with fears of American prudery, which in turn went hand in hand with fears of American whorish trendiness.

In point of fact, in the matter of Hall's invitation Freud's paranoias were not unjustified. On the very same day that he'd sent out the letter to Freud, Hall wrote an invitation to his own former teacher, William Wundt, the star of Leipzig who'd set up the world's first institute of experimental psychology and had been William James' mentor. To Wundt, Hall offered an honorarium of $750 (3000 marks), almost double what he'd proposed to Freud. Hall indeed was trying to hustle Freud to Worcester on the cheap.

Matters might easily have ended there. And the history of psychology in America could have veered off in any number of other directions. Putnam, for one, might have been dead by the time opportunity rolled around again for Freud to visit America. And without Putnam's impassioned Fifth Column defense of analysis from within the ranks of Boston's medical elders, the reception of Freud's theories in America might have been very different.

However, in mid-February Hall sent Freud a second letter saying that the financial situation had changed (hmm), enabling the Clark board to double Freud's honorarium (to exactly Wundt's quotient of $750 or 3000 marks), and also announcing that the date of the conference had been changed to September.

Freud now happily accepted, but the pattern of lurching between extremes of hope and hopelessness that would characterize the whole trip was in place. Freud had fallen straight into the classic American bipolar rake's progress—a kind of Hogarth saga sans morals: back alleyway poverty to limelight lottery-winner on a whim of blind fate.

THE DOCTORS SAILED to America on a North Lloyd liner named the *George Washington*. As their ship entered New York harbor, Freud, Ferenczi, and Jung watched the approach of envy-green Lady Liberty, the ghost necklace of the Brooklyn Bridge, and the panoply of downtown scrapers circa 1909. Tired and ill after their ten-day passage, they floated through the East River mist toward the approaching land mass of America. Suddenly, Freud turned to his companions and said, "Don't they know we're bringing them the plague?"

Three weeks later, they were on their way to Putnam Camp.

As Freud came closer to Keene Valley, Putnam paced in an accelerating fluster around Camp's rocky, uneven ground. It's a March Hare picture with long-legged Putnam substituting for the rabbit's cry of "Oh the Duchess! Oh the Duchess!" the lament of "Oh the Professors! Oh the Professors!"

Putnam was above average in height, trim and hale, with bony cheeks, a close-cropped white beard, and spectacles. On an average day, dressed in a well-worn black suit, jogging at a dogtrot along the Charles from his house in Back Bay to Mass General, he looked the picture of spare, conscientious, post-Calvinist pluck. And yet, this was not a typical day and his lucid vigor was imperiled. When Putnam felt the convergence of too many conflicting demands he tended to go a bit blurry, and unfortunately such was the case on the 15th of September in 1909. He'd arrived at Camp much later than planned—only a couple of hours in advance of the doctors—because he'd had to tend Molly, his favorite daughter, as she recouped from an appendectomy back in Boston. Putnam himself had performed the emergency operation on the kitchen table right on Marlborough Street, with light streaming in pale milk from the dusty street level panes. He'd wiped clean the table's wooden grain himself. He could still see the bloody incision and bare glow of Molly's 16-year-old body.

Yet, even before that medical crisis, things had been off kilter and overcharged. The decision to go hear Freud had been last second. Neither he nor his close friend William James was planning on going to the Clark

Conference at all. Putnam had warned Jones that if Freud lectured at an off-the-beaten-path location like Clark he'd be neglected. Though logistical demands would never stand in the way of the grail of intellectual enlightenment for Putnam himself, he had sufficient misgivings about the materialist course Hall was championing to consider skipping the celebration. Hall's advocacy may well have detracted from Freud's already limited appeal. Basically, Putnam agreed with James' assessment of Hall as a figure whose personal psychology was "queer and torturous" and who could not bear clarity in any form because clear-mindedness offered his fearful nature no avenue of retreat.

Whereas Putnam enjoyed the feistiness of Ernest Jones and had been interested enough in Freud's work for several years to read most of his papers that made their way to the States, he felt that analysis took too much time and demanded too thorough and degrading a penetration of patients' histories to constitute any sort of redemption of psychotherapy. Elements of the treatment could be useful, but nothing truly seized the higher Boston imagination.

Further complicating matters, Hall had incomprehensibly not bothered to publicize the final dates for the conference until the summer, so that everyone in the effulgent squint and squirm of New England chandelier society had already booked their Septembers. Putnam himself had planned a long overdue trip the weekend of the Clark Conference to Cazenovia, New York, to visit the most stimulating woman he knew, his ex-patient and philosophical mentor Miss Susan Blow. Putnam saw no problem with the fact that this brilliant lady had gone from being his medical charge to being his spiritual guide in the wilderness of contemporary philosophy. He paid homage to her genius and hoped he'd done something to help free her to use it. More than that, he acknowledged the vital place of her teachings in his own understanding of the universe. Just as she was dependent on him in ways that required trustful, homely attentions, there was no conversation that gripped him more strongly than hers in the glassy twilight languor of her lake country verandah.

But then Putnam and James had met up in Cape Cod at the end of the summer to spend a few days talking and pacing Cotuit's raked sands. The upshot of their conversations had been that they convinced each other that maybe they'd better look in at Clark after all. Hall had assembled a rather extraordinary array of scientists: twenty-nine lecturers in disciplines ranging from mathematics, history, and psychology to physics and pedagogy. Even two Nobel laureates were on the roster: Ernest Rutherford, who identified the nucleus in the atom and did pioneering work in radioactivity, and Albert Michelson, whose advances in optical precision instruments led to breakthrough spectroscopic investigations. In line with Hall's own specialization, psychology had been made a focus of the conference. It was true that Hall had a tendency to obsess, indeed to drone on about the role of sex in mental life. Apart from the genital-jammed epic of his 500-page *Adolescence*, Hall's major work, *Education Problems*, had one 150-page chapter alone entitled "Sexual Pedagogy." Putnam insisted there was something in all the erotic welter nonetheless. James felt that whatever there was tended to be confused with a great deal that wasn't. They debated back and forth while the soft waves trilled in and out between their old, curled bare toes, and offshore their children captained tiny gay turnabouts in a two-reef breeze: "Sneaker," "Hoolet," "Crab," and "Bob" racing this way and that between the bright buoys across the gray combers.

IN THE END, sacrificing the chance to put a little fire to his soul out of fealty to his professional conscience, Putnam canceled on Blow. He could hear her quiet disappointment quaver through the miles of barren air dividing him from Cazenovia. The chain of events then being that Putnam stood up Susan Blow only to almost have to miss Freud anyway because of Molly's morbidly enlarged appendix. As though one had caused the other and the other had caused the one. Why was it that these subterranean connections always seemed to proliferate for Putnam when it came to the fathomless needs of intriguing females?

But things had been sorted out—in a fashion. And the lectures had proven riveting beyond his dreams. Professional and private quandaries that had been haunting Putnam for years seemed to be directly addressed by Freud's words, to the point where he'd decided that nothing was more vital than to hear more from Herr Professor. Which was why his wife Marian had now taken over sickbed duty in order to allow Putnam to tear off on the six-hour journey from Boston to the Adirondacks. He'd made it ahead of the foreign doctors—just—only to find that Cousin Selma Bowditch, wife of one of Camp's co-founders, and Putnam's medical colleague Henry Bowditch had decorated the entire grounds of Putnam Camp with a fluttery parade of red, white, and black German flags. Confused by the intricate patchwork of pre-World War I national identities, she'd organized flag-sewing parties to celebrate the fact that all the doctors were denizens of Deutschland, despite the fact none of them were. So that less than an hour before Freud's arrival, with Putnam having had no chance whatsoever to compose himself and review even one of the myriad questions he was yearning to ask, he was still consumed in tearing down Teutonic emblems from unexpected places, between hemlocks, behind pillows, under sundials, and above suits of armor. The maniacal whimsy of the women in Putnam's family could be a terrifying thing.

It's hardly surprising that minutes before the carriage conveying Freud, Ferenczi, and Jung swerved off the main road onto the Camp driveway, Putnam was just managing to strip free of his city clothes to wriggle and strap himself into his signature Putnam Camp leather lederhosen, carefully crowning the whole ensemble with a special felt cap and twitching a cocky feather into the brim. Someone started ringing the Camp triangle bell.

It was two-thirty in the afternoon and as he bounded down the grassy path to meet the doctors' conveyance, Putnam was thankful at least that Camp was largely deserted so that the distinguished guests didn't have to confront the full battery of eccentric Putnams, Richardsons, Lowells, Lymans, Bowditches, Lees, Grinnels, and Greggs then in residence. Ten guests were off scaling a series of high peaks known as "The Range"; another six had raced away on a lengthy overnight hike for "The Lakes"; and a smaller contingent had gone tromping up Indian Head, where frequent stream crossings gave hikers a chance to indulge in the rock hunting that the youngest of Putnam's four daughters, Frances, referred to as the "labradorite craze" sweeping Camp.

Putnam was even grateful that Marian was back in Boston, tending Molly and orbiting on her endless planetary circuit of social calls to relatives. He wanted full peace so that the doctors would be most at their ease, with nothing to distract them from the free flow of profound conversation. Now at last they were here all together and, after shaking their hands and showing them their cabins, Putnam wasted no time introducing the foreigners to the Putnam Camp way of life. He invited Freud, Ferenczi, and Jung to accompany him on a hike. He promised it would be undemanding. What could the exhausted men say?

Freud prided himself on his walking skills. Even in his fifth decade, when he traipsed the Tyrol with his boys, Freud often vaulted ahead, leaving them panting far behind. His oldest son, Martin, was, by his own admission, *frightened* by his father's speed. Other holidays Freud handily scaled the broken marble wonders of antiquity while his contemporaries staggered like blind men below.

Off they charged, following the brook bordering one side of Camp up a hill, straight into what Jung called "a northern primeval forest." It didn't take long for Freud to realize he'd entered a whole new genus of hiking. Rain had been falling intermittently for days, and bitter wind was still gusting through the trees. As the doctors scrambled over snake dens of roots buckling up from black mire, and scaled a series of rude wooden ladders propped against boulders, Freud realized that he'd sorely miscalculated his conditioning for Adirondack exercise. He informed his family with masterful Viennese sarcasm of how his host had instantly given the foreigners "the opportunity of becoming acquainted with the utter wildness of such an American landscape." He confessed that they'd taken trails and slopes "to which even my horns and hoofs were not equal."

Adding insult to injury was the sight of Putnam himself, spry and cheerful, skipping ahead in his preposterous lederhosen, expounding on the natural beauties of their surroundings without a stitch in his side. There was no talk of analysis now. Putnam rolled off the names of the peaks they viewed from different overlook ledges, like nightmares sprung from Fenimore Cooper's unconscious: "Upper Wolf Jaw," "Sawtooth," "Panther Peak," "Iroquois," "Nippletop."

The men struggled up yet another and another precipitous forest-clad slope to finally reach a violent cliff edge. When the clouds were effaced enough to glimpse the view, there was nothing to see but further layers of thick foliage, huge moss-covered boulders, and tall trees—endless other chains of remote, uninhabited mountains stretching off to infinity—what Jung described as a "wild glacial landscape" coated as far as the eye could see in virgin forest.

But what was it the doctors were actually seeing as they stomped about above Keene Valley? As Thoreau said, "It is in vain to dream of a wilderness distant from ourselves." The question of the true relationship between civilization and nature in the United States haunted Freud for years as he tried to envision the future of analysis in the New World.

WHEN FREUD, JUNG, and Ferenczi were in the Adirondacks they were still viewing nature which, by European standards, was untrammeled. But to the degree that they took the experience as an immersion in true wilderness, even in 1909 they were also registering the dominant metaphor of American romanticism.

Presidents from Andrew Jackson to Abraham Lincoln to Theodore Roosevelt extolled the ways in which American civilization derived its potency from the natural world. Yet the invocation of American nature as the salvation of American civilization often appeared in close proximity with the most virulent efforts by that civilization to eradicate nature. "The more rapidly, the more voraciously, the primordial forests were felled, the more desperately poets and painters—and also preachers—strove to identify the unique personality of this republic with the virtues of pristine and untarnished, of 'romantic,' Nature," the historian Perry Miller wrote in reference to America in the mid-nineteenth century. Was it then really quite so wild as the foreigners made it out to be in letters home?

In 1909 the entire Adirondack region was, in fact, in development frenzy. The lumbering and woodbuilding industries that had sustained Keene Valley throughout much of the nineteenth century had ceased to function, as serious economic engines and tourism, particularly the summer crowd, had now become the region's lifeblood. A series of new railroad lines circled the region around Putnam Camp without ever quite getting it into its crosshatches. The objection to finishing a line right through Keene reiterated in books and newspapers was that the arrival of the railroad would shatter the area's wilderness *atmosphere*—not any actual sanctuary from civilization. In the same breath in which different contemporary writers praised the influx of business connected with the building of the new summer resorts now studding the region, they criticized the prospect of a railroad as contrary to the romantic spirit of development unique to the High Peaks. A nineteenth-century historian wrote that although the colonization of the Adirondacks had become a source of employment for hundreds of men and women, catalyzing the "interior transportation business" and nourishing "the local mercantile and manufacturing interests," even area inhabitants who were direct beneficiaries of the new dynamism bemoaned the fact that "the scream of the locomotive whistle will drive away a large portion of these temporary residents and the large sporting element," just as it would "the deer from the forest." Nonetheless, there were periodic efforts up to the time of Freud's visit to have railroad tracks laid up to the summit of mountains as a crowning touch to the creation of trolley systems linking all the important rail heads throughout the North Country.

What really made the elaborate public transportation schemes obsolete was not incipient environmentalism, but the arrival of the automobile and the consequent proliferation of new roads. Notwithstanding Freud's lurching passage from Lake Placid, massive, ambitious road-building projects designed to make the area a more attractive destination were in full swing. By 1909, the difficulty of arriving in Keene was largely part of local mythology. Putnam's brother, Charles, wrote in a sketch of Camp about how in earlier years it could take all day to travel there just from Westport, New York. "We walked up all the hills, the horses walked down them, dust rose in clouds, and I cannot imagine how our parents survived." However, he continued, "Our compensation for the slow journey was that when people arrived, they stayed. Three weeks was a minimum and five about right. . . . Guests could be trusted not to leave early or stray away to other centers."

In fact 1909 was later singled out by the *New York Times* as the historic year in which numbers of automobiles in New York State hit a new height of 24,000 and road construction went into overdrive. In another ten years, the number of cars would catapult to 571,000, cruising 7,000 miles of completed state roads. Indeed, the campaign to foster ease of travel to the region through automobile-negotiable roads worked so well that it actually backfired. Not only could travelers arrive with celerity and comfort, they could depart again just as precipitously. The hotel industry was devastated by the very roads that brought a new flood of visitors to the mountains. Tourists came and went like locusts consuming the aura of nature and moving on.

Artists looking for a shot of the sublime had been making their way to the Adirondacks since the 1830s when Thomas Cole first traveled to Schroon Lake and began painting portraits of the prototypical American wilderness. By the late 1860s, the Adirondacks were seen as a resource of far greater import than simply scenery for artists. During the Civil War, the Adirondack Park was designated the nation's first protected wilderness area. The tract was linked conceptually to New York City as a kind of backyard of scale appropriate to the Empire State. One editorial writer in the *Times* dubbed the Adirondacks "Central Park for the world," and compared the region's riches favorably with its international counterparts.

It's true that the Adirondacks were the first parcel of land in America to be designated by official governmental legislation "forever wild." However, though the addition of this article to the New York State Constitution proved a touchstone for conservationists down to our own day, its passage was primarily a response to academic research of the late 1800s predicting that the result of giving free rein to lumbermen and railroad magnates would be the transformation of the entire region into a desert. This translated into the loss of vital headwaters, the eventual drying up of canals, and the evaporation of springs for drinking water. Even the Hudson itself abandoned to the engines of immediate profit would one day dehydrate. All of which meant that transportation of goods, entrée to the West— indeed, the entire waterway system and groundwater reserves on which the East Coast's urban centers depended—would be decimated. The Adirondacks were, in the end, protected not because of ideals of nature worship, even though these notions played a crucial role in the culture of Adirondack life, but in order to sustain the momentum of civilization's progress as it radiated out from the American metropolises.

BY THE TIME of Freud's visit, a second generation of urban intellectuals had supplanted the romantic landscape painters. Putnam Camp, with its mixture of philosophers and medical doctors, typified the new breed of retreats. Felix Adler, who founded the Ethical Culture School, stayed about a half mile from Putnam's sanctuary for a number of summers and attracted members of other Ethical societies around the East Coast to camp out around his lodging where they discussed the logistics of leveraging nature to revitalize culture and inspire social reform. Another important Adirondack intellectual community formed at Summerbrook, a retreat that became the region's foremost bastion for socialists and feminists. Among its famous guests were Upton Sinclair, author of *The Jungle*, Lillian Wald, whose pioneering social work on the Lower East Side included the founding of the Henry Street Settlement, Jane Addams, the Nobel Prize winner activist who founded Hull House in Chicago, and Charlotte Perkins Gilman, the feminist poet who composed a washing song for Summerbrook extolling the joyous virtue of communal laundering with a refrain that went "wring brethren wring." Three years before Freud traveled to the Adirondacks, right after the failed 1905 revolution in Russia, Maxim Gorky and his lover, the actress Maria Andreyeva, visited Summerbrook. During his four-month stay, he wrote the novel *Mother*, which was a best-seller back home and was subsequently dubbed "the first cornerstone of Soviet literature."

Even if Freud didn't have the faintest idea about the existence of activist colonies buzzing away behind the walls of hemlocks surrounding Camp, he had inklings of the complex interplay of forces at work in the culture. When he wrote his family about how everything was at once "rough and natural," seemed "artificial," yet somehow "came off," he was identifying the aesthetic of cultured renunciation of culture that characterized early turn-of-the-century intellectual camps all across the region.

EVENTUALLY, AS THE men stood gazing out over the Park, to Freud's relief, black clouds began to converge. Putnam had no choice but to allow the hiking party to march back home.

When they staggered back to the cabins, dusk was upon them and yet their physical initiation into Camp life was not quite over. Frances, 12 years old and by all accounts the most vivacious of Putnam's children, rushed up to the three men and baited them into a game of tetherball. The letter she wrote later that evening to her mother back in Boston includes one of the most withering assessments of the founders of psychoanalysis ever recorded.

> Dear Ma—
>
> How is your arm? And your daughter? Alfred got here this morning. It rained last night and part of this morning. The doctors are killing. You should see them at tetherball! One of them didn't try it, but the others hop round like kangaroos, but almost never hit anything! Awful hurry.
>
> Lots of love, F.C.P.

CHAPTER 2

To Find One's Porcupine

*This is a perfect "day in June." And more perfect here I believe
than in any other place in the world. Jim and I have been
working hard all the morning digging, raking and moving
stones on the small domain we call our own; and I am surprised to find what an absorbing interest manual labor has
when you are beautifying your own grounds. . . . It is too
lovely tonight—there is really nothing to say except to string
along a lot of adjectives, about the place and the people and the
flies, the former two sets all complimentary, the latter too
improper for a letter. . . . There is a snake however in every
paradise and this is no exception.*

Marian Putnam writing a cousin from the Shanty, June 1887

FIFTEEN MINUTES BEFORE seven: the cook dusts the flour from her
hands, leaves the red and brown farmhouse, crosses the patch of thyme
and clover to an iron triangle fixed to a wooden post, and begins violently
whirling the striker within the triangle's border, ringing out the warning
for dinner. Freud, Jung, and Ferenczi hurry to complete their grooming
as best they can, crowding the little mirror, pinching and rubbing—they'd
been warned that it was best to be punctual.

The picture of Freud, Jung, and Ferenczi on this peaceful mountain
slope peppered with rustic cabins, clambering over one another in the
tiny Chatterbox, each trying to get at his luggage, tripping and poking
one another, while the New England natives went whistling efficiently
through their brisk ablutions in nearby cabins, evokes the Marx Brothers: *A Night at Putnam Camp*, with Sigmund Freud playing Groucho, Jung

playing Chico, and everyone's favorite, Sandor Ferenczi, as Harpo, puffing out his cheeks and honking a bicycle horn.

The doctors finished their flurry of scrubbing, combing, and collar straightening and slid out the door. It wasn't dark yet, but the mountains swallowed the sun quite early and already it was decidedly dim. They crept down the narrow path between boulders and wildflowers, catching a pale yellow kerosene flicker from within the windows of the dining room and overhearing the animated chatter of guests. Good God, could they have arrived late after all?

AT FIRST IT must have been so disorienting as to be barely assimilable. A rectangular room with a low ceiling, dimly lit. Long, Robin Hood-green tables fit end to end to form a square, at the center of which stood an old cast-iron stove. Here and there about the walls hung various chivalric accoutrements—a shield with a face painted on it, a claymore, a crossbow, an entire suit of armor—only it appeared as though all of the knightly artifacts were made of garbage.

Over dinner the doctors would learn that the entire collection in fact was created out of refuse from a dump. The suit of armor represented Sir Guy Witherington Fitz-Bowditch Shantum, sixth Baron Shantum, fourth Viscount Putney, and the face painted on the shield represented the wife of Brennus the Gaul, an image intended to terrify his enemies. Each article in fact had a complex chivalric history, which every guest could relate in infinitesimal detail and with infinite glee. The entire display was created by Putnam's close friend and medical school roommate, Edward Emerson, the youngest son of Ralph Waldo Emerson, one long dull afternoon when everyone else was off hiking.

Even before taking in the fact that they were in a baronial hall decorated with mock medieval detritus, the visitors would probably have noticed that many of their fellow diners were dressed in the peasant costume of different countries. You go to dinner, you dress like an Albanian. You have your steak while swaddled like a Swabian fieldhand. The doctors must have glanced down at their own drab suits. Beacon Hill matrons in dirndls might not have exactly constituted formal dress, but casual didn't fit the bill either.

However, there was little time to linger on their sartorial inadequacies; the doctors were being hustled along by fresh waves of guests behind them to choose a napkin ring from the great box by the entrance and sit down. I remember that box well. How much fun it was as a child to rake through the bin among all the fanciful wooden rings carved by disparate guests on their own bored afternoons—some sporting wolves, others sprouting squirrels and mountains, eagles, or savage bears. Perhaps Freud got a stump or a turtle or a deer with its antlers poking him all through the meal. Other guests were expertly plucking the ring they most desired from the box, hurrying for a free chair. Putnam hadn't even kept a seat for Freud, abandoning his distinguished visitor to be planted between a frightening member of the maiden aunt militia and the tetherball tigress, Frances. The entire table, in fact, was crammed full, brimming over with eager merriment when the door swung open and the last guest of the night walked into dinner.

Suddenly the diners exploded in song, banging their cutlery in time, stomping their feet and chorusing out at deafening volume:

> Little popsy-wopsy, chick a biddy chum
> He shall have a pysie wysie and a sugar plum
> He shall yidey-pidey in a coachy woachy too
> All around the parky warky with a cockle doodle doo.

The poor guest stood in the entrance until the last chorus was done. Punishment had been meted out. Then, smiling sheepishly, totally humiliated, the straggler slunk to the last seat at table.

Hattie Shaw herself, Camp cook for over 50 years, with her renowned black Irish eyes, and what my grandmother described as a "queenly carriage," in conjunction with a plentiful dose of "horse-sense," customarily served the entree. She got up at three in the morning to bake two loaves of bread, one graham and one white, and may well have prepared for the foreign guests her special roast beef with a white caper sauce topped by a sprig or two of fresh wild mint picked from the lush drainage patch near the pigpen.

Whether it was meat or Yorkshire Pudding or Hattie's own high country fried chickens clumped with corncake, Putnam Camp staples like popovers would have accompanied the meat in abundance. In a typical American meal circa 1909, starch was king. Along with breads and muffins, dinner

often included a variety of potato dishes—baked, boiled, mashed, escal-
loped, and puffed—along with hominy and perhaps a side order of sweet
potatoes. For the entrée, middle-class homes might serve a weighty roast
at lunch or dinner, while the rich enjoyed more exotic, but no less robust
dishes like cold and hot ham in champagne sauce with sides of pig's jowl.
Adirondack Camp fare was somewhere in between and singular as well,
offering specialties from both ends of the spectrum with a faux primitive
flair. This was a dough-heavy diet beyond even the most plugged-up nightmares of Freud's Eastern European forebears. Oh for the razor of a little
Rhine wine now.

Over dinner, Freud lightheartedly explained that he'd come all the way
to America to see a porcupine and was disappointed that he'd not yet
found one. In return, he was given a primer on Putnam Camp history. He
would have heard how, periodically throughout the 1870s, Putnam, his
pediatrician-philanthropist brother Charles (also in attendance during
Freud's visit), Henry Bowditch, an important experimental physiologist,
William James, and a handful of others used to escape from Boston for male
walking trips through the New York State mountains.

In the course of their peregrinations, the men happened at last upon
Keene Valley. In the words of my grandmother, Putnam's eldest daughter, Elizabeth, they "knew that they had found one of the loveliest spots on
earth." The year of Freud's visit, James wrote, "I love it like a person, and
if Calais was engraved on the heart of Mary Tudor, surely Keene Valley
will be engraved on mine when I die."

In 1941, as the world was going to hell, Elizabeth wrote a kind of elegiac rhapsody on the beginnings of Putnam Camp that she read aloud
at the annual meeting of the Keene Valley Historical Society: "At the head
of the Valley, on the eastern side, a modest farmhouse, a one-room shanty
and a barn stood by the road in a bit of pasture-land cleared from the
forest on Giant's bosom and sheltered by her arms to north and south,"
the address began. "A brook with enchanting waterfalls and pools came
down from the mountain through spruce and maple, balsam and arbor-
vitae, and out across the pasture into the Valley. This was Beede's Boarding House; and here the young men stayed. They bathed in the brook
before breakfast; they climbed the near-by mountains and bathed in the
brook again. In the evening they sat on the farmhouse piazza, with the

brilliant stars overhead—always more stars here than anywhere—the outlines of Noonmark, Sawtooth and Hedgehog clear before them, and talked and talked and talked—for they were filled with an infinite curiosity as to the ways of the universe and the workings of the human mind and heart."

A year after discovering Keene Valley, the four doctors purchased a small piece of land bordering the woods above the farmhouse. Soon after that first acquisition, the men bought Beede's Boarding House (the Beedes themselves had moved on to the construction of a luxury resort across the road) and another four acres. "Buildings of the simplest type were put up from time to time," my grandmother wrote. "First the Stoop—our parlor and library—set high among the trees." In 1877, women were brought into the equation—Mrs. Henry Bowditch, Putnam's sister, Miss Lizzie Putnam, and another cousin, Miss Annie Putnam. The doctors now created additional shelters, like the Coop, the Nursery, and the Parents Assistant to house the Bowditch and Putnam families. The Log was launched, rituals of daily life began to evolve, and Putnam Camp officially came into being.

James, Bowditch, and the Putnams were modeling their summer place on the original Adirondack retreat for Boston intellectuals: the Philosophers' Camp. The Philosophers' Camp was created one generation prior to the arrival of James and Putnam in the North Country and involved the pilgrimage of members of the famous New England intellectual Saturday Club in Boston to Follensby Pond, a remote spot near Saranac Lake. Ralph Waldo Emerson was a founding member of the Saturday Club, and the Philosophers' Camp experience had a pivotal effect on his reflections about the relationship between man and Nature, which the Putnam Camp founders would have read while at Harvard where two of their teachers, Louis Agassiz and Jeffries Wyman, had participated in the enterprise. They'd have heard of it too from Edward Emerson.

Even at its inception, the model for whimsical wilderness living adapted at Putnam Camp had as its basis not an organic relationship to the environment—or even to the platonic idea of nature as such—but an aspirational relationship to a previous philosophical experiment in nature by America's foremost sage, which itself had been at least partially conceived by an artist and journalist who wanted to create an image of the American philosopher in the wilderness.

———

AS DINNER FINISHED, Freud's neighbor at table, Frances, may have told him about the bonfires staged outside the Stoop where guests had recently organized a marathon Wagner sing-along at which young and old pounded out the choral rhythm with burning brands. But this night was drizzly and the party retired to the Stoop.

The Stoop resembled a hunting lodge. Two of the walls swung out and up to form a roof above a piazza looking over Gothic Mountain and the western range. With its enormous hearth, piano, organ, card tables, library, and even a curtained stage, the Stoop has always served as the center of post-prandial entertainment. A few days before Freud's arrival, campers had staged a Noah's Ark party there, at which each guest played an Ark-bound animal.

Putnam's cousin Annie doled out bowls of bitter, strong coffee, while Freud, Jung, and Ferenczi warmed themselves at the fireplace and sat on crude chairs fashioned from tree branches. Freud described to his family how "the unmarried sister of Dr. Putnam (Lizzie), a well-preserved lady of middle age, accompanied on the piano a young girl who sang English songs." Jung rose to his feet to perform a cycle of German lieder. The family was charmed.

For the final activity of the evening, Frances and another cousin cornered Freud and Ferenczi and insisted on teaching them how to play a new board game. Perhaps they were introduced to the wildly popular "Don'ts and Old Maids," a board game that worked as a kind of humorous self-help guide on how to avoid a "woman's worst fate"—spinsterhood. Or they might have played "Sociable Telephone, A Game for the Smart Set," which reflected America's obsession with manners. Players answered a "sociable telephone" (two blocks connected by a string) to respond to questions about proper behavior in various social situations.

Despite his exhaustion, Freud found the pastime surprisingly amusing. In fact it was all rather cozy with the fire in the great hearth crackling away indoors, the roar of the brook without, and the different guests stationed about the Stoop engaged in making "ghost pictures" (a process achieved by signing one's name along a fold of paper with a full pen of ink and then doubling the page over without using blotting paper), solving puzzles, reading books, playing cards, and engaging in conversation and song, like a painting by Breughel depicting the varieties of human recreation. Just before going off to bed a further round of sweets was distributed to the guests. The three doctors were stuffed beyond measure by the time they finally tottered back down the hill to their cabin.

Next morning, Freud was probably woken for the second Camp meal of the day (there were four in toto): "Forky Breakfast," (short for Déjeuner à la Forchette) announced at quarter past eleven by a series of slow notes struck on the iron triangle, followed by a "rapid rat-tat-tat" at eleven-thirty. Hattie Shaw's famous griddlecake flag decorated with pictures of pancake announcing that this was Griddlecake Day and everyone had better leave "plenty of room" was as much a threat as a promise. Griddlecakes would have been served with maple sugar from Camp's own sugar-bush, along with cereal, cream, perhaps a maple sugar pie, and yellow muffins with "apple snow," a compote of apples mixed with egg whites and cream and topped with red jelly.

Freud seems to have been in good spirits. He was amused by Forky, and extremely pleased about the weather. The dark clouds of the day before had burst into a formidable downpour. Though a party of Campers had nonetheless dashed off to climb Mount Marcy, New York State's highest peak, he was not going to be dragged up another slope. Before long, Freud learned, even that band of masochists had to surrender their expedition, working off untapped energy by "racing the carriage" on its way home.

But at some point early in the afternoon, to Freud's dismay, the showers abated, the clouds lightened to a milky gauze, and doors began slamming to the accompaniment of merry voices as the Putnam Camp villagers began stepping outside. He was sitting with Ferenczi and Jung in the Chatterbox when a knock on the door announced the arrival of Putnam's giggly eighteen-year-old cousin, Miss Mary Lee, and a female friend, both dressed in bloomers and sailor blouses. Cousin Jim had asked the two of them to show the doctors around, they trilled. They knew where a porcupine had its nest near the maple sugar camp. Freud had, after all, proclaimed that the purpose of his voyage was to lay eyes on the animal. Now, alongside Jung, confronted with Putnam's proxy, what could he say?

Freud agreed to make the trip, confining his resentment to a sardonic glance at the costumes of the two girls, followed by a comment to his colleagues about the unusual, if not outright bizarre taste evidenced by

American female fashions. Mary Lee still remembered the slur when she was eighty. Having made his point, Freud donned a stiff straw hat and took up his gold-headed cane.

Of course the hike was not in the least undemanding or brief. It was long and excruciating. It began gently enough, with the two girls babbling away and Jung going along with their silliness for the sheer sex thrill of it all, but soon the ridge became steep. After a time, the doctors' panting breaths began to be met with a fetid smell. Mary's friend suggested that they change course so as to be walking downwind. Freud refused to shift direction. The girls had insisted on dragging him out on this walk and now they would go forward as planned. On they trudged until the stench became unbearable, and suddenly—there it was. They had found the sought-after porcupine. Its carcass lay before them, bloated, swarming with flies. Freud walked forward and gingerly poked the end of his cane into the porcupine's body. Then he turned to the others and proclaimed, "It's dead." As he made his way back, he remarked on the family classification of the American porcupine. The comment sparked a spirited debate among the three doctors about the taxonomy of porcupines.

Mary Lee suggested that they should move on to the maple sugar camp. Freud ignored her. It was only after Dr. Jung intervened on behalf of the young ladies that Freud at last consented to start moving again.

All in all, as Mary Lee concluded from her Olympian octogenarian perspective, with his superior English and general manner, Dr. Jung was "much more like folks" than Dr. Freud. Putnam concurred in this assessment in a letter home to Marian from Camp, describing Jung as the hands-down favorite among the guests, a "big, jolly man" quick to laugh and play.

BY COFFEE THE next morning a series of different hikes had been plotted. Jung signed on for a climb with Henry Bowditch, Alfred Lowell, and Putnam's son, James Junior. Ferenczi agreed to take part in a less rigorous trip to a lake. Freud announced that he felt sick and wasn't going anywhere. In response to Putnam's worried inquiries, Freud explained that he was experiencing stomach pains. He didn't need to be put to bed, but it would not be advisable for him to leave the Camp grounds. Though Putnam had been planning to take part in the Haystack expedition, he announced that he would stay behind with Freud. He couldn't have been more thrilled by the opportunity Freud's digestive difficulties presented.

In point of fact, Freud's internal woes began well before reaching the Adirondacks. As soon as they'd arrived in New York, all three doctors took turns fasting to soothe a spectrum of stomach ailments. Just days after landing, Freud was writing Martha, "In a few weeks, I shall be back home and I would not want to leave again. . . . Day before yesterday was the turn of Ferenczi to go without food, yesterday Jung, today my turn." The problems did not end on leaving New York. In a letter to Emma about leaving New York for Fall River City on their way to Clark, Jung wrote, "Our vessel set sail from the West River around the point of Manhattan with all its tremendous skyscrapers, then up the East River under the Brooklyn and Manhattan Bridges, right through the endless tangle of tugs, ferryboats, etc., and through the Sound behind Long Island. It was damp and chilly, we had belly aches and diarrhea and were suffering from hunger besides."

According to Jones, Freud actually had a long history of gastrointestinal distress. And yet, the United States in general and Putnam Camp in particular marked a new chapter of his illness. Whatever the precise configuration of symptoms (to Ferenczi, he reported suffering "a mild attack of appendicitis"; to Jones he talked about a stomach catarrh; to Putnam he spoke simply of indigestion), after returning to Europe Freud insisted for the rest of his life on referring to his "American Colitis." He blamed the New World for ruining his digestion. What was going on?

FREUD WAS PERENNIALLY focused in his work on issues of what can and cannot be eaten, on what we desire to incorporate into ourselves—on orality as central to psychological development and our interaction with the outside world. At least as early as *Three Essays on Sexuality*, published in 1905, Freud was writing about the significance of the fact that infants did not differentiate between sexual activity and the ingestion of food. The different ways in which we identify with our love objects as adults are foreshadowed and modeled on the infant's actual consumption of the mother's body. In *The Ego and the Id* (1923) he compared the primitive belief that the eating of animals would result in the animals' strengths being transferred to the eaten with the concept in Holy Communion of ingesting Christ. (Cannibalism, he believed, operated on the same principle.)

Colitis, and the earlier term by which the illness was known, dysentery, carried with it a host of allegorical implications of which Freud would have been well aware. Above all, dysentery, in the nineteenth century, had been viewed as a problem of conversion: the stomach of an individual suffering from the disease was not able to properly convert dead matter into living matter (food into the body's organic system) or convert that living stuff back into dead matter again (waste into excrement). Digestion, in essence, is a process of assimilation, particularly in the large intestine where colitis occurs.

Jewishness itself was often depicted as a disease in anti-Semitic literature of Freud's day, in which the illness of Judaism could only be cured by a kind of physiological removal of Jewishness from one's being by conversion of the antiquated "dead" matter of the Old Testament personality into the living vitality of a New Christian.

Given the wealth of anti-Semitic material in the popular press of Freud's time playing on the Jewish desire to assimilate, and Freud's own familiarity with the biological racial theories of his day, it would have been difficult for him not to see his digestive troubles as suggestive of deeper problems of digesting his own identity. In America, the question was always before him: Who's cannibalizing whom? It's not surprising that Putnam Camp, which forced on Freud a round-the-clock immersion in Gentile society such as he'd never before experienced, would have brought all these issues to the fore.

Freud in America was sick, and then he ate, and then he was sick again and he ate more. In the Adirondacks he ate of the "plentiful and original" fare until doing so made him ill enough that he could exclude himself from the group, taking inside the physical nourishment that would forcibly expel him from the communal physical culture. One distinguishing feature of colitis is that its symptoms include both a spasmodic knotting up and a dramatic flushing out. Freud's "American Colitis" thus enacted his wish to make the primal choice about the New World both ways.

THE WEATHER REPORT heading the log entry for September 17, 1909, reads, "Very clear and sunny." All the length of that long, deep blue day the two older men strolled slowly about the different stations of Putnam Camp, hands clasped behind their backs, perhaps on especially uneven ground arm in arm, peeking in on little vignettes of Camp life, stopping at one porch or another to drink a lemonade and soak in the magnificent view of the mountains, pausing to analyze an unusual lichen or mushroom spotted by a tree base. And all the while they meandered the grounds they discussed the mysteries of the human mind.

They might have started their tour with a walk down to the brook where Putnam's brother Charles was overseeing construction of a new shed to contain the forge at which Putnam's female cousins fashioned silver settings for the trove of labradorite dredged up from the mountain brook. Reveling in his Yankee know-how, Charles had developed a scheme for making the shed's foundation out of empty tin cans set in cement. Perhaps it was here that Putnam asked Freud to go into more detail about the axioms of psychoanalytic theory that he'd outlined in his lectures, from repression and dream interpretation to the different paths of sexual development characteristic of normalcy and neurosis. Putnam was an adroit questioner and he was not afraid of having to be corrected as he tested his grasp on Freud's arguments. Freud was impressed with this self-abnegation before the truth. It was not what he was used to from colleagues, let alone his elders, in Europe.

The men ambled down the path in the cool shadow of trees fringing the brook toward the barn-workshop in which guests concocted inventions that seemed straight out of Grimm's fairy tales. It was here that Bowditch constructed a device involving a miniature waterwheel set in a tiny waterfall meant to extract the web from a spider and spool it onto an even more minuscule reel.

Posed before this magical laboratory, Putnam might have turned the conversation to the topic of greatest interest to him: sublimation. At Clark, Freud had argued that the same energies of the libido which, when misdirected, might conjure neurosis, could be rechanneled to fuel man's elevation. Owning up to one's subterranean desires thus need not be debasing, Putnam reasoned; such frankness might even be liberating. If Freud hadn't figured it out for himself already, Putnam would have made clear that, even beyond himself, sublimation was a great selling point for analysis in America at large. The idea resonated with the popular optimistic movements of the day—both the new Progressivism and the older hybrids of Emersonianism—along with a slew of more dubious mind–body fads capturing the mass imagination.

Putnam's enthusiasm on this point was so exaggerated that Freud felt it necessary to caution him that the opportunity to sublimate was not available to everyone. For men like himself and Putnam, obviously yes, sublimation was the goal. However for the common, uneducated hoard. . . . But Freud could sense Putnam's discomfort with this line of thought and was politic enough not to pursue it.

At some point in the day the issue of power in the therapeutic relationship arose. Putnam wanted to know how Freud was able, without abusing his authority, to spur patients on to keep revealing more of themselves. He was troubled by the growing prevalence of suggestion-based therapy in which doctors tried to forcibly train patients' thoughts like so many unruly vines. Freud assured Putnam that no one could be more opposed to this practice than himself.

At last, Putnam decided it was time to show Freud the "Men's Pool": a small bathing-hole formed by an artificial dam along the brook in which a handful of sun-bronzed men and boys just back from a hike were disporting themselves in the buff with great glee, like a painting by Eakins come to life—posturing, diving, and splashing each other, while shrieks from the females frolicking in the Ladies Pool some twenty yards downstream ricocheted up through the trees.

In an address she delivered to the Keene Valley Historical Society in 1941 my grandmother acknowledged the idiosyncrasy of social codes defining relations between the sexes at Putnam Camp in the era of Freud's visit. "Those were the days," she recalled, "of an innocent adherence to conventions which forbade our [young men and women] spending the night on Giant unchaperoned, but permitted us to start at 5 minutes past midnight and go up for breakfast!"

The two men made their way back from the Men's Pool along the loamy tree-flush path, back to the long grasses, wild herbs, and wooden cabins of Camp proper. Freud's measured responses to Putnam's inquiries about even the most disturbing topics, his patient insistence that one need not be afraid of sexuality of any variety (including one's own), won Putnam's trust and faith. The relief of being able to speak out on topics that had tortured him all his adult life was profound. Most exciting was the notion that all of man's dark yearnings could serve as so much coal to fuel his self-development. Putnam found himself embracing a fresh hope after many years of doubt and confusion.

By dusk, almost everyone had long since returned from different mountainsides. Everyone except Jung. Alfred Lyman and Harold Bowditch had made it back from Haystack at half past five, collapsing beneath the farmhouse in happy exhilaration. It was moments before the dinner bell rang that Jung at last panted into Camp. Grouchy and appalled by the way the other members of the party had abruptly accelerated into a breakneck pace, he pronounced their "record-mania, thoroughly American."

For Freud to see Jung's physical prowess brought down to size must have been the perfect denouement to a lovely day.

AS THE DOCTORS prepared to leave the following morning, Putnam told Freud that he had a parting gift for him: a small metal porcupine. It would sit on Freud's desk all his life, still remaining in the Freud Museum in London to this day.

It was typical of Putnam that he would have felt so troubled by Freud's coming all the way to America to see a porcupine only to discover one dead carcass that he'd manage somehow to procure for Freud an immortal porcupine icon on the brink of his leave-taking.

Freud accepted the keepsake with real delight. In the best Putnam Camp tradition, the present was as fanciful as it was meet. Handshakes all around. Freud thanked his hosts once more and prepared to get into the carriage. It was a neat surprise ending. Putnam, too, must have felt gratified. Yet he had no idea just how resonant the relic actually was.

In most biographies of Freud that mention the porcupine incident, the anecdote is related as a charming instance of Freud's sly, humorous approach to ambition and of Putnam's concomitant, eccentric generosity. Freud's hunt for the porcupine is viewed through the lens of his statement to colleagues before leaving Vienna. As Freud explained to his followers, whenever you have some large objective in mind, it's always good to identify a secondary, less demanding goal on which to focus your attentions in order to detract from the anxiety associated with the search for the true grail. "So, before leaving Europe he [Freud] maintained that he was going to America in the hopes of catching sight of a wild porcupine *and* to give some lectures," Jones recounted. "The phrase 'to find one's porcupine' became a recognized saying in our circle."

But why had Freud chosen a porcupine from the bottomless drawer of possible subsidiary goals for his quest to conquer America? Porcupines had long preoccupied Freud, not because of any special zoological fascination with the creatures themselves, but as a result of the metaphorical use to which they were put by one of Freud's most significant philosophical forebears, Schopenhauer. Schopenhauer used the porcupine to allegorize the problematics of intimacy: the animal was condemned to seek the warmth that came from physical proximity with other porcupines and yet, upon snuggling close, would invariably be pricked by the quills of its brethren. Much of Freud's work can be read as a study of the hunger for and barriers to intimacy; he was fixated on Schopenhauer's parable, which perfectly allegorized the complexity of his relationship to America. Freud craved the warmth and overall communal support of the New World, but constantly felt stabbed, injured, and generally violated in consequence of whatever proximity he did manage to attain. Thus, in relation to America and, critically, to the subsequent American psychoanalytic endeavors, Freud was compelled to adopt an odd position of self-imposed isolation within a group that he helped to form.

To understand the American reaction to this picture of Freud up against the New World one can juxtapose it with the image of the "Philosophers' Camp" at Follensby Pond. William James Stillman, the artist journalist who organized the Philosophers' Camp, painted a famous portrait of the undertaking. "There are two groups; on one side, Agassiz and Dr. Jeffries Wyman dissecting a fish on a stump, with John Holmes, doubtless with humorous comment, and Dr. Estes Howe, as spectators; on the other, Lowell, Judge Hoar, Dr. Amos Binney, and Woodman trying their marksmanship with rifles," wrote Edward Emerson in his description of the painting for his book on the Saturday Club. "Between the groups, interested, but apart, stands Emerson." The historian Richard Plunz has described how Emerson's position of isolation confronting nature, of self-imposed exile within the group, became paradigmatic of a new character: the American "poetic voyeur" before the wilderness. It was, in fact, a role that proved essential in defining the U.S. wilderness as a romantic mirror to the psyche of the atomized individual.

In the same way that Emerson's position as solitary, intense observer of the scene at Follensby Pond played a crucial role in establishing the American landscape as an archetypal wilderness, Freud's self-created image as the isolated heroic scientist confronting human psychology—isolated even within the psychoanalytic associations he founded—enabled Americans to envision the mental landscape in analogous, romantic, nature-based terms. Indeed, Freud made America see the human mind as its own true wilderness. The image of the American mind as Wild Nature, mysterious, sublime, teeming with resources, danger, and romantic potential proved, in fact, a far more tenacious legacy of Freud's in this country than did any kind of purely sexual unleashing.

In both Emerson and Freud's case, it was the willed construct of an observer, a speculative voyeur outside the scene, that made such a leap of interpretation possible. Freud's face on its own or glowering out of group scenes is the epitome of penetrating, quill-studded rejection of the too-intimate approach. His isolated, orphic status is a prime example of the porcupine factor.

HOWEVER, IF SCHOPENHAUER was so profound an influence on Freud's choice of an ancillary goal, imbuing the porcupine with a resonance that made it only questionably secondary, why didn't Freud explain this fact to anyone at the time? It's true that the implications of the parable as regards Freud's determination to retain a "mean distance" from the Americans, however much warmth they might have wanted to convey to him, meant that he might have preferred not to explain to his Adirondack hosts why he was bent on finding a porcupine. Yet that doesn't explain why he would have felt it necessary to hide the backstory from his colleagues in Vienna. They were hardly strangers to his mistrust of America. The inner circle would have relished the irony inherent in the bold gesture of Freud declaring his purpose in going to the New World to be the sighting of an animal that allegorized the impossibility of his ever getting too close to the Americans. And yet, so far as we know, Freud was as mum to the Adlers, Reitlers, and Stekels as he was to the Halls, Jameses, and Putnams.

The explanation for this reticence would seem to lie in another realm of questions of intimacy, the intimacy of intellectual influence, that Freud was constantly musing on, never more so than in his relationship with America.

Schopenhauer played an almost incalculable role in the development of Freud's theories. Only Nietzsche came close to the same degree of relevance for Freud—and Schopenhauer had an impact on the evolution of Nietzsche's theories as well. Much of Schopenhauer's description of the psychology of the unconscious will expressed through sexual longing reads almost as though it's in Freud's voice, stripped of a certain drum-and-cymbal Jewish joke syndrome. Indeed, scholars have argued that Schopenhauer's influence on Freud's theories goes beyond foreshadowing toward a first enunciation of them. Curiously, though, Freud denied ever reading Schopenhauer until he was an oldish man. The year he settled on from which to date his exposure was 1915, when he was fifty-nine, long after his own ideas were not only conceptualized, but fleshed out. From that point onward Freud made frequent mention of the affinity between Schopenhauer's ideas and his own: "We have unwittingly steered our course into the harbor of Schopenhauer's philosophy," he wrote in 1920. Five years later, Freud set out his position on the matter with finality: "The large extent to which psycho-analysis coincides with the philosophy of Schopenhauer—not only did he assert the dominance of the emotions and the supreme importance of sexuality but he was even aware of the mechanism of repression—is not to be traced to my acquaintance with his teaching. I read Schopenhauer very late in life."

Freud invoked Schopenhauer, in other words, to establish the credentials of his own parallel discoveries, rather than to suggest any sort of debt. However, Freud himself, at the launch of his career with the publication of *The Interpretation of Dreams* (1900), cited Schopenhauer's works directly three times. Two out of three of these references presented Schopenhauer in a regressive light, as part of the benighted generation before Freud's arrival.

The overt evidence of Freud's prior knowledge of Schopenhauer's work is supplemented by contextual suggestions of further exposure. The years that Freud was a student were the same ones in which Schopenhauer's popularity reached its zenith in the Habsburg Empire. In the prevailing intellectual climate, it's virtually inconceivable that Freud could have avoided substantial exposure to the philosopher's writing in secondary school and university.

These traces of intimacy give special poignancy to Schopenhauer's discussion on lapses in remembrance, as well as to Freud's own extensive work on the operation of memory in the neurotic character. The omissions of credit in Freud's record of the genesis of psychoanalysis cast light on his famous lapidary remark, "hysterics suffer mainly from reminiscences." Whether with regard to the trail of lost, fervent male friendships Freud left behind him in the course of his life, or with respect to the chain of unacknowledged thinkers who influenced his work, the notion that sheer forgetfulness of past intimacies lay behind the lacunae is unimaginable. After all, a core premise of Freud's work is the idea that *nothing* is ever truly effaced from the slate of anyone's mind. By virtue of Freud's own theories we have to suppose that a Roman Forum of precedent lay under the foundation of his own edifice of thought, molding the topography of the visible structure. Yet clearly Freud could not bear to be reminded of his being in intellectual arrears to Schopenhauer, and had to compensate by insisting against the written proof of his own writing that Schopenhauer's temporal priority didn't mean he was one of Schopenhauer's intellectual offspring.

All these problems converged in Freud's obsession with questions of the fertility of his own ideas for future generations. Thus, at the same time as he was using the porcupine as a kind of joke to allegorize the issue of his ambivalence about drawing near to America, the porcupine also perfectly embodied the problem of a whole other register of intimacy: the intimacy between different members of the tribe of porcupine intellectuals over time. Here, also, one could only come so close to others before the quills (this time of their pens) pierced one's skin.

NOTHING COULD HAVE been more charged with significance than Freud's Great American Porcupine Hunt. And thus, also, nothing could have been more packed with meaning than Putnam's Great Putnam Camp Porcupine Gift at the visit's end. As would happen time and again over the course of their nine-year friendship, Putnam succeeded in hitting the nerve most likely to startle, amuse, and mystify Freud. The very animal embodying the principle that Freud could not come close to Putnam was transformed by Putnam into an instrument for displaying their bond of intimacy—into a gift from host to guest.

Many years later, Anna Freud, describing the porcupine in a letter, noted, "It is several inches big, has very impressive [quills] striking out and has since stood on his desk, where it still is. Curiously enough, when you pass your hands over it, the quills they give out a nice musical sound."

The symbolism couldn't be more perfect. The porcupine has "impressive" quills all standing out off the beast's back in the very position meant in Schopenhauer's parable to ward off closeness, and yet, curiously, when they're stroked the quills make music. In fact, the quills are bristling to *invite* touch and intimacy—to spark a duet.

And so with this little metal porcupine with its paradoxically melodious quills, the metaphor of the actual porcupine for Freud's relationship with America is taken one step further. It's not a *real* porcupine he finds, just as Freud didn't feel that what he got from the Americans was real psychoanalysis. It's a psychoanalytic figurine—comic, yet well meaning, which makes harmonious sound on contact instead of giving injury. Putnam's porcupine present was America itself to Freud; the optimism that anything was possible (*porcupine ex nihilo*), the silliness, kindness, artificiality, success, faith, bizarreness—enough. It may well be that the whole cluster of possibilities, of potential unintentional and willed meaning is the reason Freud kept this little bit of bric-a-brac on his desk with such an intimidating array of more impressive artifacts. The porcupine was, at least, the question of America. Which was, in turn, Freud knew, the question of the future of psychoanalysis. And with all this sense of uncertainty about what lay before him, there was also the matter of what lay behind the porcupine, the strange fact that this overdetermined gift had been presented to him all unknowingly. This points to the final vein Putnam opened in that visit: the vein of the uncanny.

THE DOCTORS AT last stepped into their conveyance. As the driver waited for the men to settle in, the Putnam Campers arranged themselves in a line before the farmhouse. The driver flicked the reins. Freud revolved to face the rear of his departing carriage and watched as the guests gave him the traditional Putnam Camp sendoff.

The guests all draped their arms around each other's shoulders; then, switch-kicking with panache high to the right and the left in synchrony, the Campers sang, as they sing to this day: "*We'll dance like a fairy and sing like a bird, sing like a bird, sing like a bird. We'll dance like a fairy and sing like a bird, and while the hours away.*"

Then the guests all picked up crabapples and flung them in a hailstorm at the back of the receding carriage.

How could Freud help but smile? Well—I suppose he could also have stared in horror. But I like to think of Freud, Jung, and Ferenczi chuckling, patting each other's thighs, and shaking their heads as they bounced out of the Putnam Camp driveway to once more hit the treacherous road that would take them down to the Lake Placid train station and back the long journey to New York City. All in all, the visit had been a resounding success. Hadn't it? A month after returning home, Freud wrote to Jones of his experience in America: "My fatigue vanished together with my stomach catarrh which I brought home with me. The memory of the trip becomes more and more wonderful."

Putnam who, within a couple of weeks of the guests' departure was immersing himself in Freud's work with gusto, was surprisingly moderate in his report of the visit. In his own letter to Jones, written two months after the doctors' departure, Putnam noted, "The visit of Freud and Jung to the Adirondacks was on the whole satisfactory. They were curiously unlike most of the other persons gathered there, but I believe they found the experience an interesting one."

Here, if nowhere else, one wishes one could detect a note of irony in Putnam's voice. Did he really imagine that a formal Viennese Jewish doctor was going to be at home among the likes of Cousin Selma, along with cousins Louisa, Clair, Mary Lee, Arthur, and Harold, while they carried on their ritual and athletic hijinks in an atmosphere of unrelenting open-air amusement? It seems inconceivable. And yet, the truth is that in the grand universalizing American optimistic tradition, Putnam probably *did* believe that at his Adirondack camp everyone, meeting on the level plane of wholesome, natural higher values, could coexist in cohesive stimulating harmony. Indeed, Putnam's faith that there could be a complete reconciliation of his own perspectives with Freud's views carried right through the nine years of their friendship.

For Putnam, the music of the porcupine's quills always played louder than any note of human difference, whether cultural, professional, philosophical—or psychological.

And was Freud in reality as different on this point as he made himself out to be? What could be more universalizing than the core premises of psychoanalysis? The notion that *all* slips and dreams reveal unconscious motivations? The idea that *every* dream is an instance of wish fulfillment, the inevitable role of sexual repression in the development of neuroses?

Indeed, in a strange way, it may be the case that the American predilection for universals was one of the points that made Freud uncomfortably aware that his quills were headed for a quiver in the New World. In fact, the Americans may have anticipated him in different ways. After all, he hadn't brought a porcupine to them. Freud himself had to go searching for a porcupine in the American wilderness.

CHAPTER 3

Casa Medici

*What fun we shall have—playing house, and how can any old
pleasures and associations but become doubly dear!*
                                    James Jackson Putnam to Marian Cabot,
                                    on their engagement in 1885

MY MOTHER VISITED 106 Marlborough Street while Marian, her grandmother, was still living and recalls the acute narrowness of the house. "One
room on top of another room, on top of another room, on top of another
room—and nothing off to the sides," was the way she described it to me.

The house still stands at the corner of Marlborough and Clarendon in
the somewhat apprehensively genteel heart of Back Bay, along with all its
upright neighbors on unprepossessing, flat land reclaimed from the pesti-
lent, marshy fens in a massive mid-nineteenth-century earthwork project.
Though conceived in civic idealistic terms as a means of cleaning up an
unsanitary area and dealing with the overflow from a population explosion
in Boston, the planners' vision for Back Bay was never especially democratic. Following the grail of maximum profits, the new neighborhood
quickly emerged as another site at which the wealthy could cluster and
compete. To the relief of real estate developers, the legendary remark of
one Beacon Hill patriarch who told his son-in-law that he would never
consent to have his daughter reside on "made land" never gained social
traction. Well-off Bostonians squeezed out of the Hill continued to settle
in Back Bay until the 1920s. The 145 dirt cars working 24 hours a day to
load gravel from Needham, transport it to Boston, and dump it along the
expanse of swamp ended up providing foundations for blocks of fancy
townhouses, an orgy of Unitarian churches, and the occasional odd secular

institution, like the gargantuan Peace Jubilee Coliseum (1869) in which, after post-Civil War fetes began to seem stale, less proximate conflicts began to be celebrated as when, in 1872, Johann Strauss conducted a concert to herald the end of the Franco-Prussian War. There were exceptions, of course, to the dominant Brahmin tone. One of Back Bay's most prominent populist buildings was constructed just a few blocks from Putnam's home— Mary Baker Eddy's gray Mother Church, modeled after St. Peter's if without a mote of that masterpiece's sublimity.

The brick façade of 106 Marlborough Street has now been sandblasted to a peach tone less gloomy than its dark red shade in Putnam's day, but the building still looks pinched and towering. The top of the townhouse is sharply peaked, like a witch's cap. It was on the uppermost floor, in the attic, that for many years Putnam maintained a laboratory where he carried on the vital neuropathological experiments for which Harvard didn't yet have facilities. Putnam's home laboratory became the basis for Harvard's own neuropathological center.

When Putnam himself was not at work in the laboratory, assistants were hunched above the attic microscope day and night. The first floor was almost entirely taken up by Putnam's office and consulting rooms. All day long, patients streamed in and out of the office by passing through a small adjoining parlor. Putnam's children were instructed to walk swiftly and soundlessly through the hall by the office. Indeed, though the house was large, it was also always crowded, to a degree that we associate now in America only with impoverished new immigrants. Stray female relatives were often nesting with the immediate family; Putnam's sister Lizzie had a permanent home in the townhouse. Between cousins and workspaces, Putnam's five children shared rooms throughout the years they lived at home.

Constance Worcester, the daughter of the Reverend Elwood Worcester, one of the founders of the Emmanuel Movement (a sophisticated Christian communal organization offering free psychotherapy and progressive mind–body spiritual healing), lived just a few blocks down Marlborough Street from the Putnams and was best friends with Frances. She described Putnam's house as having "bare, uncarpeted floors and scanty furnishings." Constance had also been shocked to discover that on Sundays, the children were fed only bread and milk for supper. Putnam's home was nicknamed "Casa Medici" by a patient because it was so dark and gloomy; this nickname carried enough resonance for others that it stuck.

WITH ALL PUTNAM'S effusive optimism, what was it that made his domestic environs so bleak? It's especially jarring given the warm interior tastes of his local Boston mentors. Putnam modeled many of his life attitudes on the example of Ralph Waldo Emerson. Edward Emerson was probably Putnam's closest adult friend and Putnam spent many hours absorbing the atmosphere at the Concord residences belonging to the Emerson clan. At Emerson's home in Concord, "Bush," the rooms are comfortably broad and the prevailing color scheme is steeped in leather browns and tea-shades. Everything feels layered, carpeted, and close pressing. Indeed, there's something vaguely Eastern in its profusion of oriental carpets and low furniture.

This may not be surprising when one considers the remark by Emerson's friend, the Episcopal priest Phillips Brooks, "A large part of Boston prefers to consider itself Buddhist rather than Christian." Excerpts from the first substantive history of Buddhism ever published, the work of a French scholar, were published in Emerson's journal, *The Dial*, almost simultaneously with its European appearance. Emerson adopted different themes from the Eastern canon to formulate his own theories of ultimate unity and the metempsychotic character of material being—ideas which, in turn, would prove crucial to Putnam's own spiritual philosophy. Perhaps the Asian resonance also reflects the commercial roots of so much New England wealth. American Victoriana is marbled with the plunder of the seafaring community's travels across the Pacific.

IN DESCRIPTIONS OF Emerson's funeral in 1882, there are accounts of how the artist responsible for Concord's famous Minute Man sculpture hung a white robe over Emerson's body to contrast with the black walnut coffin in which he was carried from his home. Local women made black and white rosettes to decorate houses along the route of the funeral procession to the First Parish Church of Concord, the floors and galleries of which had been reinforced to support the crowds, while the walls and pews had been decorated with hemlock and flowers. Mourners marching to the church carried pine branches. All this was done to evoke Emerson's beloved American wilderness, perhaps even the Philosophers' Camp itself.

In reports of the elaborate roles played by his admirers at the funeral, with Louisa May Alcott preparing a lyre of jonquils and Bronson Alcott reciting poetry specially composed for the occasion, and the children of Concord dropping floral displays into the open grave, there's no mention of Edward. Was Putnam beside him, pressing Edward's hand as the two thin men in their black suits blurred into the background drizzle of New England's perpetually deferred spring?

Edward never had an easy time of it. Six of his seven children predeceased him. His decision to administer ether to his father when Emerson was suffering a bout of pneumonia may have been an act of euthanasia provoked by Emerson's deepening dementia. After his father's death, Edward never worked another day of his life as a physician, though he was only 38 years old. Beginning in 1909, Edward dedicated himself to editing his father's journals, the kind of employment his father had kept him from while he was alive in favor of his sister, Ellen. Edward's labors editing Emerson's endless journals occupied him the last lonely years of his life.

What did it say about Putnam himself that his closest friendship was with a haunted man who had to settle for second choices all his life?

PUTNAM DIDN'T MARRY until 1884 when he was 38 years old, long after the majority of his friends had surrendered their single stature. Speaking of the woman he finally proposed to, William James wrote his brother Henry, "she is a serious old maid, exactly like him. He would have done better to run off with a ballet dancer." To Putnam himself, James naturally put on a better face, albeit a bemused one, hinting at Putnam's own vulnerability to greater befuddlements down the road. "Benedicto te!" he wrote on hearing the news. "But what depths of duplicity thy nature contains! It positively gives me gooseflesh to think how you told me last summer that 'the fact was' you cared for nobody enough to give up your bachelor comforts. . . ." Declaring that Marian would have "the best husband of all the men that are still running loose," though "there *have* been as good, no doubt, but they're all gone now" he let drop one admonition before the close. "One thing! Don't get into a habit of philosophical discussion together—it never ends."

There may be a clue to the mystery of Putnam's late marriage in the verses Edward Emerson wrote the couple to celebrate their silver wedding anniversary. Emerson's poem describes how, in the mid 1860s, Putnam had said to him:

"Though her face were fair and her fancy bright, no comfort could I
find
In a maid who should give her life to me, without —a logical mind."
Said the idle wight [Emerson] —yet not then light in rede or in thought was
he —
"Now the just Heaven guarde thee, friend, or dreary thy lot shall be!
Would you wipe from the sky God's rainbow, to scan but the spectral prism?
Shall the bride of thy youth veil love and ruth in a cramping syllogism?

The poem seems to reiterate the point James had made that in Marian Putnam found his dreary doppelganger with the added insinuation that it was hard work locating a "serious old maid." But in reality Putnam "found" Marian years before their engagement. In relating the story of her parents' marriage, Molly wrote of how they'd known each other through many years of joint philanthropic work. They also "often had met with a small group of his [Putnam's] cousins and friends to read poetry and discuss philosophy; but above all they had been companions at the 'Shanty' in the Adirondack Mountains for two or three weeks each summer." Thus, they'd not only had a glancing social and charitable association, the two had shared a life in the incredibly intimate, indeed cramped Putnam Camp cabins for substantial stretches of time over a period of years.

The girl with the logical mind was lying just a bunk away from him through many cool, full-mooned mountain nights. If Putnam did use words akin to those Emerson attributed to him in his mock epic, might he not have been using them defensively? Putnam claimed to be holding out for a maid with a logical mind, but hadn't he been sitting all the time smack in the center of logically minded maid paradise? The cup of his reform and charity meetings overflowed with syllogism-drunk virgins. It could be that notwithstanding his statements to Edward, Putnam was dreaming of finding precisely the vampy dancer James retroactively prescribed for him. Only how could he ever meet his exotic fantasy match in the constrained world of Boston society?

There was only one location where Putnam could meet a type of woman distinct from those above the flashing needles of the Cabot-Lowell-Bowditch-Higginson sewing circles: his clinic at Mass. General. Even though he had risen to prominence rapidly in the emerging field of late nineteenth-century American neurology, Putnam's hospital workspace consisted of a single, small, bare room paid for by a meager annual allotment. The patients he saw were often indigent, and, in many cases, were recent immigrants. Illnesses he treated ran the gamut from problems of partial paralysis to the kinds of hysteria cases Freud and Breuer were soon to write about on the other side of the Atlantic. Given Putnam's keen sensitivity and openness of mind, it's not difficult to imagine him being gripped by the charms of a dark, foreign beauty very different from the practically minded Boston ladies. The glimpse of a more affecting loveliness than he could discover among members of his society may have made it hard for him to settle for a Cabot, even though he was ostensibly searching for coals at Newcastle.

In a move that would prove typical, Putnam swerved his romantic passion into the fight against social injustices oppressing the lives of the lower classes from where he took the majority of his patients. Thus it was that he undertook demanding research into the damaging effects of lead in water pipes and arsenic in wallpaper. His findings led him to launch crusades that lasted for years and excited the wrath of plumbers and wallpaper manufacturers; his muckraking essays in the 1880s on cases of chronic arsenic poisoning became classics in the field. Putnam also identified other symptoms of the neurological and physiological effects of the industrial revolution such as "a disturbance of the subjective sensibility of the skin, giving rise to what is known popularly as numbness, recurring periodically . . . and affecting one or both hands." With this diagnosis, Putnam became the first person to identify one of the most prevalent complaints of the keyboard era: carpal tunnel syndrome.

AND THEN, SUDDENLY, in 1884, Putnam folded his hand. Whatever fleeting fancies he may ever have entertained of being whisked away on lunar wings into a Midsummer Night's dream far removed from the realm of eligible young maids in sensible, low-heeled shoes, he dismissed them once and for all.

Marian was born into a family of eight children. Her brother, Fred, who gave away my grandmother, Elizabeth, in marriage, became the lead judge in Boston's juvenile courts and President of the Boston Symphony Orchestra. She grew up in Brookline in comfortable, if not wealthy circumstances, surrounded by her immediate family and countless cousins. Of this Brookline clan, descended from John Cabot, one member wrote, "Lees, Cabots, Jacksons, and Higginsons knew each other well in Essex County, and had a satisfying belief that New England morality and intellectuality had produced nothing better than they were; so they very contentedly made a little clique of themselves and intermarried very much, with a sure and cheerful faith that in such alliances there could be no blunder." Marian's sensible goodness comes through in every letter, along with a certain deflating practicality. And there are so *many* letters, riddled with so many pressing, exhausting, day-to-day demands.

By the end of the century, the Putnams had produced five children: Elizabeth Cabot, b. 1888; James Jackson Junior, b. 1890; Marian Cabot, b. 1893; Louisa Higginson, b. 1895; and Frances Cabot, b. 1897. With respect to Putnam's children as well, James dispensed tart observations. In a letter to a cousin, he discussed the children of Putnam's brother Charles as "an absolutely happy family" who had made a wonderful picture as they tromped off for a climb "barefoot and barelegged." They were "delightful young creatures—such a contrast to Jim P.'s little old maids."

After the thrill of Putnam's New Year's letter about playing house, the weight of the home that they actually were compelled to play in, with so much that was dismal and dowdy, and an endless quantity of diurnal business to attend to, must have become oppressive. "Be sure and ask Papa for some money to travel with, and give a doucer to the two maids at Mrs. Coolidge's—are you coming down here at all before the exams and when? And where after the exams?" Marian wrote in one typical letter to Molly. "I hope your wardrobe is in good condition . . . Mrs. Quigly could wash a few things on Friday (tomorrow) if you want them for Monday or could finish some things Monday if you do not go till Tuesday if you speak to her *yourself* about it. . . . Coz Grace comes tomorrow afternoon. Coz Marian comes Sat. and possibly Coz Amy—Ask Elizabeth to write to me."

Imagine poor Putnam trying to disentangle himself from this kind of knot to ponder metaphysics. In photographs depicting him up through the first years of his marriage, Putnam looks positively robust. In one, which shows him reading beside Marian in the Pigpen at Camp, his heavy shirt spreads around a barrel chest. His head looks sturdy and chiseled, a veritable

Adirondack mountain face of rugged angles. The dark beard resembles a trowel. Drop the book and substitute an axe and Putnam could pass for a North Country logger.

But over the years something happened. By the time Putnam met Freud, the big eyes magnified by his round silver spectacles never quite compensated for the hollow, gaunt cheeks. Fourteen years after wedding Marian, Putnam had grown too spare of form. What his countenance calls to mind in the days of Freud's visit is the public fasts of petition that marked New England law books until an astonishingly late age. Massachusetts had an official annual statewide fast codified in its law books until 1893! The same year that Bell lost the patent on the telephone, spawning a multitude of competitive independent telecom carriers, two full years after basketball was invented, and three years before the Klondike Gold Rush, Massachusetts legislators finally struck the last annual state fast from the books. An unbelievable profusion of fast dates used to riddle the American law books and enjoy spontaneous proclamation throughout the year with the frequency that today we observe holiday sales at the mall. A number of our Puritan and colonial forebears, including Putnam's own ancestor Increase Mather, apparently destroyed their digestive tracts by conspicuous bouts of fasting.

When one looks at Putnam's "bare, scantily furnished" physique along with that trademark sunken cheek, one suspects he may have been the kind of person who actually *liked* fasting, who got more corporal pleasure from denying the flesh than from feeding it.

Yet at 63 years of age Putnam could bask in the knowledge that for the past sixteen years he had performed with unstinting dedication and great distinction his duties as Harvard Medical School's first full professor of diseases of the nervous system. He was only three years away from being declared professor emeritus. Two decades before Freud's visit, Harvard conferred on Putnam one of its highest marks of confidence by creating a new professorship to formalize the status of his specialty as its own discipline. Outside of academia, Putnam had been a founding member of the American Neurological Association. In 1888, he served as president of the Association. The roster of other professional associations in which he was a member is exhausting—the Association of American Physicians, the American Medical Association, the American Association of Pathologists and Bacteriologists, the American Academy of Arts and Sciences, and so on—and this is only to adduce the professional groups he belonged to in direct conjunction with his vocation; there is also the record of his philanthropic work and attendant group memberships.

But the marks of Putnam's achievements weren't only registered in a hollow roll call of names. The spontaneous testimonials Putnam excited from his peers and colleagues in recognition of his honorable, productive life are often moving: "In all these fifty years I have no memory of you that is not delightful, and [that] I have never known a more absolutely unselfish, pure hearted and high minded man," wrote Putnam's lifelong friend, the jurist Moorfield Storey in 1909.

In the year of Freud's visit, Putnam's practice was flourishing. On top of teaching and handling a heavy caseload of patients, he was writing papers at the same prolific clip he had sustained all his life. Among his literary projects was a more ambitious article series than he'd ever undertaken before. In the summer of 1908, Putnam arranged to compose a series of lengthy articles for a prestigious new magazine, William Belmont Parker's *Psychotherapy: A Course of Reading in Sound Psychology, Sound Medicine and Sound Religion.* These essays were intended to lay out the true, ideal relationship between philosophy and American psychotherapy, both in detail and as a sweeping vision. "It is truly grand to see you in extreme old age renewing your mighty youth and planing yourself for flights to which those of the newest airships are as sparrows fluttering in the gutter!" wrote William James to Putnam on hearing the news. "Go in, dear Jim! It is magnificent."

But in truth, the scale of the project suggests a sense of something urgent left undone. Four of the articles in the series attempt nothing less than a new definition of the "Psychology of Health." Among a good deal else, these essays posit that the true path to mental health, and hence the psychotherapist's responsibility in treatment, includes an element of metaphysical education. Doctors are charged with the mission of helping patients become aware of their place in the ultimate, infinite universe. For all their expansive implications, these articles, it turns out, were conceived as but the opening shot in Putnam's new crusade. So far from being ready to be put out to pasture, he was convinced that his greatest work still lay before him. One wonders at times, reading his letters and papers around 1909, whether Putnam took any satisfaction whatsoever in his accomplishments to that date. This lingering hunger doesn't indicate that he was one of those people who simply can't garner satisfaction from their work no matter what its effect. Rather, Putnam's winter of discontent reflected the fact that his sense of purpose swerved dramatically in a two-stage process some time before he met Freud, yet well after he'd established himself, in the words of an American Neurological Association biography, as "the primary native Bostonian of early American neurological history."

Why was it that all his professional and societal validation on the verge of retiring, Putnam felt it necessary to plead the case of philosophy? His shift can be usefully contrasted with Freud's roughly contemporaneous abandonment of the seduction theory. It throws into stark relief the opposing vectors of American and European thoughts relevant to the evolution of psychoanalysis in the U.S. And, as was the case with Freud's theoretical reorientation, Putnam's was partially fueled by personal factors.

Another lens on Putnam in 1909 would depict a man crushed on all sides by the tremendous scaffolding of bourgeois family and professional life he'd inherited and erected for himself. Here was an individual dying to cast off all his worldly rewards if only that meant breaking free to the starry heavens where ultimate questions burned lustrous. Putnam didn't become thinner as he grew older out of the classic desiccated scholar's gastrointestinal convolutions but because of a desperate, at times desolate spiritual struggle. When Putnam met Freud, he was yearning for a conversion—not only in the spiritual sense of the word, but also in the sense registered in the discipline of physics—a radical transformation of one type of energy to another.

CHAPTER 4

The Energies of Men

*Go! child of perdition, fill thy belly with the East wind, froth
at the mouth in doubly-re-relational-compound-coördinated
Spencerian phraseology, subscribe to the Popular Science
Monthly, hang at the breasts of "Cosmism" (—breasts yclept
"falsehood" and "inanity,") go to bed with the Persistence of
Force, the unknowable, the Realism, the Empiricism, the
Substantialism the correspondences, the fatalism, and all the
other brats of the chromo-philosophy, and if you can sleep
quiet through their fratricidal strife, be it so, you are not fit
for better things!*

William James to Putnam, May 26, 1877

THE PERIOD LEADING up to and immediately succeeding the year of
Freud's visit marked the single most dramatic surge in economic productivity and overall industrial dynamism in America's history. Between 1900
and 1914 the amount of track laid in this country increased the size of the
national railroad network by over a quarter of a million miles. The production of coal between 1870 and 1900 quintupled. Crude oil, in the same time
span, increased a boggling twelve-fold. Chicago doubled its population.
Fueled by immigration of indigent rural populations from Ireland and the
backcountry of New England, Boston's population jumped from a peaceful couple of hundred thousand in Putnam's youth to a metropolis of over
a million by the turn of the century. One of the most complex webs of street-
cars and trolleys in the country linked together the city's outlying neighborhoods in a proto-suburban sprawl. To feed the nation's track habit, the steel
industry experienced the most astronomical growth of all. The production

of steel castings and ingots for rails, wire, pipes, plates, sheets, and a host of industrial tool parts increased *140 times* in three decades. At the same time as there was an enormous surge in the country's urban population, the number of farms supplying the swollen population with calories doubled; wheat, cotton, and corn cultivation increased by 250 percent.

Talk of energy, whether in terms of new production capabilities, of needed resources, or as part of some loftier effort to define energy's ideal nature, was rampant in turn-of-the-century America. There was much deliberation on the sacrosanct trust of natural resources as a symbol of the nation's superior destiny, which paralleled discussions of the American wilderness that were so influential on settlements such as Putnam Camp. America's energy capacities were understood to be unprecedented in the history of the world, but the question of how this potential could be most effectively realized was charged. As Theodore Roosevelt stated bluntly in 1907 in a message to Congress concerned with the development of the country's dams and waterways, "The conservation of our natural resources and their proper use constitute the fundamental problem which underlies almost every other problem of our National life."

It was in this context that Putnam composed his Shattuck Lecture, "Not the Disease Only, But Also the Man," written shortly before Roosevelt's Conservation address but long after the issues raised there had become pressing national concerns. In the course of this talk in which Putnam argued, in essence, for a holistic approach to psychological and physiological treatment, he invoked metaphors involving water flow dynamics no less than six times.

In the concluding words of the lecture, as he beseeched his physician audience to go out into the world independently and function as individual centers for the spread of enlightenment, he noted that even when effects of such labor were not immediately measurable, they "may, nevertheless, work upheavals in social sentiment, as the water which trickles into the crevices of the rock may, one day, freeze and burst it asunder."

So pronounced a repetition of metaphor is not accidental. Rather, Putnam was articulating his points about mental process in the prevailing national idiom of energy-speak, within which the dynamics of water flow represented one important dialect. Indeed, near the opening of his talk Putnam pointed directly to the larger concept within which his thoughts were being framed, one he could count on his audience at once grasping and imbuing with the right national political-economic resonance: "The energy set free by the magic agencies of hope, courage, desperation, fanaticism, or by the enthusiasm for a great cause, may reveal the possession of a force undreamed of, or so husband the resources of the body as to keep the flame of life burning for a time when the oil seems exhausted."

PUTNAM WAS HARDLY alone among the Americans in his insistence on the central role of energy distribution and access thereto in the dynamics of psychology. The term *neurasthenia*, a coinage from the Greek signifying lack of sufficient energy in the nervous system, was given international currency by a neurologist colleague, George Beard, as a catch-all phrase for nervous disease. When Freud was beginning to study hysteria, Beard was looking at the depletion of vital energies affecting "nearly every brain-working household" and the consequent proliferation of neurasthenic illnesses. The overlaps in terminology between writers speaking from within the American industrial revolution (including those involved with management issues of natural resources) and the early American psychologists (particularly the new school of psychotherapy) attempting to chart the dynamics of mental process are striking.

This is a conspicuously different register from the references to energy ideas found in European psychological discourse of the era, such as those expressed, for instance, in the work of Wilhelm Wundt, James' old instructor who also lectured at Clark. On the Continent, the psychology of energy was associated with the archaic forces of myth, rather than with wilderness-based industrial resources. "Myth is affect that is converted into idea and action," Wundt wrote in 1904 in his work, "Ethnopsychology." The bonding of these notions to theories of the *Volk* were, of course, central to Hitler's success.

In America, Morton Prince, a well-born New England psychologist who studied the unconscious, pioneered a form of investigative talk therapy that probed personal history as a prelude to "sidetracking" negative thoughts, and was one of Putnam's closest professional associates pre-analysis, extended Freud's association of libido with energy to include ideas. Prince posited that ideas had an active neurological force similar to Freud's concept of instinctual drives. In an introduction to the new field of psycho-therapeutics published in a collection of essays that he helped edit in the months before Freud's visit, Prince devoted an entire section to emotional energy as a primary fuel source for mankind's vital functions. After discussing how positive complexes of ideas engender a "wakened state of energy" and depressive ideas with their accompanying "feeling tones" a corresponding reduction therein leading to "fatigue, ill-being and disintegration," Prince used the language of conservation to explain how networks of positive ideas could be interwoven with the patient's old ideas: "Finally the whole complex, by repetition, emphasis, and the stimulus of emotion, is firmly linked and organized until it becomes conserved as unconscious brain residua and a part of the individual's personality. . . . To be effective ideas must be fixed, conserved, else they become the sport of every passing thought and feeling." The danger Prince perceived in careless expenditure of useful ideas is close in tone to that of Roosevelt when he warned Congress that "there must be a realization of the fact that to waste, to destroy, our natural resources, to skin and exhaust the land, instead of using it so as to increase its usefulness, will result in undermining in the days of our children the very prosperity which we ought by right to hand down to them amplified and developed."

MOST INFLUENTIAL OF all writings in this period on the ecology of energy in relationship to psychology was Williams James' essay, "The Energies of Men," published in 1907, the same year as Roosevelt's conservation address. James' essay opened with the question of why it was that "the amount of energy available for running one's mental and moral operations by" ebbed and flowed dramatically at different times. He bemoaned the fact that scientific psychology had made no systematic study of the real and artificial limitations to mental energy and called for a "topographic survey" to rectify this situation. The findings of this survey should ultimately enable psychologists to "construct a methodical inventory of the paths of access, or keys, different with the diverse types of individual, to the different kinds of power."

The thesis of "The Energies of Men" amounted to a jeremiad: there exists abundant evidence that "We are making use of only a small part of our possible mental and physical resources." It's as though the human mind were somehow equivalent to resource-rich American Nature—were somehow an alternative or even coextensive reality with that landscape—yet this other interior, with its concomitant reserves, remains practically virgin. "Of course there are limits," James wrote. "The trees don't grow into the sky. But the plain fact remains that men the world over possess amounts of resource, which only very exceptional individuals push to their extremes of use."

As proof of his contention, James cited various case histories, such as that of a friend who broke free of what sounds like manic depression ("a circular process of alternate lethargy and over-animation") by immersion in an intensive program of Hatha Yoga.

Beyond individual cases, James invoked the general power of conversions to unleash our bound energies, whether these conversions "be political, scientific, philosophic or religious." Putnam, coursing with the ideas in this essay, was *thirsting* after a conversion experience at the moment he met Freud. What's more, the initial encounter with Freud convinced him that he was actually having this experience and that it was the promised fulfillment of an earlier, primary conversion he'd undergone in the 1890s.

In his essay, James wrote about the "very copious unlocking of energies by ideas, in the persons of those converts to 'New Thought,' 'Christian Science,' 'Metaphysical Healing,' or other forms of spiritual philosophy, who are so numerous among us to-day." He was referring to the wildfire of proto-New Age mind–body therapeutic movements spreading across America in 1909, with Boston serving as conflagration epicenter. James lambasted his colleagues' drive to critique what they neither were willing to investigate on their own with truly scientific experiments, nor were able to outdo with treatments they developed from within what they define as the true realm of science.

The popularity of the different "mind-cure" movements began to demand a response from the professional medical community in the late 1890s. The "irregulars," as they were called, were sucking patients from the clinics into the meeting halls at an astonishing clip, reflecting a mounting awareness among the general public of the psychological establishment's failure to actually cure. Alienists (the nineteenth-century term for mental doctors originating in the idea that the insane were estranged from their proper mental faculties) in charge of psychological care at public hospitals actually recorded a decline of 50 percent in the rate of healing between the time Putnam began his career in the 1870s and the year of Freud's visit. There were multiple theories as to why the numbers were turning against the profession, the most prominent of them shifting blame for the spike in mental illness from the individual and his or her doctor to an overall social pathology—the besieged nervous system of modern life.

But none of the justifications made the threat of the new healers any more palatable to the doctors losing business. By 1898, the sick-brain drain had become pronounced enough that a powerful lobby of professionals was pushing for legislation to cordon off the irregulars' influence and prevent any further poaching of patients.

Even though Putnam was himself increasingly fixated on the importance of taking a holistic mind–body approach to treatment, he was opposed to the mind healers on account of what he saw as their demagogic tendencies. It took James' staunch defense of a strategy of non-intervention to make Putnam back away from the proposed legislation and accept the utility of leaving them alone. On March 2, 1898, James wrote to Putnam, "Why this mania for more laws? Why seek to stop the really extremely important experiences which these peculiar creatures are rolling up?" In an article published the same day in the *Boston Evening Transcript*, James issued an even starker, general challenge: "Do you dare to thrust the coarse machinery of criminal law into these vital mysteries, into these personal relations of doctor and patient, into these infinitely subtle operations of nature, and enact that a whole department of medical investigation (for such it is), together with the special conditions of freedom under which it flourishes must cease to be?"

Basically, James was challenging his colleagues to prove that there was no value to the treatment mind-curers offered patients, goading them to demonstrate that their own protocols consistently succeeded, something he knew was impossible. James later declared to Putnam that he had no affection for the mind-curers, but he did have a real respect for the way these movements flung open the floodgates on humanity's reservoirs of energy and got the vital forces cataracting.

Putnam's response to James' charge conveyed the clash of emotions to which he was so often subject. "I think it is generally felt among the best doctors that your position was the liberal one and that it would be a mistake to try and exact an examination of the mind healers and Christian Scientists," he wrote to James. "On the other hand I am afraid most of the doctors, even including myself, do not have any great feeling of fondness for them, and we are more in the way of seeing the fanatical spirit in which they proceed and the harm that they sometimes do than you are. Of course they do also good things which would remain otherwise not done, and that is the important point, and sincere fanatics are almost always, and in this case I think certainly, of real value."

The decision to refrain from legally prosecuting the irregulars had a number of positive repercussions. If the efficacy of the cures worked by the irregulars themselves remained debatable, the pressure on the professionals exerted by the popularity of the mind-curers spurred the former to hone their clinical skills with a vengeance. Indeed, the eminent historian of American psychoanalysis, Nathan Hale, goes so far as to say that this competition was *the* driving force behind the development in Boston of "the most sophisticated and scientific psychotherapy in the English-speaking world."

It also must be noted, however, that by withdrawing their protest the mental professionals conferred a backhanded legitimacy on the mind-curers, enshrining them as agents in the free market of healers in ways that continue to play out in America down to the present day. Religion as such, in James' schema, was defined as "the feelings, acts, and experiences of individual men in their solitude, so far as they apprehend themselves to stand in relation to whatever they may consider the divine." When everything is judged relativistically, by virtue of its usefulness for a given individual in terms that the individual defines, what sometimes gets lost—and what Freud clearly saw as another American pitfall—is the capacity for a communal skepticism.

Be that as it may, Putnam's deferral before James' position marked the close of only the first skirmish in a struggle between the professionals and the irregulars that flared up periodically at least until the First World War. And whereas he might not have been ambivalent regarding his own distaste for a figure like Mary Baker Eddy, Putnam had also become tortured by the thought that he was not tapping the depths of his reservoir of powers. By the time of Freud's arrival, everywhere around him champions of industry were trumpeting the fact that American energy was being released, produced, and harnessed for work as never before in the history of the world. What was more, the spectacular rise of the Progressive Movement made plain that large numbers of Americans recognized that giving a moral dimension to economic growth made that expansion even more potent.

FOR YEARS, THE onrush of discoveries in Putnam's own field of neurology had been steady enough to make it consonant with the spirit of the age. But gradually, leading doctors like himself came to realize that purely material brain pathology was not adequate; an ethical dimension had to be incorporated into therapy in order to balance conservation with production. From there the need arose to ground these ethics in a higher cause. But now all this had arguably been achieved. Putnam no longer had any excuse for his own personal failures as a doctor and a man. What was wrong with him, he wondered, that his own floodgates of energy had not yet burst open?

Hardest of all, perhaps, was the sense that he'd already had his great life revelation. For a time, Putnam had felt himself in the eye of epiphany. Indeed, his program of essays for Parker's *Psychotherapy* journal was not only an attempt to preach truth to the world against the encroaching forces of superstition; it was also an effort to convince himself that the transcendent discoveries he'd made in the 1890s were still valid. What more did he want? Why wasn't he at peace yet? After all, Putnam had his medium, mentor, and prophet constantly awaiting his arrival to regather the threads of their talk and weave cosmic fate itself between them.

CHAPTER 5

The Absolutism of Thought

*I hope that through this study the thought I love may prove
the truth I seek. If not, then I suppose the honest thing would
be pluck out the right eye through which has come what light
I have.*

Susan Blow to "Mrs. Hitchcock" in the 1880s

SUSAN BLOW WAS an American Dorothea Brooke, the heroine of
Middlemarch, raised in a mansion called "Old Southampton" in the flush,
stuffy St. Louis suburb of Carondelet by a jealous mother and a domineering businessman-politician father, who was obsessed with his daughter. A
painting of Blow in her teenage years depicts a quietly stunning young
woman, with clear, classic features and a self-possessed, amused, penetrating gaze. Her frock is simple and light. Her arms are folded at her waist
and her left hand is clutching an open book.

This book, no doubt, was one of the innumerable volumes on philosophy, history, and religion with which her father's enormous library was
stocked, and which Blow was said to have devoured en masse by about her
sixteenth birthday. Her favorite was the Book of Parables from the Bible.
She seems to have become fluent in German while still an adolescent, and
the densest writings of the most formidable Teutonic intellects soon ran a
close second in her heart to Solomon's epigraphs.

By the time she was 20, the alacrity of Blow's adolescent countenance
had given way to an expression more ponderous—and sad. Posing for a
formal portrait, she wore a black dress of bombazine and curled her finger
around the finial of a baroque chair; her tiny chin jutted forward and her
stare was at once far away and long suffering. But in her thirties, the fire in

her gaze was back. She looked gamine and pubescent, with Joan of Arc–style willfulness.

Unlike Dorothea, Blow never married. When Putnam was making his first discoveries as a neurologist and commencing his courtship of Marian, Blow was performing the theoretical and practical pedagogical work for which she is most remembered. After a European Grand Tour during which she immersed herself in studies with disciples of the Idealist philosopher Friederich Froebel, Blow returned to St. Louis to found America's first kindergarten, becoming the leading advocate for early childhood education in the Midwest. The focus of her work, derived from Froebel's theories, was on the instrumentality of play in learning, both in helping children absorb knowledge and in fostering their socialization. For many years after creating the original kindergarten she continued to refine the curriculum of training programs for young teachers, participated in the establishment of new kindergartens elsewhere, and tirelessly proclaimed the crucial responsibility of teachers and parents to promote children's "creative self activity." Blow became America's "Mother of the Kindergarten."

Just over a decade before Blow met Putnam, Elizabeth Harrison, who herself became a prominent early childhood educator, establishing the first rigorous training college for kindergarten teachers in the country, had her own introduction to Blow. She wrote about Blow's appearance at a special ten-day course for fledgling teachers that included talks in education and philosophy: After a "foreign-looking" man completed a talk on Herodotus, Harrison noted, "people began whispering 'Miss Blow has come!' The woman who entered was "small in stature with a slight, well-rounded face and graceful figure, a refined and keenly intellectual face, light brown hair, and expressive blue eyes. She was altogether attractive and distinguished in appearance."

"She had a compelling personality which would ray itself out into her environment," wrote Denton Snider, a St. Louis philosopher, after seeing Blow speak at the same conference in the late 1870s. She "became the queen of the audience. Not by any display of jewels and wardrobe, (she was the worst dressed in that well-gowned company, hat lay somewhat askew, hair riotous, shoes unshined) but everyone, in spite of a little feminine jealousy, acknowledged secretly her supremacy, I, the teacher, being therein the foremost. She knew her peculiar power, when I aimed my eyeshot at her, and I could not help it, her red face turned redder with a defiant smile and seemed to flash, 'Come on, I am ready.'"

By the time Blow met Putnam, she was in her late forties and had become a renowned lecturer on topics ranging from Dante and Goethe to Shakespeare and the Bible. She divided her time between Manhattan and the pristine upstate watering hole of Cazenovia, New York. She had friends everywhere. Yet Blow's letters and essays are filled with the note of a high-keyed, suppressed anguish. In the last images of her, taken around the time of the beginning of the First World War, Susan Blow's face, beneath a snowy crown, seems to consist only of weary, melancholy eyes and a frighteningly high pale brow. What on earth happened to make this brilliant, lovely, and wealthy woman so blue?

ON THE DAY Blow slipped into Putnam's office for her first consultation, with her self-effacing step and mournful gaze, she may well have appeared to him a kind of star. Even if he didn't know much about her organic approach to childhood education combining intellectual, spiritual, and creative learning, Blow was a popular speaker on the podium circuit that made for the favorite filler of Boston's leisure hours. Though Putnam's circle of friends and family composed Boston's best society, and Boston, "The City of Beautiful Ideals," still boasted the best society in America when it came to the world of glowing concepts rather than glittery things, Putnam quickly intuited that Blow possessed an intellect of an unfamiliar and marvelous species. However modest she might have been, the blade of her intelligence slashed through her emotional veils. The acuity of her thought was matched by the breadth of her education. He'd never met a woman like her.

And Blow, poor Blow, saw Putnam, so kind and compassionate a listener, so curious and striving an intellect, as the man who could restore her to this worldly hope. He would save her from the low spirits that had no place in her capacious philosophy, and yet that threatened at times to consume her vision.

Blow had come to Boston to consult with Putnam on the urgings of her intellectual mentor, Dr. William T. Harris, after a failed course of treatment at a sanatorium in Danville, New York. This institution was primarily devoted to treatment of illnesses with a nervous component. Blow's diagnosis seems to have involved a combination of depression and Graves' disease. Around the time of Blow's stay, the sanatorium passed into the control of a specialist in neurasthenia who combined a spectrum of hydropathic therapies with diet treatments. Dr. James Jackson was a disciple of Sylvester Graham, creator of Graham Crackers, who had linked the consumption of over-refined foods, in particular white bread, along with spicy dishes and the wearing of tight corsets, to the erosion of genital health. Above all, Graham argued, an improper diet stimulated the eater to acts of "self-pollution" that promoted everything from simple acne to "a body full of disease" and a "mind in ruins."

Jackson took Graham's teachings as incitement to create a new food source that would embody the principle of healthy nutrition against the degenerative qualities of Graham's list of destructive foods. He ground up stale loaves of unleavened whole grain bread, soaked the hard crumbs overnight in milk, and served the resultant concoction for breakfast the following morning under the catchy name of "Granula." Thus was born the world's first cold breakfast cereal recipe.

Blow's confinement within an institution that was becoming a hub both for the water-cure and for experiments with diet aimed at promoting moderation of the passions was an indication of how serious her condition had become. Not long after she first came into contact with Putnam, Blow's longtime friend, Laura Fisher, wrote to Dr. Harris that Blow's symptoms were so extreme that "she is pretty near the end." Given Blow's ferocious capacity for stoic self-denial, it's hard to imagine how overcome she must have been to reveal such desperation. This was a woman who believed that old-fashioned self-sacrifice could accomplish much of what the new psychotherapeutics claimed to achieve. "Fasting is the conscious exercise in a moral form of that activity of inhibition whose unconscious and semiconscious influence is now so strongly insisted upon in treatises on psychology," she observed in her journal.

THOUGH PUTNAM WAS years away from his encounter with Freud, he understood the importance of personal history in treatment. Talk was already central to his psychotherapy. A time may have come early on when Blow revealed that once in her life she had been passionately in love.

Through a combination of circumstance, economic opportunity, and ideological transformation, the Blow family had left their roots as rich Southern agrarian slave owners, moving to St. Louis to become Midwestern Republicans with commercial interests in mining and paints. Dred Scott eventually became the property of Henry's brother Taylor, a convert to Catholicism, who was responsible for freeing Scott as soon as he acquired possession of him. Scott's funeral expenses were paid for by Susan's father.

In the Civil War, Henry was active in committees that oversaw military spending and acquired considerable influence among army authorities in Washington. As mobilization went into full gear, St. Louis' Jefferson Barracks, one of the country's important ordnance depots and medical facilities for Union soldiers, became a teeming center of young soldiers. To entertain the troops, and perhaps the town's ladies as well, dances were held throughout the year. Blow, then 20 years old, was not so bookish or so repressed as to stay away from the more elite of these gatherings. At a ball for officers, she met William H. Coyle, a promising young colonel. The two seem to have fallen immediately in love.

Though Henry was based in Washington, he came back to St. Louis often enough to hear of his daughter's passion and to demand an interview with the young man. Perhaps Henry was offended that the soldier had begun courting his daughter, one of St. Louis' foremost heiresses, without first being given his paternal blessing. More probably, given Susan's later difficulties, the sheer yearning Susan felt for Colonel Coyle was enough to disqualify him in Henry's eyes. He refused to give his consent to their courtship. But when Henry took the long train back to the nation's capital, the couple resumed their rendezvous.

Blow's parents began spreading rumors that Colonel Coyle was hiding some nameless fatal, health problem. But their daughter's ardor did not cool. And then, abruptly, Coyle was transferred, Uriah like, to the deadly frontline at Pea Ridge, Arkansas, where, in contesting Missouri's status as a Union State, more than 4,000 troops died in a few days. Coyle was duly wounded in battle, but not killed, and Blow visited him throughout his convalescence.

In the winter, her father sent her money and ordered her to come live with him in Washington. There, Henry introduced her to a high-ranking officer, thirteen years her senior, whom he'd designated a fitting suitor. Still, Blow stayed loyal to Coyle. Against her family's wishes, she returned home to St. Louis in the early spring of 1864, and when she couldn't see Coyle, continued to insist on writing him letters, at least one of which her mother,

Minerva, intercepted in fury. Minerva reminded Blow of the dangers of Coyle's elusive illness and informed Henry about her daughter's stubborn passion.

And then, mystery of mysteries, in May, Coyle was decommissioned and sent home to Kentucky for unspecified "medical reasons." Contact between Coyle and Blow never resumed, and Blow never openly confessed to romantic interest in another man.

This story may have come out only very gradually in her talks with Putnam, as she began to expose the intensity of her relationship with her father. Given Putnam's empathetic understanding of her, it's likely that he prompted her to first speak about the philosophic subjects to which she'd devoted the desires that had not found an outlet in a love relationship. He may well have recognized that by proving the sincerity of his interest in her ideas he would gain access to her emotional inner life. In truth, for Blow the membrane between personal feeling and belief was so thin that once Putnam peeled back either side he would have confronted her heart.

Even when she was preoccupied with visits to schools and the preparation of new lectures, she was always engaged in extremes of soul searching. We must only focus on personal experiences insofar as they can be "transfigured into general insights," she wrote one close friend in 1882. "Ungeneralized personal experiences" can become a source of repulsive self-centeredness, just as the claim of "individual independence" often masks simple "defiance." This sentiment is uncannily close to that of the Puritan ancestors both she and Putnam could claim who believed that, as one Calvinist theologian put it, "Every man, individually is an epitome . . . every natural man (who in a natural consideration is called *microcosmus*, an epitome of the world), in whose conscience God hath his throne . . . may be called *microchristus*, the epitome of Christ mystical." For Blow herself, as for Putnam, hope lay in pursuit of "unity in thought."

At the same time, though, as she struggled with this challenging intellectual ideal, Blow expressed anxiety about the deleterious effects of the "fever of questioning" filling the minds of women on the East Coast. She praised the "girlhood" of White Sulphur Springs for its serenity. "It is graceful and considerate and not self-assertive." This conflict between her own intense speculative nature and her sense of the conservative domestic role women were meant to play tortured her all her life.

As well as writing letters to friends, Blow kept a commonplace book for herself, where she would write such epigrams as, "The absolutism of character is as repellant as the absolutism of thought is inspiring," or "The Almighty Dollar—nay—the almighty idea. A man must live—nay—Sometimes a man must die. The world owes every man a living—nay—Every man owes the world his service."

The relentless insistence upon self-denial and willed sublimation of desire bespeaks a woman who not only had experienced, vividly, the ripe tug of passion, but who had actually built around this intimate knowledge a learned, rigorous philosophy of salvational asceticism.

BLOW APPEARED AT the very moment when Putnam had begun to wonder whether his long years in the laboratory and clinic were simple failures by the transcendent Emersonian standards he'd pledged himself to as a young man. She made him realize how much he had yet to learn. Froebel was the least of it. Putnam came to see in Blow nothing less than another route to faith. With her pockets stuffed with reading lists, she embodied the German high road that would keep him out of the demagogic movements like Christian Science and Spiritism, yet still bring him at the end of the day to the absolute.

Given Putnam's stringent ethical standards, it can be startling to see the readiness with which he allowed the patient–doctor relationship to slip into something more intimate. But in fact, the establishment of a friendship was, for him, the ultimate sign of treatment's efficacy. At this moment in American psychotherapy, when the whole definition of madness was being reappraised and the deficiencies of treatment acknowledged, doctors like Putnam called into question the legitimacy of the physician's stance of omniscient authority. The ideal of talk therapy was dialogue, and the foundation of dialogue was a democratic give and take. Putnam would have seen himself serving Blow better when he was able to draw from her ideas that obviously helped *him*. Doing so demonstrated her capacity for real world service, and it was axiomatic that this would be the true goal for them both. An equal exchange on profound topics took both physician and patient out of the self toward a greater end of working to heal society at large.

Miraculously, for many years, both Blow and Putnam's hopes about what the other would bring seem to have been largely fulfilled. After having suffered progressively more debilitating depressions for over a decade, Blow felt that she'd been cured by Putnam. She was able to return to her life mission in all its various demanding capacities. "I only wish I knew how to express my deep and grateful realization of the fact that for any and all work I am able to do, I am in large measure indebted to your skill, fidelity, and kindness," she wrote him at the beginning of 1894. Shortly thereafter, Putnam made his first solo visit to her upstate home in Cazenovia.

Blow was suffering increasingly from problems with her vision. As she began to lead him more mentally in conversation, Putnam found himself serving as her physical guide. He helped her on their circuit from chairs on the porch to her bookshelves, and back to the open air again. For years, Putnam had been fixated on Helen Keller as the modern allegorical model of self-transcendence through a synthesis of science and spiritual will. In Blow, on many levels, he'd found his own Helen. Each time they went indoors, she'd bring her face very close to the accordion of bindings, then draw another volume down from the shelf to hand over to him. In her *Study of Dante*, a book she wrote in 1886, Blow described how Virgil introduces Dante "to the stern warden of Purgatory as one who is seeking liberty." It is only when Dante has been through the first volume of education in the Inferno and is near the apex of the purgatorial mountain that he feels "For flight within him the pinions growing." Virgil was an "instrument of Grace." These instruments, wrote Blow "are the mighty institutions which, revealing and enforcing ideal standards, enable the individual to measure his own defect and inspire him to overcome it; a 'store-house of grace' is that great 'deposit of faith,' the true literature of the world . . . 'channels of grace' are all honest experiences of sorrow or joy; 'ministers of grace' are the strong things who redeem our feeble thought—the heroes who spur our languid wills and the saints whose ardor fans into fresh flame the dying embers of our devotion." All these roles Blow played for Putnam.

Why was it, however, that Blow's strange, ponderous philosophical vision proved such formidable armor for Putnam when he went to do battle with Freud? And if Putnam's deeply American fantasy was one of self-fashioned, self-help salvation—a new faith through self-obliteration, a new hope that the world could be transformed overnight through true understanding—what was Freud's complementary vision?

CHAPTER 6

The True Mask

*I would so much like to give the picture a place among my
household gods that hang about my desk, but while I can
display the severe faces of the men I revere, the delicate face of
the girl I have to hide and lock away. It lies in your little box
and I hardly dare confess how often during the past twenty-
four hours I have locked my door and taken it out to refresh
my memory. And all the while I kept thinking that somewhere
I had read about a man who carried his sweetheart about with
him in a little box.*

Sigmund Freud to Martha Bernays, June 19, 1882

IN 1876, FREUD published his first medical paper, a study of eels, go-
nads, and intersexuality. His essay tackled the question, as old as Aristotle,
of whether the mature male eel had testes. In choosing to make his first
professional subject the problem of whether or not sexuality was anatomically determined in a slithery phallic male creature—the problem, indeed,
of what masculinity consisted in and of what anatomy disguised—all of
Freud's work was microcosmically prefigured.

It's no more accidental that ambiguous sexuality in eels was Freud's
initial subject than it is that his first official psychological study, published
ten years later, was on the then reasonably novel topic of male hysteria.
Although doubt has been cast on the degree of astonishment that he later
claimed his talk on the subject elicited from Vienna's *Gesellschaft der
Aerzte*, or Society of Medicine, the idea of male hysteria was certainly
not the most conventional lecture material for a young doctor at the outset of his career in 1886. Did it really happen as Freud asserted in his

autobiographical study that an old surgeon, on hearing Freud's paper, cried out, "But my dear sir, how can you talk such nonsense? Hysteron [*sic*] means the uterus. So how can a man be hysterical?" Even if that anecdote is apocryphal, Freud's decision to devote his earliest professional study to the idea that men, too, could suffer from a disease linked historically and etymologically with women and the womb remains suggestive. What brought Freud to focus on this topic of male hysteria in the same year that he married?

Freud referred repeatedly in his writings to the fact that the most formative relationship of his life was a passionate, love/hate bond with his nephew John; the relationship had, Freud wrote in *The Interpretation of Dreams*, "a determining influence on all my subsequent relations with contemporaries." The mutual desire was often triangulated through a female playmate, who was Freud's age. Ernest Jones, Freud's hagiographical biographer, remarked of an early incident from Freud's self-analysis in which John and Sigmund assaulted this girl to steal some flowers she'd gathered that it was "the first sign that Freud's sexual constitution was not exclusively masculine after all." "Since those youthful days," Freud observed, "John has had many reincarnations which revived now one side and now another of his personality."

One of these was Freud's adolescent companion, Eduard Silberstein, with whom he spent all his free time, taking "secret walks" and playing games in which they spoke in a private language based on Cervantes' *Don Quixote*. "I really believe that we shall never be rid of each other; though we became friends from free choice, we are as attached to one another as if nature had put [us] on this earth as blood relations," Freud wrote to Silberstein from the University of Vienna in 1875. When Silberstein began to be drawn to women, Freud's jealousy was savage. He wrote philosophical denunciations of women's character to try and warn Silberstein off females: "A thinking man is his own legislator, confessor, absolver. But a woman, let alone a girl, has no inherent ethical standard," he declared in one letter.

When Silberstein married six years later, in 1881, Freud was incensed. He derided the woman Silberstein had fallen in love with as unintelligent, rich, and spoiled. Either Freud himself broke off their correspondence, or Silberstein was so appalled by Freud's reaction that he ended it himself. One of the most disturbing incidents in Freud's life story occurred ten years later. Pauline, Silberstein's wife, became depressive. Silberstein and Freud must have resumed contact because Silberstein eventually sent Pauline to Freud for treatment. Not only was Freud unable to cure her, Pauline committed suicide in Freud's apartment building by throwing herself down the stairwell. Given Freud's blistering resentment of Pauline, it's possible that he told her something about Eduard's desire and her own inability to fulfill this passion that proved the final blow to her self-image.

On a theoretical level, Freud's male-centric tendencies culminated in his argument that women's desire for a baby was only a substitute for their desire for a penis (the reverse argument might be easier to defend). In a literal sense Freud postulated, as the French philosopher and analyst Luce Irigaray wrote, a "homosexual structure," in which women were solely vehicles for the reproduction of men and an exchange between men. There were nothing but penises and shadow penises in this model whichever way one turned.

Although Freud lived his life outwardly as a heterosexual family man, and it would never have occurred to him to say, "I am a homosexual," he would have been equally unlikely to say that he was devoid of homosexual longing. "You are right in supposing that I had transferred to Jung homosexual feelings from another part but I am glad to find that I have no difficulty in removing them for free circulation," Freud commented to Jones at the end of 1912 after that particular attraction had broken down. To be a homosexual meant, at least in some of Freud's later essays, to be arrested at the anal stage of sexual development. To have within oneself a homosexual capacity meant simply to be human in Freud's schema, where people were less *homo sapiens* than *homo phantasias.*

The encounter with homosexuality thus became essential to the whole paradigm of education as it referred to the realization of individual potential. In 1910, at a meeting of his Vienna circle, Freud commented that few teachers are adequate to the task of instructing children on the question of sexuality. The difficulty, he remarked, "is connected with the growing proscription of homosexuality in our time." He added that, "In suppressing the practice of homosexuality, one has simply suppressed the homosexual direction of human feeling that is so necessary for our society." The loss was pedagogical: "The best teachers are the real homosexuals, who actually have that attitude of benevolent superiority toward their pupils."

If Blow and Putnam turned to Virgil and Dante for their educational model, Freud turned to Plato and his boys. Furthermore, male-on-male intercourse in a comprehensive sense played the muse to Freud's personal fantasies. He could not have been unaware of this overwhelmingly masculine cathexis. And if homoeroticism structured Freud's fantasy life, what bearing does that fact have on the development of psychoanalysis?

In 1881, Freud graduated from medical school. His betrothal to Martha Bernays commenced in 1882, at the same time that he began working in Vienna's General Hospital. Three years later, Freud went to Paris for a year to study hysteria under Charcot at the Salpêtrière. On returning to Vienna, he launched his private practice and married Martha. In the early 1890s, he began working with Josef Breuer on various case histories in hysteria. In 1896, Freud's father died and he began his self-analysis. Three years later, he published the book that he would always consider his masterpiece, *The Interpretation of Dreams*, a book that used descriptions of his own and patients' dreams to, in Freud's words, chart the "royal road to the unconscious."

Only after his writing had failed to stir substantial interest (the first edition of *The Interpretation* sold 600 copies over eight years) did Freud throw himself seriously into a series of non-literary measures designed to make a movement out of psychoanalysis. In 1902, he founded the Wednesday Psychological Society. Over coffee, cigars, and cakes the group discussed Freud's approach to the dynamics of mental life. Six years later, after many changes in membership, the remaining nucleus of the group was renamed the Vienna Psychoanalytic Society, which in turn would evolve into the International Psychoanalytic Association.

Throughout the years that he was building his movement, Freud was obliged to fix a conventional bourgeoisie mask to the exterior of his existence. He drove to visit patients in a *fiaker* (the BMW of its day), rather than a cheaper mode of conveyance like a bus or tram, and did so wearing an elegant suit, because doing otherwise would be considered an insult to the status of the patients themselves. (Legend has it that in the Emperor Franz Josef's final hours in 1916, when his health abruptly took a turn for the worse, his physician was contacted and told to rush to the sick bed. The designated doctor flew to the Emperor's side with no regard for his own appearance, and at the sight of the disheveled physician, Franz Joseph remarked, "Go home and dress correctly." Perhaps on account of the resultant delay in treatment, those words were purportedly the Emperor's last.) In Freud's home, meals took place like clockwork at their appointed hour. Martha supposedly kept a cloth ever ready by her cutlery and would leap up, on the instant, to apply the rag to any spill. Her devotion to the task of organizing Freud's life went so far as selecting and laying out his daily clothes, and to putting his toothpaste on his toothbrush.

Indeed, just as Putnam was always trying to break out of his petrified, New England shell to reach his own freer, more powerful, truer inner persona, Freud was constantly seeking to clamp a conservative, scientifically reputable mantle onto his private and professional practice in order to achieve societal validation. Though Freud's insistence on middle-class regularity may have pointed to his sense of personal susceptibility to the *tohu* and *bohu* of ancient, subterranean powers, it's still necessary to ask why such fears should have held sway for a person of his station in turn-of-the-century Vienna.

THE DIFFICULTY OF distinguishing the role of fantasy relative to that of memory in shaping the contents of mental life played into my own family's Viennese history. Within the tiny collection of surviving photographs from my father's life in Austria, one picture was the hands-down favorite of me and my siblings. In this image, my father is standing on the sidewalk at the age of 7 or 8 alongside a heavy building made of large, rusticated stone blocks. He's smiling dreamily, and though he's still obviously in Europe (clear from his age, the architecture, and the fact that there's a sign reading *Confection Manufacturwaron* on the wall behind him), my father is dressed in a fantastic American Indian costume. His buckskin suit is festooned with wampum and feathers. He's wearing an elaborate feather headdress. In one hand he's swinging a tomahawk back over his shoulder. In the other he holds an extraordinary round shield made of leopard skin.

When we were young we liked the picture simply because the costume was so elaborate and it was funny to see our little father dressed up as an Indian. Later, some of the irony inherent in the image of this little Jewish boy in Vienna wearing the outfit of the native people of the land to which he was destined to flee began to be apparent: my father was playing Rousseau's idealized Savage, unaware that he would soon be joining the tribe. The picture never ceased to intrigue me as an adult. It said so much about my father's character. He became more American than the Americans in a classic new immigrant move, and to see that evolution foreshadowed in his pre-America love for fringed deer hide was uncanny. And then, of course, it suggested something about the privileged nature of his life in Vienna as well—the notion that playing fancy Indian was even imaginable. Perhaps a parallel could be found with the Putnam Campers dressing up in peasant costumes of different peoples for dinner. Finally, there's the Freudian register of resonance, the idea of my father in Vienna in the 1930s embodying in Indian guise the wild unconscious itself, which Freud restored to the New World. My father, in this paradigm, represented a kind of savage cupid of the Id.

The family joked about my father as a juvenile Native American in Nazi Vienna all the years of my growing up. I was, thus, surprised when, as an adult, I asked my father where exactly the photograph was taken and my father told me he couldn't actually recall the circumstances behind the portrait. The costume might have been a birthday present from his parents. It also, he suggested for the first time, might not have been given to him in Vienna at all. The photograph could have been taken in Zurich immediately after his family fled Austria. I said that I was surprised his family would have had the wherewithal, in any sense, to buy their son an Indian outfit after having just escaped from the Nazis. Well, my father mused, the costume might have been distributed to him by some nice Swiss social services organization. "My parents couldn't possibly have afforded it. They had to leave all their money behind in Vienna. I just don't remember."

It seemed a rather lavish and atypical present for refugee children— "Welcome to Switzerland, here's your Indian costume"—but who knew? And in a sense the ambiguous nature of this apparel—was it my father's longed-for choice, or was it imposed on him as a token distraction from all he'd surrendered in Austria—points toward other rich questions of destiny evocative of Freud's Central European experience as well. Fate or free will? Chooser or chosen? The mystery of disguise. The question of the availability of Native American costume in post-Anschluss Vienna.

On the latter score, my father's costume choice was less idiosyncratic than it had appeared to me growing up. Hitler himself might well have encouraged the production of such apparel once he'd occupied Austria (at least for young Aryan braves), given his own boyish fascination with the American frontier. Karl May, the immensely popular German adventure

writer who set more than eighty works in the Wild West without ever having traveled there himself, was a personal hero of Hitler's who claimed to
have learned geography from May's books. One of Hitler's schoolteachers
later even suggested that Hitler patterned his behavior toward his school-
mates on "May's tales of Red Indians." In 1906, just after Freud had published *Three Essays on Sexuality*, and Hitler had turned 17, the famous
American circus show starring Buffalo Bill toured Hitler's hometown of
Linz. Among the 800 performers with their 500 horses, the 100 real American Indians in full warrior costume who galloped the ring whooping and
firing off their bows and arrows must have set the heart of the future Fuhrer
aflutter. Jung's kindred fascination was manifested in his obsession with
parallels between the Adirondack landscape and that of the Wild West. A
certain register of New World fantasy life was, thus, inscribed at the heart
of early twentieth-century Teutonic mythology.

EVEN IF HITLER didn't manage to do away with his loved ones, my
father's link with the past and personal history was tenuous, typical in this
way of many Jews in Vienna who'd come from the East only a generation
or two before. And although my father's attitude toward most members of
his ethnic group was summed up in the slightly puzzling slogan he often
repeated, shaking his head sadly as he read news related to Jewish affairs,
"I don't care how smart they are, a lot of them just don't have the sense to
come inside when it's raining" (an expression that left me picturing sullen
Jewish men wearing little round glasses hanging around outside buildings
with their arms folded in the midst of downpours), there was loyalty at his
core. He demanded of us, in principle, that we absorb everything we could
about our Semitic heritage. Why, then, didn't we know more about his past?

For all the wrath that Freud's idea of repression has inspired, there's
no question but that during the time I was growing up much of my father's
past was buried for him because of the sadness and ambivalence it kindled,
inaccessible to his conscious mind as such.

The limitations of memory are apparent even in the photographs he's
preserved, perhaps half of which have no caption. This makes the images
function like found photographs. On the one hand, the power of found
photographs derives from the way they've been violently torn out of context and have no relationship to any known world. On the other, they're

often not so different from our own clusters of family images. We are slightly senile or repressed parents and descendents of the whole found photograph clan. These faces express some profound failure of transmission.

The study of dreams in the early days of psychoanalysis, in the first years of the twentieth century, was always two-fold. The less studied aspect of research by Freud's followers into dreams involved, in fact, a violent *disassociation* of the dream from the dreamer's specific life history. This tearing from background was meant to distill the pure symbolic quality of the dreamed events.

In different ways, then, the semi-found photographs of unknown family ancestors can offer a peculiarly apt entry into Freud's city with its intimate relationship to dreams and ghosts, ghosts of dreams, and dreams of ghosts. There was no question of context that haunted and stimulated Freud more potently than that concerned with whether Vienna represented his own rightful setting.

At the very beginning of their five-year engagement, as early as 1882, Freud wrote to his fiancée, "Must we stay here, Martha? If we possibly can, let us seek a home where human worth is more respected. A grave in the Centralfriedhof is the most distressing idea I can imagine." The idea that Vienna would never grant him his due, that the city was an agent determined to perpetually forestall his achievement of independence, recurs in his correspondence over the years.

Long before Freud had any personal connection with the United States, his sense of being fatally constricted in Vienna had made him subject to a certain classic American Dream. The New World extended the abstract promise of bringing fulfillment to his ambition. In 1883, Freud's sense of disenfranchisement in Vienna inspired him to dream of actually immigrating to America. He became excited by the idea that his title of docent would translate into greater status in the States than would ever be accorded him in Austria. "So they lived happily ever after, fortunate and highly respected in the United States," he wrote to Martha. But, as Freud put it to Jung years later: "Unfortunately things went so well in Vienna that I decided to stay on."

Whereas at a certain stratum of his psychology Freud felt himself almost coextensive with Vienna, this was not typically a positive sensation. "I hate Vienna almost personally, and in contrast to the giant Antaeus I gather fresh strength as soon as I remove my foot from the soil of my urbs patriae (father's city)," he wrote in March 1900 to Wilhelm Fliess, an ear, nose, and throat specialist who created elaborate theories of cosmobiology and was Freud's closest friend in the years that he was articulating the foundations of psychoanalysis. The reference contains a complex oedi- pal twist because, as Freud certainly knew, though Antaeus is reinvigo- rated when he is thrown down onto the Earth (the Earth is, of course, his mother, Gaea), the source of strength is feminine. Here, another form of ambiguity is being introduced into the relationship, one based on the heterogeneous influence of male-female principles on character. With this, Freud would have to have considered the question of what kind of strength, exactly, he would be imbued with on removing himself from the father soil. Would this severance from the environment that formed him leave intact his own power of generation? One of Freud's most mov- ing articulations of this problem came near the end of his life in a letter written to Max Eitingon, one of his early disciples, immediately after escaping to England in 1938. "In spite of everything I still greatly loved the prison from which I have been released . . . the happy anticipations of a new life are dampened by the question: how long will a fatigued heart be able to accomplish any work?" The matrix of earth mother and soil of the father's city immures us, but is yet the primal source and object of love; as such it is also the muse of productivity.

THE *CENTRALFRIEDHOF*, OR Central Cemetery—the place Freud de- scribed as the most distressing fate he could imagine, the decontextualized symbol of a life spent entirely within Vienna—was founded in 1874 under the reign of Franz Josef. From the beginning, the cemetery's scale was such that the site in the outlying neighborhood of Simmering was referred to as a "city for the dead." Though it has been some time since Vienna could boast any sort of imperial scope, the site, with its more than 3 million dead, remains the largest burial ground in Europe. The cemetery's old Jewish section—the only Jewish section in Freud's day—stands in atmospheric contrast to the adjacent, more recent Christian graves.

Today, the grave plots are dramatically overgrown and neglected. Many of the tombstones are broken or collapsing, tilting inward in that way graves do, as though they are being dragged down to the subterranean realm by hands already underground. The state of lyrical abandonment might not be so striking if it weren't for the spotless, manicured rows of Christian gravestones, paths between the markers all neatly mown, situated just a stone's throw from the tangled heart of the Jewish section, where gravestones indicate who lived to foresee the end and who was spared the vision. One grave belongs to a middle-aged man who died on the day of the Anschluss, another of a young woman whose death was recorded late in 1939. Many old people seem to have died in the awful year of 1938. They seem fortunate next to the elderly inhabitants of Nazi Vienna like Freud's four aged sisters who perished in Theresienstadt.

In Freud's day, of course, the Jewish section was an altogether different kind of place, a grand and imposing one. Though there are plenty of gravestones indicating no special financial resources, the old Jewish section of the *Centralfriedhof* is distinguished by a handful of gargantuan tombs. Among these, none are more spectacular than two built in the style of gothic cathedrals, complete with gargoyles. They constitute a sort of annunciation: these Jews have emerged in death, through some sort of virgin birth process, within the womb of Catholic architecture. What did Freud think as he wandered between the impressive mausoleums? Did he buy into their premise? Or did he classify them as instances of a wish-fulfillment dream? When he wrote Martha that there was no worse fate he could imagine than being buried among these graves was he gesturing beyond the mere fact of dying in Vienna to the delusional nature of the cemetery itself?

In the dreaminess of their structure, the graves also invoke the larger fantastical architecture of Vienna. Freud took in a wildly different environment from the one Putnam absorbed through his circular spectacles as he dog-trotted the prim brick blocks of Boston: the unassimilably massive Hofburg palace, the bloated toad of the Burgtheater, the vertigo-inducing museum blocks, that preposterous perpendicular neogothic town hall, and Parliament's neoclassical convulsion—almost every building supported and crowned by armies of statues of humans and gods. Hitler described in *Mein Kampf* how intoxicated he was by the sight of the Ringstrasse on his first visit to Vienna. "From morning until late at night I ran from one object of interest to another, but it was always the buildings that held my primary interest . . . the whole Ring Boulevard seemed to me like an enchantment out of 'The Thousand-and-One-Nights.'" The critic Hermann Bahr wrote, "If you walk across the Ring, you have the impression of being in the midst of a real carnival. Everything masked, everything disguised."

The mask was long conceived of as an essential instrument of self-presentation in Vienna. Kraus, the great early twentieth-century Austrian satirist whom Freud venerated until Kraus began to broadcast his disgust with the analytic project to his wide audience of readers, repeatedly sketched the duplicity and mask-wearing endemic to the operation of Austrian government and society.

Though the laws and social codes with regard to sexual deviance were Draconian, the reality was notoriously licentious. Many of the city's restaurants featured curtained-off back rooms where diners could retreat for a cannibalistic extra course on their companion. Though the law books prescribed twenty years of hard labor for sexual relations with a minor, in truth child prostitution, at least in working-class districts of the city, was widespread and generally winked at. It was understood that given the deplorable living conditions that dominated these neighborhoods, corruption of youth was inevitable. Thus, one muckraking journalist described how, in his trip to the lower class quarter of Brigittenau, he "found a stable that had become too inadequate for animals, as an abode for ten people, among them three children, who lived in random fornication among entirely run-down lumpenproletarians."

How *could* the New Englanders have come up with the same theories as the Viennese? If the streets of Boston invoke any Freudian category, it would be the withholding, impacted spirit, whereas Vienna might represent the triumph of hysterical fetishism. This was a city in which fantasy held sway with unusual force, creating a very special relationship to the threat of madness.

THE IDEA THAT the imagination could overwhelm sanity was not, of course, original to Freud. Franz Anton Mesmer, the Viennese physician whose ideas of the subconscious and hypnotism were an important influence on Freud's theories, had himself been attacked by the Académie Royale des Sciences for the imaginary nature of the invisible magnetic fluid that he pretended to control. Mesmer's ability to affect patients was attributed by a host of French enlightenment scientists and physicians first and fore-most to the "terrible power" of the imagination.

Freud, however, went farther than Mesmer in suggesting in places that our psychological make-up as such might be a product of the imagination. Though he wavered on that point (in part because he was caught as his Enlightenment forebears had been on the dilemma of how imagination could function both as the source of creativity feeding mental fertility and as the flush demon that inspired madness), Freud demonstrated again and again that fantasy could be as effective a trigger of psychological distur-bance as memory.

Indeed, Freud's most vital legacy may well be a new understanding of fantasy's place in psychological reality—this understanding derived in large measure from an insight into homosexuality. "Give a man a mask," Oscar Wilde once quipped, "and he will tell you the truth."

AT A MOMENT when American psychotherapy was focused on overcoming fatigue and domesticating what we would today call obsessive-compulsive disorders through a mixture of electrical treatments, hypnosis, and behav-ioral reeducation, Freud's subject matter must have appeared exhilarat-ing. Reading through lists of books and essays on American psychology circa 1900 and then coming across his titles, *The Interpretation of Dreams*, *Three Essays on Sexuality*, and *Jokes and Their Relation to the Unconscious*, it's as though one has suddenly discovered a graphic pulp novel stuck between dusty tomes on a desiccated academic library shelf.

In his grasp of the double, multiple, and often inverse relationship be-tween the apparent and actual significance of our actions Freud sounds his most familiar note: the tone of gay urbanity in our time. Perhaps noth-ing lingers with us from Freud more compellingly than a certain stylish irony, an inability not to see dual meanings everywhere. The lag he identi-fies in the letter to his intimate friend Fliess between hearing and under-standing as a trigger to fantasy is central, also, to the operation of wit, as Freud demonstrated in *Jokes and their Relation to the Unconscious*. By using psychoanalysis to bring out the double entendres in our own language and lives we become an acute audience to ourselves, transforming our mundane and hysterical behaviors into Wildean dramas of which we are at once, author, star, and merciless critic.

IN THE FIVE years between 1900 and 1905, Freud learned to extract the ideas from *The Interpretation of Dreams* and implant them into the dream of daily waking life.

Even his earlier breakthroughs depended on the deployment of a new vocabulary suggestive of the stage more than the clinic. It occurred in tandem with his abandonment not only of the seduction theory (which proposed that actual as opposed to fantasized erotic violation was at the root of most neuroses), but also of a language for mental processes with parallels in the contemporaneous American lexicon.

Freud had his own set of energy ideas. His pre–self-analysis energy psychology was based on an ideal norm in which "currents" flowed between the different points of brain activity in a state of harmonious, low-stimulation equilibrium. In Freud's mode, however, the peaks of possibility that in America gave energy psychology a theological, self-help luster were lacking. In "Project for a Scientific Psychology," published in 1895, Freud described the operations of psychology in terms of "resistance to discharge, contacts for paths, zero levels and stimulus escapes." To the extent that he defined the ego, it was as a kind of filigreed complex of channels.

Ironically, Freud's revelation took place with the *discarding* of the energy metaphor that Americans were viewing in increasingly epiphanic terms. In place of that descriptive model, he began to adopt a language based on epic first names. Indeed, his psychology really became Freudian when he started to label the dynamics of mental activity with words that functioned as icons for humanity's canonical narratives. Instead of abundant stores of energy, here are limitless stories of tragic character. The most famous of these structural namings obviously involves Oedipus, the protagonist lifted from Greek theater. However, it wasn't only classical myth that Freud picked over in order to name, as Adam did the animals, the bestiary of the modern mind. Eight dramas from Shakespeare, as well as plays by Goethe, Schiller, Ibsen, and Kleist also make their entrances and exits over the course of *Interpretation of Dreams*. Freud's work came alive when he conducted the abstract electrical currents of the age into footlights.

PUBLISHED IN 1901, when his relationship with Fliess had passed its zenith and was in danger of ending altogether, *The Psychopathology of*

Everyday Life can be seen as the climactic work under the emotional sway of their friendship, and one that lays the groundwork for the books Freud published in 1905, most notably *Three Essays on Sexuality*. It's also, arguably, the most Wildean book in Freud's canon, in which the trivial bunglings of daily being are each assigned repressed significance—generally a sexual one. The forgetting of names, mistakes in speech, mistakes in reading and writing, erroneously carried out actions, and other instances of inadvertent clowning are each dissected for their "real" meaning. "It is full of references to you," Freud wrote to Fliess on its publication, "manifest ones, for which you supplied the material, and concealed ones, for which the motivation goes back to you. The motto, too, was a gift from you."

Why would Freud have wanted to implicate Fliess so heavily in this particular book? Freud's strategy in the manuscript, as a rule, is to flip everything upside down. What appears to be forgetting is actually a con conducted on the remembrance of what is most important to us. What appears to be slip of the pen is the instance when we express what we really mean. *The Psychology of Everyday Life* is based on the principle that our lives encode an inverted vision of the world. The purpose of this destabilizing may be to open up the ground beneath the feet of people in conventional relationships. However, it serves likewise to intensify the frisson of the sexually ambiguous affair, which itself provokes a particular relation to memory. The topsy-turviness of ordinary life reflects a sexual disorientation that we would rather forget.

Of the book, Freud wrote to Fliess, "Apart from anything that might remain of the content, you can take it as a testimonial to the role you have played for me up until now." If the whole book can be read as a palimpsest tribute to what Fliess has been in Freud's life, this is because Freud ascribes to Fliess the role of Platonic instructor who taught Freud to see through the everyday appearance of events to the drama underneath. It's a didactic relationship invoked even before the book's first chapter, in the epigraph taken from *Faust* that Freud says he "borrowed" from Fliess, "Now fills the air with so many a haunting shape / That no one knows how best he may escape." In Goethe's play this plague of black fantasy began when Faust "fell to searching the dark with curses world and self besmirching," a moment in which he damned all the "everyday" joys of human existence. Rather than Faust, however, the accusatory tone of Freud's letter to Fliess suggests Oscar Wilde's character Cecily when she admonishes Algernon in *The Importance of Being Earnest*, "I hope you have not been leading a double life, pretending to be wicked and being really good all the time. That would be hypocrisy."

Mention of Wilde is not arbitrary. His work and persona were an obsession in the German-speaking world in the years during which Freud was developing his theories, and in Vienna most of all. The story of Wilde's undoing fascinated the Mittel European audiences at least as much as it did the English. In fact, the first transcription of part of his trial was published in German, and this became the only version in circulation for a full ten years. Even more influential than the scandal per se was the corpus of Wilde's actual writing, of which there were multiple German editions released more or less simultaneously with their English editions. Wilde has been credited as being the principal influence on Karl Kraus' methodology in the most important satirical journal of early twentieth-century Vienna, his *Die Fackel* (*The Torch*). Apart from consciously modeling his own satirical voice on Wilde, Kraus, in *Die Fackel*, printed numerous translations of Wilde's original works. For years, Freud read *Die Fackel* religiously; he corresponded with Kraus about different articles and quoted him directly in *Jokes and Their Relation to the Unconscious*. Hitler expressed his disgust at the Austrian love of satire; yet the supposed "Jewish roots" of that medium owed as much to the London West End stage as to any Semitic tradition.

THE TWO CORNERSTONES of Fliess' theory of bisexuality, on which Freud (and, notably, Otto Weininger) based parallel speculations were first, the idea that both men and women have menstrual periods (a notion that while not unique to Fliess was given unusual emphasis by him) and second, the idea that the nasal cavities were organically allied with the genitalia. In Fliess' view, the nose was also the central organ implicated in male menstruation. (This focus on the nose, of course, calls to mind stereotypes regarding Jews. In fact, one contemporary trope of the anti-Semitic caricatures involved rendering the Jew's nose as a penis.)

Sandor Gilman has explored ways in which the figure of the Jew was equated both mentally and physically with women in *fin de siècle* culture. This perception of a deep affinity operated both on a broad, generalized level and with respect to specific details of the Jew's body. So, for instance, women were stereotypically described as weaker than men in terms that overlap closely with the pejorative vocabulary used to catalogue Jewish inferiority. This inferiority reflected the fact that Jews and women were similarly members of a separate species that had been arrested at an earlier phylogenetic stage of development. One frequently cited example of the more primitive stature of women and Jews was the charge that both groups were distinguished by their smell. The production of odors, in turn, was viewed both by medical writers and early advocates of the public sanitation movement as proof of the presence of disease. In the case of women, the basis for their offensive smell, and a core piece of evidence for the female's proximity to the animal, was menstruation.

The extent to which female menstrual discharge was viewed as a source of olfactory contamination paralleling the poisonous smell of the Jew casts a suggestive light on Fliess' project. If Fliess were able to prove the existence of ethnically indifferent male menstruation—of, in fact, universal periods—one whole avenue through which Jewish primitiveness was diagnosed would be closed off. Along this same line, if the nose, which was such an overdetermined site of Jewish identity going beyond the stereotypes of an exaggerated, atavistic sense of smell, could be given universal gravitas as the seat of sexuality, this, too, would take the spotlight off the Jew.

Freud's position was not, be it said, invariably heroic in this struggle with prejudice and the chain of associations that bound Jew with woman and both with a regressive animal organism. Furthermore, Freud was surely aware that by categorizing female identity in terms of the missing male genitals, he was making a parallel to the Aryan view of Jewish circumcision. The Jewish penis was defined in the same way that Freud defined female genitalia, in terms of lack or absence. The missing foreskin represented the missing masculinity of maleness in Jewish men.

With respect to how this feminized character of the Jew played out in the external world, nothing was more strongly emphasized than the Jewish man's vulnerability to disease. And the disease most often cited as Jewish in nature was a quintessential malady of modernity: nervous illness. Not only was neurasthenia viewed as a particularly feminine complaint, it was also characterized as *the* "American illness," because of America's association with overstrained, sexually dissipated, materialist urban existence. Viennese Jews were thus perceived metaphorically, also, as ultimate Americans.

This completes the chain: as woman is to the Jew, Jew is to the American. This identification must have functioned as another reason Freud was apprehensive about being embraced by the Americans. What, exactly, would the American acceptance of his ideas confirm?

Part of Freud's purpose in taking up the study of nervous illness lay in the effort of universalize the Jewish, feminine, American disease. By tracing the roots of the disease back to foundational experiences of childhood, and, indeed, to archetypal structures of society, he sought to remove its Jewish taint. The royal road to the unconscious also leads to family romance.

THE SAME YEAR that Freud wrote *The Interpretation of Dreams*, he wrote a short essay entitled "Screen Memories," which analyzed the way a memory acceptable to the ego can mask more upsetting recollections in which our psychic energies are actually invested. The prime example he adduces of this phenomenon involves his memory of the flower picking scene with John (itself masked as the memory of a patient). Freud writes of how he and John, seeing that their female cousin had a better bunch of flowers than they did, took action: "as though by mutual agreement, we—the two boys— fall on her and snatch away her flowers." In analyzing beneath this memory to a more troubling substrate involving memories of his father's business failure and loss of authority, Freud concludes that "it may indeed be questioned whether we have any memories at all *from* our childhood: memories *relating to* our childhood may be all that we possess. In those periods of revival, the childhood memories did not, as people are accustomed to say *emerge*; they were *formed* at that time."

Ten years later, in a footnote to a discussion of homosexuality in *Three Essays on Sexuality*, which also sheds light on his fascination with antiquity, Freud made a point about desire that began to explain why fantasy trumps memory: "The most striking distinction between the erotic life of antiquity and our own no doubt lies in the fact that the ancients laid the stress upon the instinct itself, whereas we emphasize its object," Freud wrote. "The ancients glorified the instinct and were prepared on its account to honour even an inferior object; while we despise the instinctual activity in itself, and find excuses for it only in the merits of the object."

Once this idea is grasped, a host of prejudices based on everything from individual sexual proclivity, to conventional marks of attractiveness, to ethnic stereotypes with their associated sexual clichés are shaken—exposed—even overthrown. Vienna, city of fantasy, rife with disjunctions on every level between convention and reality, appearance and underlying structure, was an ideal city in which to cast into doubt the most primal conjunction (in the sense of reproduction) of drive and object. This space between the two is the womb of fantasy itself.

CHAPTER 7

An Enormous Fair

*A dose like that within your guts my boy, And every other
wench is Helen of Troy*
Line from Goethe's *Faust* quoted by Freud
in a letter to Jung on April 16, 1909

THE BOAT TO the United States left from the mist-swaddled, medieval
port town of Bremen. Freud and Ferenczi met up there ahead of Jung.
Freud's mood was rotten because he'd failed to sleep on the overnight train
from Vienna. A couple of beers en route hadn't helped. He found an excuse to begin disparaging America immediately as Ferenczi, in his efficient
manservant manner, had already managed to change some money into
dollars. Freud found the bills unclean and weird. He described in his travel
diary, with condescending amusement, how the U.S. notes had "a picture
in the middle like that of a buffalo or some other animal."

Long before stepping onto the New World shores, Freud had diagnosed
the national malady as anal eroticism. In his 1908 essay, "Character and
Anal Eroticism," Freud traced in detail the age-old association between
money and filthiness, specifically the equation between lucre and feces.
This symbolic affinity would have been playing in his mind when he recorded Ferenczi's possession of a "large bundle of dirty notes"—Freud's
first American property.

The two men ate breakfast. Ferenczi pulled out a Baedeker. Exhausted
and grumpy, Freud seems to have agreed that the best thing to do was sublimate through tourism. The men bumbled out into the notoriously foggy,
winding streets of the Schnoor to sightsee. No doubt they took in the
old Merchant's guild building, the gothic Rauthaus, the fourteenth-century

Cathedral of St. Petri with its statues of Old Testament figures like Moses and David. But how enthused could Freud really have been expected to feel? The city was steeped in the old Teutonic enchantments, which had such unfortunate present-day implications for the disenchanted Semites. Its latter-day history as export city central for Christianity northward to the Scandinavians was hardly more inviting.

Nonetheless, Ferenczi, in his desire to impress the master, had memorized a comprehensive litany of names and dates that he proceeded to recite, while Freud doggedly jotted down notes, as they stopped before each site.

Midday, or thereabouts, they abandoned their scavenger hunt and headed back to their lodgings to write postcards and collect mail. Jung strode in on the men, in Freud's words "beaming as he always does," and immediately took charge of the Bremen itinerary. He knew Bremen like the back of his big hands. Because Freud and Ferenczi were exhausted, Jung declared that they would all go out for lunch at the city's most renowned restaurant, the Essignhaus, an ancient establishment near the docks.

Over lunch, Jung announced that his abstinence days, imposed by the director of the Burgholzli on all staff as part of the institute's strict code of discipline, were over. Freud took this as a sign that Jung had decamped definitively for the Viennese analytic circle. Wonderful! They would all drink wine. It was a celebration. Freud ordered a slab of salmon. The three men were bound together. Someone called for a toast. They were on the eve of their American voyage. They were about to conquer the New World.

The conversation rambled over different topics, but Jung kept steering them back to a discussion of the *Moorleichen*, mummified corpses that had been found in the peat bogs not far from Bremen. As they refilled their glasses and cut fresh slices of moist flesh, Jung persisted in speculating on the nature of the *Moorleichen*. Freud stared at him with mounting alarm. At last he broke out, "What is it with you and the corpses?" And still, Jung wouldn't let it go. Abruptly, Freud keeled over, fainting into the skeletal remains of his fish. Jung leapt to his feet and carried Freud's limp body to a couch.

"Naturally, we will not let Papa pay for us any more," Jung said.

FAINTING IS A classic symptom of hysteria. Hanging over Freud's couch there was an etching by Brouillet in which a woman collapsing in a faint falls into the arms of a physician. The scene is being watched by rows of doctors, supervised by Charcot himself.

Jung later claimed that Freud had confessed his fear that Jung's discussion of corpses signified a death wish for Freud. If Jung is telling the truth, that accusation alone seems hysterical. Bearing in mind the etching Freud hung over his analytic couch, we might also imagine that the faint represents a desire for salvation at the hands of a strong man. This would suggest a fantasy of inhabiting the typically symptomized female body.

Freud himself, in his own accounts of the event, eliminated the underlayer of deeper meaning. He explained away the faint as the result either of his having drunk too quickly or of having the effects of his sleepless night catch up with him. The excuses ring lame. Even Jones, who came to abominate Jung, accepted Jung's claim that an argument concerning death wishes preceded Freud's collapse. He too envisioned Freud playing out an interior opera of deadly enemies and lovers.

NEAR THE BEGINNING of James' novel, *The Europeans*, there's a description of the protagonists' first stroll along the streets of an American city during which the "Baroness Munster's" reactions resonate powerfully with Freud's initial impressions of New York: "She said very little, but she noted a great many things, and made her reflexions. She was a little excited; she felt that she had indeed come to a strange country, to make her fortune. Superficially, she was conscious of a good deal of irritation and displeasure. . . . It seemed to her now that she was at an enormous fair—that the entertainment and the *désagrements* were very much the same. She found herself alternately smiling and shrinking; the show was very curious, but it was probable from moment to moment that one would be jostled."

The handful of days that Freud, Ferenczi, and Jung spent in New York after the days at sea reads like a parody of the frenetic Gotham itinerary. The men toured the Lower East Side, ate in Chinatown, visited the Met (where Freud scrutinized with special care the cases of Cypriot antiquities), and shopped at Tiffany's. At night, their entertainment included an excursion to Coney Island and Freud's first trip to the movies.

The trio stayed at the mid-priced Hotel Manhattan at the dreary, aggressively anonymous corner of Madison and 42nd, just down from the New

York Public Library and up from Grand Central. Freud was unimpressed by the city's scale. "They're not beautiful, whatever else," he said of the skyscrapers on Broadway. On their first afternoon, Freud and Jung struck out for a long walk through Central Park. It was warm and breezy and both men found relief from the city's jostling pace in the expanse of green. But Freud was obsessing about Jewishness—questions of his own acceptability as a suitor of American love that found fodder everywhere he turned. "Signs are posted which, besides being in English, are in German, Italian and Yiddish with Hebrew lettering," Freud wrote in a letter home. "The park swarms with Jewish children large and small."

Jung wrote to his wife that during the walk the pair talked "at length about the sociological problems of psychoanalysis. He [Freud] is as clever as ever and extremely touchy; he does not like other sorts of ideas to come up and, I might add, he is usually right. . . . We spoke a good deal about Jews and Aryans, and one of my dreams offered a clear image of the difference. But one really can't go very deep into anything here, because the general hustle and bustle is so overwhelming." We know from Jung's other writings that one point he probably broached in this conversation—a notion Freud was justifiably afraid of—was Jung's belief in the biological distinction between Jews and Aryans.

Jung described to his wife their evening meal at Brill's home with Brill's "nice, uncomplicated" American spouse, without mentioning, as Freud did to Martha, that Brill's wife was also lovely, tall, gracious, and slim. In describing the remarkable oddness of the food, Jung asked Emma to picture a salad made of "apples, head lettuce, celery root, nuts, etc."

Around midnight they all drove down to Chinatown, "the most dangerous part of New York." Brill arranged for "three sturdy rascals" to accompany them as bodyguards. The men marveled at the fact that all the Chinese wore dark blue clothing and styled their hair in long pigtails. They visited a Chinese temple housed in a sinister den, and suspected that around every street corner people were being murdered. At last they ended up in a Chinese teahouse, drinking exceptional tea and a rice dish involving bits of meat "smothered in earthworms and onions." Thankfully, the worms turned out to be Chinese potatoes that were surprisingly tasty.

As the night wore on, the Chinese began to look less menacing than the ethnically nondescript hoodlums managing the neighborhood's underworld commerce. Jung noted that Chinatown was made up of "9,000 Chinese but only 28 women," for which reason, "swarms of white prostitutes" plied the streets, occasionally interrupted by police sweeps.

The evening ended with a visit to a genuine Apache Indian music hall where, despite the gloominess of the scene, the appreciative audience showered the Apache singer's feet with money.

THE DARKEST MOMENT for Freud of those first days was that on which he accompanied Jung to visit Brill in his offices up at Columbia. Afterwards, the pair strolled along the Palisades, looking down from the high cliffs at the immense thoroughfare of the Hudson. No doubt, Freud was trying to turn their conversation to the military status of the campaign to date. What ought they do in preparation for their departure to Worcester the next day? Jung, however, kept twisting their talk back to their own dream analyses, the loose mix of group and self-analysis that seems to have succeeded the men's psychoanalytic efforts on board the *George Washington*.

The weather was very warm but stirred by soft winds off the water. Deep in talk, Freud and Jung clambered along a narrow path bordering the Palisades. The view toward the northern horizon of the great river was quintessential Hudson River School, the landscape of Cole, Church, and Durand—that American wilderness sublime that Freud was reframing in the vistas of the mind.

Freud was anxious, and probably spent by the action of the past several days. Here he was bordered by the most primitive landscape of his trip to date, next to the man who wanted to kill him—whom Freud wanted to kill. They were walking along the edge of the cliff. And then there was that unruly bit of homosexuality cropping up and crossing all wires. With Jung pushing harder for Freud to expose himself, something irresistible began creeping into the scenario—irresistible and unbearable. Abruptly, Freud began urinating, releasing uncontrollably into his pants, an event which, exactly like the fainting fit in Bremen, put Freud in an infantile dependent state relative to Jung.

In his essay angled at America, "Character and Anal Eroticism," Freud posited a connection between urethral eroticism, enuresis, and "burning ambition." The moment on the Palisades was not the first time he'd suffered such an attack; what happened there fit with the one larger neurosis that Freud was willing to diagnose himself with in *The Interpretation of*

Dreams: overweening desire for success. (This is so even though as Jung recalls the incident, when he made this equation between the eneuretic symptoms and ambition, Freud protested violently and said that in no way had he ever been an ambitious man.) Freud's attacks of helplessness were just the obverse face of the eroticized will to power. In his system, all aberrant sexual behaviors occur in conjunction with their reverse (sadism and masochism, scopophila and the urge to expose oneself, etc.). Freud's diagnosis bundled together the active and passive roles in sex to culminate with the bisexuality of desire as such.

In later writings, Freud made the relevance of enuresis to these questions explicit in his bizarre theory that civilization began when man learned to control himself from urinating on, and so extinguishing, fire. Authority was vested in the tribal leader who could restrain the urge to urinate as a wrongheaded display of potency. Near the end of his career, Freud completed this chain of associations for modern man by equating the pen with the penis, the ability to modulate one's writing with the ability to control one's urge to micturate. Writer's cramp, the inability to hold and manipulate a pen without pain, became another cipher for castration and impotence. In 1938, the year Freud left Vienna, he wrote Marie Bonaparte a letter in which he returned to the trip to America. He described to her how his handwriting had recently been disturbed in consequence of a bout of urinary trouble. "There is an inner connection between urinating and writing, and assuredly not only with me. When I noticed the first signs of prostatic hypertrophy in the functioning of the bladder, in 1909 in New York, I suffered at the same time from a writer's cramp, a condition foreign to me until then."

The New York visit ended with a night trip to Marine Park's classiest attraction, Dreamland, built only a few years before the doctors' visit. The main entrance to Dreamland was through the "Hall of Creation," a gaping maw crowned by a colossal racy statue of a woman draped only in a loose robe covering her frontside from the pubis down. Her more than semi-nude state was deemed permissible because, as the guardian spirit of the Hall of Creation, she was intended as a Biblical reference. Five times a day, the opening chapter of Genesis was restaged inside the dark opening directly behind her inviting form.

More than any other attraction at Coney Island, Dreamland recalled the Ringstrasse and the ways in which the Ringstrasse itself foreshadowed the latter-day American theme parks like Epcot Center and the fantasy hotels of Las Vegas. Visitors to Dreamland rode through the Swiss Alps and floated along the Canals of Venice; they sipped tea in Revels of Japan, wandered the Streets of Cairo, and watched with horror as Hell in the End of the World consumed the damned. For, in that true American spirit, sights of the apocalypse were somehow thematically equivalent to attractions representing the world's greatest wonders.

AT HALF PAST three on the 4th of September, the European doctors hopped onto the El at 42nd Street and rode west to the piers where they boarded a five-story steamer and sailed down the Hudson, around the tip of Manhattan, then on up through Long Island Sound. Their boat traveled through the night and made Fall River, Massachusetts, Sunday morning. It was pouring rain as they boarded the train for Boston. But en route the storm passed away, the clouds broke, and they found themselves in a landscape Jung pronounced "charming." The austere lyricism of the American scene enchanted him from the start. He described to his wife the train's passage through "low hills, a great deal of forest, swamp, small lakes, innumerable huge erratic rocks, tiny villages with wooden houses, painted red, green, or gray, with windows framed in white (Holland!) tucked away under large, beautiful trees."

After switching trains in Boston, the men made it to Worcester a little before midday. They checked into the Standish Hotel, and succumbed, for a few hours, to exhaustion and gastrointestinal misery. Around six, they dressed for dinner and moseyed out along the broad, shady sidewalks of the town (which seemed to the men notably clean, civilized, and peaceful after Manhattan) to the home of the conference organizer and Clark's president, G. Stanley Hall.

At the time of the Clark Conference, Hall was 65, two years older than Putnam. In a photograph taken at the time he conferred honorary degrees on Freud and Jung, he looks dour and long-faced, with a high forehead and a partially electrified snowy white beard. Indeed, his appearance calls to mind that of the archetypal unhinged visionary behind any number of America's interminable religious revivals. In fact, however, though not without his own admixture of moral self-torturing, Hall was another spry, forward-groping New Englander, obsessed with health, his home institution's global destiny, and the complexities of adolescent sexuality. He was given to promulgating "zests" among his disciples such as walking everywhere barefoot. Jung's first impressions of him were of a "refined, distinguished, old gentleman," with, "a plump, jolly, good-natured, and extremely ugly wife who, however serves wonderfully good food." The Halls' home was busy with people going in and out, and stuffed with books and boxes of cigars.

CONJOINED WITH THE national fixation on questions of energy was a related passion for pedagogical reform. The whole concept of the Clark Conference was conceived in a spirit of educational idealism stamped with American self-improvement mania. Where the Habsburgs had their cases of gold and gems, the Americans displayed their chalk and slate collectibles of plundered knowledge. Hall's plans for the Vigentennial gala were unbelievably ambitious and moralistic. As he wrote in his autobiography, "we were again able to bring a number of the most eminent pioneers in science from Europe and elsewhere besides many from this country, believing that this type of academic celebration and festivity is more dignified and more worthy of a real American university than processions, banquets, and merely formal public exercises."

In line with this idea of a moral program, the entire first week of the Clark Conference was devoted not to experimental science, but to a discussion of the current state and future needs of child welfare operations in the U.S., with, as Hall noted, "27 different types of child welfare organizations, fifteen sessions, and forty-seven addresses," as if the value of debate were a quantifiable matter of industrial production. One outcome of this initial week was the formation of the first effective national association of child welfare organizations. The second week was devoted to a series of lectures featuring top international scientists in the fields composing Clark's principal departments of study: mathematics, chemistry, physics, biology, and history. Most of the guests were eminent figures in their respective disciplines. Two of the physicists, Rutherford and Michelson, were Nobel Prize winners. Lectures on psychology, Hall's own field, consumed the final week of the Conference. Freud's name received top billing.

The gathering was also a mecca for radicals of every ilk. The droves of anthropologists, neurologists, psychologists, physicists, and representatives of other established sciences, as well as interdisciplinary oddballs, who cut out from their regular lives to make it to Clark, turned the conference into a kind of middle-aged, intellectual Woodstock, if one where an understanding of German was an asset.

The American infatuation with sophisticated European knowledge was already a cliché. When Bertrand Russell came to the U.S. in 1924, he said of the women attending his talks, "They try to rape the mind of every lecturer that comes along." Some of this tendency seems to have been operative at Worcester. "Today I had a talk about psychoanalysis with two highly cultivated elderly ladies who proved to be very well informed and free-thinking," Jung wrote to his wife. "I was greatly surprised, since I had prepared myself for opposition. Recently we had a large garden party with fifty people present, in the course of which I surrounded myself with five ladies."

At the same time, the consuming fever for knowledge at the Clark Conference was clearly more than ornamental and not only, in the case of the interested females, a matter of sexual compensation. The event embodied that American faith in the possibility of gathering the fruits of the globe, transmogrifying and then re-exporting them to universal, salvational effect. Hall's belief that education had become "the chief problem of the world, its one holy cause" was widely shared by contemporaries as disparate as Putnam, James, Dewey, and Roosevelt. It could be argued that the public-minded, national pedagogical obsession in America between the 1880s and World War I tapped the same spirit that would later manifest itself in our own, individualist rage for self-help.

Thus, even the Bohemian element at the Conference has to be seen as much more than an exercise in proto-radical chic. The most notable guest with a revolutionary agenda was Emma Goldman: "Plump of person, demure of manner, chastely garbed in white and bedecked with rimless glasses, she might have passed as a visiting teacher," as the *Boston Evening Transcript* described her. She arrived with her anarchist consort, Dr. Ben Reitman, known as the "King of the Hoboes," and characterized by the paper as looking like "a good-natured pirate." Goldman tried to rent a public hall from which to deliver her own remarks, but was refused on the grounds of her "indecent character." She and Reitman, who had his own troubles with the local police, ended up camping out on a lawn and making open-air extempore appeals for radical reform to small but devoted audiences. The questions Goldman leveled at Freud penetrated to the heart of the educational debate then (as now) occupying America. She stood in the audience at one of his lectures to ask him: "Is not pedagoguery today filling the mind of the child with predigested food, instead of aiming to bring out his individuality? Is it not most important that he should learn his own ability and be equipped to understand his relation to the world about him? Do not women's colleges neglect to take up the most important subject, that of sex psychology, and so unfit their graduates, who become teachers, to get in touch with pupils? Does not successful teaching depend on individuality rather than method?"

In fact, Goldman's sympathy for Freud's project seems to have been matched by Freud's own, unacknowledged affinity for Goldman's platform. Both of them believed that release from conventions of sexual hypocrisy afforded the individual more human dignity and the possibility, at least, of a more engaged social existence. But it was her American perspective that led Goldman to focus responsibility for this release on the institutional education system.

CHAPTER 8

Where Is the Savior?

The Americans were indeed fortunate to hear all this in the spoken word!

Karl Abraham to Freud, April 28, 1910

ONE HAS TO tip one's hat to Freud for his cool in having forgone the crutch of preparing his lectures in advance of the most important professional opportunity of his life. As matters turned out, his extemporaneous composition method gave the talks a spontaneous appeal particularly suited to the American temperament. Each morning, Freud would leave Hall's home, walking past its borders of flowering shrubs "overgrown with virginia creeper and wisteria" to meet up with Ferenczi for an early constitutional. As they strolled past the stately lawns of the neighborhood around the University and perhaps wandered as far as Worcester's aging mills and wire factories, Freud would orally compose his remarks for the day. Jones, who had joined the party in Massachusetts, stated that Freud claimed on the eve of his first lecture to "have no idea what to talk about." Jung suggested that Freud speak about dreams. Jones lobbied for him to lecture on something of wider relevance. Freud eventually accepted Jones' recommendation not because dreams were an overly restricted subject, but because their impracticality might repel the Americans.

From the outset, Freud was striving to shape his themes to the tastes of his audience. Quite apart from the subtler personal strains affecting the men's relationships, the question of what Freud's subject matter should be in representing the movement to the Americans exposed theoretical divisions among members of Freud's inner circle. Jones was making a dig at Jung in dismissing dreams as a subject of too limited application. For

Jung, Jones knew, dreams reflected the most profound stratum of the psyche. Jung rejected Freud's interpretation of dreams as a "façade" behind which lay meaning and identified them instead as a "part of nature" free of the tricks of consciousness. In Jung's autobiography, *Memories, Dreams, Reflections*, almost the entire section on his American visit is taken up with descriptions of dreams he had over those weeks.

FREUD DELIVERED MOST of his five lectures from Clark's art library, a simple mid-sized room illuminated by a large, impressive skylight. He lectured in his native tongue without a translator. The fact that the rooms where he spoke nonetheless stayed packed with listeners demonstrates the proficiency in German still expected of American scientists five years before the Great War. Over his starched white shirt with a stiff, low collar and ready-made butterfly tie, Freud wore a dark vest and a long black jacket with broad lapels. Emma Goldman described how Freud, "in ordinary attire, unassuming, almost shrinking among the array of professors looking stiff and important in their university caps and gowns," yet "stood out like a giant among pigmies."

His talks offered a highly simplified answer to the question: What is psychoanalysis? Their tone was self-effacing, and cosmopolitan, and they were addressed not just to the physician but to the lay listener. By discounting the need for a medical education as a prerequisite to fathoming analysis, Freud did not mean to undercut his movement's scientific legitimacy, but to make universal common sense the great arbiter of its conclusions. From his opening lines, Freud established mastery by way of a feint. "Ladies and Gentlemen, it is a new and somewhat embarrassing experience for me to appear as lecturer before students of the New World. I assume that I owe this honor to the association of my name with the theme of psychoanalysis, and consequently it is of psychoanalysis that I shall aim to speak." Freud let the audience in on an imagined act of orientation that discreetly highlighted the fact that analysis had already attained sufficient stature to gather a crowd.

In the first of his lectures, Freud went through the case of a hysterical female patient, humbly ascribing her cure to Breuer's treatment. He described the case of this 21-year-old as the original application of the talking cure. By teaching the young woman to express emotions and articulate suppressed neurotic associations Breuer had relieved her symptoms. The lecture closed with an emphatic self-denigration—one specifically aimed at establishing his empathy with the audience's own doubts. "I am afraid that this portion of my treatment will not seem very clear, but you must remember that we are dealing here with new and difficult views, which perhaps could not be made much clearer. This all goes to show that our knowledge in this field is not yet very advanced." But, he added, "complete theories do not fall from Heaven, and you would have had still greater reason to be distrustful, had any one offered you at the beginning of his observations a well-rounded theory, without any gaps; such a theory could only be the child of his speculations and not the fruit of an unprejudiced investigation of the facts." Freud argued that the gaps in his theories and the audience's mistrust were proof of the objectivity of his findings. If they had been more complete and carefully proven, Freud implied, *then* one could accuse him of unwarranted speculation.

In his second lecture, Freud turned to the pioneering role of Charcot and Janet in the psychological treatment of hysterics. He introduced the concept of repression and the mechanism whereby a repressed thought could remain active in the formation of symptoms.

The third lecture was the chattiest, full of humor and stylistic twists that made the audience feel, with him, like men and women of the world. Freud used a joke to explain how wit operated by way of condensation and allusion: Two unscrupulous businessmen thought to enter good society by having their portraits painted. When the works were completed, they held a gala viewing to which they invited an influential art critic. The critic gazed for a long time at the two portraits as though trying to find something, and then pointing to the gap between the two pictures asked, "And where is the Saviour?" Freud then moved on to offer a confession. "I might say, esteemed hearers, that for a long time I hesitated whether instead of this hurried survey of the whole field of psychoanalysis, I should not rather offer you a thorough consideration of the analysis of dreams: a purely subjective and apparently secondary motive decided me against this. It seemed rather an impropriety that in this country, so devoted to practical pursuits, I should pose as an 'interpreter of dreams' before you had a chance to discover what significance the old and despised art can claim."

By this time, Freud knew that his audience had so enjoyed themselves taking part in his salon-style conversation on mental dynamics that they would be prepared to laugh at their own stereotypical devotion to practicalities. And this is where Freud's rhetorical genius emerges because he *did* hold off for precisely for the reason he adduced. We're all such good friends now, Freud winked, that I can reveal my little game to you. Having drawn his listeners into complicity with him, he was able to launch into a reasonably intricate discussion of his theories of dreams and the psychopathology of everyday life.

What Freud did in America was to let out, in a controlled fashion, his own Viennese ambivalence and skepticism. By channeling the aspects of his personality given to doubt even his own central findings, he managed to use them in the creation of a persona (Karl Kraus would say the donning of a mask) for whom charismatic self-questioning served as a badge of authenticity.

THROUGHOUT THE WEEK of Freud's lectures, Putnam dashed back and forth from Back Bay to Worcester, distracted by an even more than usually demanding litany of family duties and anxieties. Molly's swollen appendix appeared first and most worrisomely, followed hard on by Jamie contracting bronchitis. Then Elizabeth went to a house party at the Wigglesworths' and nearly put an eye out by racing into a rustic gatepost in the middle of the night and smashing her glasses into her cornea. Whereupon Marian, who had foregone her philanthropic rounds to stay home nursing Molly and Jamie, slipped on the bedroom floor and ended up with a wrenched shoulder that put her in bed for three days. On top of that, two close relations and friends were having a wedding, the very day the Clark Conference opened. And Putnam was already supposed to be up in the Adirondacks tending to relatives and his remaining children there. To crown everything, he was supposed to have traveled to Cazenovia to visit Susan Blow.

No wonder Freud's talks transported Putnam. Here he was surrounded by broken, sprained, maimed, beseeching loved ones—from the reclaimed marsh land beneath Beacon Hill to the northern high places—when suddenly, *poof*! The whole slapstick circus disappeared behind a spreading genie cloud of cigar smoke, dissolved before the sang-froid of worldly European knowledge. Here, no false prudery about the labyrinth of human desire. This, the elegant dispassion of classicism. The prospect of psychology's rebirth. A hint toward the ultimate significance of hidden universal energies. Even the possibility that greatness had not yet eluded him personally, though he was 63 years old.

Many of Freud's discoveries brushed close to ones Putnam had seen evidence of in his own practice—and then boldly went a step further. Freud's idea of different mental "groupings," which knew nothing of one another, as exemplified in the unconscious, was not so different from Putnam's theory of the co-conscious. And yet, the idea that the unconscious actually dictated the *whole* of waking psychological life represented a startling leap from Putnam's position.

Since his student days, Putnam had cherished the image of the great, revolutionary man in conflict with convention-bound contemporaries. His youthful heroes exemplified the principle that history's most consequential discoveries were produced by a small group of visionaries and thus, as he wrote in one essay as a Harvard undergraduate, "we should be careful how we reject a doctrine because its supporters may be few." Freud's remarks on the nature of resistance to psychoanalysis in the third lecture struck home. Among his opponents, Freud said, there were those who "would not reject the result of a microscopical research because it cannot be confirmed with the naked eye"; yet the odds were stacked against acceptance of the insights of analysis. "Psychoanalysis will bring the repressed in mental life to conscious acknowledgement, and everyone who judges it is himself a man who has such repressions. . . . It will consequently call forth the same resistances from him as from the patient, and this resistance can easily succeed in disguising itself as intellectual rejection." The fact that psychoanalytic theory was bound by definition to provoke rejection made it an ideal cause for a champion of unpopular truths. Freud represented for Putnam nothing less than the radical unbound ideals of youth.

IF PUTNAM FOLLOWED the mainstream press reports on the Conference, he would have been pleased to see that they were generally sympathetic, if tending, predictably, toward frivolity. "Men with Bulging Brains Have Time for Occasional Smiles," read a headline in the *Worcester Telegram*. Freud gave one lengthy interview, to Adelbert Albrecht of the *Boston Transcript*. "His (Freud's) high forehead with the large bumps of observation and his beautiful, energetic hands are very striking," Albrecht wrote before making a note on Freud's appearance which, given Freud's horror of old age, would have been the most offensive possible. "Students of Dr. Freud's books on psychic analysis have doubtless fancied him a cold and cheerless person, but that prepossession vanishes when one confronts the man, bent and gray, but wearing the kindly face that age could never stiffen." The interview went on more gratifyingly to position Freud as the voice of the future in psychology and the hero of young doctors of mental illness worldwide.

The good will Freud met with in the press was no index of the prevailing response from his New World professional peers. The Dean of the University of Toronto said of the lectures when they were published a year after the Conference, "An ordinary reader would gather that Freud advocates free love, removal of all restraints, and a relapse into savagery," a response Jones characterized as "by no means atypical."

A division Freud would fight throughout his career in America was already manifest, whereby scientific arbiters afforded him less credit for specific insights than the popular sensibility accorded him for his general validation of a new world of hidden psychological urges. Albrecht's comment in the interview that Freud had shown great insight into the "mechanism of the sick soul" since the "conscious will reaches as far as the conscious psychic processes, and every psychic compulsion is caused by unconsciousness" pointed toward Freud's identification of the wilderness of the American mind. Acknowledging a barbarism within us is a far cry, however, from having advocated a return to that savagery, and at least in the initial decades of the American popular response to Freud this distinction was clear. The early American newspaper response made him sound more like an honest exposer of hypocrisy, in the American vernacular a muckraker of the mind, than a traditional doctor.

In his fourth lecture, Freud abruptly switched tacks. As he introduced the idea that the roots of all neurosis lay in sexuality and that the origins of individual sexual disposition lay in infancy, he dropped his modest tone. Freud shared with his listeners how difficult it had been for him to accept the primacy of sexuality in psychological constitution, and related how even his close followers often suspected that he overstated the role of sex.

Freud insisted that he had no a priori investment in assigning to sexuality such a dominant place in human psychology. "I was converted to it when my experience was richer and had led me deeper into the nature of the case." Freud suggested that his audience consult the other psychoanalysts who'd accompanied him to Worcester: None of them wanted to believe in it either, Freud averred. "Ask them, and they will tell you." His own adherents were doubtful about the key premise of psychoanalysis, "until they were compelled by their own analytic labors to come to the same conclusion." Even then it wasn't easy. Patients are committed to concealing their sexual life "by every means in their power . . . they wear a thick overcoat—a fabric of lies—to conceal it, as though it were bad weather in the world of sex."

From acknowledging the difficulty people had accepting the reality of sexuality, Freud went on to say that he had a yet more incredible disclosure to make, namely, that the creation of symptoms related to sexuality "in every case goes back to the adolescence and the early childhood of the patient." He executed a ringmaster flourish, making his argument leap through the hoop one way, then the other, and then both directions at once as the hoop burst into flames. As he wrote long afterward in "An Autobiographical Study," of his presentation at Clark, "it seemed liked the realization of some incredible day-dream; psychoanalysis was no longer a product of delusion, it had become a valuable part of reality." The sense of a fantasy come true, a "derealization" that proved the reality of his success, resonates with other key events in Freud's biography, such as the moment on the Acropolis in which his sense of reality dissolved before the realization that he'd definitively surpassed his father.

"Now I can at any rate be sure of your astonishment," Freud said. "Is there an infantile sexuality? you will ask. Is childhood not rather that period of life which is distinguished by the lack of the sexual impulse?" No, he answered. It was not true that sexuality only began at puberty, "as the devils in the gospels entered into the swine." Enough is enough, gentlemen, Freud was saying. I've been the picture of tolerance until now, but here I must draw the line. I will not accept this manifestation of willful blindness and hypocrisy. In fact childhood sexuality is not hard to believe in at all. What's truly incredible is the *denial* of its existence. "It is not very difficult to observe the expressions of this childish sexual activity; it needs rather a certain art to overlook them or to fail to interpret them." Not only that, Freud said. An American doctor had already made a similar observation: Dr. Sanford Bell of Clark University had published in an article 1902 citing "2500 positive observations" of the "amorous condition" in children.

Having begun his lecture by acknowledging that his listeners might find it hard to accept his arguments, Freud concluded by asserting that the Americans were leading the way in collecting hard data on the reality of childhood sexuality. Doesn't this go against everything we've been taught to think of the Americans recognizing the importance of childhood sexuality years ahead of Freud? What is the truth about turn-of-the-century Americans and sex?

CHAPTER 9

The Great Sex Symphony

Everything in the world is for the most part a repetition of
something else. We have the same sorts of bodies with our
neighbors, learn the same things with them . . . and in general
seem striving to make the poor old world go on repeating itself
year by year. I have a well-written French book, lent me years
ago by Miss Blow that tells all about it. . . . In the reason, the
imagination, the will (one of them trained through Philosophy)
alone is bliss.

Putnam in an undated letter to a cousin around 1909

THERE'S A PERVASIVE sense that Freud somehow imported sex to America. He arrived on these shores with panting lust in a little hairy black box and opened the lid, whereupon *it* went crawling off on a billion pink, wriggly legs to conquer the U.S. In truth, despite the prevailing "civilized morality" documented by Nathan Hale with all its anti-sexual ethos, from the latter half of the nineteenth century up to the time of Freud's visit and beyond, a considerable swath of the American medical and reformist elite was to some measure aware of the inevitable vicissitudes of human desire, and of the fact that sex could not simply be ignored or extinguished. Hysteria and neurasthenia both were often traced to sexual frustration. George Beard assigned to neurasthenia an etiology grounded in the detrimental habits of contemporary existence. One of the most flagrant of these was the disruption of domestic intimacy caused by the industrialized, accelerated pace of urban life. Freud was hardly the first to declare that the origins of hysteria lay in the marriage bed. His theoretical decision to fix the wellsprings of hysteria in unrequited sexual longing complicates his special interest in male hysteria, as well as the implications of his own hysterical episodes. If women's pleasure in his schema was a factor of synchronizing desire with anatomical structure, what did the male inability to find pleasure even in heterosexual genital sexuality indicate? With regard to the male, fantasy and the failure of fantasy operated on something closer to a blank slate than the female body. Indeed, the stubborn challenge of trying to define what exactly hysteria was reflected to some extent the question of what sexual dissatisfaction signified. Did it, for example, mean, in regard to the female, that she was nymphomaniac, or did it suggest a problem with respect to the spouse?

The broad American recognition that unconsummated erotic need played into a host of nervous diseases raised endless questions. Many of these boiled down to the conundrum of how much release was too much release? Along with the moral religious framework that people were often squeamish about transgressing there was, once again, the field of energy dynamics to consider. Orgasms represented an expenditure of a finite energy stock. Even if the Christian code was faltering in places, there remained the grave danger of exhausting one's energy supply. In numerous cases, men counted on female sexual reticence to safeguard them from their own profligate tendencies. Debates about how to negotiate the balance between excessive sexual tension and wastefulness in both a physiological and religious-ethical sense were raging in America long before Freud had developed his theories of sexual psychology.

(Today's women's magazines with articles such as "7 Secrets of Highly Orgasmic Women," suggest that in classic American fashion we've simply flip-sided the problem faced a hundred years ago. Along with empowering and giving control, we've created at least as much pressure on women to hypersexualize themselves as existed in Putnam's day to contain and neutralize female desire. The silken fetters are surely a more pleasurable form of bondage than were the hard chastity devices of earlier days, but they are not necessarily for that reason a form of liberation. The debate about balance has been eliminated, but only in favor of the glutted mentality of consumer culture.)

Many American doctors did not need Freud in order to believe that the subject of sex was of vital importance and that the current dynamics were pernicious, in spite of the fundamental sexual powerlessness of women in *fin de siècle* social structure. Medical figures were making their respective benighted and relatively enlightened cases in every imaginable context. They were also treating the problems of unfulfilled and unfelt desire with surprisingly direct tactics.

Doctors of the mind like Putnam couldn't help confronting the importance of sexuality in neurosis as they regularly saw patients who complained of sexual problems. Near the outset of his career, Putnam received a letter from a man who pleaded that he be "fitted for marriage" because his "generative powers" had been devastated by "self-abuse." The model of chastity, Susan Blow herself, eventually told Putnam about the crippling incestual overtones to her relationship with her father.

Putnam's therapeutic practice in the early years relied primarily on electrotherapy and hydrotherapy. Rachel Maines' book, *The Technology of Orgasm*, which traces the astonishingly suppressed history of women's medically supervised, technological sexual stimulation, implies that both Putnam's shock therapeutics and "water cure" methodologies would almost certainly have included therapy specifically aimed at bringing patients to orgasm. Maines has collected a set of illustrations and firsthand accounts indicating the extent to which a portfolio of douches (especially "douches upon the loins") and water jets were employed at spas and clinics to produce in women "the most extraordinary effects, as weeping, laughing, trembling, &tc," as one practitioner put it. Electrotherapy used a variety of devices (from the full-size "jolting chair" to hand-held vibrators) to generate mild shocks for the purpose of tonic, usually genitally focused massage. These devices had long been seen as an excellent means of relieving "pelvic congestion" and its accompanying neurasthenic symptoms. John Harvey Kellogg, cereal magnate of Battle Creek, was a great enthusiast of the effects of contractions in treating neurosis. In an address he gave in 1904, he describes how, in his own latest experiments, "with one electrode placed in the rectum or the vagina, and the other upon the abdomen, strong contractions of the abdominal muscles may be produced, and even of the muscles of the upper thigh, without any sensation other than of motion." In the year of Freud's visit, Maines notes, Kellogg's *Good Health* catalog dangled before doctors "a vibratory chair, a vibrating bar, a trunk-shaking apparatus . . . apparatus for percussion and mechanical kneading, and a very impressive electromechanical 'centrifugal vibrator.'" Some of these sorts of tools, such as the luxury "Chattanooga Vibrator," honed for both rectal and vaginal penetration, were also applied to male neurasthenics.

Putnam's work at MGH employing such instruments was then the typical first line of defense treatment for a variety of neurasthenic complaints. No one, however hidebound by the conventions of the age, could have mistaken this welter of penetrating nozzles and nodes as anything but forms of sexual treatment. Some physicians argued that the generation of pelvic contractions, instead of releasing tension, could spark a proliferating desire (with all the consequent access of neurosis), but these naysayers did not bring about a reduction in such forms of treatment. Despite the pathologization of sex implicit in all this, matters become more ambiguous in the early 1900s, still before Freud's visit, with the increasing sales of consumer vibrators for home usage. The American Vibrator Company, based in Blow's hometown of St. Louis, produced a home vibrator in 1906 that was promoted on the basis of its depth of access and spectrum of untiring motions. The ultimate selling point was the fact that the "American Vibrator" could be administered alone, "in the privacy of dressing room or boudoir, and furnishes every woman with the very essence of perpetual youth." Even *had* Freud sought to bring a legitimization of sexual energy and ecstasy to America, it would appear that in households furnished with a device like the American Vibrator, he would have been bringing coals to Newcastle.

At the least, the question of what Freud *did* bring America becomes more—congested. As Freud himself noted, the Yankees were acutely conscious of childhood sexuality. Indeed, Putnam was so concerned with the reality of children's sexuality that, as Molly stated as an adult, he had adjusted his daughters' bicycle seats out of concern that the friction might be unduly stimulating. He was so scared of triggering any kind of father–daughter sexual response that he forbade his daughters to sit on his lap. This is a notion of children's erotic potential that seems even to out-Freud Freud himself. (Jones reports that Freud was physically warm with his children.)

For all of Putnam's extreme caution when it came to his own female offspring at home, he did not consider sex an omnipresent evil to be avoided. In 1898, in an essay entitled "Neurasthenia," Putnam insisted that a physician ought first to discuss with patients both the "difficulties and possibilities" of "self-restraint" for the phobias and impotence that could accompany sexual neurasthenia. However, in advocating that the physician act as a counselor who would then turn over to the patient the decision about which course to pursue, Putnam was a long way from mandating a course of chastity. Indeed, by pointing out both potential advantages and the hardships of self-restraint, the physician was working equally with "a view to the stimulation of the will" in those who could fortify themselves for the moral struggle and "the counteraction of morbid self-reproach" among those for whom the high road was too strenuous. Even if what was taking place in these counseling sessions was a far cry from the "talking cure," it's apparent that a reasonably candid conversation about sexuality was part of treatment. As Hale points out, there was a growing cognizance in the last years of the nineteenth century that an inability to speak about sex could itself have debilitating consequences.

In the 1870s, Putnam was willing to take the advice of a colleague in treating symptoms of neurotic "cerebro-spinal exhaustion" in prescribing "the fat of beef and mutton to be eaten freely; butter and cream likewise. Sexual intercourse to be absolutely abstained from. Mental labor to be made as regular and unemotional as possible and sufficient sleep to be obtained: nerve tonics; phosphorus or zinc phosphate, oxide of iron, arsenic, strychnia, for relief of spinal pains, electricity and the emplastrum, belladonna, etc." By 1898, these sorts of pacifying somatic regimes were insufficient. Although he made the point in the essay "Neurasthenia" that patients need to understand that "sexual intercourse is not the main object of marriage," he also stresses that "an unnatural struggle for extreme abstinence is not good for the neurasthenic patient, and the physician can often bring material aid to the patient in arriving at a wise conclusion as to the detail." Couched in qualifiers and abstractions, Putnam was saying that one sensible prescription for sexual neurasthenia was sex.

In another essay on neurasthenia, published in 1908, Putnam expressed a progressive—in the sense of being anti-hereditary—theory of sexual perversion. He suggested that environment and social causes were at the root of tendencies that many doctors attributed to degeneracy and "manifestations of an implacable destiny." By this point, Putnam was fully cognizant of the link between adult neurosis and youthful sexuality: "The sexual instincts, though not consciously recognized as such, are the basis of much of the emotional instability of early puberty and middle life," he wrote in 1908.

Some popular religious organizations of the age, such as the Emmanuel Movement, also acknowledged the role of environment as opposed to innate depravity in sexual deviance. *Religion and Medicine*, which was written by three of the movement's founders (who cite Putnam as a key early supporter) and published in 1908, contains passages deploring the rise of prostitution, along with "temporary and irresponsible unions," which the industrialization and fragmentation of American society was spawning. But rather than critiquing the sexualized individuals themselves, the authors chose to highlight the damaging effect of sexual hypocrisy in the American climate. They decried the "effects of a 'double life' upon the nervous system" and invoked as their authority none other than Oscar Wilde, who wrote, "'He who lives more lives than one, more deaths than one must die.'" They criticized the victimization of women endemic in the prevailing social structure.

It may have been inconceivable to posit having good sex as a life goal, as we do today, but sexuality as such had to be given its due.

THE MAGNUM OPUS of G. Stanley Hall, *Adolescence*, published in 1904, was largely concerned with the constitutive role of sexuality in human psychology. Whereas Hall had obviously read Freud and alludes to him directly with regard to the dominant etiology of sexual trauma in neurosis, Freud is primarily invoked to buttress Hall's own homegrown interpretation of the importance of sexuality, not the other way around.

Hall can hardly be considered a feminist, and he was taken to task by leaders of the women's rights movement. Of his concept of woman as a transcendent mother figure, Kate Gorden of Mount Holyoke College wrote in 1905, "To adore this naïve being, passionately to worship an unconscious divinity (the roots of whose being are so penetrating), is it not a very apotheosis of the vegetable?" However, for all Hall's undoubted sentimentality and refusal to countenance women's capacity for certain vocations, he nonetheless devoted a great deal of space to arguing in support of women's higher education (albeit in the humanities). What's more, much of the fifty-page chapter "Adolescent Girls and Their Education" in the book *Adolesence,* consisted of a call for a greater recognition of female sexuality. In an exhaustive review of contemporary writing on the subject he made clear his condemnation of the lingering view of menstruation "as a disagreeable function or a badge of inferiority." He cited approvingly the work of Dr. F. C. Taylor in the *American Journal of Obstetricians* in the 1880s who had stated that "if the sexual life [in women] is lowered or suppressed, a tonic needed for vigor in all directions is lost." Hall implicitly supports Taylor's position that when women are kept "in a suppressed semi-erotic state with never-culminating feeling" they lose their ability for concentrated work or affections of any kind.

Hall argued that happy marriage can't be purely sentimental and "should be bulwarked by mental affinity" between husband and wife. Whereas "women are weaker in body and mind than men" they can nonetheless "achieve great things even intellectually, and might take courage from examples like that of Darwin, who did much of his best work in years of such weakness that he could apply himself for only an hour or two a day." Along with the need to grant women greater intellectual relevance in marriage, Hall alluded to another author who promotes the importance of recognizing the "animal basis" in its pure and wholesome capacity. If American women are not nurtured in that regard, Hall writes, startlingly, "there will have to be a 'new rape of the Sabines,' and if women do not improve, men will have recourse to emigrant wives."

Part of the blame for the lack of stamina necessary to preserve the animal basis is laid on ignorance. Great suffering and unhappy marriages can result from teachers' ignorance on the subjects of puberty and sex. Hall cites a German physician as his source for the crucial idea that "definite instruction in sexual hygiene" should be provided to middle school pupils. This education was to be, in some fashion, egalitarian, or at least responsive to the separate integrity of female erotic concerns. "Neither sex should copy nor set patterns to the other, but all parts should be played harmoniously and clearly in the great sex symphony." He criticized the agendas of women's colleges to date and remarked that in conferences on the subject of how to better the state of female education, despite "rare, striking exceptions," the "proceedings are smitten with the same sterile and complacent artificiality that was so long the curse of woman's life." The reason for this is, at least partially, that "public opinion is still liable to panics if discussion here becomes scientific and fundamental, and so tend to keep prudery and the old habit of ignoring that pertains to sex in countenance."

Though Hall was neither a champion of modern women or of sexual liberation, he clearly understood that a crisis was afoot and that the crisis was due in large measure to near total inhibition of female sexuality along with general ignorance about the erotic domain. The question of sexuality in turn-of-the-century America came down, like so much else, to a question of education. What was it that men and women needed to be taught about their bodies as a way of safeguarding and nurturing both their physiologies and minds?

Despite Hall's belief in the merits of learned "sexual hygiene," the problems he experienced actually acting on his faith revealed the lingering sway over him, like so many of Putnam's circle, of the pent-up New England past. In 1904, Hall tried to teach a weekly course on sex psychology at Clark. However he soon abandoned the effort for two reasons: "First, because it was difficult to exclude those I deemed unfit since too many outsiders got in and even listened surreptitiously at the door, and second, because two or three of my students developed an interest in the subject which I deemed hardly less than morbid." A third reason, never quite acknowledged as such, was tendered at the end of this autobiographical passage: "It is, of course, impossible to treat such a theme scientifically without at least some plain speaking upon perversions . . . and this I found it most unexpectedly hard to do although all women were excluded." In other words, one's own recognition of the centrality of sex did not translate into instant acquisition of an appropriate vernacular for communicating the subject to others.

PUTNAM WOULD HAVE read Hall's book on *Adolescence* with acute interest given his overweening sense of responsibility for his daughters' development, along with his preoccupation with the question of their sexuality (the older ones were just then entering puberty). But he would also have been annoyed with Hall's pugnacious materialism—his contention that, once the social fuss had been pooh-poohed away, the whole business came down to particulars of a purely biological nature.

Freud's lecture on sexuality, for all its insistence on a strict materialist approach, clearly presented a different field of questions and a more honest response to the ones Hall had raised. In fact, Freud seemed to be calling for adults to step in at the right moment and help complete the "childish investigation" into sex that has such a "determinative significance in the building of the child's character, and in the content of his later neuroses." At the end of Freud's fourth lecture, he issued an explicit plea for pedagogical reform on these matters that would have appealed to Putnam: "great problems," in the matter of promoting a healthy sexuality, "fall to the work of education, which at present certainly does not always solve them in the most intelligent and economic way."

And still, Putnam would have left the lecture hungry, uncertain exactly what a healthy sexuality meant in the larger scheme of the universe. Of course it was important to do all one could to lessen human misery. Freud's noble words on the importance of ridding the field of hypocrisy may have explained how to draw one's fellows out of the pit, but how did one fulfill the ultimate pedagogical mandate of helping them draw nearer to the heavens? And each night after hearing Freud he returned to 106 Marlborough, and to Molly's prostrate 16-year-old body, her convalescence under his sole care.

By the time Freud delivered his fifth and final lecture he'd already received his honorary degree from Clark, and cabled home to Martha in Vienna a one-word telegram: "Success!"

His reception in the U.S. was very different from that in Vienna. There has been, in recent years, a reappraisal of Freud's assertions of having been ignored in Austria. Challenges to his account are largely based on the reviews (mixed in nature) that his studies did in fact garner, sometimes in prominent publications. However, given that professional Viennese society, at least up until the dissolution of the Habsburg Empire, established value through institutional hierarchies, Freud's demonstrable marginality in that official labyrinth lends legitimacy to his claims.

Freud's frustration with his slow rise in the university did not reflect any structural disapproval of the system itself, but was due rather to the fact that his advancement was supposed to take place through the operation of the uniform mechanism that dictated life in the empire, and yet his Semitism had somehow impeded the action of the cogs.

The American idea of infinite stores of energy hidden within the self, only awaiting the right touch to be released and so revolutionize the individual's place in society and the universe, made little sense to Freud. Indeed, it wasn't long after he received his honorary degree that the absence of obvious hierarchies in American society—ones based anyway on a principle other than wealth—began to aggravate him. He didn't like the free-for-all character of a democratic exchange in which social distinctions fell by the wayside. What was the point of having received a degree or social rank of any standing if those things counted for nothing in society? If anything other than money did give standing in America it was youth, and

Jones mentions an incident underscoring Freud's age as exemplary for him of the distasteful "free and easy manners of the New World."

In between giving his lectures at Clark and visiting Putnam in the Adirondacks, Freud took a trip to visit Niagara Falls, a tour he'd been looking forward to even before leaving Europe. The sublimity of the sight impressed him even more than he'd anticipated. In the midst of his marveling, however, as his tour group entered the Cave of Winds, the guide abruptly held the other visitors back with a condescending gesture to Freud. "Let the old fellow go first," he prompted.

This is the context for Freud's climactic lecture at Clark. The idea of sublimation that he introduced there with singular emphasis must be looked at through the lens of Viennese social hierarchy, not the system of advancement Americans favored: a market-based, Darwinian "jungle" or ideal meritocracy (depending on one's perspective).

Habsburg imperial rule was based, in part, on the legal guarantee of equal rights to all the empire's multifarious nationalities. This particular model of enfranchisement was also dependent on the idea of holding all Austro-Hungarian peoples at saber's length from the inner sanctum of authority. As Joseph Roth wrote in *The Radetzsky March,* "Our Kaiser is a secular brother of the Pope, he is his Imperial and Royal Apostolic Majesty; no other is as apostolic, no other majesty in Europe is as dependent on the grace of God and on the faith of the nations in the grace of God." The last bitter line of the passage underscored the nontransmittable essence of the Kaiser's power: "But God has abandoned the world."

In the Freudian model, sublimation of one's desires didn't involve only an exercise of willpower; the achievement also signaled possession of an elite mental endowment. In this sense, there are echoes in Freud's belief system of the Calvinist notion of a predestined elect. Though Freud might have challenged the license accorded the aristocracy in the *Hofburg* (hence his daydreams of overthrowing imperial authority [Roman and monarchial]), he did so in favor of empowering an eternal aristocracy of the mind, the ranks of which could not be broached by dull petitioners. Threats to the power of this elite arose primarily from within the individual. Freud's model of tragic heroics was, thus, both classical, based on an inscrutable system of fatal dispensation, and Shakespearean, in the sense of being set in motion by a fatal character flaw. In the expanded later introductory lectures to psychoanalysis (published with an introduction by Hall in 1920), Freud employed martial metaphors to describe the state of sublimation. "[But] the structure thus built up [through sublimation] is insecure, for the sexual impulses are with difficulty controlled; in each individual who takes up his part in the work of civilization there is a danger that a rebellion of the sexual impulses may occur, against this diversion of their energy. Society can conceive of no more powerful menace to its culture than would arise from the liberation of the sexual impulses and a return of them to their original goal." By the time Freud published this statement, with psychoanalysis booming in the New World, he'd conceived of a paradigm in which the psychoanalyst served as general, ensuring the containment of a perpetual erotic insurgency. By now, the potential for sublimation was the political capital of the analysts.

When Freud talked about sublimation in America, he was not describing a common goal toward which any random neurotic could work; he was defining a process which, through a purge of complexes, analysts could prepare the minds of the chosen to undertake. One suspects that Freud's real concern in the talk was to sugarcoat the pill of sexuality by suggesting that the same energy that went into lust also, on occasion, found civilized applications. Fear of mass American squeamishness about the erotic was his greatest motivation for introducing sublimation.

Putnam, however, took something very different from the lecture and in doing so forecast the deeper American interest in psychoanalysis. Freud's theory of sublimation completed a circuit. On the one hand there was sex, very much present for him as for many of his peers and present very much as a problem. On the other hand there was a set of transsexual, Blowian, Bergsonian, Royceian ideals to which *every* individual ought to aspire, though there was no formula for doing so. How did one harness the power in the individual toward worthy Platonic ends? Unlike some, Putnam did not believe that it was enough to say that there were two ways forking out from each person and it was up to the individual to simply "choose life." He'd seen too many cases in his clinic of patients who *wanted* to choose the good, but didn't have sufficient strength or understanding of their better instincts to know how to act on them.

At the beginning of the lecture, Freud made a blunt statement about the role of sex in the neuroses. The individual becomes ill, he said, "when

in consequence of outer hindrances or inner lack of adaptability the satisfaction of the erotic needs in the sphere of reality is denied." The flight
into sickness is a quest for "surrogate satisfaction for that denied him."
Putnam knew in his own person the ways in which, when life failed to bring
the fulfillment for which he longed, he could turn up a side of himself that
was antithetical to all the values he cherished. Freud's summary of this
phenomenon introduced the idea of repetition—backsliding to an earlier
stage in the patient's own psychology and to a more savage collective an-
thropological moment. "The flight from the unsatisfying reality into what
we call, on account of its biologically injurious nature, disease, but which
is never without an individual gain in pleasure for the patient, takes place
over the path of regression, the return to earlier phases of the sexual life,"
wrote Freud. Given Putnam's heartfelt philosophy of progress, this would
have had to have been the most frightening of all scenarios.

Freud then shifted from the dark abyss of regression toward Purgatory.
He pointed out that, in fact, "the deeper you penetrate into the pathogenic
of neurotic diseases" the more you find that there are connections between
the neuroses and other aspects of mental life including "even the most
valuable." Because Freud had just carefully equated disease with the thwart-
ing of erotic desire, and his audience was being guided to follow the implications of this fact for an understanding of the neurotic personality, it must
have appeared a surprising, bold twist when he said, in effect: But gentlemen you know yourselves in your own persons the phenomenon I'm describing. "You will be reminded that we men, with the high claims of our
civilization and under the pressure of our repressions, find reality generally quite unsatisfactory." It's not just the neurotic who finds life disappoint-
ing, Freud said; we all do. Hence our tendency to fantasize. Because of
this frustration every one of us is prey to, we all "keep up a life of fancy in
which we love to compensate for what is lacking in the sphere of reality by
the production of wish-fulfillments." It is "these phantasies" that in fact
define our psychological constitution, "repressed in real life." But this production of fantasies is not by definition neurotic. In a statement with parallels to the thought of James, Freud went on: "The energetic and successful
man is he who succeeds by dint of labor in transforming his wish fancies
into reality." Fantasizing is universal—is, indeed, the inevitable response
to reality—the proof of a fantasy's value is in the individual's capacity to
make it real.

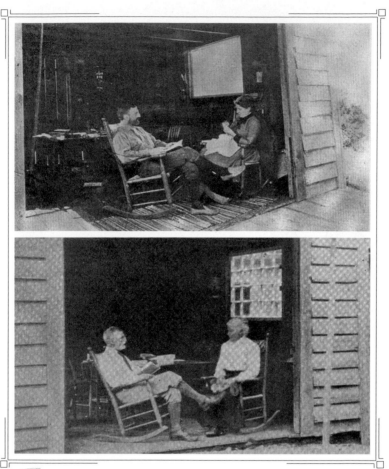

*J*ames Jackson Putnam and Marian Cabot Putnam on the porch of the "Pen" at Putnam Camp in the summer of 1886, and in 1910. Originally a pigpen, the building was converted into a writer's retreat. Its walls were embellished with a frieze of pigs' tails vanishing behind open books.

*P*artial view of Putnam Camp in 1907, probably photographed from William James' ledge, a small, precipitous rock outcrop discovered by James on a slope just above Camp.

*T*he bristling, musical metal porcupine that Putnam presented to Freud at the end of the latter's Adirondack visit, shown here in its prominent place among the ancient bibelots on Freud's desk in London.

*W*illiam James (on right) and a companion near the central farmhouse at Camp in 1907.

(A Hungarian song)..

1) Ritka árpa, ritka búza, ritka rozs —
Ritka kis lány takaros.
Lám az enyim - takaros,
Jetike, pienke - nem nagos.
Hej! Kis lány. Kis lány, kis lány!
Mondd meg az anyádnak:
Ha egy kicsit, nagy kicsit nagyobb volnál —
Mindjárt megcsókolnálak!"

Ferenci:
Budapest.

Translation:

Rare (pre) oats, rare (is) wheat and scarce is barley
Rare is the little girl who is pretty
See my maiden how charming she is
Tiny tiny — not too tall
Hey little girl — tell this to your mother
If you were a wee bit taller
I would kiss you right away.

Sat. sept. 18   clear

*S*andor Ferenczi's transcription and translation of a Hungarian song in the Putnam Camp log, inscribed on the eve of the foreign doctors' departure.

Top Left: The Putnam family in December 1899. Clockwise beginning in the upper left: James Jackson Putnam, Elizabeth, Louisa, Frances and Marian, Molly, and James Jackson, Jr.
Top Right: Frances Cabot Putnam in lederhosen on the Camp farmhouse steps in 1907.
Bottom Left: Unidentified Putnam Campers at studious post-prandial labors in the Stoop.
Bottom Right: The Putnam children in 1909. A certain brooding gravity sets in. Left to right: Louisa, Elizabeth, James Junior, Molly, and Frances. This picture became the final lantern slide in the series Elizabeth prepared for her parents' silver wedding anniversary in 1911.

*P*utnam Campers sending off a party of guests in 1903. James Jackson Putnam is the third figure in from the right.

*U*nidentified Putnam Camp guests at a meal in the dining room. On the wall hangs part of "Sir Guy's" suit of armor, built from junk heap refuse one long afternoon by Edward Emerson.

*D*ramatic amusements at Putnam Camp. ***Top:*** A children's theatrical production. James Jackson Putnam, Jr. is the central figure. ***Bottom Left:*** A fanciful, winged aerial conveyance, probably made in the Camp workshop. ***Bottom Right:*** Molly Putnam stilt-walking along Camp's uneven, rocky ground.

A dreamy Molly at Put-nam Camp around the onset of puberty in Native American costume.

My father on the street in Vienna or Zurich in his own Native American tribal regalia.

Top Left: Susan Blow looking like an Edith Wharton heroine at about the age of twenty-one. *Top Right:* Susan Blow approximately ten years later, buttoned up in the role of kindergarten pioneer.

An undated entry from Blow's commonplace book.

———

PUTNAM MIGHT HAVE heard these lines of Freud and thought not just of the larger American Protestant ethic but of his own relentless labors and the question of what fruit they bore. Along with publishing volumes of papers every year, teaching, taking part in innumerable professional associations, and handling a full case load, he remained ever active in the lives of his children and engaged with the family's vast social circle. He could not have found it easy to maintain the delusion of still holding anything back in the way of will to work. "It is a great thing," he wrote Marian a few months before the Clark Conference, "to learn to give up, gracefully and quickly, the attempt to reach goals that can't be reached, and to go in for goals that can be reached." This is something, he said, that he himself still must learn "painfully to do." There are, he reminds himself, "many sensitive people" who "teach themselves to do it, but I don't think it is quite fair. It is rather a 'war-measure.'"

It wasn't, then, more of the same garden-variety energy that Putnam needed, but access to energy of an altogether different nature.

FREUD AVOWED THAT analysis would never be guilty of "a disturbance of the cultural character by the impulse which has been freed from repression." The whole purpose of the practice he advocated was in fact to weaken those revolutionary impulses within the self, a type of urge "which is incomparably stronger when it is unconscious than when it is conscious. . . . The work of psychoanalysis accordingly presents a better substitute, in the service of the highest and most valuable cultural strivings, for the repression which has failed."

This opened the door to Putnam's revelation. "Now what is the fate of the wishes which have become free by psychoanalysis, by what means shall they be made harmless for the life of the individual?" For the most part, Freud said, "repression is supplanted by a condemnation" carried through in an economic manner. So far from letting the dark side of the self out into the society, one learns how to vilify it openly. This condemnation, according to Freud, is less psychologically costly than repression.

There is, however, a further service psychoanalysis offers society. Unconscious impulses once exposed can be redirected toward the meaningful goals that they should have been abetting all along. Rather than trying to eliminate these sources of energy, analysis supports "a far more purposive process of development ... so called sublimation, by which the energy of infantile wish-excitation" enables "a higher, eventually no longer sexual, goal" to be established. Putnam's Eureka moment came as Freud proclaimed that "the components of the sexual instinct are especially distinguished by such a capacity for the sublimation and exchange of their sexual goal for one more remote and socially more valuable."

With these words Freud had unknowingly created an ideal ecology. For years, Putnam had wrestled with the fact that repressed sexual impulses caused mental disturbance. Yet the expenditure of these impulses willy-nilly was wasteful of energy—or worse, morally corrosive of the community. At the same time there was a grander unsolved puzzle: Where did individuals find the energy to rise above their own foibles of character and so fulfill their supernal responsibilities to society and the universe? Freud's idea of sublimation suggested that the solution to one enigma also resolved the other.

By learning to sublimate erotic desire, humanity would be able to expel the sexual energy which, when jailed inside, ate away at the individual's sanity. But so far from just going into exile, the libido could serve as the missing catalytic converter to fuel the individual's ascent toward labor of a higher purpose.

For Putnam, Freud wasn't the one who brought sex to America, he was the one who *took sex away*. By an alchemic reaction, sex through sublimation became spirituality. Thus, Putnam's embrace of Freud signified no less than his investment in the future of psychology, a desperate effort to save the American transcendental nineteenth-century religious past.

CHAPTER 10

Derealization

*The apotropaea are entirely in our possession, they are always
consolations through sexuality. . . . All watch charms —pig,
ladder, shoe, chimney sweep, etc. —are sexual consolations.*
Freud to Jung, November 21, 1909

FREUD WAS APPROACHING the question of sex from an opposite landscape, in which spirituality itself metamorphosed into an erotic sublime.

IN HIS ORIGINAL plans for travel to the New World, Freud had lobbied
to sail from Trieste, a route that lapped Palermo and other sun-washed
haunts of the ancients. There were deep emotional reasons for trying to
piggyback this scenic point of departure onto the most important professional expedition of his life. The last time Freud had departed from Trieste
was in August exactly five years earlier, on a visit to Corfu with his younger
brother, Alexander, that unexpectedly led to Freud's first trip to the Acropolis. While in Trieste, Alexander had called upon a business acquaintance
who dissuaded them from traveling on to Corfu because of the summer
heat, recommending Athens instead. Freud later wrote in a letter to Romain
Rolland of an experience he underwent on the Acropolis in which he was
overcome with a strange kind of wonder. He described the sensation as,
alternately, a disturbance of memory or a "derealization." At the climactic
moment in his account, Freud "cast his eyes around the landscape" and
suddenly became seized with the remarkable thought, "So all this really
does exist, just as we learnt at school!"

Dissecting the event for Rolland's benefit, Freud wrote, "the person who gave expression to the remark was divided, far more sharply than was usually observable, from another person who took cognizance of the remark; and both were astonished, though not by the same thing. The first behaved as though he were obliged, under the impact of an unequivocal observation, to believe in something the reality of which had hitherto seemed doubtful." Freud likened this first figure to someone who abruptly catches sight of the Loch Ness Monster "stranded upon the shore and found himself driven to the admission: So it really *does* exist—the sea-serpent we always disbelieved in! The second person," Freud continued, "was justifiably astonished, because he had been unaware that the real existence of Athens, the Acropolis, and the landscape around it had been objects of doubt." But why did Freud speak of himself as double or split?

A PRIMARY SYMPTOM invoked in diagnosis of the hysterical condition since at least the eighteenth century, and one that Freud himself invoked in his writing, was possession of a dual personality. Charcot, under whom Freud studied prior to writing his paper on male hysteria, defined this phenomenon as a "second consciousness." Theories as to what spawned the second self were various, but sexuality was implicated in many of them, generally an unappeased erotic appetite of one sort or another. Was Freud confessing to a moment of hysteria?

His analysis of the event for Rolland began with a recognition of the inaccuracy of his apostrophe on the Acropolis. In fact, Freud tells us, there was never any point in his school days when he "doubted the real existence of Athens. I only doubted whether I should ever see Athens." He linked this distrust to a bout of depression which, he says, both he and Alexander succumbed to in Trieste on contemplating the prospect of a voyage to Athens. "We discussed the plan that had been proposed, agreed that it was quite impracticable and saw nothing but difficulties in the way of carrying it out. . . . We spent the hours that elapsed before the Lloyd offices opened in wandering about the town in a discontented and irresolute frame of mind." Freud traced their skepticism about the voyage back to his father. "It must be that a sense of guilt was attached to the satisfaction in having got so far: there was something about it that was wrong, that was from earliest times forbidden," he wrote. "It seems as though the essence of success were to have got further than one's father, as though to excel one's father were still something forbidden." Eventually, Freud attempted to parse the character of what he called "derealization," the generalized phenomenon in which one loses the ability to believe that whatever is taking place is actually happening. The two forms of derealization refer to the seminal category of infantile experience: the desire to incorporate an object or to keep it outside of one. In a moment of derealization, "the subject feels either that a piece of reality or that a piece of his own self is strange to him." However, Freud says, "There is another set of phenomena which may be regarded as their positive counterparts—what are known as *'fausse reconnaissance,' déjà vu, déjà raconte*, etc., illusions in which we seek to accept something as belonging to our ego, just as in the derealizations we are anxious to keep something out of us." Derealization, Freud goes on, leads specifically to "the extraordinary condition of *'double conscience.'*"

The *déjà vu* element in the Acropolis story links it with the uncanny moment when, on Freud's fiftieth birthday in 1906, less than a month after he'd begun his correspondence with Jung, his disciples presented him with a medallion engraved with his own effigy and on the obverse face an image of Oedipus before the Sphinx, along with a line from Sophocles' play: "He who solved the famous riddle and was a most powerful man." Jones wrote how Freud, on being presented with the bronze medallion "grew pale, became agitated and, with a strange voice, asked who had chosen the inscription. He reacted as if he just met something again; actually, it was this that just happened . . . Freud let them know that, as a young student at University in Vienna, he was accustomed to walk around the great court and look at the busts of the old famous professors. It was then that he not only had the phantasy of viewing his own future bust (that should come as no surprise from an ambitious student), but also had imagined this bust with precisely the same quotation on the medallion."

For Freud, the notion of encountering ghosts included the idea of self-division—of being confronted with the fulfillment of one's own fantasy self from an earlier point in time. The moment of his "disturbance of memory" constitutes a fantasy in which Freud seeks to accept something as the rightful possession of his own ego, rather than a derealization, which would imply the wish to reject the experience from the boundaries of his own anatomy (as destiny). What Freud wants to accept before the temple of the gray-eyed goddess is an occult cannibalization of his father.

At the conclusion of the letter to Rolland, Freud drove home the defeat of his father consequent on his own presence in Athens. First, Freud mentioned that there was a particular aspect of the Athens experience that "contained evidence of the sons' superiority." Then, in a single sentence, he made a triple assault on his father's memory. "Our father had been in business, he had had no secondary education, and Athens could not have meant much to him." This gratuitous elaboration turns the next sentence into a non sequitur: "Thus what interfered with our enjoyment of the journey to Athens was a feeling of *piety*." What kind of piety is expressed in this exposure of the father's nakedness? Even the slur on Jakob Freud's lack of education is misleading. Whereas Freud's father was, it is true, self-taught (discounting a substantial religious education), he was hardly a man lacking in intellectual interests or abilities. He himself served as Freud's teacher until Freud entered a private school. If there were any professed lack of interest on Jakob's part in the Acropolis, it would likely be an ideological one having to do with the opposition between Hellenic and Semitic values. Jakob Freud's learning as a Jew was strong enough that at the age of 75 he could still inscribe a complex Hebrew dedication in a bible he presented to the 35-year-old Sigmund, threading together different quotes in classic rabbinical fashion. It seems doubtful that Freud himself would have been able to read this inscription without his father's help, and so in the context of the gift would have been made aware of the limits of his own education.

Athens is, of course, the city of Pallas Athena, and the Acropolis is dominated by the temple dedicated to her, the Parthenon. Freud had a long-standing fascination with Athena. The bronze figure of the goddess that he eventually acquired was given pride of place in his art collection, and in the final hours of his life in Austria, when it appeared that he would have to sacrifice all his material possessions in order to escape, the Athena was the sole object he chose to smuggle out with him. In 1922, Freud wrote a short essay on Athena focused on the figure of Medusa typically engraved on her breastplate, an emblem that is, indeed, plainly visible on the statuette in his collection.

Freud's departure point in the study is his symbolic association of decapitation with castration. The severing of the subject's head signifies the absence of a phallus and, hence, the possession of female genitalia (themselves defined negatively by the missing male organ). Freud writes how many analyses have taught him that when a boy who has been "unwilling to believe the threat of castration, catches sight of the female genitals, probably those of an adult, surrounded by hair, and essentially those of his mother" he becomes instantly as it were a convert to the faith. The Medusa's head on Athena's armor is obviously decapitated. However, Freud says, the angst provoked by the icon of castration is compensated for by the writhing snakes that surround Medusa's head. The snake is a substitute for the penis. Though Freud does not here work out the implications of this dual possession he's just identified, elsewhere he notes that Athena seems to have originally been a hermaphroditic deity.

In his 1922 essay, Freud explains Athena's decision to wear the "symbol of horror" on her dress because by doing so "she becomes a woman who is unapproachable and repels all sexual desires—since she displays the terrifying genitals of the Mother." He follows this remark by noting, "Since the Greeks were in the main strongly homosexual, it was inevitable that we should find among them a representation of woman as a being who frightens and repels because she is castrated." It's a significant jump to say that because most of the Greeks were homosexual they idolized the image of a sexually terrifying woman and in fact made this castrated/castrating figure the center of their cultic worship at Athens. Freud in fact has given us a series of truncated—castrated—memories and associations.

In analyzing the malaise into which he'd sunk in Trieste in 1904, Freud omitted to mention perhaps the most obvious explanation: a flare-up of his lifelong travel phobia. This phobia kicked in, by Freud's own admission, in connection with the other major voyages of his life, such as the aborted expeditions to Rome before 1900 and the trip to America five years after Athens.

In a letter to Fliess on March 10, 1897, the same in which he made his famous renunciation of the seduction theory and acknowledged the role of sexual phantasy in psychological complexes, Freud explained the origins of his travel phobia. It began, he says, in the course of his childhood move to Vienna, when he was traveling to his new home in Austria from Leipzig. During this overnight trip, which he spent with his mother, Freud writes, "I must have had the opportunity of seeing her *nudam*. . . . My anxiety over travel you have seen yourself in full bloom."

In other words, Freud's travel phobia originated in the sight of the female genitals, the very image he describes as being symbolically encapsulated in the Medusa on Athena's breastplate. Furthermore, in his account of the event an additional allusion makes the Athena analogy still stronger and shows Freud himself as a new kind of myth maker. Freud's story of seeing his mother's nakedness is preceded by another item in his laundry list of revelations from his self-analysis, "that my 'primary originator' [of neurosis] was an ugly, elderly but clever woman who told me a great deal about God and hell, and gave me a high opinion of my own capacities." (Some have speculated that this woman was Freud's own primal seducer.) The stories of the old woman and the mother accounts were prefaced by the statement, "I can only say that in my case my father played no active role." The arousal of libido at the sight of the "terrifying genitals of the Mother" is then a particular sort of Greek self-empowerment—of ambition vis-à-vis supplanting the father. Similarly, the fear of castration that Freud binds to the sight is oedipal, the fear that his exposure to his mother's sexuality puts him in conflict with his father and hence in danger of suffering the father's vengeance. At the moment when Freud sees her nakedness he knows that he is in the secret privileged place of the father, which excites him—despite the terror of the genitals themselves—but this excitement is immediately connected to the terror that his father will decapitate Freud's own genitals in consequence.

The fact that in Trieste Freud's fears would have been aroused in anticipation of a visit to the ultimate site dedicated to the "woman who is unapproachable and repels all sexual desires since she displays the terrifying genitals of the Mother" is predictable. However, the story does not end with his indulging this fear. After the gloom, the anxiety, the fear of the father to which he succumbed in Trieste, Freud is stunned to find that once he sets the process in motion, there is no difficulty whatever in actually making the travel arrangements. Suddenly, he has arrived and is standing upon the Acropolis. This is the point at which, in order to explain his sensation, Freud divides his persona in two.

At the edge of the site, Freud envisions the multiplicity of difficulties like the profusion of different snakes surrounding Medusa's head. He says of Medusa's writhing hair that it is a "confirmation of the technical rule according to which a multiplication of penis symbols signifies castration." However, he continues, "The sight of Medusa's head makes the spectator stiff with terror, turns him to stone. Observe that we have here once again the same origin from the castration and the same transformation of affect! For becoming stiff means an erection. Thus in the original situation it offers consolation to the spectator; he is still in possession of a penis, and the stiffening reassures him of the fact."

Following this sensation, Freud finds himself on top of the Acropolis—flourishing. He now likens his experience to that of someone catching sight of Loch Ness, a "transformation of affect" identical to that described in relation to Medusa. The stranded serpent is a stiff serpent as well. And so the spectator, Freud, is "still in possession of a penis" (though he's on forbidden ground), and a gigantic one at that. There are many divisions being invoked: Athena and Medusa. The multiplicity of snakes and the single sea serpent. Freud's own astonished self, and the self astounded at the astonishment. The two brothers. The two locations—Vienna and Athens. The old woman and the mother. The father and the son.

The divided self Freud himself experiences at this moment on the Acropolis relates to a pair of classical concepts: exstasis and the sublime of Longinus. So far from suffering a sense of loss of control and transgression, once Freud is on the Acropolis he achieves a state of extreme elevation, of "transport," the feeling of being carried outside himself. In the moment of ecstatic sublimity inside the Acropolis, Freud is also inside Athena, no longer afraid of her or what she represents vis-à-vis the father because he is embodying her, standing victorious, staring back at the patriarch. Freud himself comes to hold the shield of Athena as a defense against his father's wish to destroy him. Indeed, the icon of Athena that Freud kept next to him all his life is itself, were the arms removed, unmistakably a phallic figure. Athena's helmet makes a perfect crown on the erect penis.

At the conclusion of his essay on Athena and Medusa, Freud talks about how "what arouses horror in oneself will produce the same effect upon the enemy against whom one is seeking to defend oneself." If the mother's genitals terrify him, they can also be used against his enemies—especially as he inhabits them he becomes himself the figure of terror. The penultimate paragraph makes one final twist. "The erect male organ also has an apotropaic effect, but thanks to another mechanism. To display the penis (or any of its surrogates) is to say: 'I am not afraid of you. I defy you. I have a penis.'" So the arousal of libido in relation to the nude mother, the figure of castration, becomes a defiance of her and the father both. And in carrying around the little apotropaic phallic statuette of Athena Freud had things both—indeed, all—ways at once. Apart from wanting to revisit the ruins of classical civilization, he wanted to embark from Trieste to reexperience an ecstatic potency in preparation for America.

Psychoanalysis was always poised between an effort to invoke the dead and stand apotropaically against the powers of the underworld. Sexuality had an axial place in this equation. Just as Freud erased the boundaries between the antipodal perversions, proclaiming that a sadist was always, also, a masochist, on the Acropolis the desire and repulsion associated with the father and the rest of the retinue of departed spirits effaced; Freud felt himself standing with one foot on either bank of the Lethe.

But there was another figure who was willing to take these ideas further, erasing the borders between classicism and the spirits antedating the gods of Olympus; in the most dangerous symmetry conceivable, he occupied the place of Freud's son. More terrifying even than the absence inscribed in the mother's genitalia is the idea of a cosmos swarming and everywhere infested with sensate being. This state, worse than primeval chaos, Lucretius warned of as threatening mortals "with horrible aspect"; it was also the realm Jung increasingly devoted himself to summoning before Freud.

THE LAST TIME Freud and Jung were together in Vienna before traveling to America, Jung had wanted to hear Freud's views on the paranormal. Late at night in Freud's study, as Jung tells it, he asked Freud what he thought about the occult. Freud responded out of his "materialistic prejudice," relegating the entire complex of ideas to the realm of nonsense, and what was more, doing so, Jung says, "in terms of so shallow a positivism that I had difficulty in checking the sharp retort on the tip of my tongue."

Suddenly, a strange sensation overcame Jung. He felt as though his diaphragm was made of iron. It was becoming "red-hot—a glowing vault." At the moment he registered this, "there was such a loud report in the bookcase, which stood right next to us, that we both started up in alarm, fearing the thing was going to topple over on us." At this point, one can picture Jung folding his powerful arms and glaring triumphantly as he proceeded to confront Freud. In his account he proclaimed:

"There, that is an example of so-called catalytic exteriorization phenomenon."

"Oh come," Freud exclaimed. "That is sheer bosh."

"It is not," Jung replied. "You are mistaken, Herr Professor. And to prove my point I now predict that in a moment there will be another such loud report! . . . Sure enough, no sooner had I said the words than the same detonation went off in the bookcase."

Jung later wrote that he still did not know what had given him this conviction, or what was passing through Freud's mind as he "stared aghast" at Jung. All that was certain, Jung recounted, was that the incident had "aroused his mistrust of me, and I had the feeling that I had done something against him."

Two grown men sitting together in the agnostic's home arguing about the reality of parapsychological phenomenon are interrupted by two loud, inexplicable noises within the bookcase at climactic moments in the debate. No wonder Freud looked shocked!

Jung's explanation for Freud's stubbornness about acknowledging the reality of what had just transpired drew on another conversation between the two men that took place in 1910, in which, according to Jung, Freud said, "My dear Jung, promise me never to abandon the sexual theory. That is the most essential thing of all. You see, we must make a dogma of it, an unshakeable bulwark." Jung reported that Freud made this command with great emotion, like a father admonishing his son to go to church every Sunday, whereupon Jung, "in some astonishment," asked Freud, "'A bulwark against what?' To which he replied, 'Against the black tide of mud'— and here he hesitated for a moment, then added—'of occultism.'"

In trying to make sense of why Freud would feel "compelled to talk of sex continually," of Freud's apparently blind recourse to a "monotony of interpretation," Jung identified Freud in flight from himself (another image of self division). Jung claimed that Freud's own susceptibility to mystical experience made his theories of sexuality defensive. Freud was afraid "that the numinous light of his sexual insights might be extinguished by a 'black tide of mud.'"

Jung hit on Freud's need to distance himself from the occult as from a realm of "horrible aspect." Freud held up sexuality against the occult in a manner evocative of the injunction of his hero (and Jung's ancestor) Goethe:

"Only a God can prevail against a God." When mysticism runs rampant, Freud knew, it's never good for Jews. By persistently reminding people of the sexual, pathological roots of their mystical fantasies, Freud hoped to defuse their amorphous power over the psyche. Precisely this denuding drove Jung crazy.

Along with the sexualization of mysticism, Freud demystified sexuality. By showing how all sexuality partook of odds and ends from practices conventionally deemed deviant, Freud stripped behaviors designated perverse of their mystically repelling/galvanizing social aura. In doing so, he universalized his own vulnerabilities.

One function of his art collection was purely defensive, in a manner again reminiscent of Goethe's philosophy. In this schema a figure such as the head of Medusa became a symbol of the victory of classicism over the nameless chaos of humanity's dark past. When Goethe acquired a plaster mask of a well-known antique marble head of Medusa for his collection, which he'd admired while living in Rome at the palazzo of the Rondanini, he wrote to a friend of how contemplation of the image "by no means turned one to stone, but rather enlivened one's artistic sense exceedingly and magnificently." Along these lines, the objects in Freud's collection were meant to conjure the sublimation of mystical energies, not the original powers themselves.

IN THE SPRING of 1909, when Freud wrote Jung his own analysis of the mysterious banging in the bookcase, thoughts of America were more dominant than they'd been that winter when Jung visited. Freud now contextualized the supernatural experience entirely in terms of transmission, of the profound filial stature he bestowed on Jung that night. Repeatedly in the letter he described himself as the father and Jung as the son. "It is strange that on the very same evening when I formally adopted you as eldest son and anointed you—'in partibus infidelium'—as my successor and crown prince, you should have divested me of my paternal dignity." This divesting, Freud observed, seemed to give Jung as much delight as Freud himself had received from the *investiture* of Jung's person with so superlative a tribute.

It's not surprising that Jung blanched at the call. He would have found confirmation for his suspicions that Freud took the psychoanalytic mission religiously in every word Freud wrote. Even Freud's description of where the anointment took place, *in partibus infidelium* (in the land of the unbelievers) is an ecclesiastical term applied to a see given to transplanted Latin bishops. The element of irony in his terminology becomes more tenuous with each repetition and in consequence of the fact that Freud never steps out of character.

Above all, the letter conveys the anxieties of the older man infatuated with a younger, free-spirited rascal. He acknowledges to Jung that the events of the night made a deep impression on him. He notes that when he continued his investigations alone after Jung's departure, he realized that there was a "constant creaking where the two heavy Egyptian steles rest on the oaken boards of the bookshelves." One of the Egyptian objects would have been the important limestone, Ptolemaic-period donation stele in Freud's collection. The text of this stele recorded the events in which Egypt's first Greek-speaking leader tried to form a base of support among the Egyptian elite: the Hellenistic spirit sought domination over a more ancient Semitic mysticism. In the beginning, Freud wrote Jung, he was prone to accept the creaking as evidence of Jung's power to invoke the supernatural. However, he averred, in that case, the noise ought to have ceased once Jung had gone. "But since then," he wrote, "I have heard it repeatedly, not, however, in connection with my thoughts and never when I am thinking about you or this particular problem of yours. . . . My credulity, or at least my willingness to believe," he concluded, "vanished with the magic of your personal presence."

In openly admitting the "magic" of Jung's "personal presence," Freud was confessing the mystical aura to which a certain register of the erotic is vulnerable—specifically the erotic, which cannot be acknowledged as such because of its social illegitimacy. In another striking allusion, Freud described how, with Jung no longer there, "I confront the despiritualized furniture as the poet confronted undeified Nature after the gods of Greece had passed away." Freud then shifted from the magical back to the patriarchal-filial terms of exchange. "Accordingly, I put my fatherly horn-rimmed spectacles on again and warn my dear son to keep a cool head, for it is better not to understand something than make such great sacrifices to understanding."

Nonetheless, citing the privilege of age, Freud took the liberty of citing one more matter "between heaven and earth" that surpassed their rational grasp. He described how before going to Greece he'd arrived at the conviction that he would die between the ages of 61 and 62. To Jung he gave a very different explanation for the gloomy agitation he subsequently underwent in Athens from the one he would offer Rolland. On arriving in Greece with his brother, Alexander, Freud reported that "it was really uncanny how often the numbers 61 or 60 in connection with 1 or 2 kept cropping up in all sorts of numbered objects, especially those connected with transportation." The strange coincidence depressed him, but he hoped that his state would improve once they reached their lodging in Athens.

Freud's letter to Jung revealed that he was worried about his *own* death in connection with the trip, not angst regarding the defeat of his father. Jung, with his unironicized mysticism, went beyond Freud, just as Freud went beyond his own father with his un-Jewish classicism. Just as Freud somewhere knew that he had projected onto his father the death wish he himself felt for the old man, now Jung had inspired a fear that this adopted son wanted to see him dead. In that complex spring of 1909, part of Freud's wish to go to America encompassed the wish to get "beyond" his son before his son could outstrip him. This was his chance to break the mold and circumvent the same death wish he'd once deployed. By planting his own seed in the States he would be hedging his bets on the problem of transmission, adding a trans-Atlantic dimension.

UNLIKE PUTNAM AND the Americans who sought a way to free themselves from sex, Freud found in the erotic itself a source of personal aggrandizement. By projecting the hidden play of others' sexuality onto the big screen of mythology, Freud became the father of the sexual pantheon. Paradoxically, however, he could only attain this position because of his own ecstatic alienation. When it came to sex, Freud's Byzantine historical hysteria set him apart from the crowd; he was the stranger in the land of sex who became king. "Incapacity for meeting a *real* erotic demand is one of the most essential features of a neurosis," he wrote at the end of his case history of Dora. Yet, in Freud's system, real lust was always a product of fantasy. Freud's sexuality is the ultimate arena of derealization.

Freud claimed to have only stumbled on the erotic wellspring of neurosis by the sort of felicitous accident commonly granted an outsider; it was his segregation from the common condition that allowed him to see what everyone else was staring at blindly. Freud's account of how he came to an understanding of the role of sex in psychology in A *Short History of the Psychoanalytic Movement*, makes him sound like an ambassador from another planet *à la* Voltaire's Micromégas. "The idea for which I was held responsible had not at all originated with me. It had come to me from three persons, whose opinions could count upon my deepest respect," Freud wrote. "All three men had imparted to me an insight which, strictly speaking, they had not themselves possessed. . . . But these identical communications, received without my grasping them, had lain dormant within me, until one day they awoke as an apparently original discovery." These were two instances of double consciousness: that of the two men in relationship to their own understanding, and of Freud's own in relation to his belated discovery of what he'd grasped the men were saying. (Freud's whole notion of sexual trauma was likewise based on a repetition that shifted the topography of the past.)

The first of these promptings occurred when, in answer to Freud's questions as a young hospital doctor about a wife who'd begun to suffer from nervous illness, his colleague Breuer remarked, "Those are always secrets of the alcove." "Astonished," Freud wrote, "I asked his meaning and he explained the expression to me ('secrets of the conjugal bed'), without realizing how preposterous the matter appeared to me." Next, Freud described a scene involving a couple in Charcot's care. "The wife was a great sufferer and the husband was impotent, or exceedingly awkward. In discussing the case with a colleague, Charcot said suddenly and with great vivacity: 'Mais, dans des cas pareils c'est toujours la chose génital, toujours—toujours—toujours.' And while saying that he crossed his hands in his lap and jumped up and down several times, with the vivacity peculiar to him. I know that for a moment I was almost paralyzed with astonishment. . . ." Finally, a year later when Freud had begun work in Vienna as a private docent in nervous diseases, and was still "as innocent and ignorant in all that concerned the etiology of the neuroses as any promising academician could be expected to be" (i.e., of sex), he received a call from the university gynecologist, Chrobak, about a female patient who resisted all treatment. With Freud once more playing the holy fool, Chrobak remarked, "The only prescription for such troubles is the one well-known to us, but which we cannot prescribe. Penis normalis dosim Repetatur!" "I had never heard of such a prescription and would like to have shaken my head at my informant's cynicism."

Unlike the Americans who'd long recognized that sex played a role in the neuroses but didn't know what to do about it, Freud claimed that his own delayed revelation enabled him to see that sex played *all* parts in the drama of the nerves. The obscuring of this fact was precisely the pathogen. Other, more worldly men actually made the discovery for him; Freud just listened to their words with the literalness peculiar to a non-native speaker, or a schizophrenic.

If Freud helped Americans exorcise the spirit of sex en route to self-transcendence, he used sex to draw people down from the heavens to earth and to show how everyone was possessed by an unconscious, split into two by their own inner unknown. Like the hysteric, the demonic, the ecstatic, the father, son, and unholy ghost, the analysand discovered the vastness of the self they were divided from; as Longinus wrote, "Sublimity is the echo of a great soul." The doubling of the self born of the sexual unconscious was one Freud felt he could control. While others wallowed in the pink, Freud himself remained atop the Acropolis, sprung, in a mitosis of myth, from Athena's helmeted brow.

CHAPTER 11

Studies in Spiritism

People's sense of dramatic reality *is what they will certainly
obey no matter how much they pretend to follow nothing but
points of evidence. They* have *differed about the interpretation
of Mrs. P., and* will *differ, until other mediums add to the
volume of the drift.*

William James to Alice Johnson, August 26, 1907

BUT IF FREUD thought he could escape the occult by playing meteorolo-
gist to the erotic tempest in America he was mistaken. Obsessed with sta-
tistics, hard facts, and logical data though the nation might have been,
America was also in the grip of a feverish mania for loose, baggy spiritism,
one peak of which coincided with Freud's visit. Across the nation, in the
homes of the poor and disenfranchised and of the highly educated, pros-
perous elite alike, seances were being staged with a zeal suggesting that if
the participants didn't act now, the dead might forever hold their peace.

Sometimes mediums were possessed by the spirits of departed souls and
the spirits spoke through human lips; at others communication around the
seance table was effected through a series of raps or knocks in which a
preordained number of sounds indicated certain words. While séance participants clutched each other's moist, tingling hands in dimly lit, thick-
curtained parlors, tables levitated, bells rang, hard surfaces thumped and
banged, voices whispered, shrieked, keened, and conversed on everything
from world history and Egyptian deities to missing family pets. The implication was plain: the dead were desperate for someone living to talk to, if
only the latter would have the courteous grace to sit down, shut their eyes,
and strain to hear. Though visual, tactile, and olfactory manifestations were

not unknown, and mediums shuddered through a number of visible physical transformations in the course of a sitting (frequently suggestive of a hysterical fit), the core séance experience was aural; the responsibility of sitters was to *listen* with an antenna-like, quivering intensity far exceeding the attention incumbent on the religious confessor.

Sociological explanations for the rise of spiritism in America from the second half of the nineteenth century until the First World War frequently point to the gradual erosion of authority undergone by America's mainstream Christian sects and the persistent mass need for evidence of immortality. They tend to downplay the fact that some of the most important investigators into the paranormal were cosmopolitan intellectuals who had never viewed events on the Cross as more credible than a slew of other, heterodox supernatural phenomena. By Putnam's day, the most influential thinkers considered themselves Emerson's children, not his coevals.

Indeed, among the most thoughtful psychical researchers it's apparent that rather than trying to replace the Church with a new, folkish form of religion that could proliferate in opposition to the dictates of scientific reason, the driving impulse behind turn-of-the-century spiritualism was the urge to extend the domain of science into an exciting unknown that transcended materialist boundaries. For these individuals, an idealistic faith in the expansive, humanistic relevance of science—not a denial of rational truth in favor of the supernatural—made plausible the idea that certain mediums might tap into hitherto neglected channels of cosmic energy, even though the majority of spirit conjurers were plainly, in Hall's words, "deadbeats and swindlers."

NOTHING BETTER ILLUSTRATES the way that an almost religious national veneration for the principles of common sense could coexist with beliefs that smack of extreme mystical indulgence than the case of William James. James, author of the theory of Pragmatism, and lecture circuit advocate of the idea that "scientific loyalty to the facts" is the sine qua non of the true philosophical mind, was also a believer in telepathic, trance-based communication from the dead. Arguably the most influential medium of the age, at least in New England, Mrs. Laura Piper became for many years an almost personal oracle to James.

The relationship between James and Piper bothered Putnam no end. And yet Putnam was inextricably entangled in the national conversation about psychic experience himself, as it was a fixation among members of his immediate personal and larger professional circle. "Henry [Bowditch] and I discussed the endless question of psychical research in relation to William James and the tiresome Mrs. Piper," Putnam wrote of one morning spent at Putnam Camp. "Then Annie came in and talked about how the chimney in the Stoop could be made to look sufficiently unkempt, and told us of some superb enamel and brass work that Madeline has been doing; then George opened the door saying that he had had enough of J. M. Barrie and found him deadly dull; and so on."

James himself was far from being the only Camp visitor for whom these questions were a consuming interest. Through James, Richard Hodgson, the English Secretary to the American Branch of the Society for Psychical Research, also became a regular guest at Putnam's Adirondack retreat. Hodgson first came to America after James, immersed in his own research of Piper, had begun writing a series of letters to the Society detailing his experiences of Piper's mediumship. The Society contacted Hodgson with word of James' studies not because of his support for the findings of paranormal research but, quite the opposite, on account of his reputation as an investigator of psychic cons. Hodgson's most famous achievement for the Society to date was an exposé of Helena Blavatsky, the enormously influential founder of the Theosophical Society, whom the Society pronounced "one of the most accomplished, ingenious, and interesting impostors in history."

However, after taking up the challenge, in sessions at which James was often present, Hodgson found himself unable to disprove the authenticity of Piper's mediumship. He did not, by any means, become an instant convert. For years, in fact, he worked to concoct more rigorous tests by which to reveal her deceit. At times, he had her tailed by professional private eyes. He made sure that when she was first entering the houses where she was to conduct sittings, she did not make surreptitious contact with servants or engage in other forms of covert information gathering. In 1892, in his first report on Piper to the Society, Hodgson adamantly refused to cede ground on his skepticism. But five years later, in his second report, Hodgson struck a new, humbled tone. "I cannot profess to have any doubt but that the chief communicators . . . are veritably the personalities that they claim to be; that they have survived the change we call death, and that they have directly communicated with us whom we call living through Mrs. Piper's entranced organism."

Hodgson puts pay to the stereotype of the psychic researcher as pale, ethereal transplant from lunar landscapes. My grandmother, in her book about Putnam Camp, describes him as "a great big man with a brown beard and a full, rich voice" who taught the children songs, climbing skills, and set them puzzles to solve. Hodgson played a leading role in the celebrated Putnam Camp masquerade pantomimes and distinguished himself, my grandmother wrote, because he "not only enjoyed them but *believed* in them."

Having this great, vivacious bear of a man taking up the cause of Mrs. Piper must have made her tempting even to an infidel. Putnam would certainly have had many conversations with Hodgson in the Stoop and on the surrounding mountain slopes about the intricacies of communication with the other world. It's not surprising that in this climate where talk about supernormal phenomena was so pervasive, and often took place with interlocutors of such earthly charm as James and Hodgson, Putnam himself joined the Society for Psychical Research and remained a member for many years.

However, the Society was capacious, and Putnam seems to have pitched his tent in the camp of the "fraud hunters," rather than among members looking to have their intuitions of spiritism validated. He held out against the seduction of the supernatural even when contemporaries for whom he had the greatest respect embraced it, just as he held out against the new forms of Christian-based faith healing. Why was it that Putnam found a wildly spiritualized philosophy more palatable than either of the popular, spiritualist alternatives raging in Boston?

After his premature death in 1905, Hodgson himself, the hero of Putnam Camp, became Mrs. Piper's principal "control." (A control was the lead spirit making a visitation from the dead to take possession of a medium.) In 1909, at the precise moment of Freud's visit, James completed a copious study of Piper's mediumship. Hodgson, as the manifesting spirit from the dead, was a major presence in the work and perhaps as much a topic of conversation in the Putnam household as he'd been when alive.

JAMES AND PUTNAM were not the only Americans Freud met with who had Hodgson and Piper on their minds. At the same time that James was putting the final touches on his mammoth study of Piper, with its largely favorable conclusions about her gifts, G. Stanley Hall was actively involved in the work of a brilliant former assistant, Dr. Amy E. Tanner, who was also writing a study of the occult centered around Piper. Her investigations would be published the following year (1910) in book form as *Studies in Spiritism*. Tanner's book, which assigns credit to Hall not just for inspiration and guidance but for actually arranging the sittings with Piper—and which contains a twenty-page introduction by Hall—came to an opposite conclusion about Piper's mediumship to that of the Society for Psychical Research. Moreover, this study, probably the first major American refutation of a psychic's powers based not on an exposure of the mechanics of trickery but on a psychological assessment of the sitter's character, used Freud as a touchstone for its argument.

It appears that James came to call on Hall in Worcester after Freud's third lecture. Hall knew that James' visit concerned a matter of more urgency than any wish to meet privately with Freud and Jung. James was making the call to hand deliver, subpoena-style, a copy of his opus on Mrs. Piper.

Hall probably primed his foreign guests for James' arrival with a pinch of irony. He had no hesitation about being brutally dismissive of James' supernormal pursuits, just as James' open aversion to Hall was partly a factor of Hall's war against advocates of the paranormal. Hall may well have told Freud and Jung that in his foolish youth he himself was an enthusiast of the world of mediums. "Spiritualists abounded" in his rural hometown of Ashfield, Massachusetts, he later wrote in his autobiography. When he went on a tour of Europe as a medical student, Hall made a point of hearing the lectures of Zollner on Spiritism and of Theodor Fechner on the mystical "besouled" condition "of plants and planets." After he'd returned to the States and launched his career, he "visited every medium who advertised in Philadelphia." Sometime thereafter he "made similar rounds in New York" and Boston. However, Hall made abundantly clear that as he matured his youthful credulity passed into a "no less preponderating adult disbelief." By the time of Freud's visit, Hall thought that for any man of science to seriously contemplate the problem of "discarnate ghosts" and their ability to "suspend the laws of matter" was not only "bad form" "but an indication of a strange psychic rudiment in their makeup that ought to be outgrown like the prenatal tail or the gill slits."

On the eve of James' visit, t　　　　　　　　　　　　'h Hall
for several days and Hall had
sympathies for the psychical
have retired to one of Hall'
ticipation of James' arriv
smelling comfortably of
season's mildness prob
cigar from one of Ha
himself had asked
　　Eventually, Ja
bered the scene　　　　　　　　　　　　　　　　　　　　　n
you might be i　　　　　　　　　　　　　　　　　　　　es
"put his hand　　　　　　　　　　　　　　　　　　　delight proved to be a

　　Even with their limite　　　　　　　　　　　　　knew of
his reputation as a relentless fun　　　　　　　　　ne whose
interest in building up the University 　　　　　　　y intellectual debate he was engaged in. Thus, as Jung 　　　　cene, James'
presentation of Mammon to Hall as the symbol o.　　all was really
interested in, seemed "a particularly happy rejoinder" to Hall's dismissal
of James' own interests in the other world. Regardless of whether the slip
was Freudian or an intentional slight, James at once "excused himself pro-
fusely and produced the real papers from the other pocket."

　　Freud must have been on his guard throughout all this. He would have
seen the debate as a potential trap in which a misstep could cost him politically. The best policy would be to express polite, noncommittal curiosity. Both Hall and James would have been happy to oblige Freud there.
However much the two Americans disagreed on the meaning of Piper's
trances, there was a consensus about what literally took place.

IN 1909, THE 50-year-old Leonora Evelina Simonds Piper presented a
humble, matronly appearance, with tiny, deep set eyes, a cumbersome jaw,
and a high, clear brow. Even her detractors agreed that Piper was not a
fraud in the usual sense in which the term applied to mediums. She derived little material benefit from her gifts. At $20 a sitting and a restricted
schedule of audiences, her earnings never much exceeded $1,000 per

LOOSCAN BRANCH LIBRARY
5830 WESTHEIMER RD
HOUSTON, TX 770575617

10/25/2012	15:50:52
Merchant ID:	000000000801893
Terminal ID:	03498548
164021937994	

CREDIT CARD

VISA SALE

CARD #	XXXXXXXXXXXXX0484
INVOICE	0003
Batch #:	000169
CLERK	8886
Approval Code:	547101
Entry Method:	Swiped
Mode:	Online

SALE AMOUNT   **$9.00**

CUSTOMER COPY

annum. Nor was there other money in the family, either inherited or earned, to sustain Piper and her husband, who was a modest store clerk. Furthermore, Piper herself seemed to receive little pleasure from the notoriety she'd attained. As she grew older, she appeared increasingly exhausted and withdrawn. Piper seemed to see her mediumship as her destiny, yet an uncertain asset.

Over the years, Piper's sittings took on a set form. She sat in an armchair and chatted with her sitters. In front of her stood a table on which lay three pillows. Conversation was superficial, as Piper was trying to empty her mind. Gradually, her breathing became slower and she began to look drowsy; her eyes took on a fixed stare. Within a minute after the onset of sleepiness, her mouth fell open; her breathing grew slower still. After several more minutes, her head would loll over onto one of the pillows. Her face would twitch slightly. At this point, her pulse was also measurably lower than normal. Now, she was inside the trance. One hand took up a pencil and began to write at the prompting of her control. Piper also sometimes spoke in the voice of the dead visitor, either separately or in conjunction with writing. This state of communication, from the afterlife or elsewhere, would last between an hour and a half and two hours and while inside the trance and "possessed by the dead" Piper would be engaged in a form of conversation with her sitters, who would ask her questions and whom she would guide toward certain interpretations of their exchange.

As she exited the trance, Piper's face went through various contortions similar to the expressions Charcot studied in hysterics. Her mouth twisted dramatically to one side; she assumed expressions of pain and repulsion. Sometimes she would gnash her teeth. Often she began weeping. The process of leaving her trance took twice as long and more as that of entering it.

For all the supernatural armature of the sittings there was another paradigm they may have suggested to Freud—one that would have made him more nervous than anything else, including his concerns about conflict with James and Jung. Freud would not have missed in the descriptions of Piper's mediumship the parallels between psychical sittings and psychoanalytic sessions. The effort to empty the mind prior to receiving the dead was not so different from the surrender of ego-based control over consciousness that the analysand undertook. The content of the control's conversations appeared to arise from very much the same underworld depths Freud invoked as his own source in the epigraph of *The Interpretation of Dreams*.

Another affinity can be seen in the word association tests employed by sitters in their talks with Piper, particularly when they were trying to ascertain the veracity of her trances. In Freud's case, the use of free association technique was intended to probe the content of a patient's unconscious. With Piper, the strategy was meant to uncover the reality or lack thereof of her connection with the dead. However, the parallels were obvious enough that Tanner, in *Studies in Spiritism*, referred directly to Freud's theory on the average length of time it took to react to a word in a psychoanalytic session (1.5–2.5 seconds) in adducing Piper's conscious word association responses relative to those of her control. Above all, the employment of a dialogue form that was simultaneously internal and external as a tool for probing remote depths of the mind—for conjuring forth the primal history of forces behind day-to-day individual life—is akin in the two practices, both being what Italo Svevo called in his *Confessions of Zeno* (published in 1922), "psychical adventures." Svevo wrote how starting an analysis was "like entering a wood, not knowing whether one is going to meet a brigand or a friend. Nor is one quite sure which it has been, after the adventure is over. In this respect psychoanalysis resembles spiritualism."

The phenomenal popularity of spiritism in turn-of-the-century United States helped prepare Americans for the dynamics of the psychoanalytic relationship, foreshadowing the special kind of listening and talking involved in Freud's practice. It's unlikely, however, that Freud would have felt confident enough at this point about the stature of psychoanalysis to suggest that the similarities between the two activities proved that psychoanalytic matters were at the core of the sitter's trance. It's more plausible that he would have felt afraid that the parallels would cast aspersions on his own methodology.

ON SEPTEMBER 10TH, in a ceremony swollen with pomp and circumstance, Hall presented Freud with an honorary degree, "the first official recognition" psychoanalysis ever received, as Freud later wrote. He did not mention the fact that another 20 lecturers received honorary degrees along with him, among them Jung, who displayed an infuriating irreverence for the whole scene. Freud savored every element of the elaborate presentation, including the citation on his degree, "Sigmund Freud of the University of Vienna, founder of a school of psychology already rich in new methods and achievements; leader today among students of the psychology of sex, and of psychotherapy and analysis; Doctor of Laws."

Sometime in the course of the same evening, Freud walked William James the mile and a half from Clark's campus to the Worcester train station. To have been singled out for this signal private moment with the then reigning figure of American psychology, testified, in Freud's mind, to his and James' collegial intimacy. James was the great elder intellectual of the past, whereas Freud represented the young future. At one point, James asked Freud to walk ahead; he would catch up as soon as he had overcome an attack of angina. "He died of that disease a year later," Freud wrote of the encounter, "and I have always wished that I might be as fearless as he was in the face of approaching death."

James' reaction to Freud, on the other hand, rather than being colored by intellectual sympathy, was marked by distaste. He encouraged Freud to explain himself and Freud, in the ebullience of the day's glory, appears to have been atypically unguarded, becoming talkative enough that he came across to James "as a man obsessed by fixed ideas." With James' own theoretical stress on pluralism, fixation was a cardinal sin. The core psychoanalytic concept of a sexual underpinning to dreams repelled James, who wrote a friend that he could "make nothing in my own case with his dream theories, and obviously 'symbolism' is a most dangerous method." These responses of James stand in sharp contrast not just to Freud's reaction to James, but also to James' enthusiasm for Jung and larger broad-minded support for any number of fresh currents in psychology.

JAMES' DEPARTURE DID not herald the end of Freud's exposure to American spiritism fever. Hall, for all his belittlement of the men of science who felt compelled to probe the supernatural, was himself obsessed with psychic investigation, even if his ostensible purpose was to find evidence disproving the claims of believers. On Freud's last night at Clark, Hall arranged for another exchange about the occult. This time, the men were to actually have the chance to examine a medium themselves.

Although when Jung wrote his wife about the encounter he described it as a "private conference" about the "psychology of sex," the conference in fact had as its object a would-be medium. Tanner described the young woman in her book: "an impressionable, dreamy girl, the constant companion of a mother who was born with a veil and who, true to that heritage and to the teachings of her own seeress mother, saw visions and talked with spirits." This woman had also been studied by James.

By 1909, her control was none other than Lucifer, familiarly called Zezy. Hall and others had been working with Zezy for some time to try to bring back Clark University's founder from the dead. Zezy succeeded in the initial sessions in manifesting the spirit of this gentleman. But in the sittings he could only speak about his life with the American Indians in the wilderness, despite the fact it appears highly unlikely that the Founder in life had ever so much as met an Indian.

Hall anticipated that the session would give him the chance to study how Freud used psychoanalytic theory to dismantle the woman's psychical claims. But the Europeans were so quick to determine that the advent of the young woman's mediumship was coincident with the start of an unrequited passion "developed as an agency by which she might become attractive to this man," that the drama of the scene was lost. Even Jung was unable to view the girl's supernormal character as anything but a manifestation of repressed sexual fantasy. Freud added that she was "slightly paranoiac." In Hall's report of what happened in the séance some years later, there's a suggestion that he was more credulous than he liked to think. "The erotic motivation was obvious and the German savants saw little further to interest them in the case," he wrote of the events later. "I was a trifle mortified that now the purpose so long hidden from us was so conscious and so openly confessed."

Because the young woman's complex was so immediately transparent to Jung, he considered her unworthy of a place in the larger debate about spiritism and proof of nothing but Hall's own lingering ignorance. Freud might even have suspected that for Hall to bring up a case as primitive as this one as conceivable evidence for the spiritism cause showed him up, in Hall's worst nightmare, as, in fact, a covert agonistic on the topic—himself a gullible man stuck with gills.

FOR ALL TANNER'S sense of indebtedness to Hall, her *Studies in Spiritism* strikes a distinctly more sophisticated tone than Hall was capable of. In this sense, the book calls to mind James himself. And, in fact, because of James' sponsorship of Piper's mediumship, Tanner is in a kind of cool dialogue with James throughout the work.

In her preface, Tanner notes that when her research with Piper began early in 1909 she did not set out to dismantle Piper's claims, but rather entered "in a spirit of doubt that inclined toward belief." She expected, at the least, to come away with a faith in telepathy. Instead, she writes, "the more I have read and seen of such experiences, the more amazing has it come to seem to me that two theories like telepathy and spirit communication, which are unsupported by any valid evidence, should have obtained credence today; and the more incomprehensible has it come to be that men should be willing to stake their professional reputations upon the inaccuracies and rubbish that pass for 'scientific' facts in these matters."

This is a direct jab at James, who had famously said of Piper, "Practically I should be willing now to stake as much money on Mrs. Piper's honesty as on that of anyone I know, and I am quite satisfied to leave my reputation for wisdom or folly, so far as human nature is concerned, to stand or fall by this declaration." At the end of her preface, Tanner cited James directly, noting that his observation about the "marsh of feebleness" in which much supernormal research was mired received too little attention. Instead, people focused on James' idea of a "stream of veridicality," a symbol for this worldly intervention of the beyond. "A stream lost in a marsh is a very different thing from a flood inundating a land and tearing down all the old landmarks, and, far from rising in the mountains or descending from the clouds, it is more likely to be merely the drainage of the lowest part of the marsh," Tanner opined.

However well-meaning intellectual authorities such as James were in lending their support to spiritism, they were opening the door to a larger, mob-style debunking of science. The license given exclusively to people within the psychical camp to define the terms of what constitutes proof of occult phenomena was what Tanner set out to challenge. (This notion that only those within the folds of the spiritist movement are in a position to critique it also calls to mind a principal charge leveled against the psychoanalytic movement.) For the most part, *Studies in Spiritism* proceeds by way of what Freud humorously referred to as "the American method" (i.e., the aggregation of hard data). Tanner's massive accumulation of bare-bone facts and figures on sittings with Piper and, to a lesser extent, other contemporary psychics, is enlivened by patches of biographical narrative on the mediums and by Tanner's interpretative comments.

Piper, Tanner writes, developed an ovarian tumor (the first of many such tumors) when she was still an adolescent, not long after a sledding accident injured her internally. Following the birth of the first of her two children, Piper's father-in-law, in a fairy-tale scene, "persuaded her to consult a blind medium, Dr. Cocke, in order to get advice as to the tumor from which she was suffering."

At the first sitting, "she felt twitchings in her hands and feared that she might become unconscious." Six weeks after the child's birth, Piper returned to Cocke, and when he placed his hands on her head "she did become unconscious, seeing as she went off a flood of light, strange faces, and a hand moving before her. She had seen a similar flood of light as she was fainting from the effects of the blow from the ice sled. She had several other sittings with Dr. Cocke, and each time was controlled by Chlorine, the same spirit that appeared at first. Then came a period when many controls appeared, notable characters such as Luther, Lincoln, Washington, Bach, and Commodore Vanderbilt. Eventually, all these controls were supplanted by one French physician, Dr. Phinuit, who had forgotten his native tongue. Cocke's control "was also a French doctor, named Albert G. Finnett." Dr. Phinuit appears to have had no great physiological skills when it came to Piper herself. Her general health and, specifically, her gynecological health, continued to be fragile. Nine years after the birth of her first child she had her fallopian tubes and ovaries removed. A couple of years after that, she suffered a hernia that required another operation.

Tanner links highlights in Piper's ongoing health crisis with dramatic shifts in the character of her mediumship. So, for example, at the beginning of 1892, George Pelham, "a young and prominent lawyer, a friend of Hodgson's, greatly interested in the problem of personal immortality, died suddenly and accidentally." Several years before, under an assumed name, Pelham had had several sittings with Piper. But right around the time of Piper's major operation (end of 1892 beginning of 1893), Pelham suddenly began appearing at several sittings in company with Phinuit. Pelham and Phinuit "continued to be the dominating controls until 1895–97, when again Mrs. Piper's health was unsettled," and a new control began to play a major part in her repertoire: Stainton Moses, before his death a prominent English spiritualist. Tanner writes that as Piper's health began to improve there was a period of "steady deterioration in the sittings until the onset of the climacteric," a reference to menopause.

Hall's tone in regard to the whole affair, from the introduction onward, is one of frustrated mockery. "Would that she [Piper] would give the world her own utterly candid *biographie intime* or a confession of her honest womanly reactions to all this business!" he wrote. For all his recognition of the importance of sex, he couldn't overcome his own squeamishness, indicated by the break into French at this critical juncture. Women's sexuality has to be somehow dealt with, but Hall wishes that women would take care of it themselves.

Tanner, on the other hand, turns immediately to Freud in her summation of the Piper case, regretting the fact that Piper's sittings couldn't take place in a waking state like the "confessions" Freud receives. She suggests that Piper suffers from "disassociation," a split-self triggered by her pubescent injury and subsequent shocks to her sexual physiology. All this has led to a "greatly heightened suggestibility" on Piper's part. Faulty record keeping and "ordinary laws of the mind as seen in apperception, inference, etc." explain the rest of what psychical researchers have attributed to the supernormal in sittings with her.

In the conclusion of *Studies in Spiritism* Tanner went several steps further toward a societal diagnosis. In the same way, she writes, that children find it easier to explain thunder by the idea of barrels rolling in heaven than to understand its relation to electricity, to "very many minds today it seems far simpler to assume spirit communication than to study the manifold hereditary and social relations, the conditions of nerve cells and sense organs" that actually lie behind the phenomena. Ultimately, she ties American Spiritism circa 1909 into a larger course of world history culminating in the radical shifts in social organization that have taken place in the country, from the invention of the sewing machine to that of the telephone and the arrival of the railroad. Tanner lambastes the failure of the clergy to accommodate the reality of the changing world around them. "The conflict thus precipitated between science and religion led to probably more speculation and reshaping of religious ideas than at any time since the days of Luther and Melanchton. But at this modern time no great leaders like them arose to keep the people out of the mire. In our country culture was at its lowest ebb, the clergy, who should have guided the people aright, alienated them by their severe doctrines and lack of sympathy with the great trend of events, and so these alienated ones, untrained in thought, and yet realizing the empty bottles of the old doctrines, wandered everywhere in search of spiritual food."

Tanner's mire is identical to the black tide of mud Freud worried about with Jung. But like Putnam, she went beyond Freud in recognizing the role played by the atomized industrial society and isolation of the individual in generating susceptibility to selfishness and spiritism. Where Freud universalized the problem of human loneliness and narcissism as a kind of psychological bedrock, Putnam and Tanner saw the structures of everyday life that nurtured those conditions as ameliorable. The contents of the unconscious were the real point of contention between Freud and the American medical leaders from James to Putnam. By helping patients stare further and further backward, the psychoanalytic situation becomes pregnant with meaning. But Freud himself never firmly decided what was actually inside the womb: the archaic residue of history, an engine of fantasy, or an underworld inhabited by real ghosts.

TANNER WROTE THAT the nature of subconscious ideas and their influence upon the waking self was "at present one of the most disputed and uncertain points in psychology." Spiritism became implicated in what was a veritable land-rush to claim "ownership" of the unconscious, alternately known (among other labels) as the subconscious or co-conscious. Freud gave the Americans the unconscious as Wilderness—sublime, dangerous, dark, fertile, and a territory to which a principle of internal manifest destiny could be applied: where Id was, Ego shall reign.

James' world of unconscious life was far more capacious than Freud's, and the relative amount of space dedicated to painful memories—to memory as such—was reduced to a minor province (except in cases where people were very ill). Far more than a storage realm for uncomfortable recollections, James describes that which lies outside the conventionally defined field of consciousness as a "transmarginal field of consciousness" operating in a numinous fashion "like a 'magnetic field,' inside of which our centre of energy turns like a compass-needle, as the present phase of consciousness alters to its successor. Our whole past store of memories floats beyond this margin, ready at a touch to come in; and the entire mass of residual powers, impulses and knowledge that constitute our empirical self stretches continuously beyond it." The transmarginal field is the whole fabric of our potential being—in James' schema, an infinite element. There is nothing like the Freudian mechanism of repression to contend with when reaching this other side. Indeed, it's already present, albeit "inattentively realized." A special kind of attentiveness is, therefore, key to overcoming the barrier.

James did not explain why in such a perfect, if intricate, contiguity there was any division between the realms at all, or what that division really consisted in. For all of Jung's admiration of James, in his later writing he sharply criticized James on this score. "So vaguely drawn are the outlines between what is actual and what is only potential at any moment of our conscious life, that it is always hard to say of certain mental elements whether we are conscious of them or not," he wrote in "On the Nature of the Psyche."

But James needed this boundary-free democracy of the psyche, in which the dead founder of Clark, along with Commodore Vanderbilt and Jesus, might be equally likely to burst into the brain at any instant, both as a portal for the "energies of men" and to counter theories that would limit the unknown contents of the mind to primitive biological drives. It was this danger James had in mind when, in an extended footnote to the *Varieties of Religious Experience* (published in 1902), he lampooned the fashionable linkage of sex and the mystical. "It seems to me," James wrote, "that few conceptions are less instructive than this reinterpretation of religion as perverted sexuality. It reminds one, so crudely is it often employed, of the famous Catholic taunt that the Reformation may be best understood by remembering that its *fons et origo* was Luther's wish to marry a nun: the effects are infinitely wider than the alleged causes, and for the most part opposite in nature." Of course, James continued, "in the vast collection of religious phenomena, some are undisguisedly amatory." He singled out, among other examples of this, "ecstatic feelings of union" with the divine. Part of what was so infuriating about the vogue for assigning sexual significance to mystical experience was that there were plenty of cases where that connection was, to any enlightened believer, old hat. Yes, religious speech uses metaphors drawn from sexual life, he wrote, but it also takes from the vocabulary of eating, drinking, and the respiratory function.

As for the notion that many religious mystics evidence neurotic symptoms, James accepted the coexistence but saw no reason to therefore assume a causal relationship. The neurasthenic personality, by definition, was

a hypersensitive one, and James was perfectly willing to accept that neurotics were more likely to have extreme religious experiences than possess-
ors of "your robust Philistine type of nervous system, forever offering its
biceps to be felt, thumping its breast, and thanking Heaven that it hasn't a
single morbid fiber in its composition." (Given Hall's notorious relish for
fitness, James may have been taking another swipe at him here.) Our obligation is to examine "the immediate content of religious consciousness" as
such. "Who does not see that we are likely to ascertain the distinctive significance of religious melancholy and happiness, or of religious trances, far
better by comparing them . . . with other varieties of melancholy, happiness, and trance, than by refusing to consider their place in any more general series, and by treating them as if they were outside of nature's order
altogether?" The more James knew of Freud's work, the more he was convinced that it was in the tradition of those who would "snuff out Saint Teresa
as an hysteric, Saint Francis of Assisi as an hereditary degenerate."

If Freud felt himself in anyway "menaced" by James, then, it would
apparently have been on the grounds of James' antimaterialism. And yet,
when the subject of James came up with Putnam in the Adirondacks—
which it surely would have done given both James' intellectual prominence
in American psychology and his imprint on the world of Camp itself—
Putnam might well have expressed concern that James' work had a tendency to become *too* materialist. James' insistence that the proof of a
religious phenomenon lay in "THE WAY IN WHICH IT WORKS ON
THE WHOLE" was a form of empiricist criterion that could make everything seem relative. Putnam was neither sure that every belief that "works"
was thereby true, nor that beliefs that failed to be objectively productive
were thereby untrue. He was more willing than James to return to the notion
of Platonic, a priori truths in philosophical theory building.

Freud intuited that he was entering unstable ground as he made his way
through the American materialist–antimaterialist debate in which questions
of spiritism formed but one crack in the earth opening into a vast subterranean realm containing everything from the individual unconscious to the
primal herd, God and Doctor Phinius. Freud may not have fully grasped
the foundation of American idealist perfectionism grounding both Hall's
and James' sides of the debate, but in throwing out a sop to those who felt
he was too focused on sex as sex, he weirdly positioned himself in the middle

of the argument and created a "third way" that directly addressed Putnam's particular nexus of concerns.

At the end of her book, Tanner praised a series of advances in scientific understanding. Just as hysterics are no longer considered witches, Tanner wrote, "many secondary personalities have been reunited, and many other incipient ones have been prevented from dividing, and, with increasing familiarity, such phenomena will be recognized as not opening the door to another world but rather to the insane asylum." And yet, like Putnam, Tanner acknowledged the legitimacy of the larger national fascination with the untapped potential energies of humanity, a fascination of which James was the principal exponent. Tanner developed the idea of a nonmystical "store of infinite energy that is stored up within every man. . . . Even the most hard-working genius does not one-millionth part of what his brain is capable of doing, because there is friction, loss of connections, etc. . . . But if we only knew the way, we could knit together these warring factions and have an army against which nature and sin and disease and death itself could not stand."

After several hundred pages of bottom-line scientific observation of mediums, the conclusion of Tanner's book can appear jarring. In fact it is key to the whole. In her coda, Tanner issued a kind of plea that can be read, simultaneously, as a call for psychoanalysis and a call for a new spiritualized philosophy. It's no wonder she says that people turn to mediums when they confront a personal crisis that they cannot share with their families, particularly given that pastors and the like may be unwilling or unable to offer much comfort. The yearning for spiritual solace cannot be neutralized by intellectual arguments. "No faith dies because it is unreasonable, but only because the instincts which it has satisfied find more complete and permanent gratification in other directions," she wrote. Tanner's answer was to nurture the growth of a sort of ideal community of mutual care: "in proportion as man draws near to his fellow-man, and in proportion as he works for and with him, he realizes that the 'other side' can wait till the morrow, while salvation is here and now."

These words, the last in her book, could be taken straight from the charter of various New England charitable movements, whereas the first part of her explanation for the current popularity of psychics resonates with the mission of the new Boston psychotherapeutic schools. On both counts, she'd issued a manifesto that Putnam would have wholeheartedly applauded, calling for new, integrated forms of social and individual healing as a means not just to health, but to redemption.

However, Tanner's exposure to Freud's work was limited. Putnam's gripe with spiritism coincided with the risk he gradually came to identify in psychoanalysis itself: both had the potential to nourish a virulent strain of American narcissism.

CHAPTER 12

The Supreme Reality

Your visit to America was of deep significance to me, and I now work and read with constantly growing interest on your lines. In general I find myself in complete agreement with your ideas, except in some details, but I am looking forward to the day when I may venture to form an opinion of my own, with greater confidence.

Putnam to Freud, November 17, 1909.

AFTER HIS ENCOUNTER with Freud at Camp, Putnam returned to Boston, rolled up his sleeves, and retrofitted his entire clinic as a psychoanalytic laboratory. What was this like, one wonders, for the typical patients who patronized his office?

Among the first group of psychoanalytic patients Putnam described, two offer insight into treatment methods common in America before analysis took hold. One patient, a "well-balanced, intelligent, middle-aged, business-man," in five years of marriage had never had "satisfactory coitus, a cause of mortification and regret." Putnam treated him "carefully and energetically" using a portfolio of somatic techniques. Along with "electricity in various forms," Putnam tried "stimulant perineal douches combined with other hydrotherapeutic measures, full doses of johambin— long continued—strychnea" and hypnotic influences. Bodies were stimulated, relaxed, and shocked again in response to sexual dysfunction and generalized nervous sickness. Psychological "mortification" resulting from impotence was attacked in apotropaic fashion by mortification of the flesh. Alternately, in the case of an adolescent stammerer, Putnam tried a religiously inflected form of suggestion therapy. His pre-Freud treatment "consisted partly in suggestions and exercises calculated to mitigate some of the more specific difficulties of enunciation (including certain exercises advised by Scripture)."

One day patients were being treated with a grab bag of physiological treatments and unthreatening, vaguely religious, talk-based psychotherapies; the next they found themselves on the couch speculating about why they wanted to sleep with ma.

In Putnam's case, however, the transformation was probably more gentle than his enthusiasm for Freud's ideas sometimes implies. Although he would have encouraged patients to probe back into their roots for the sources of present-day neuroses, and would even have been willing to broach associations with disturbing Freudian reverberations, Putnam would never have made patients feel they were being forced to strip under the searchlight before an omniscient figure of authority. Indeed, as he would later admit, there was an admixture of empathetic identification in his approach to analysis distinct from the Viennese ideal.

Furthermore, whatever Putnam was putting his patients through he was going through himself as he launched his self-analysis, no doubt in a more harrowing form than he would ever impose on anyone else.

IS THE WHOLE notion of self-analysis just a less credible version of the largely implausible practice of psychoanalysis as such? It's revealing that self-analysis is the one core aspect of psychoanalytic practice that even the movement's bureaucracy came to view as obsolete—too demanding to be a prerequisite, or even a reliable preparation for serving as an analyst for others. For all intents and purposes no one psychoanalyzes him/herself today. And we must wonder how different a "psycho-sphere" the founders of psychoanalysis inhabited when we reflect not just how many of them viewed self-analysis as central to their own psychological development, but how much of their foundational theoretical work came from a form of analysis that was abandoned in the initial decades of the movement's existence.

Whatever hostility one might feel toward psychoanalysis, one has to feel a certain sympathy, even admiration, for the risk that the first generation of self-analyzers took with their sense of personal dignity. After all, psychoanalysis gave no guarantee of release, let alone absolution, at the end. To try to trace one's dreams as far back as the associative chain will lead at the very least immerses one in a sea of untoward desires, aversions, and memories, where one would rather not dawdle. Whatever one learns, the experience must be exhausting. For many people in analysis, a point is reached where the sense of a Dantean topography with different levels to aspire to gives way to the feeling of being in a hall of mirrors. In self-analysis, where one does not have even the pretense of an interlocutor, that danger must be dramatically amplified.

Nonetheless, Putnam persisted in the effort, sometimes with over-whelming emotional consequences, often with frustration and anguish, for years.

BUT AT THE beginning of his correspondence with Freud, whatever he was encountering in that division of self into analyst and analysand, Putnam was more excited than anything else. In his first letter, he informed Freud that he was sending him photographs of the Adirondacks as a reminder of their trip, and reported, like a good pupil, that he had carefully studied Freud's paper on *Analerotik*, though he was still not sure what Freud meant by the "Geld complex." Putnam told Freud that he dwelt on this point because, "it shows me that in my own 'Analysen' I have not yet learned to go deep enough to find all that can be found." Less than two months after Freud left America, Putnam's self-analysis had already gone so far that he could feel surprised at evidence that he'd not yet plumbed the depths of his being.

The core of the essay to which Putnam referred, Freud's 1908 paper, "Character and Anal Eroticism," laid out the theory that character traits of "orderliness, parsimony and obstinacy" represent the sublimation of a "subsidiary" infantile pleasure in defecating. People with these traits are, Freud says, "born with a sexual constitution in which the erotogenicity of the anal zone is exceptionally strong." By the time Freud wrote the study, he thought that he was defining a syndrome with particular rel-evance for the Americans.

Part of the explanation for this, once again, was anxiety on a cultural level. Jews in Europe were also targets of accusation regarding veneration of capital. Arthur Trebitsch, a bourgeois Jew who, like Otto Weininger, came to formulate racial theories foreshadowing aspects of Nazi anti-Semitism, wrote an important attack on Freud charging him with a failure to sublimate as revealed by his emphasis on sexuality. This inability to raise the mind above the level of "erotomania," he said, was characteristic of the Jews' inferior form of intellect, another symptom of which was the tendency to hoard money. As was the case with nervous illness in general, anal eroticism as Freud defined it exhibited symptoms consistent with stereotypes that caricatured Jews and Americans equally.

Putnam's home life at the time of the Clark lectures suggests why Freud's description of anal eroticism might have struck a chord as, despite the fact that his career was booming, he felt beset with budgetary anxieties. Near the end of August, Putnam wrote Marian to express his concern at the size of their "table-expenses." "We have had but little company and I have been away more than usually, I think. Probably Mary [a house servant] is not a good manager, and gets things out of season and not when they are cheap. I suppose we need more housekeeping than I give." A few weeks later, Putnam agonized about whether to replace or restring Molly's tennis racket. "Even the exchange for another second hander would not pay; because the question of case comes in. . . . After all, the whole cost will only have been 5.00 + 2.25 = 7.25, and we have had several good years of wear." At most, he was looking at a bill of seven dollars. As Putnam himself confessed on more than one occasion, he could be awfully cheap.

But why was Putnam so quick to admit this failing, with its special erotic significance, to Freud? To have written James, Emerson, or Bowditch about ways in which his behavior betrayed the excremental nature of his infantile sexuality would have been inconceivable. Yet, he felt trusting enough of Freud that in his very first letter he could make the connection with no hint of embarrassment.

Perhaps Putnam's unguarded confidence in Freud reflected, in part, sensitivity to Freud's own vulnerabilities. Though Putnam experienced rapid success with Freud's methods, he was troubled by the lack of a teleological dimension to analysis; the fact that Freud had things to learn made Putnam less afraid of appearing dependent. He felt, he told Freud, that "the psychoanalytic method needed to be supplemented by methods which seek to hold up before the patient some goal toward which he may strive. Thus, I am now treating a lady of much intelligence—a schoolteacher—who is a great sufferer from morbid self-consciousness and blushing. I am making good head-way and tracing out the origin of these symptoms, but find that I have also to meet the difficulty that she has lost all interest in life and living. . . . I feel that it ought to be possible for us to work up ways of dealing systematically with such a state of mind as this."

Although the patient's identity is concealed, several factors point toward Susan Blow. Blow's reputation was built initially as a brilliant schoolteacher; one of her initial problems involved overwhelming self-consciousness. Though Putnam's first sessions with her produced positive results, her struggles with depression recurred. In 1904, after an especially taxing bout of "despondency," Blow wrote Putnam to thank him for giving her words that inspired "fresh courage." This was a gift more of philosophical, than of psychological comfort, just as Blow had offered Putnam the consolation of metaphysics. Two years before Freud's visit, writing, as she did time and again of her excitement at an impending visit of Putnam to Cazenovia, Blow promised, "We shall have a grand time talking over these grand subjects and getting our minds away from the questions which are perplexing because they deal not with what is universal and necessary but with what is uncertain because contingent. If I were asked what was the great good of Philosophy I should say that one chief good was that it gave us a sky where we can look forever at steady guiding stars while we try to steer our ship over a rough and stormy sea." Putnam's personal affirmation of these sentiments, as well as his experience of Blow's route to health through philosophy, stands behind his plea to Freud for a method that held up a goal for patients to work toward.

Behind his challenge to Freud also lay a sense of guilt. It would have been impossible for Putnam not to feel the gravitational tug of Blow's need for him, and to feel that he had been inadequately attendant. Over and over, she wrote him to express unconstrained hunger for his presence. "As I realize that I am at home I remember with great pleasure your partial promise to come to me for another little visit. When will you come? Any time between now and Sept. will be perfectly convenient for me," she wrote Putnam in the summer of 1907. In the fall, she was pleading: "October is here and I am hoping that it is still in your mind to come to me for that little visit. Could you come in the middle of next week—either Wednesday or Thursday (Oct 16 and 17) this would be a time when my one guest chamber would be free and it is also a time when we might hope for good weather. If this time is not convenient for you how would it suit your convenience to come any time between Nov 16 and Dec 1?" The pang in her tone was even more palpable the next summer. In mid-August, 1908 she wrote Putnam, "The sooner you come and the longer you stay the more pleased I shall be." On the 19th, her tone had become feverish. "Again tell me when you are coming," she begged him. "There will be fifty things to talk about. . . . We are on the eve or rather at the morning twilight of a new constructive era, which will force re-statements of religion, philosophy, medicine, education and politics."

Few of Putnam's letters to Blow have survived. Molly spoke in an interview of how, after her father's death, she hunted for Putnam's side of the correspondence to no avail. I suspect that the letters were returned to Putnam after Blow's death and that he destroyed them. Nonetheless, the tenor of Putnam's intervention comes through in Blow's own passionate apostrophes. "It's good to have a bracing word from you," she wrote in 1909. "Even were things as bad as many fear, courage and kindness would still accomplish their miracles." Whether she is alluding to his own courage and kindness, or the courage and kindness that he often tried to teach to others, part of the comfort he offered lay in the fact that he never pretended to occupy an Archimedean point in relation to his patients. These thoughts gave me strength; perhaps they can help you as well, he often seemed to be saying.

Even before Putnam met Freud, he was trying out Freudian terminology on Blow. "I can verify from my own experience what you say about misdirected repressions and concealments," Blow wrote to him. "I suffered tortures in my childhood because of this and can give you any number of instances when, should they interest you. I know too that 'dread' was natural to me and made me take blue Presbyterianism hard." However, as would be the case in all of Blow's arguments—and Putnam's redaction thereof for Freud—acknowledging the reality of these "misdirected repressions" was not in itself a sufficient form of treatment. "I am greatly interested," she continued, "in your recognition of the connection between religion and philosophy and the relation of both to science. I hope that the period on which we are entering is to do a great work in understanding the reality and supremacy of that level of human experience whose chief concern is with the questions of whence, wherefore and whither."

Blow contended that the true work of healing went on beyond the psychotherapeutic clinic and encompassed not just the roots of neuroses but the ultimate destiny of being. Nothing less than this "great work" could touch her real identity. In a beautiful passage she wrote, "I have often a rebellious feeling that my hopes and despairs and struggles and self-corrections and aspirations and moral imperatives are not accorded the respect given to pebbles and beetles, clouds and crystals. I AM AS MUCH A REALITY as any physical thing—and my loves, faiths, struggles, hopes are the supreme reality of me."

Blow's words got to the heart of the objection Putnam raised in his first letter to Freud. By giving patients a higher goal toward which they could aim, he suggested, one was only recognizing the ideal aspirations already innate in them. The "supreme reality" of Susan Blow encompassed far more than what was covered in the papers of Freud that Putnam had pored over so far (notably "Character and Anal Eroticism," "The Sexual Enlightenment of Children," and "Collected Short Papers on the Theory of Neurosis"). Of course it was all true about sex and no doubt there was much more to learn along these lines, but what about the sublimation of sexuality Freud had mentioned at Clark?

Freud left it to Ferenczi to tell Putnam that there were no "general rules" by which patients could attain sublimation. "Methods of sublimation differ in each case," Ferenczi warned Putnam at the end of November. When patients reached a certain depth in their analysis, "ways and means of sublimation" would always come into the conversation. "But these must not be *forced* on a patient."

BACK IN VIENNA, Freud was still trying to calculate the results of the voyage to America. He wrote Jones that Putnam "was a most gracious host, but the interminable climbing about brought me to the point where I finally went on strike and stayed at home, especially since I was not quite well either." Freud had, however, noted with pleasure Putnam's facility with psychoanalytic ideas, which was greater than he had expected. The analyses he reported having undertaken, along with his efforts at dream interpretation, had been proficient, if not comprehensive. Nonetheless, Freud concluded, the practical challenges of psychoanalytic treatment still seemed "to scare him a great deal."

To Ferenczi, Freud complained cheerfully about how busy he was, especially on account of the labors his trip to Clark had engendered. "It's an

entirely American exploitation; I hardly have time to live, never mind work."
To Jung, Freud was more caustic. "Quite against my will I must live like an
American: no time for the libido."

When Freud answered Putnam at the beginning of December, he
clamped down on any feelings of ambivalence he may have carried away
with him. "Our stay at your home was perhaps the most interesting part of
our American experience, and the exchange of ideas with you, in spite of
its brief duration, particularly strengthened my hopes that there might be
a future for psychoanalysis in your country," he wrote. Ever on the look-
out for opportunities to broadcast his youthfulness, Freud continued, "Although you are a decade older than I am, I found in you a high degree of
general open-mindedness and unprejudiced perceptiveness to which I
really am not accustomed in Europe." He did not ask that Putnam concur
with psychoanalytic theory "in every particular," but that he consent to
reserve judgment until he'd had the chance to "undergo the experiences"
on which psychoanalysis was based. Psychoanalysis was not yet fully fleshed
out and there remained "ample room left for the contribution of others."
Putnam must have read those words with a sense that Freud was validat-
ing his own argument that psychoanalysis needed supplementing.

Freud could not, however, resist a dig at his host country. "The attitude
toward money should be especially revealing in the United States, where
anal eroticism has undergone quite interesting transformations," he wrote
in response to Putnam's request for more detail about the "money complex." When Freud took up Putnam's case history, a more serious resistance emerged. He told Putnam that his complaint about the inability of
psychoanalysts to compensate patients for surrendering their neuroses was
unjustified, though this was not quite what Putnam had charged. Freud
went on, "It seems to me that this is not the fault of therapy but rather of
social institutions. What would you have us do when a woman complains
about her thwarted life, when, with youth gone, she notices that she has
been deprived of the joy of loving for merely conventional reasons? She is
quite right, and we stand helpless before, her, for we cannot make her young
again. But the recognition of our therapeutic limitations reinforces our
determination to change other social factors so that men and women shall
no longer be forced into hopeless situations."

Freud's rebuttal is startling on account of the many biographical points
he's interpolated into Putnam's account of his patient (all ones that jibe

with Blow's case). Where did Putnam imply that this woman's youth was gone? Or that she "has been deprived of the joy of loving for merely conventional reasons?" Freud's denunciation of the causes that have blocked a woman like Blow from living a fulfilled life seems to refer to the overly stringent moral codes that defined the sexual ethics of the era. The implication is that if people would accept the findings of psychoanalysis, social factors themselves would change (just as individual patients, once far enough along in analysis, would find the path to sublimation on their own). Thus, at the very same time that Freud was ostensibly acknowledging the limitations of his therapeutic method, he was also advocating the extension of psychoanalytic perspectives into other sectors of life far beyond the clinic—as in fact a *weltanschauung*. "Out of our therapeutic impotence must come the prophylaxis of the neuroses," he declared to Putnam. Because of what we cannot accomplish on the couch, it's all the more important that neuroses are never allowed to form—a prescription that would necessitate mass education in psychoanalytic theory.

The ardor of Freud's tone here was driven by his aversion to American women. He agreed with Jung's assessment of American women as "ravening wolves," dominating the Yankee men who had become, in consequence a "flock of sheep," at least on the home front. In Freud's estimation, coeducation was responsible for the fact that American girls grew up feeling better than boys. At one point, Freud mused that in America the "father ideal appears to be downgraded, so that the American girl cannot muster the illusion that is necessary for marriage." Psychoanalysis was clearly not only about removing illusions, but also about fostering necessary ones, among them the father ideal. Putnam's family was the only one Freud spent enough time with to get any real sense of father–daughter interaction in America. Was Putnam himself the model for the patriarch who had failed to propagate an adequate image of himself as a "father ideal"?

Freud was not arguing to Putnam that social factors ought to be changed to enable a more progressive role for women in society. If anything, he was making the opposite point. By acknowledging woman's desire more openly, and by making a place for that within the culture, the conservative family structure had a better chance of surviving. Putnam said to Freud, help me marry your psychoanalysis to my philosophical understanding and my loveless woman patient will be saved. Freud replied to Putnam, help me make analysis a social reality and your woman won't need to be saved because she'll be equipped to find love.

Ironically, Blow would have agreed with Freud on this main point. Her immensely active career in education and philosophy coexisted with a strident social conservatism about the proper role of women. "I am increasingly sure that nothing will so contribute to the overcoming of nervous tendencies as the revival of domesticity," she wrote to Putnam in 1909. "It is not natural for women to be competitive in industrial employments—neither is it normal for them to gyrate in a round of selfish pleasure. A woman is a nurturer and soother and helper and women will never be normal again until they can consciously accept only those forms of life and activity which are consonant with the impulses bred in them by all the experiences of love and maturity."

Was it Blow's own life, lived so much outside of the home sphere, that prompted these musings? Putnam, who wanted to help women sublimate to some point of ideal individual, familial, and communal fruition, probably did not know what to do with her remarks. They went against his tendency to an unconventional egalitarianism in marriage. Putnam embraced the role of nurturer and helper in his own person alongside Marian, in the same harness.

Freud was shrewd enough to sweeten his remarks on the hopelessness of the therapist before women bereft of the opportunity to love by invoking sublimation. The position of therapeutic impotence was only a dialectical stage. "The more energetically one attacks the sexual problems in such cases, the more one is able to palliate," he wrote. "Where the conditions are not so hopeless, sublimation creates new goals as soon as the repressions are lifted." As long as your female patient isn't a lost cause, after you've dealt with her sexual neuroses the goals which you long to make part of therapeutic practice will crystallize of their own accord.

NOTWITHSTANDING the conceptual questions that remained, Putnam threw himself wholesale into the psychoanalytic cause. By the time he received Freud's letter, he'd almost completed a 30-page work entitled "Personal Impressions of Sigmund Freud and His work," the first of more than two dozen major essays that Putnam wrote on behalf of the Freudian cause in nine years.

Putnam began by deploring the failure of Americans to learn more of Freud's work as both a mark of insufficient application of energy and a mark of mental slowness. "Though little known among us," Putnam wrote, "Freud is no longer a young man, and indeed he outlined his life work and 'laid his course' so many years ago that it is a reflection on our energy and intelligence that we have not gained a closer knowledge of the claims and merits of his doctrines." He characterized all Freud's work as concerned, one way or another, with "the belief that the hidden motives which help to rule our lives, and which frequently show themselves as prejudices, are made up of 'attraction,' 'desire,' 'acceptance,' on the one hand, and, on the other hand, of 'repulsion,' 'repression,' 'denial,' mixed in equal parts." After a competent summary of the evolution of Freud's theories through the study of hysteria, Putnam turned to sexuality. Here, he was completely defensive of Freud and his call for tolerance had a clarion ring.

Putnam wrote that Freud's patients, under analysis, "uniformly referred to one or another manifestation of this great passion as the ultimate source from which these motives sprang; and no wonder, for it is the basis of most of what we care for in this world." His own purpose, he said, was to "make a plea for open-mindedness." The distasteful nature of the topic of sexuality cannot be used as an excuse to ignore it. "There are many subjects intensely disagreeable for discussion, from the social standpoint, which nevertheless the trained man of science studies eagerly and without a trace of unpleasant feeling. This is true, for example, of the bodily excretions."

The aversion to the subject was itself, Putnam argued, an indication "that the topic has or has had a sort of hold on us or a right to demand our interest and attention." Putnam compared Freud's detractors to Darwin's opponents. What was the use, they asked, of demonstrating that "we once were little animals, having no touch with the things that now make life so sacred." Rather, they proclaimed, we ought to "press constantly forward into the free air and more abundant light, and let those who have a dark history forget it. Look forward and not back." This is the great cry of classic American optimism down to our own day. But Putnam, for all his own buoyant idealism, saw through the weakness of the position. "This is a fine cry," he continued, "but unfortunately it has served the cause of ignorance, narrowness, and prejudice as well as that of progress." Echoes of the cry had drowned out the voices of those who tried to address the problems of sex, regardless of the sincerity of their efforts. With a touch of asperity,

Putnam added that "this outcry against one or another sort of investigation is never raised except with regard to our neighbors' efforts to find the truth; the purity of our own motives, the value of our own inquiries, provided they are genuine, rarely come in question." Ultimately, "a fool's paradise is a poor paradise," and no investigation undertaken in earnest could be immoral. "It is a piece of narrow intolerance, cruel in its outcome, to raise the cry of 'introspection' in order to prevent an unfortunate invalid, whose every moment is already spent in introspection of the worst sort, forced on him by the bigotry, however well meant, of social convention, from searching, even to the death, the causes of his misery, and learning to substitute the freedom, liberality, tolerance, and purity that comes from knowledge for the tyranny of ignorance and prejudice."

Near the end of the essay, he introduced the idea of sublimation and revealed the New England inflection that the idea had already taken on in his thinking: "The pressure which all of us are under to make individual interests subservient to community interests finds its strongest, its most fundamental expression at the point where the problem is in question, how to raise to what may be called a higher level, the intense and varied emotions and tendencies that cluster round the great instinct and function of reproduction. This process of transforming our instincts into what may be called by courtesy nobler forms is designated by Freud as one of 'sublimation,' and he is surely right in saying that in it, that is, in the repression of our instincts in the interest of other sorts of gain, the march of culture toward a higher culture virtually consists."

Putnam here blurred the line that Freud sets up between the instinctual renunciations on which civilization depends and the concept of sublimation. At Clark, Freud didn't say that sublimation was a matter of noble self-denial, but rather that "after the removal of repression the way to sublimation is open again." Our highest cultural achievements are a kind of by-product of the "personal character development" and "life adjustment" that result from sublimation. Ferenczi had underscored these points to Putnam in his letter at the end of November. There he reminded Putnam that Freud argued for "conscious condemnation" taking the place of repression, and (invoking an economy of personal pleasure that would have been alien to Putnam) noted that when consciousness has intervened on behalf of the libido that has not found erotic satisfaction "the patient then instinctively will look for and find objects from which he can derive sublimated pleasure." Putnam, on the other hand, framed the act of making "individual interests subservient to community interests" as the overriding, conscious *aim* of sublimation. Thus, from the outset, for Putnam personal sacrifice was the route to sublimation, and sublimation itself was a practice meant to elevate one's capacity for communal contribution.

In the penultimate lines of the paper, he came close to repeating the lines he'd written Freud in his first letter. He expressed his belief "that the intimate knowledge of ourselves, which is essential, needs to be supplemented by more or less distinct study of motives of a social and ideal sort." From the very beginning of his work for the psychoanalytic movement, Putnam set out his real ideal: Oedipus Philanthropus.

Freud wrote Putnam at the end of January 1910 to thank him for the article, which was published in Morton Prince's *Journal of Abnormal Psychology*. "What I read did not surprise me in view of our correspondence," Freud noted. "But it has given me pleasure and satisfaction. I hope your words will make a strong impression in America and will secure for psychoanalysis the lasting interest of your country men." Freud also gestured toward the question of religion. In a line that may have been a toss-off for Freud, but that filled Putnam with hope that Freud would one day be brought to see the light, Freud wrote, "Probably my attitude toward religion is very different from yours. However, I do feel that all honest men share the same faith." If Freud had any idea how literally Putnam would read these words, he would have resisted the urge to make such an assurance to his new acolyte.

CHAPTER 13

The Infancy of Our Movement

*An ethical fraternity, with its mythical Nothing, not infused by
any archaic-infantile driving force, is a pure vacuum.*
Jung to Freud, February 11, 1910

BEFORE THE NEW YEAR, Putnam had his first taste of blood in defense of
the movement. Jones was present at the Harvard psychotherapeutic conference largely dedicated to Freud's work where the gauntlet was tossed. Passions, both serious and silly, raged in all directions. Jones related remarks by
two women that served as fodder for Freud's gleeful ridicule of the Americans. "One wild female flourished two dreams at me that were 'entirely altruistic,'" Jones said, "and declared there was nothing selfish in her, even in her
subconscious." Another woman supported her, protesting against the psychoanalytic effort to generalize about egocentric dreams. "What was true of Aus-
trians might not be true of Americans!"

Putnam himself presented a philosophically inclined paper comparing
Freud's idea of the unconscious to that of Putnam's hero, Henri Bergson.
The climax of the meeting occurred when another Boston psychotherapist
and sometime colleague of Putnam's, Boris Sidis, made an extended, savage attack on psychoanalysis, deriding the "mad epidemic of Freudism now
invading America." It was, he said, a gross regression in psychology that
took the science back to the dark Middle Ages. Calling Freud "one more
pious sexualist," he expressed comfort at the thought that at least it would
prove a "passing craze."

Sidis' assault is intriguing, first in that it implies that "Freudism" was
gaining traction in America just months after the doctors' visit, and second
because in his choice of descriptive terms, he came very close to Freud's

own rhetorical line. The "mad epidemic" Sidis identifies sounds very much like Freud's plague.

This was a pivotal juncture for Putnam. Throughout his mature professional life, he'd striven to serve as a peacemaker. At the Harvard meeting, however, he became so incensed "that he couldn't trust himself to speak," as Jones told Freud. Finally, he rose to Freud's defense in high dudgeon. "It becomes you very ill," Putnam charged, "to criticize a movement you yourself have appropriated with only petty variations and a too scant acknowledgement for so long." Freud could not yet grasp what it must have cost Putnam in psychic terms to lash out for the cause, rather than to retreat into the carapace of his good manners.

A few months later, in the spring of 1910, Putnam evinced the same impulse to do battle when, at a meeting of the American Neurological Association in Washington, he himself was set upon for his new Freudian viewpoints by a well-known New York neurologist. An essay Putnam presented at that meeting was vilified by the neurologist Joseph Collins as a collection of "pornographic stories about pure virgins." Putnam's measured, yet persuasive response to the points raised against analysis led to a backlash against Collins and new support for psychoanalysis. Jones told Freud how someone had remarked that the Association "should be thankful that a man of Dr. Putnam's high ethical motives had probed and tested it [psychoanalysis] for us." This remark "aroused the heartiest applause."

In fact, Putnam's feisty stance at these meetings marked the reawakening of the spirit which, as a boy, had made him choose St. Francis of Assisi and Kepler as guiding spirits. The young Putnam's passion for figures who overthrew conventional opinion indicates that enfranchisement within Boston's established first families did not guarantee conservatism. Yes, there was a heavy Calvinist heritage to contend with, but in New England, unlike, say, Catholic Vienna, the tradition of the burghers themselves contained an element of revolutionary sympathy, which in the Habsburg Empire only marginalized groups like the Jews could be expected to entertain. The fact that Freud named his second son Oliver, after Oliver Cromwell, the foremost general of the Puritan revolution and hero to both settlers of Plymouth Colony and leaders of the American Revolution, may hint at another discomforting affinity with the Americans Freud had to reckon with. Nathan Hale is right to point out that Putnam's New England inheritance would have included, along with the stereotypical emotional reserve, an equal measure of "judicious radicalism." One turn-of-the-century writer, eulogizing Marian's brother, Fred, described how he was a "surviving type of fervent Puritan, who was defined by nonjudgmental liberality of spirit." This, of course, does not mean that the two strains of tradition harmonized with each other.

The opportunity to fight for Freudian truth galvanized the old Puritan warrior spirit in Putnam that had lain dormant for decades. By the end of the winter of 1910, Putnam had added a busy speaking schedule to his arsenal of activities in defense of analysis. His correspondence with Jones shows him constantly engaged in strategizing about how to conduct the campaign for analysis in the New World.

This makes Freud's response to news of the first round of fights and Putnam's paper all the more bewildering. He wrote to Jones testily, "Actually I am not fully recovered from the journey, and have been suffering since then from appendix pains. Let us hope that in exchange something respectable will emerge for our movement in America. . . . The bit in Putnam's essay—'He is no longer a young man'—hurt me, and this outweighed any pleasure I was able to get from the rest of the paper."

Freud's claim to have been so upset by this one sentence that 30 pages of ringing praise brought no gratification at all reveals both hysterical vanity and terror for the future of his theories. It put Jones in the ridiculous position of having to explain why Freud shouldn't have minded the comment. "I was much touched by your reference to Putnam's remark," Jones wrote soothingly, assuring Freud that Putnam's intention had been purely laudatory. "People are apt to think that every revolutionary investigator must be 'only a young man,' and he wished to indicate that you are a man of vast experience." Yet on some deep level, Putnam's paper had inspired in Freud an urge for revenge.

WHATEVER SHOCK OF conflict Putnam experienced in the first year of his work on behalf of psychoanalysis, it was nothing compared to the fray Freud presided over within the analytic camp itself. The second annual "International Psycho-analytic Congress" (a grand title for what was still a rudimentary outgrowth of Freud's home-based Wednesday Psychological Society) was to be held in Nuremberg at the end of March 1910. In his retrospective history of the movement, Freud described his role in

Nuremberg in terms reminiscent of King Lear. He'd decided that the time had come to properly organize the movement, and that he would be happier withdrawing into a position free from its day-to-day cares. To accomplish this, Freud wrote, he'd resolved to "transfer its center to Zurich, and place it under a head who would take care of its future." Freud felt that the connection with Vienna and his own leadership were obstacles to the movement's success. "I was no longer young, I saw a long road before me and I felt oppressed by the idea that it had fallen to my lot to become a leader in my advanced age. . . . It was now my desire to transfer this authority to a younger man who would, quite naturally, take my place on my death. I felt that this person could only be C. G. Jung." Freud had privately conferred on Jung the title of "Crown Prince" on the evening when they were disturbed by occult noises; now he wanted to publicly pass on the scepter of psychoanalytic authority.

From the start, however, everything went wrong. Just three weeks before the Congress was to take place, Jung, who was also to be the event's keynote speaker, received a call to come to America from the mother of a New York patient, which he decided to accept. Topping off the insult, Jung asked his wife to pass on word of this change of plans rather than confessing to Freud himself.

Jung had already shown a capacity to disappoint Freud by postponing gratification, particularly when it came to letters. In November, Freud had written Jung, "It probably isn't nice to keep me waiting 25 days (from October 14 to November 8) for an answer—as though the promptness and length of my last letter had frightened you away." In the midst of his anxieties, Freud descended into a mire of Fliess-based male menstruation talk, blaming the problem on their respective times of the month. "But I can't help responding to my own rhythm," Freud cried. "And the only compromise action I am capable of is not to post the letter I am now writing until Sunday."

Now, Jung knew, he was risking something much more extreme. "Don't get cross with me for my pranks!" he finally wrote Freud, "*I have arranged everything so as to be back in time for Nuremberg.*"

Freud was enraged—and scared. To Oskar Pfister, the Swiss Protestant pastor and psychoanalysis enthusiast, Freud moaned, "What will happen if my Zurichers desert me!" To Jones, he bitterly complained, "Perhaps it will be news to you, as it was to me, that Jung has left Europe for America yesterday on board the *'Kronprinzessin Caecile.'* . . . Smart, is he?" Freud was left feeling so vulnerable by the turn of events that at the close of the letter he even referred to Jones' assurance about his youthful spirit saying, "After all Putnam may be more correct as regards my age than you."

Freud's aggravation reflected the fact that the grand scene of transmission that he'd fantasized about for so long might now never take place. The very concept of forming an official international body to serve as "central command" for psychoanalysis had only been suggested to Freud by a local Viennese pharmacist's scheme to establish an "International Fraternity for Ethics and Culture." Now to have the intended recipient of that transmission fail to show up for the hand-off would turn the affair into outright travesty. Instead of inscribing the success of their New World junket on the canvas of Europe, the event threatened to expose the impotence of America to affect his fate at home.

In the end, Jung strode into Nuremberg at the same moment as Freud opened the Congress with an address called, in a flourish of heavy-handed irony, "The Future Prospects of Psychoanalytic Theory."

BUT THE RESTLESSNESS of the Viennese was not assuaged by Jung's last-second arrival. They huddled together in one corner of the hotel, puffing their pipes and pounding their psychoanalytic papers. The air was heavy with smoke; the breath was thick with bratwurst. Despite its international imprimatur, the Congress was basically split in two: the Viennese circle pitted against the Swiss. Adler and Stekel, both men more than ten years younger than Freud, led the Austrian side, while the delinquent Jung (supported by Jones and Ferenczi) dominated the other.

Alfred Adler, the small, chubby, unkempt leftist son of a corn merchant, had always been conscious of his origins on the wrong side of the tracks relative to most analysts. His proletarian background was the catalyst for a more consuming political agenda than that burdening the rest of Freud's inner circle. Much of the psychological turmoil that Freud blamed on the clash of inner drives Adler attributed to the individual's struggle with social forces. Adler's wife was a good friend of Trotsky's, and he remained a socialist throughout his career. Ever since 1907, when Adler published his opus on organ inferiority and its compensation—the foundation of a psychological theory that downplayed the twists and turns of libidinal fortune relative to that of childhood feelings of helplessness in the genesis of neu-roses—relations between him and Freud had been growing strained.

As for the diminutive, melancholy Wilhelm Stekel, though he'd come to Freud as a patient and been so smitten by the experience of analysis that he'd declared himself "the apostle of Freud who was my Christ!," then going on to do valuable pioneering work on the nature of dream symbolism, Freud had long harbored doubts about his stability and intellect. To Jones, for example, shortly after returning to Vienna from America, Freud wrote that Stekel was "weak in theory and thought," even granting that he had a "good flair for the meaning of the hidden and unconscious." On a theoretical level, against Freud's belief that masturbation released pathogens and endan-gered health, Stekel argued for the complete harmlessness of the act from a physiological standpoint, blaming social stigma for any deleterious effects of onanism.

There were, indeed, a host of reasons Freud had stacked the deck in favor of the Zurichers. The Swiss knew what was coming at the Congress and basked in humble confidence of impending victory, whereas the Viennese suspected skullduggery, but did not yet have evidence to back their paranoias.

The first half of the Congress was dedicated to essays on the latest dis-coveries of psychoanalytic theory. As a culminative event of this portion of the program, a committee was formed to study the origins of all symbols. It was to be a joint Swiss-Viennese venture, the only one to emerge from the Congress. Polite applause came from both sides. And then, at the end of the first day, March 30th, discussions on the future organization and administration of psychoanalysis began.

Ferenczi advanced to the lectern. It was his great hour. He'd been prim-ing himself for weeks. This was the moment at which he advanced from playing Sancho to Freud's Don Quixote to a role more akin to Lady Macbeth's. At the beginning of February, he'd written Freud an overheated letter fantasizing about what the world would be like once the psychoana-lytic perspective was accepted—revolution waited in the wings. "Once society has gone beyond the infantile, then hitherto completely unimagined possibilities for social and political life are opened up. Just think what it would mean if one *could tell everyone the truth,* one's father, teacher, neigh-bor, and even the king." One can just imagine tiny, plump Ferenczi waltz-ing up to Franz Josef himself, plugging thumb to nose and fluttering the fingers. This would be the end, Ferenczi declared, of all artificially imposed authority. In its place would be only what is *"rightful."* Ferenczi mused, "I do not think that the psychoanalytic worldview leads to democratic egalitarianism; the *intellectual elite of humanity* should maintain its hegemony." He concluded the thought with a modest sniff: "I believe Plato desired something similar."

Freud responded to Ferenczi a few days later, reporting that he'd also made the connection with the Platonic rule of philosophers. He extended only one caution to Ferenczi: "I ask you in your own interests to please be careful with organization." From the moment Ferenczi began to speak at Nuremberg, it was clear that in the thrill of battle Freud's prudent admonition flew straight out the window.

Perhaps he was just overexcited by the idea that he'd been chosen to define the establishment that would transform the world into a court ruled by Platonic princes. Instead of explaining Freud's larger tactical purpose in shifting the center of analysis to Switzerland as a means of universalizing the image of the movement, Ferenczi began leveling insults at the skills of the Viennese analysts. Psychoanalysis couldn't remain based in Vienna—the Viennese had no idea what they were doing! The International Association would be controlled by the Swiss because the Swiss were superior! Jung would be president. Riklin, another Swiss, would be secretary. What was more, Ferenczi expostulated in a pitch of totalitarian frenzy, from here on in, no psychoanalyst anywhere in the world would be permitted to publish a paper or deliver a lecture that hadn't been personally vetted by the president of the International Association! However prepared Ferenczi was to incur martyrdom, neither he nor Freud anticipated that his speech would incite a confrontation so violent that all meetings had to be called off until the next day.

The Viennese gathered in Stekel's hotel room to plot their next move. What had happened was grossly unfair. They'd stood by Freud's side when the entire psychoanalytic movement was essentially a once-a-week postprandial game of cards and cigars. Now was the center of the movement to be plucked from its roots? In truth what *was* the psychoanalytic movement? Many of the men already held substantially different views from Freud on key points. What were they doing bowing down in Freud's court to begin with?

Someone let Freud know that the Viennese were holding a war council around Stekel's bed. He rushed to their hotel room, burst in on the men, and made a desperate appeal. Beginning on what had to be the least promising note possible, Freud announced, "Most of you are Jews, and therefore you are incompetent to win friends for the new teaching." But he forged onward. "Jews must be content with the modest role of preparing the ground. It is absolutely essential that I form ties in the world of general science! I am getting on in years. I am weary of being perpetually attacked. All of us are in danger!" And then, in an extraordinary gesture, like something in a painting by the French neoclassical artist Jean David, right there at Stekel's bedside in the presence of the men who'd helped him found analysis. Freud ripped open his coat and cried, "My enemies would be willing to see me starve! They would tear my very coat off my back!"

Freud was 54 years old. Jones, describing him two years earlier, noted his grayness, his diminutive stature, the "strikingly well-shaped head" crowned with thick hair, "a handsome moustache, and a full pointed beard." Freud, Jones said, was a little "rotund" and Jones "dimly sensed some slightly feminine aspect in his manner and movements."

The shock of seeing this slight, white-bearded man who was nominally their king prostrate himself before them in a manner that evoked the fainting fit in front of Jung—the trauma of seeing the master play dead—had a sobering effect.

And then, with deft political instinct, Freud made his tactical bait and switch. Though the International Movement would remain the domain of Zurich, there was no reason that Adler couldn't be president of the *Viennese* Psychoanalytic Society. And Stekel could be secretary. After all, he no doubt suggested, this doesn't mean that Vienna won't continue to be the theoretical capital of the movement from which all the important discoveries are to be made that the Swiss will then transfer to the globe at large.

The gambit worked. The Viennese calmed down. As one further sop to the Jews, Freud announced the formation of a new journal that would allow them a mouthpiece to compete with the original Movement publication (the *Zentralblatt fur Psychoanalyse*) over which Jung exerted control.

But after the Congress was over, Freud admitted that it had been a Pyrrhic victory. "Your impassioned pleading had the misfortune of unleashing so much opposition that they forgot to thank you for your significant inspiration," he wrote Ferenczi. Noting that every society was "thankless," but that they were both a bit to blame for not having adequately reckoned with the effect Ferenczi's speech would have on the Viennese, Freud closed on a hopeful note. "The infancy of our movement has ended with the Nuremberg *Reichstag*, that is my impression. I hope that a rich and beautiful youth is now coming."

If the movement was out of infancy, it seemed to have gone straight to adolescence. Jung was not dependable. The Viennese were crazy and Freud felt an aversion toward them that had in fact been building for a long time. Increasingly, he must have been gazing back toward America with a suspicion that the Movement's best prospects might lie in the place where he'd experienced the most powerful internal revulsion of his life.

But how sure of Putnam could Freud really feel?

WHILE FREUD WAS caught up in preparations for the Nuremberg campaign, Putnam had sent him another long letter in which a discussion of consciousness dissolved into a disquisition on religion. In the course of trying to show Freud that theories of the unconscious entertained by Freud's perennial target of scorn, Morton Prince, were not so different from Freud's own, Putnam equated consciousness with self-consciousness in a manner paralleling the Calvinist doctrines in which his ancestors were schooled. Indeed, the commandment to self-awareness Putnam adapted from Freud's writing had less to do with the mythological fate of a figure like Oedipus than with such Hebraic excoriations as those of Putnam's ancestor, Cotton Mather. "To get good Knowledge, let that be the First Care of them that would be Saved," Mather had cried. Putnam's jump from a struggle to articulate the "complex conditions" of consciousness to a theological confession was not so great as might first appear. "You speak of my religion as probably different from yours," he wrote Freud. "I do not know how this may be, but until recently I have had no religion at all, properly speaking, and was ready to let 'natural science' be the arbiter of everything. Within the past few years I have changed in this respect and I hope, some time, to have the chance of studying these matters over with you at some length."

Putnam received the faith to which he refers from Susan Blow. But why had he felt obliged to discard the purely "natural science" with which he'd hitherto been occupied? What was the genesis of Putnam's first, pre-Freud conversion?

CHAPTER 14

The Terms of Pacification

*It is hard to fight with the demon in his moment of power. I
believe the best one can do is to fix in the mind a conviction
that the black and motley crew of despondent thoughts are of
fleshly origin, and not, as they would pretend, from a spiritual
source. And second to engage the mind as much as possible in
some occupation.*

Dr. James Jackson to Anna C. Lowell, November 12, 1843

FOR A YOUNG man freighted with Putnam's particular species of idealism, the primary emotion inspired by the Civil War was disgust. The years
of the war coincided with his Harvard undergraduate education, a time during which Artemus Ward, Lincoln's favorite satirist, laconically noted,
"Harvard was located at the Parker House bar." In a more sober vein,
Samuel Eliot Morrison observed, "College life went on much as usual, and
with scarcely diminished attendance. Public opinion in the North did not
require students to take up arms, as in the World War, there was no mass
movement into the army or navy, and draftees who hired a substitute were
not despised." Putnam would never have been so flippant as Ward's objects of caricature, or as passive as Morrison's "business as usual" under-
graduates, but there's no hint that he ever considered interrupting his
education to mingle in the great national struggle. To the contrary, his response to the war seems to have consisted in throwing himself into his studies more relentlessly than ever. Putnam's surviving letters home during the
war years are often terse requests for study aids. He wants a new chair for
his desk. He wonders whether his family might be able to help him save

toward a microscope. He details the progress of his grades and outlines his upcoming courses.

The Civil War forced a brutal reckoning with the limitations of medical science in the New World. In 1861, a substantial percentage of American surgeons had never performed surgery at all, let alone had experience treating a gunshot wound. A poor understanding of the importance of hygiene and antiseptics in surgery led to huge numbers of deaths from typhoid and dysentery throughout the conflict. Indeed, diarrhea and dysentery resulted in almost double the number of fatalities as battle wounds. Estimates run as high as 995 cases of chronic diarrhea or dysentery per one thousand soldiers.

The grossly ill-equipped medical corps on the battlefield had its origins in the inadequacies of America's institutions of medical education. During the years Putnam was an undergraduate at Harvard, and for at least a portion of the time he was a graduate student, Harvard Medical School (considered the best in the United States) didn't possess a single microscope or stethoscope.

Putnam wrote college essays rhapsodizing over the model of the German pupil who dedicated his life to rigorous experimental work. Disparaging the abstract worship of the fossilized classics, young Putnam extolled the virtues of the applied sciences. One of his few surviving comments on the Civil War is a cool critique of Northern romanticism. In "The Terms of Pacification with the Rebels," written in 1865 when Putnam was at Harvard, he foresaw the impending crisis of Reconstruction: "The spirit which has been fighting so long against making the Negro a man, even as a military necessity, and that too in the midst of a stupendous war, will blaze out with renewed vigor now that peace is established, against making him a citizen," he wrote. Putnam argued that it was incumbent on the *North* to surrender the "fatal idea" that "Lee is a magnanimous hero, and Davis and others misguided patriots." The success of Reconstruction depended on his fellow Yankees abandoning the mystique of the Confederate leaders as great men, and accepting that they were treasonous murderers.

On finishing his initial round of neurological studies in 1870, Putnam couldn't wait to get out of America and continue his education in the cosmopolitan swirl of the European centers of learning. After a summer spent bounding through castles, galleries, and palaces, dutifully examining the masterpieces of Northern European art and architecture, respecting the penetrating austerity of the grand Dutch portraitists, and being revolted by the fleshy eruptions of Rubens, he'd had his quota of aesthetic pleasure and was ready to buckle down to work. Putnam studied first in dusty laboratories in Leipzig, then migrated on to Vienna, and finished his two-year sojourn abroad in Berlin, living with Emerson in "two scraps of rooms" notable for their lack of sunlight. All the time, he was transforming himself into a veritable young turk of microscope-focused materialism.

THERE WAS IMPORTANT family precedent for Putnam's dedication to the European scientific standard. Of all the heroes in his canon, the most important in Putnam's gallery was his mother's father and his own namesake, the great man closest to home, Dr. James Jackson.

Dr. Jackson had been a colossal figure in the early history of American medicine. Like Putnam, Jackson was renowned for his prescience and diplomatic persistence in importing vanguard European medical advances to the New World. Most notably, Jackson played a key role in importing smallpox inoculation techniques and the larger fruits of the European vaccination movement to America. He was also a prominent founder of Massachusetts General Hospital.

In 1905, when Freud was putting the finishing touches on *Three Essays on Sexuality*, Putnam was publishing an enormous history of his grandfather and his grandfather's family. In the book, Putnam described Jackson's situation following the Revolutionary War in words that resonated with his own position following the Civil War. The confusion that followed the conflict created, Putnam suggested, an opportunity whereby "men of energy and public spirit" could come forward and serve as leaders. But Putnam noted of Jackson that he never let his embrace of that leadership role blind him to the fact that the principal responsibility of high office was an enlarged capacity and obligation to serve on behalf of others.

Jackson's prescription for the ideal physician was based on humility and self-sacrifice. "The true physician . . . cannot fail to be modest in his pretensions," he wrote in an introductory chapter to an anthology of his medical writings, "for he is aware how his knowledge and power are limited, while he feels the magnitude of his task." Jackson asked whether it was the physician's business to cure *all* his patients, and answered that indeed the doctor's mandate was nothing less than this as the word "cure" in its original, true sense means to unstintingly provide nurture and so-lace. "The priest had the parish for his cure, the physician the sick for his." Jackson noted that he *never* pronounced a patient "cured," but that all the patients who came into his hospital were perpetually to *be* cured, "that is taken care of."

Jackson's acute personal scrupulousness extended to matters of faith. When one of his sons, Putnam's namesake James, died suddenly in Europe while studying medicine, Jackson refused to write in eulogies that he was a good Christian. To William Ellery Channing, Jackson explained, "It is common enough for people to strain matters in order to say that a man died in the full faith of Christianity. I would not say so—I stated the exact truth. But I ask, which is the best, that a young man should adopt the principles of the Christian religion and endeavor to conform to them, while he is uncertain whether the evidences will bear strict scrutiny; or, that he should wait to be satisfied as to the evidences before he adopts the principles?"

These were the standards that Putnam was concerned with upholding as he launched his own career.

A pivotal scene of Putnam's youth occurred exactly three months after Jackson's death. Putnam was still in medical school. On an early fall day in 1867 he arranged to meet a family friend and cousin of his future wife, Anna Cabot Lowell, who'd told him that she had an important legacy to pass on from his grandfather. Perhaps the two agreed to rendezvous at "the Delta," the centrally located triangular plot of ground just outside Harvard Yard defined by the intersections of Cambridge, Kirkland, and Quincy streets. Though the cornerstone ceremony was still some years away, by 1867 the Delta had already been consecrated as the future construction site of Memorial Hall, Harvard's monument to its war dead. This "Ruskian-Gothic" edifice, which Henry James described in *The Bostonians* as having "rather too much brick about it," and being "buttressed, cloistered, turreted, dedicated, superscribed" like nothing his Southern protagonist had ever seen, would become the largest building on the Harvard Campus, its scale suggesting a guilt offering to the kernel of truth in Ward's gibe.

Anna was brimming to discharge her sense of obligation to the deceased (who had looked after her during a prolonged illness). Putnam hardly had the chance to greet her before she thrust into his hands his grandfather's key and seal. When she later explained the gift, Anna reminded Putnam how many of Jackson's family had "nobly justified" his grandfather's example, "uprightness and honor being their ideal of true happiness." "May it serve," Anna wrote Putnam, "to keep his love, and holy, spotless example ever before you, so that you may live to be truly worthy of the name you bear."

It was the most intimidating bequeathal imaginable.

WHEN PUTNAM MADE his own educational foray to the Continent he had access to the leading celebrities of European medicine. The three principal figures he studied with would each in his own way prove essential to the theoretical development of Freud ten years later: Theodore Meynert, John Hughlings Jackson, and Jean Martin Charcot. In the critical years of their early education, Freud and Putnam trod virtually identical paths. Both began their respective explorations of the human mind through the study of brain anatomy as a faithful recorder of heredity and physical injury.

Putnam came of age in the grand heyday of the "somatic style." Mental disease was viewed as an exclusively physical phenomenon. Just as a deformation at a particular point on the brain could trigger a whole host of psychological disorders, a "battery doctor" might treat a given set of symptoms through specific applications of electricity. Under this overarching rubric, there were, however, different lines of inquiry pursued by different schools of research. For some of the preeminent figures, such as Charcot, the rich efflorescence of hysterical/neurasthenic symptoms could all be traced back to a single source: hereditary degeneration. There might be various immediate precipitating causes of the disease, but none of these could operate, or were even truly relevant, apart from the fundamentally weakened neurological system inherited by the hysteric.

Though respecting Charcot, Putnam was never as interested in this avenue of theory as he was in the other great field of research occupying European neurologists in the 1870s: the localization of brain function. The most memorable sight for Putnam of his entire tour was that of Theodore Meynert at the University of Vienna single-handedly slicing, dicing, and weighing on the scales more than eight hundred brain specimens to deepen his grasp of the regional action of neuropathology.

Putnam's tour coincided with the moment when hope crystallized in the labs of Meynert, Jackson, and others that the origin of every psychological expression might be pinpointed on a map of the brain, much as, in our own time, the human genome is taken to offer an encoded predictive history of humanity.

FOR ALL OF Putnam's Germanophilia, he and his fellow medical pilgrims from New England never intended to set up shop in Europe. They returned to America to apply their newfound knowledge on Yankee patients and specimens with the goal of transforming the state of science at home to at least a more credible likeness of its utopian promise.

At heart Putnam always preferred the American scene, and his spirit never left the North Country wilderness. Just after he arrived in Rome in the autumn of 1870, he wrote his mother, "Hurray for the Adirondacks! Your 2nd letter and Lizzie reached me yesterday glowing with autumn colors and breezy with primeval forests, two points on which, as far as our experience goes, the new world goes ahead of the old. . . . The solitude is greater so that one feels a sort of ownership or at least companionship with the woods and mountains, a sort of first settler-right to all the nooks and corners instead of feeling like a mere spectator of somebody's else's property. I own that feeling is snobbish but I really enjoyed the St. Theodora Pass knowing that it is not every traveler who goes over it. Every turn of the road has a history of its own and bears the stamp of civilization and one feels like an interloper sometimes or rather I won't say that but at least one misses the feeling of a discoverer." It was to the feeling of being a discoverer that Putnam's soul always thrilled.

On his return to Back Bay, Putnam threw himself into the labor of quantifying the qualities of the human brain. If sheer volume of work could pick the lock on the remaining mysteries of the human psyche, Putnam was poised to scoop the secrets of the Sphinx thirty years ahead of Freud. In his absence, his older brother, Charles, had established himself as one of Boston's principal pediatricians and a leader in the hyperanimated social world of the city's charities. In late nineteenth-century Boston, meeting hall get-togethers of philanthropic cabals and reform groups devoted to everything from vegetarianism to feminism, socialism, abolitionism, temperance, spiritualism, and quirky new education curricula played a role analogous to that of the music hall, vaudeville, saloon, brothel, pleasure-hopping circuit in the ex-Dutch business metropolis further south. For

Putnam, champing at the bit to do his own part toward revolutionizing reality, the scene was heaven.

In the fall, he was appointed "Electrician" at Mass General. The first machines he used to administer low-voltage shocks to patients were the size of pianos. Putnam would have manipulated a crank to turn glass wheels inside the device. These wheels were in contact with a brush, thus building up a spark that issued in an electrical charge.

From the title of Electrician, Putnam's position gradually evolved to that of "Instructor of Diseases of the Nervous System." In 1874, he became a founding member of the American Neurological Association.

Putnam's dedication to the somatic style was such that in 1876 he elected to participate in a historic debate with George Beard on the topic of the usefulness of the new, emerging psychotherapies relative to strictly physiological treatment. Putnam staunchly defended the pure somatic style, arguing, in effect, that however much more work needed to be done to perfect treatments based on organic brain anatomy, he had never seen evidence of mental therapeutics eliciting a cure.

The one hint of the future turn Putnam's thought would take lay in the terms he chose to repudiate Beard's therapeutic experiments as "unscientific." Beard's work failed, Putnam averred, because it attempted to isolate the emotions. As much as Putnam championed the localization of brain function at this stage, he increasingly was pushing beyond even Jackson in focusing on the dynamic interaction of different neurological regions. Even if one could say that a specific anatomical area appeared to be responsible for a given cognitive function, if that area never operated in isolation, but was always actually registering the action of an elaborate network, an element of profundity crept into the equation.

Putnam's evolving late nineteenth-century concept of dynamic neurology foreshadowed his later thinking about the individual in relation to society. It was impossible to isolate the solitary emotion from the larger, crowded field of mental being, just as it was impossible to isolate the individual from the fabric of the community that both threatened and constituted the soul. Research being done in Germany on aphasia convinced Putnam that "a thought is actually compounded of vast numbers of these sensory and motor ideas associated together in a network of infinite complexity, and any disturbance of this association must involve a disturbance of the thought." The moment Putnam could use the word "infinite" in describing the material operation of the brain, the fissure was visible into which the Divine was eventually destined to seep.

Perhaps creeping doubts about the conclusiveness of somatic theory helped goad Putnam to a fury of labor aimed at shoring up its foundation. In the late 1870s, he began teaching at Harvard, establishing the University's first neuropathological laboratory and helping to shape an entire discipline on the subject of nervous diseases. He worked long hours seeing patients in his clinic at Mass General, and carried on a host of experiments in his home lab. Between 1890 and 1895 he plunged into clinical research of infectious diseases of the nervous system with a manic gusto unprecedented in the history of modern neurology. He reported completion of no less than five thousand case histories in this single five-year period. Putnam single-handedly produced the most comprehensive portrait of physiological nervous system damage the world had ever seen.

And still he could not deny to himself that he'd failed to save his patients. According to some studies, rates of mental illness in America were actually rising. Putnam eyed Jackson's seal on his desk like a melancholic staring at a skull. He was neither curing his patients in a modern sense, nor "taking care of" them in conformity to Jackson's definition of the physician's role. The hunger for solace was not assuaged.

As a young man, he'd tried to save Boston from its mystical namby-pambyness with an injection of pure European materialism. But now he suspected that he'd gone too far. His lack of attraction to Christianity didn't make him a sanguine atheist. All he'd developed over the years was a profound sense of deferential self-doubt. The confidence of Putnam's youth withered. He began to experience symptoms of nervous disease himself. With a new child popping into the austere environs of 106 Marlborough Street every couple of years and he himself getting, frankly, old, the time in which to become great was shrinking. It was true that he'd kept an open mind and increasingly found himself experimenting with new techniques of psychotherapy that he'd once rejected, but though these methods were promising, he couldn't see them building toward the kind of grand synthesis he craved.

In late middle age, Putnam found himself, like Dante, "in a dark wood, for the straight way was lost."

CHAPTER 15

Just God and Kindly Nature

Fortunately, in any case, the world is not built on pleasure,
but on accomplishment and affection and insight, and the
"sensitives" may in the end get their full share of these.
Putnam to Marian in an undated letter.

BY THE TIME Putnam wrote Freud to express his yearning for the day
when he and Freud would be able to sit down together to study religion
"at some length," his own faith was firm. He could grant Freud the fact
that we might "get the *formal* explanation for our religious conceptions (idea
of God, etc.) through 'projection' of our anthropomorphic ideas," but this
did not mean that the formless supernal to which we aspire was any less
real. What was more, as Putnam informed Freud, the royal road to knowledge of this other consciousness ran through philosophy and metaphysics.
"Psychologic observation of ourselves teaches us much, but it teaches *nothing* with regard to the essential nature of the universe or of ourselves."
Putnam declared, "Our psychopathic patients need, I think, something
more than simply to learn to know themselves. If there are reasons why
they should adopt higher views of their obligations, as based on the belief
that it is a morally conceived universe, and that 'free-will' has a real meaning, then these reasons ought to be made known to them." Coming to the
brink of mentioning Blow, Putnam told Freud that he could refer him to
"books where these arguments are set forth with all the convincing logic
and *reference to experience* that you have shown adherence to in your own
work."

Freud was willing to humor Putnam on the religious question—up to a
point. "It would be a great delight to me to discuss religion with you since

you are both tolerant and enlightened," he wrote in March. "Perhaps we shall have occasion to do so at the next Congress." And yet, Freud felt obliged to add, "I am afraid that it may be only a pious wish-fulfillment." In a remark calibrated to, at once, advertise the superiority of psychoanalysis to a religiously informed world-view, even while catering to Putnam's fascination with the idea of sublimation, Freud explained, "'Just God' and 'kindly Nature' are only the noblest sublimations of our parental complexes, and our infantile helplessness is the ultimate root of religion." Freud's personal animus came through in his closing comments. "What we see around us gives us little evidence for the existence of an ethical order in the world. But this is not a logical consequence of psychoanalysis; one may or may not graft religion onto it; as a matter of principle I should not like to have psychoanalysis placed at the service of any specific doctrine."

Putnam had never suggested doing any such thing. On that point he agreed with Freud completely. This only made it harder for him to understand why Freud's discomfort with claims to an exclusive monopoly on truth signified the banishment of philosophy as such. It was beyond Putnam's ken to grasp the long history of anti-Semitic persecution that lay behind Freud's hostility. Freud's resistance on this point shows him at his ecumenical best, displaying an instinctive empathy with the unsanctified that would make him chary of the Zionist project as well. Putnam's ethical idealism was touching, but in Freud's estimation, Putnam's admirable character in no way meant that his ideas had anything to do with the real world.

EIGHT MONTHS AFTER the Clark Conference, Putnam claimed to have already treated "more or less thoroughly, sometimes quite imperfectly, about twenty patients, suffering from anxiety-neuroses, hysteria, neurasthenia, fears, impulsions." Something significant had taken place in his clinic. The Americans had been groping in the direction of Freud's theories for years. Freud synthesized different strains of popular new psychotherapy and supplied an engaging mythological lexicon to the whole system. For people who had never had what we would today call a "personal narrative," the sheer process of connecting desires and habits with past frustration and trauma into a coherent story was liberating.

However startling his rate of treatment might appear, when Putnam declared that psychoanalysis worked, he was registering a tangible alleviation of symptoms and of the suffering attendant on that anguish. Because many of his patients had been in his care for years, he was able to directly compare the results of Freud's methods with previous therapeutic protocols. "In almost every instance the new results have been materially better than the old," Putnam reported in an essay entitled "Personal Experience with Freud's Psychoanalytic Method," the second he wrote for the movement. "I soon became convinced that my earlier acquaintance with those patients' lives, characters, capabilities and needs had been utterly superficial."

At the core of Putnam's sense of the psychoanalytic mission was the imperative to externalize conflicts taking place deep inside the individual. "Every watchful observer can trace, from infancy onwards, the working and the conflict of these two great influences, natural instinct and the repression of this instinct for the sake of society as a whole," he'd written in his first essay. "This conflict complicates and underlies all the great movements by which the emotions, the hopes, the fears of men are stirred. . . . The greatest problem of psychopathology of the future is to learn how to detect the subtle workings of this conflict and the principles which it implies." Not flight. Not even resolution. But *recognition*, a form of confession that enables the self-aware individual to make the ethical choices that together articulate a life of meaning.

In the contemporary dedication to pacifying discontent, we've abandoned the idea that there is a value to conflict. As Elizabeth Roudinesco has written, "The power of medicines of the mind is the symptom of a modernity tending toward the abolition not only of a desire for liberty but also of the very idea of confronting that experience." The exhilaration Putnam felt at being able to help patients find words for experiences that had been burrowing into them their whole lives was replaced by an impetus to shut everyone up.

EVEN AS HE transformed himself into a psychoanalyst, Putnam never felt obliged to follow Freud in every detail. For example, he saw no reason to adopt Freud's method of procedure whereby the patient was to "lie down in a recumbent or semi-recumbent position, under the real but not the apparent inspection of the physician." He called the Freudian model "a species of soliloquizing." Instead, Putnam and his patient both moved about inside the little clinic in his townhouse, circling, pacing back and forth, occasionally talking to each other, sometimes apostrophizing into the air.

The case histories that Putnam records in the second paper are among the first real analyses to have been conducted in America. As many of the individuals with whom he began analyses had been long-term patients, they also tell us something about the kinds of people and sufferings Putnam typically encountered at the height of his career.

The very first patient he chose to discuss came to Putnam with a philosophical complaint. She was "a studious and high-minded woman, now 41 years old, of the conscientious, somewhat neurotic type so common in New England, who filled a sedentary and literary position in a country town." Putnam recounted that she'd originally come to him in 1907, two years before Freud's visit, and that she presented a case of "universal doubt," a "Wandering-Jew" syndrome, whereby she was unable "to find rest in any proof." When she first showed up in his clinic, Putnam noted, she "announced timidly that she could not rid herself of the idea . . . that plants and trees suffered like men, so that cutting and breaking them caused them pain." Over time, she revealed that similar doubts infected her perspective on everything, down to her own identity and name. "Argument, as is usual in such cases, proved of no permanent avail," Putnam wrote; "abundant encouragement and directions how to sidetrack her painful doubts helped more, but secured only temporary gains." Despite the fact that she continued to perform her work with dedication, she was "never, even for a moment, free from a painful sense of nervous strain, a haunting dread of insanity and sometimes even suicide."

Putnam explained how for the past year he'd undertaken a systematic investigation of the facts behind her mental state "with steadily increasing interest on both sides." After concerted probing, Putnam was able to confirm that her generalized tendency to uncertainty was the result of doubts on "certain particular moral questions involving a sense of personal mortification."

The woman had a happy childhood, he reported, though after her father's premature death, she'd come entirely under her mother's influence. The household habits her mother cultivated were exclusively ones of "wholesomeness and refinement," a seeming blessing, "yet the very fact that this was so played its part in intensifying certain of the patient's morbid traits." As his patient recalled her past she began to see that what she'd conceived of as simply an unusually imaginative, fanciful nature was also one riven with ardent desires "which had the sexual instinct as their central points."

Thus a conflict arose between her mother's standards and her own "assumed backsliding." She suffered silently from a conjunction of private mortification with an "unanswered curiosity about sexual facts." Putnam related that "when a very small child she was induced, as a bit of fairy-story play, to make a mock marriage with a small-boy playmate, and this was attended with certain ceremonies that seemed at first trivial, but at once induced a sense of guilt." (The ceremonies involved "passing water in common, the patient being in a tree overhead.") "Then there came a period of masturbation, with sexual visions, and although this experience, like the other, was overcome after a time, and for a time, almost forgotten, yet subsequent events brought both to active life."

As a grown woman "there came a few trifling indiscretions, not of act but of thought." After glancing at a book connecting masturbation with insanity she began to have emotional thoughts linked "with the brute-animal creation"; dreams and a new sense of guilt followed on reading an Old Testament passage that also brought to mind early practices and memories "which became rekindled through a vaginal examination conducted by a physician of a stern manner who for her inflamed imagination figured as a detective." All of these different factors combined to form a "tangle, made up of natural desires gone astray, needless self-reproaches, fear of discovery, fears of insanity, the assumed condemnation of science and the Scriptures, the assumed abandonment of her maternal standards." She had entered Calvinist hell. Putnam's simile for her situation reflected his cognizance of this parallel: "In the midst of this network struggled the patient like a fly in a spider's web, feeling her life a contradiction, her mind diseased and so unworthy of trust, and yet unable to see and face the causes of her distress. What wonder, that, as the result, she reasoned herself to be incapable of reason. What wonder that she could not extricate herself unaided." Putnam could not have written these lines without recalling the most famous of American Puritan sermons, Jonathan Edward's "Sinners in the Hands of an Angry God," in which Edwards described God holding "you over the pit of hell, much as one holds a spider, or some loathsome insect over the fire, abhors you, and is dreadfully provoked. . . . And there is no other reason to be given, why you have not dropped into hell since you arose in the morning, but that God's hand has held you up."

The anguish of Putnam's patient represented the clash between a natural physicality and unrealistic standards for pure-mindedness at home, coupled with bad science, social intolerance, and insensitive doctors. Freud's theories made it easier to talk about these problems, but Putnam's fluency suggests that the essential dynamic was one he'd been aware of for some time.

By recognizing and confessing the erotic roots of her symptoms in treatment, the patient was able to reduce their hold over her. "Although her revelations were a cause of obvious and peculiar suffering, yet she has felt what everyone who seriously works by this method comes to feel, that it is a great relief to understand one's enemy; to exchange an emotion of terror for a knowledge of the facts and for problems that can be intellectually faced." Putnam stated how, along with sheer respect for knowledge, one discovered through the psychoanalytic process a "growing hesitation to pass judgments or to listen to them." In his first case history, Putnam defined psychoanalysis as, in part, an education in tolerance for both physician and patient.

Putnam's second case history involved a man "in early middle life, married and with several children," who was charismatic and enjoyed excellent health. Unlike his female patient who'd been victimized by the judgments of others, this man had become "a torment to his family from a habit of unreasonableness and exaction," a form of sadism "not unmixed with a readiness to receive blame for which the designation masochism would be equally in place."

Had it not been for "the marvelous array of data collected by Freud and his colleagues" on which Putnam could draw he noted that he might have "treated this patient forever without reading the riddle of his life." Through analytic methods, Putnam discovered that the man suffered from an "aberrant emotionalism of childhood prolonged into adult life" with a "marked but eccentrically developed erotic nucleus." He too suffered from "painful conflicts between desire" (desire often leading to masturbation) and "self-condemnation, expiation, propitiation." Sometimes his expiation took a religious form; at others it was played out in obsessive handwashing. The "maniacal seizure" that all this made him subject to "was a duplication of lesser dreams and fancies from which Dante might have found fruitful suggestions for his inferno," Putnam dryly noted. In explaining his treatment of this patient, Putnam faults himself for having tried to explain too much without letting the patient work things out piecemeal for himself.

Putnam's third patient was a younger lady, less set in her ways, which made treatment correspondingly easier. A sufferer from morbid shyness, she broke down constantly in tears and was terrified of passing urine when visiting strangers. In analysis it emerged that a broken engagement played an important part in her personal biography, but more than that, yet again, was the dynamic of her childhood home in which her strong passions as a child confronted "well meaning but narrow and bigoted parents" who brought her up "strictly and injudiciously." Throughout childhood and adolescence, she'd been dominated by "repression and outbreaks against repressions and inwardly by analogous mental conflicts. Through everything there had been a constant surging of desires and cravings which if sympathized with and guided would have made the patient a warm-hearted and affectionate person, even if impulsive."

All of the patients Putnam initially selected to report on were tortured by the residual effects of a youthful conflict between sexual desire and repressive environments. Unfulfilled erotic passion was invariably the culprit. Yet Putnam was in no way suggesting that the solution to this problem lay, therefore, in a more free expression of sexuality. He was pleading, rather, for empathetic understanding of the conflicts in the past that led to the development of patients' mental states: the need to recognize the natural presence of the sexual instinct from childhood in order to be free from its dominion as adults, not to release lusts.

Behind the plea for tolerance lay Putnam's belief that society's conservative judgment was wrong because it hindered the patient from making his or her own intellectually informed choice to sublimate erotic yearnings. On making this choice, patients were able to get beyond the self and devote themselves to the greater good.

Middle-aged and youthful, men and women, businessmen, married people, spinsters and literary types—Putnam's patients represented a catholic cross-section of turn-of-the-century Americans. In concluding, he identified the most resistant cases as those involving chronic neurasthenia, depressions, and phobias related to causal circumstances and, lastly, neuroses "for which it was impossible to secure the conditions of the sexual life favorable to improvement." In these latter instances, Putnam contended, "the resources of 'sublimation' should be fully utilized." Putnam was surely aware that failure to find carnal gratification would apply to a high proportion of patients. He was quietly calling for his colleagues to develop the one element of psychoanalytic theory that Freud himself was uncomfortable about.

IT WAS THE recital of this paper at a conference in Washington, D.C., that led Collins to accuse Putnam of telling "pornographic stories about pure virgins." Yet to his family back in Boston, Putnam revealed no hint of discord. Instead, he expounded on the fact that Washington was "a pleasant city, so it is, and no mistake," singing of the city's horticultural blessings: "This is certainly the place for trees," he wrote Elizabeth. "I suspect you'd have to go to California or England to see better specimens of old oaks and tall beeches and European lindens and that thing whose name I know perfectly but can't quite get, with composite leaves and hanging clusters of pea-shaped flowers that grows along the roadside as you go up the hill from Marston's Mills toward Cotuit."

He ate at low-priced "Dairy lunch" spots: "There is something in me, partly stinginess, partly a revulsion against swelldom (I don't approve or recommend) which makes me like these homely resorts," he wrote, "and I find it very amusing to sit without care or the need to be entertaining, with a cup of coffee and a slice of nice, warm, freshly made apple-pie balanced on the broad arm of a chair, reading Dante's Inferno with one hand, as it were, and eating with the other. The Inferno is not quite so infernal when thus mitigated."

And he observed the inhabitants of the nation's capital with curiosity and the racial outlook characteristic of his milieu in which condescension mingled with awareness of personal bias. Washington, he told his daughter, was "also the place for darkies—real ones—and I love to watch them, shambling along, if they are oldish men, or dressed up very neatly in their Sunday best, if they are youngish women. But their faces are so queer! (i.e., by our narrow standards). You only have to imagine a few rings in the noses, ears or lips and a few feathers and gorgeous amulets and a certain dearth of clothes and an environment of forests, to see them as they were, once upon a time, strange change to contemplate."

There was also professional business to report. To his wife, Putnam related that Jones had decided "the time was not yet ripe for a purely psychoanalytic society" to be founded in America. He had hence suggested to Putnam that after the planned meeting of the American Neurological Association in Washington they should set about founding a bridge group to be called the American Psychopathological Association.

On May 2, 1910, at the grandiose 341-room hulk of the Willard Hotel, the Association was duly formed with Putnam as chief officer. "I have been spending the afternoon over an executive meeting with regard to our embryo society, The American Psycho-pathological Association—which, 10 or 20 years hence, may have a glorious existence!" he reported to Marian. Putnam was careful to distance himself from the psychoanalytic side of the endeavor, adding that after the meeting he'd gone on a walk with Jones who was "highly intelligent, and satisfying up to a certain point but beyond that, not quite so." He had devoted himself "to upholding the philosophic views which Miss Blow endorses, but I must master them more fully for without something like the scheme which they imply I can see only a crippled universe."

Putnam's reticence about his newfound passion for analysis reflected the fact that its domestic repercussions were becoming apparent. Marian had by this time announced her dislike for the psychoanalytic approach. Putnam was not yet so deeply immersed that he was compelled to disclose the extent of his investment in Freud's work. It was easier to be frank about his need for Miss Blow than to confess his conversion to Freudism.

CHAPTER 16

Conviction of Sin

I shall only go where you tell me to and shall be very grateful for the guidance. After all, Freud is only rediscovering Man's "total-depravity" and as this is the one doctrine I have always held with the same firmness that I hold man's divinity, it will not be as hard for me to consider this fact in detail as it is for people who really believed man to be by nature good.

Blow to Putnam, June 26, 1910

EVER SINCE PUTNAM missed a visit to Cazenovia on account of the Clark Conference, Blow had been suspicious of Freud. By the time Putnam settled back into Boston in the late autumn of 1909 she'd already begun interrogating him about Freud and putting forward her own views about where Freud fell short. "Can we not influence the affections most effectively through educating the intellect and will?" she asked him in late November. Rejecting the idea of a purely etiological approach to healing, she insisted that "to change abnormal impulses" one had to offer up "ideals to the intellect" and help in the formation of new habits. But she was equally opposed to classic suggestion theory. "I am inclined to believe that this [the effort to form character through suggestion] is an assault upon freedom and I react with indignation at all efforts of another person to use *his* Consciousness to influence *my* subconsciousness," she wrote. "Let me make over my subconscious self by thinking true thoughts and willing true deeds. If there is a muddy reservoir somewhere in me let me send into it constantly a pure stream from the fountain of my self-activity."

With all her doubts, she also consistently expressed curiosity to learn more about Freud's work. And in a familiar lament she sighed over the fact that they couldn't join together in the sort of ethical reading circle to which her heart would always respond most strongly: "I wish you and I could study Dante's Purgatorio together. It is (aside from being great poetry) the greatest book on Moral Education in the world."

Just before Thanksgiving, she told Putnam that she was making plans to acquire a copy of Freud's *Traumdeutung* so that she could be an "intelligent listener" when they next got together to "talk about the subject in which you are so much interested." But his fascination could not intimidate her from challenging Freud's theories. Whereas she was able to accept "the value of getting patients to scrutinize their own consciousness and to become aware of their experiences which had caused their morbid or diseased state of mind," along with the idea that some experiences could be "rejected by the main personality and persist as subordinate centers of association," she viewed these as factors of diagnosis, not treatment. She could not understand why "the *recall* of the experience which created the secondary center is itself curative." She circumscribed the utility of psychoanalysis well beyond Putnam's own misgivings: "I can see that it may be preliminary to cure," she wrote.

A further difficulty Blow had with psychoanalysis related to the inconsistency with which Freudian neuroses affected different individuals. Why, she mused, should "certain suppressed experiences *produce* nervous states in one person when similar experiences have no effect on others." After all, it wasn't only remembered experience that stimulated psychological change: "I know in my own experience that an imperative ideal can have just the same effect as an imperative emotion," she argued. Blow would not countenance the notion that an urge to saintliness could itself be a neurotic trait. "Some of my worst suffering has come from the fact that I have realized that given my attained state of character I was bound no matter how hard I tried to make mistakes through which others might be hurt," she argued. "Were I wiser and better I should see ways of acting which the most earnest effort will not now reveal."

For Blow as for Putnam, although it might be possible to accept the idea that it was detrimental to torture oneself over sexual desires that were part of biological being, no criteria could be too stringent in assessing the worthiness of one's social character.

Another stratum of Blow's doubts about Freud reflected her conviction that the best aspects of his theories were already in circulation. Froebel's philosophy of education was designed to nurture "unification of life," which seemed to her to be the goal of psychoanalysis. Of course, she acknowledged, if Freud could help people get over the strain of this effort to make themselves whole that would be "a great blessing." She concluded, "I am writing you frankly my difficulties and if you show me they are simply due to ignorance I shall be most grateful. We must have some good talks this winter. And we must study Dante for when it comes to psycho-analysis of emotional states he is the 'great master of them that analyze.'"

With time, her doubts proliferated. When Putnam was about to deliver his paper in Washington, she read his essay and struggled to understand his overview of Freudian theory in the language of their existing philosophy. There were precedents for Freud's point "that a wrong thought must not be pressed or shoved aside but consciously faced and *inhibited*," but in order for the analyst to help the patient to recognize the evil or blind impulse so that it might be inhibited, the two had to achieve a frightening closeness. "I rather shrink from the intimacy it necessitates," she wrote Putnam. "It seems to me that *any* form of the confessional should be between an *unknown* and an *unknown*. The priest in his box—the sinner on his knees—There seems almost an attack on the modesty of the soul in its unveiling itself to the gaze of any known and knowing person."

Perhaps, in thinking about the patient–physician relationship Freud had structured, Blow was comparing it to the one she and Putnam forged over the years. Their exchange might not have penetrated the darkest corners of her mind, but it yet managed to plumb depths of real sadness in ways that brought vital solace. Their dialogue was based on slowly building trust, which made her feel free to speak without feeling dogmatically obligated to reveal. It was, above all, a true conversation in which Putnam paced the room with her and engaged her with his own thoughts and his own intellectual, emotional, and spiritual needs, so that she did not feel alone with her demons. The fundamental equality of the talk between Putnam and Blow put it at a great remove from the Freudian dynamic with its inevitable hierarchical cast.

The circumstances of her own fruitful treatment with Putnam may have given Blow an intuitive sensitivity to the dangers of a transference. A full analytic treatment with Putnam would have culminated in gradual disclosures of a nature fatal to the garden they cultivated together. The grace of their bond depended on a balance of openness and inhibition—inhibition in the name of speculative thought, of higher purpose, of the fundamental morality that applied equally to the dictates of divine obligation and human civilization.

However much she longed for Putnam, she knew Putnam's own vulnerability to her, and she protected him willfully in a self-sacrificing manner through the years of their friendship. "My second doubt is twofold," she wrote him, "whether the hearing of these self-revelations is good for the physician himself and whether until all great physicians become also great casuists they can be safe guides." The critique of what we would call countertransference is general, but it began, as did all her intellectual arguments, with an analysis of her own charged emotional experience.

THE LETTERS AND conversations that Blow exchanged with Putnam in the first years of his involvement with analysis struck him with sufficient force that he interpolated them into what he wrote Freud. Putnam was already dependent not just on Blow's example but on her actual ideas in articulating his side of the debate with Freud. Indeed without Blow's help, Putnam might well have been unable to sustain his relationship with Freud, as he could never accept the idea that to promote analysis it was incumbent upon him to let go of his faith. The way to keep his conversion to Freud's views on psychology from being a betrayal of his spiritual beliefs was to constantly battle to incorporate Blow's philosophy into the analytic perspective. This was also an act of loyalty to his wife and the larger Boston world they inhabited. By refusing to abandon his stake in philosophical exploration as an integral component of psychological investigation, Putnam was demonstrating that in taking up Freud he had not abandoned the "City of Beautiful Ideals."

Blow was always eager to do anything in her power to help Putnam, but it involved a strain on her psyche that he only intermittently acknowledged. "This morning I am suffering conviction of sin," she wrote him after failing to immediately answer one of his letters. "It hurts me that I have been so dilatory. Still I know when I have explained you will know there is no cause for the fear expressed in your letter and will cover my epistolary shortcomings with the copious mantle of your charity."

However sympathetic Putnam was to Blow's plight, his own exhilaration about the prospects of redemption through analysis outweighed everything. He entered a new era of personal and global optimism, even as Vienna descended into a new period of dangerous uncertainty with the death of Karl Lueger, the first mayor of Vienna to manipulate a modern form of anti-Semitism for political purposes. Lueger was buried with honors no sovereign could match and hailed as Vienna's "most beautiful corpse." Shops shut, mourning flags fluttered, and sausage stands sprang up all over town while a phalanx of almost 50,000 men framed the slow march to the cemetery. Hitler wrote of having been among the vast crowd "looking out at the tragic spectacle." On hearing of the mayor's demise, Freud wrote Ferenczi, laconically, "Lueger died yesterday. You see, all kinds of things are happening." Few people had any illusions that the attitude toward Jews would improve in consequence of Lueger's death. Throughout the spring, Freud worried about rumblings among Germany's most prominent neurologists concerning a planned boycott of clinics in which psychoanalysis was practiced.

IN EARLY JUNE, Putnam and Jones lectured at a conference in Toronto. Putnam's latest paper, "On the Etiology and Treatment of the Psychoneuroses," although again thoroughly rehearsing the arguments in favor of Freud's theories, went farther than any previous one in suggesting the need for an admixture of something distinct from analysis in treatment.

In his initial defense of Freud, Putnam made an interesting departure from the popular take on the problem of mental health in the era, as expressed in many theological tracts deploring the effects of society's industrialization on individual psychology. Putnam wrote that the strains of modern living, "the telephone, the morning paper, the noise of crowded streets, the seething competition and the pressure for a narrow and exclusive individualism such as everywhere makes itself manifest," appeared greater than they were. In a lucid vein that doesn't always characterize his writing, Putnam observed, "The pace set is set, after all, by men for men, and while it is too fast for some it is not certain that on the whole it increases faster than the power of adaptation of the majority." At the least, Putnam continued, "the strains of modern living are mostly obvious and open enemies, whereas the enemies which we have most to fear are those which, in our ignorance, we do not see. If we could but secure all the power of meeting hard conditions that belongs to us by birthright we should not have to strive so hard to make these conditions easier." This latter line is, indeed, classic Emerson with a slight twist: "the man is as it were clapped into jail by his *un*consciousness."

Much of Putnam's lecture was dedicated to unqualified promotion of Freud's work. But Putnam also struck a cautionary note. The skill and natural aptitude of analysts needed to be exceptionally high. If the physician lacked the most rigorous dedication and talent, he might "find himself standing aghast at the task before him, as Faust stood before the Earth Spirit which his magic arts had summoned." The line points to the Faustian problem to which Freud was most vulnerable: the seduction inherent in human theory making. Once the process takes off, the theory maker discovers further validation everywhere he looks. Once Fliess began to perceive the operation of bisexuality in nature, it became an all-pervasive structure. Once wish fulfillment was seen as a key explanation of dream material—once sex was seen as a great trigger of neuroses—there was no room for other causes.

Blow was plainly in Putnam's mind as he made this charge. He went on to invoke her analogy of the affinity between the psychoanalytic process and the one Dante traced in the *Divine Comedy*. "The familiar sins of 'incontinence, violence and malice' which Dante punishes in his Inferno as attacks upon social stability and progress might justly be described in medical terms as equivalent to psychoneurotic symptoms; and in the sufferings and joys of those whom this great student of human nature sets toiling up the hill of Purgatory it is possible to read the symbolized history of that typical and desirable sort of convalescence from the miseries of nervous illness which leads not only to a better personal health but to a wider sense of social opportunity and obligation." This, in a nutshell, is Putnam's perspective on the psychoanalytic mission filtered through Blow: the justification for the focus on individual psychology and personal history is as a prelude to enabling individuals to fulfill their profound social duty. Indeed, Putnam went on to say, "the community is the individual written large."

IN MID-JUNE, FREUD made a strategic decision that he knew would pay Putnam the highest compliment possible. "It has occurred to me," Freud wrote, "that only you and only Boston could be the starting point for the

formation of a psycho-analytic group to be joined by our friends in America."
In what may be one of the last such compliments paid to the city, Freud
added, "I understand that all important intellectual movements in America
have originated in Boston. I also know that no one else is as highly regarded
as you; because of your unimpeachable reputation for integrity, no one else
could protect so well the beleaguered cause of psychoanalysis." Putnam
was clearly moved by Freud's invitation and immediately wrote to thank
him for his "welcome note." But this was hardly his most ebullient letter.
Why didn't he leap to respond to the proposal that he become the founding member of America's first psychoanalytic society?

THE SUMMER OF 1910 was an especially demanding one from a fatherly
standpoint. Elizabeth was graduating from Radcliffe in June, and Jamie had
begun to suffer unexplained attacks of vertigo. Jamie's suffering increased
later in the summer when his dearest friend, Tom Bowles, a young man
from whom he was inseparable, died abruptly on a trip to Germany from
an attack of pneumonia. (It appears that Jamie's loss of equilibrium coincided with Tom's absence.) Most of the summer was spent at Cotuit, where
Putnam also had to worry about the health of the elm trees in his beloved
garden, overseeing a major spraying operation as the plague of elm disease invaded their part of Cape Cod.

    And then there was the endless succession of outings to pay visits to
acquaintances, as well as sailing trips to favorite shores for oyster picnics
and bonfires. Each summer at Cotuit witnessed the mounting of at least
one major theatrical production. In 1910 it was Thackeray's *The Rose and
the Ring* with a combined cast and audience of 114, ranging in age from
"Mr. Ropes, 86 years old, to Thornton Coolidge, 3 years old." All day long
the different families were busy making costumes and rehearsing, when
they weren't organizing elaborate boat races and swimming parties. Relatives and friends were constantly passing through Putnam's Cotuit home.
A large cluster of Lee cousins arrived mid-summer and didn't leave. Aunt
Amy returned from Italy and descended on the Putnam household, distributing Venetian beads and silver necklaces as though she were the spirit
of Old World carnival come to Cape Cod.

    It was all, in many ways, the picture of a delightful life, and it's aston-
ishing that Putnam managed to get any professional work done whatsoever.

Yet in this same period he was writing voluminous essays on Freudian theory, on top of maintaining his extensive practice and related medical association commitments. The tendency of his philosophical writing to lurch into abstractions has to be juxtaposed with the fact that his life couldn't have been more rooted in people and earth-bound duties. Putnam's speculative musings only make sense contextualized with the copious stuff of his day-to-day life, in which he was encased like a debutante in corset and endlessly layered billowing gown.

Freud's ideas—Freud himself—did not fit into the local community. Yet Putnam's ideal community was defined by knightly fealty to the cause of principled truth. If Putnam really felt that Freud's was the more honest, penetrating understanding of human psychology, there would ultimately be no way he could refrain from choosing to align himself with his movement. Most torturesome of all was the question of how he could present the decision to Marian. She had already expressed displeasure at her husband's interest in psychoanalysis. To have him then found the first American organization of the movement would be a transgression without precedent in their life together. Freeing himself from Marian's nagging needs was a challenge under the best of circumstances. Yet how could Putnam's aspiration to be a warrior for truth permit him to recuse himself from the call?

After the initial acknowledgment of Freud's offer, Putnam didn't write him again until mid-summer, when he was candid about the struggle he was undergoing. "I wish I was nearer either you or him [Jones] or some reflecting source of light." He described having read Freud's "Leonardo" with pleasure, and though he understood "that the religious conception of God is an idealized paternal complex," he still clung "to the teachings of philosophy and metaphysics as adding something indispensable to such a genetic theory. . . . I find myself compelled to ask what is the fundamental nature of the universe, and compelled to answer that it is in some sense 'eternal,' and also that the mental life is the most real thing we know." Putnam dug himself into ever deeper abstractions. "If a scheme is *really* eternal it must *as a scheme* have already fulfilled its possibilities and be a perfect scheme," he pleaded. "Otherwise it would have fulfilled its defects and have gone to pieces." Finally he had to break off. "I suppose all this sounds nonsense to you, but one must say what one thinks." And then, helplessly, he started up the speculative motor again: "I think there is a 'science' which works by certain presuppositions [laws of nature; assumption of causation, etc., i.e. by presuppositions which are arbitrary and conventional] and a 'philosophy which works by certain other sorts of presuppositions [essential laws of thinking]. Why should we discard the latter, and why should we strive to silence our instinctive desire to know the essential nature of things?" By this point, Putnam must have been staring in alarm at the Stygian stable of concepts mounded up around him, wondering why he couldn't just say what he meant when it all seemed so brilliantly clear every time he talked to Miss Blow?

At last, in what was for him the most muted, lukewarm manner possible, at the close of the whole long-winded letter, he tentatively accepted Freud's offer. "Dr. Jones and I will bring about the Branch Association meeting, but it seems to both of us that it would best take place in connection with the next meeting of our new American Psychopathological Association."

WEARY AFTER THE strains of Nuremberg and the obviously greater crises of dissension looming on the horizon, Freud made plans to take an exceptionally long summer hiatus from Vienna. He decided to take the whole family to Holland for six weeks, from where he would travel onward with Ferenczi to make a tour of southern Italy. Jones met him in Noordwijk and described how the two men took long walks along the beach: "I noticed he had to poke every bit of seaweed with his stick, his quick eyes darting here and there all the time." Jones asked him what it was exactly he expected to find in his probing to which Freud answered, "Something interesting. You never know." The trip to the seaside was one of only three he took to the beach in his entire life.

The men discussed Putnam and his noncommittal response to Freud's offer, and afterwards Jones wrote Putnam in a tone of mild needling to repeat the Master's wishes. After reporting that Freud was in excellent form ("He talked continuously and illuminating on every subject I put to him, so you may imagine it was highly instructive treat to me"), Jones observed, "Freud was a little puzzled at not having got an answer from you." Clearly Putnam's effort to finesse the subject at the end of July had failed. "He was very clear about our forming a local branch of the Verein, and produced the following argument which struck me forcibly in America," wrote

Jones. "We are so likely to have the work damaged by amateurs and char-latans that it becomes necessary to protect our interests by enrolling those with some proper knowledge of the subject in a rather official general way."

The implication was clear. If Putnam wanted to continue to be consid-ered an integral part of the Movement, he would have to consent to play the role not just of a defender, but of a leader as well.

Freud seemed to have resolved that the philosophical element in Putnam's letters was too inchoate to be dangerous. In late August, he thanked Putnam for his "promise" to found an American branch, adding that he was nonetheless "grieved that you should believe that I possibly could consider your idealist views as nonsense because they differ from mine. I am not so intolerant as to wish to make a law out of a deficiency in my own make-up. I feel no need for a higher moral synthesis in the same way that I have no ear for music." Was Freud merely being condescend-ing here? Or could it be that he was striking a true note of humility?

He was undoubtedly in an unusually reflective mood. Martha's mother was dying and he felt haunted by unfinished work and lingering exhaus-tion. Against his expectations, his situation on the Dutch coast, with its "primitive luxuriousness" was growing on him. Yet there was a hint of irony in Freud's tone of studied self-abnegation. "I console myself with this re-flection: the idealistic truths which you are not willing to give up cannot be so certain if the basic principles of the science on which we do agree are so difficult to determine," he informed Putnam. It's a savvy, backhanded in-sult. Given that our mutually endorsed psychoanalysis itself is so murky, how much stock can I be expected to put in your idealism? "Although I am resigned to the fact that I am a God forsaken 'incredulous Jew,' I am not proud of it and I do not look down on others," he wrote in a plume of acrid cigar smoke. "I can only say with Faust, 'There have to be odd fellows like that too.'"

CHAPTER 17

The Tragic Mood

Emerson says, "Fix your thoughts on the Eternal and intellect will grow." One might add by way of commentary, Fix your thought on anything less than the eternal and intellect will shrink and shrivel.

Blow to Putnam late in 1910

PUTNAM HAD NO chance to parse through Freud's allusions before registering the fact that the mantle of the American Psychoanalytic Movement had now been draped over him, Roman legion–style. But within days of his receipt of Freud's letter, he was struck an unexpected blow that allowed him to delay a response a little longer. On the 26th of August, William James died of an attack of acute angina pectoris.

The two had been close friends since their student days, first having met the year after the Civil War ended, at Harvard Medical School. Though James was several years older than Putnam, they were both part of an assembly of students who gathered every afternoon in a basement dissecting lab to listen to an anatomy instructor and recite the results of their own experiments. As Putnam wrote in the long obituary of James he published in the *Atlantic*, he remembered James from that day not only because of how James had congratulated him on a good recitation, but also because of "the frankness of his expression, the generosity of his manner, and the peculiarly attractive quality of his voice."

Putnam had been a regular visitor at the James family house on Quincy Street in Cambridge, a place of "gayety, kindliness and charm" where, Putnam recounted, James and his father shared an idiosyncratic style of expression. "A peculiarity of both was the habit of delaying speech for an instant, while the mind was working and the telling sentence was framing itself for utterance—a brief interval during which the lips would gather slightly, as for a sort of smile, and the eyes and face take on an indescribable expression of great charm. Then would burst forth one of those longer or shorter epigrammatic or aphoristic sayings which all their friends recall so well. . . . Sometimes a mere trifle would call out one of these rich, explosive extravaganzas of speech. I remember listening one day with trepidation when Mr. James, Senior, gathered his face into a half-humorous, half-thunderous expression and then rolled out a series of denunciations on the people who insisted on misusing the word 'quite.'"

In addition to being one of the original founders of Putnam Camp, James spent his honeymoon with Alice there, probably having his first sexual experience with her in the shadow of Giant Mountain, immersed in what James characterized as Camp's "romantic and irresponsible isolation." As an older man, James carried on his poignant infatuation with Pauline Goldmark, an exotic Bryn Mawr student, whose parents were refugees from Vienna and Prague, in the secret hollow of Keene Valley. He continued traveling to Camp all his life, remarking in his latter years in the midst of "Coffee," "This is a strange world; here I am with a bevy of women and children and I *like* it." He was also one of Camp's fastest hikers. Putnam described his "peculiar mode of climbing in which he raised himself largely with the foot that was lowermost, instead of planting the other and drawing himself up by it, as is so common. This is a slight thing, but it was an element counting for elasticity and grace." Marian reported that her most cherished memory of James was of him "sitting by the fire in our Parents Assistant [one of the cabins] discussing questions of philosophy with Jim late into the evening, while I darned stockings and one or more of the children slept peacefully in the room."

With all of his love for James, Putnam must also have felt himself in lifelong competition with the senior figure. Both of them, at different points in their careers, accused the other of fostering an overly materialist view of the world. Throughout the latter years of their debate, Putnam suspected that James had created a dogma of doubt that rendered all truth relative. And James was touched but unimpressed by Putnam's insistence that clear answers to the great questions must exist, even if those answers were unavailable in the present. Ironically, it was James' insistence on a kind of color-blind skepticism that made him more vulnerable to the claims of mediums than Putnam was. Though Putnam may have enjoyed a special measure of respect among hard scientists for his pioneering neurological studies, on the philosophical level that mattered most to them both, James was the pathfinder and Putnam never doubted that their vision of the cosmos was akin. For this very reason, Putnam worried that James' work had the potential to be a pernicious influence in ways James himself never intended. Part of what drove Putnam's own ferocious anti-materialism by the time he wrote his papers on psychoanalysis was an effort to counter what he worried could be the misappropriation of James' work.

Beyond their intense psychological and philosophical discussions, Putnam had for some time also been involved in monitoring James' physiological well-being. Ten years before his death, James had a severe cardiac episode while staying at Camp after climbing alone to the top of Mt. Marcy, New York State's highest peak. It took James six hours to return, and when he at last crawled back to the cluster of cabins on the stony hillside where Putnam was staying, James was scared that he'd met his end. After a physical examination, Putnam confirmed that James' heart had suffered tangible injury, and yet he stressed the psychological element in James' cardiac trouble. If James were to take care of his nerves his heart condition would improve, and he backed James' intent to seek spa treatment in Germany.

Given Putnam's swollen sense of existential responsibility for the world, he would have had to have felt personal remorse, as well as anguish, at the loss of James. He must have wished that he'd made more of an effort to focus in his last conversations with James on the ways they thought alike, as opposed to the differences in their world outlooks. Putnam served with Harvard's President Lowell as one of James' pallbearers as his corpse was carried to Appleton Chapel in Harvard Yard. Afterwards, his body was cremated and the ashes cast into a mountain brook at Chocorua.

AT THE TIME of James' death, Putnam was supposed to be at Putnam Camp, but a few days later Marian wrote to Elizabeth that Putnam had swerved his course." Papa went to Cazenovia to spend a few days with Miss Blow the day we came here," Marian wrote to Elizabeth from Putnam Camp. "I had a telegram from him saying he should go to Cambridge for the funeral (tomorrow afternoon) and probably come up here that night."

It seems likely that Putnam traveled to Blow directly on hearing the news of James' death. As news of James' worsening condition trickled down toward Boston, Putnam turned to a source of philosophical succor that he knew his wife could not supply. He may have written the *Atlantic* obituary on the verandah of Blow's home. Marian's unemotional account of James' death, notwithstanding her great friendship for him, may reflect bitterness at Putnam's attendance on another woman.

One of the things Blow was able to do for Putnam in this hour of mourning was to make him understand, in the most gentle way possible, that James' absence from the scene also meant an opportunity for him: an opening had appeared on the main stage of American philosophy.

Scrupulous as ever, in the course of the obituary Putnam felt obliged to acknowledge his worries about pragmatism. "Although the practical value of his recommendations to rigid honesty in applying the test of experience seemed undeniably of value, yet I thought the TENDENCY of his doctrine might be to encourage, among some persons, a too narrow conservatism of a materialistic stamp," Putnam wrote. In citing James' response to his criticism Putnam was also no doubt adopting Blow's hint to shape James' legacy in the direction he felt most true to James' spirit: "Surely you know there is an essence in me (whatever I may at any moment appear to say) which is incompatible with my really being a physico-chemico-positivist."

"The Energies of Men" was the work of James that meant the most to Putnam, and in the obituary, he used that paper to project James into the Freudian project. "James was one of the first among professional psychologists to recognize the full bearing of the contributions which medical observation—that is, the psychology of the unusual or the slightly twisted mind—has made to the more classical psychological attitudes and insights." The lesson Putnam had drawn from James' essay on the resources waiting to be tapped by the mind restored to health fit directly into his psychoanalytic concern with sublimation. James revealed the wellspring of energies awaiting release. Freud showed how to get at them.

Blow was more incisive in identifying the danger posed by James' theories than Putnam himself was able or willing to be. After praising Putnam's obituary, she noted, "It also conveys to me very distinctly the idea that Professor James' own marked individuality has been the efficient cause of what seems to me an over accent upon individualism in his thought. I do not think accent upon individualism produces great individuals and I greatly fear that the danger which threatens the Occident is an enfeeblement of selfhood due to emphasis upon self." In a biting finish, she concluded,

"Professor James was himself an unusual individual but his thought was not of the kind to create great individuals."

Whatever one thinks of her assessment of James' legacy, in locating the particular American danger of his work in an excess not of simple materialism but of hypertrophied individualism, Blow made an important point. A sentence in her commonplace book articulated a view that she shared with Putnam: "Insight must be inflexible but it exercises prevailing power only when mated with gracious self-surrender."

Blow foreshadowed Freud's insights into narcissism and endemic human depravity, but saw in these states an opportunity for moral didacticism that Freud never pursued. After commenting on Freud's rediscovery of man's sinful nature Blow mused, "To me life would have brought despair had it not been for comforting relics of my Calvinism." Perhaps with Freud's Jewishness in mind, she added the startling observation, "The first optimists in history were the Hebrews." Why? Because they lived suppurating with "bruises and putrefying sores. The dread disease of leprosy was the physical analogue of his [the Hebrew's] moral state." And yet, "Nevertheless he was 'the image of god.' It is holding both these truths which gives courage and communicates enthusiasm."

ALL THAT SUMMER, Freud was dreaming of orange groves in Sicily. He proposed that Ferenczi meet him at Noordwijk, whence the two could go on directly to Rome, where they would wander about the new excavations on the Palatine and meander through the Forum before embarking for Palermo. Perhaps there would even be time to see the slopes of Vesuvius and spend a day touring the charnel masterpiece of Pompeii along the way.

Ferenczi was thrilled at the prospect of three blissful weeks alone with Freud. He'd been exploring his own theories of periodicity and ebbs and flows of libido and he couldn't wait to go into greater depth about them with Freud. Responding to Freud's apparently sympathetic view of his research project, Ferenczi had bared his breast, confessing that as he knew from his own experience, "the tragic mood that one often falls into toward evening and that makes everything appear in a more elegiac light" was a "reaction to the insufficiently usable libido which has accumulated from all sense zones in the course of the day." This was why one was fresh and sober in the morning and ready for work—except work requiring fantasy. Rather than telling Ferenczi he'd gone off the rails again, Freud faulted himself for having been insufficiently receptive to Ferenczi's speculations. "Your fantasy didn't seem to me to be so unfounded according to the present constellation; it certainly deserves more attention than I have devoted to it up until now." He told Ferenczi that he looked forward to discussing the matter, and to the presence of "a friend and traveling companion between whom and myself not a hint of discord is possible."

They hadn't been together a week before Freud regretted his idealization of their relationship. Freud found Ferenczi tiresomely womanish, while Ferenczi complained of Freud's tyrannical streak. Their reciprocal snips and sniping stained the days spent amidst fallen marble columns and flowering fruit trees. Tensions culminated when Freud declared that he would collaborate with Ferenczi on his study of Schreber—a study focused, ironically, around the idea that Schreber's paranoia represented a defense against a burst of homosexual libido. As Ferenczi described the scene, Freud began simply dictating the paper aloud. "I rose up in a sudden burst of rebellion and explained that it was not at all a collaboration if he simply dictated to me," Ferenczi wrote. "'So that's the way you are?'—Freud said astonished. 'You perhaps want to take the whole thing?'"

And still, their surroundings were irresistible. Palermo offered "a wealth of color, such views, such fragrant smells, and such a sensation of well-being" as he'd never experienced simultaneously, Freud wrote Martha. "I am really awfully sorry that you cannot all be with me," he sighed. "But in order to enjoy all this in a group of seven or nine, or even of only three—in short, of *unidici, deodici, tredici*—I shouldn't have become a psychiatrist and an alleged founder of a new school in psychology, but a manufacturer of something useful such as toilet paper, matches, shoe buttons." Indeed, the only aspect of Sicily which is less than ideal, he reports, is the shopping. "There is absolutely nothing here which cannot be found elsewhere." So he asks the family, in respect to gifts, "to consider as canceled all promises made in this respect, and to accept cash as a substitute when I am back in Vienna."

THE HOMOEROTIC UNDERPINNING to the contretemps with Ferenczi became explicit as they tried to perform damage control on the trip once back home. Ferenczi analyzed his behavior with Freud in Sicily and in the process "rather ruthlessly brought to light the resistance against my own homosexual drive components." Freud, on the other hand, announced to Ferenczi that he had gone beyond the need of "opening" his own personality toward his homosexual side. "The need has been extinguished in me since Fliess's case, with the overcoming of which you just saw me occupied." Cocksure in his triumph, Freud added, "A piece of homosexual investment has been withdrawn and utilized for the enlargement of my own ego. I have succeeded where the paranoic fails." Lucky the man who in his mid-50s is still able to channel his homosexual desire into the enrichment of his own ego.

Freud went on to blame his own intestinal troubles for further complicating his mood. "And I often said to myself: he who is not master of his Konrad should not travel." "Konrad" was Freud's pet name for his own body. "As far as the unpleasantness that you caused me is concerned—including a certain passive resistance—that will go the way of memories of travel in general; small disturbances vanish through a process of self purification, and what is beautiful is left over for intellectual use." In mid-October, he played Ferenczi still more boldly telling him that there were, indeed, emotions and yearnings he was keeping to himself but Ferenczi had no way of deducing what those were. "Perhaps you are imagining completely different secrets than [those] I have reserved for myself," he teased, "or you think there is a special suffering connected with that, whereas I feel myself to be a match for anything and approve of the overcoming of my homosexuality, with the result being greater independence."

In presenting the whole affair to Jung, Freud switched from a tone of victory to a pose of sheer bemusement. He acknowledged that the trip "supplied several wish-fulfillments that my inner economy has been in need of." But it was complicated by the fact that his traveling companion, though a "dear fellow," was "dreamy in a disturbing kind of way," distinguished by an infantile attitude toward Freud himself. "He never stops admiring me, which I don't like," Freud sighed. "He has been too passive and receptive, letting everything be done for him like a woman, and I really haven't got enough homosexuality in me to accept him as one. These trips arouse a great longing for a real woman."

He and Jung were, Freud implied, of a different caliber. When dealing with the weaker members of their circle, they could afford to abandon their

defenses and allow "the witches 'Politics' and 'Diplomacy'; and the change-
ling 'Compromise' to take a hand." They would make up for the self-
effacement this required when, off on their lonesome, "we talk about these
'farts' together one day." Already there were limits. "Cases can easily arise
in which the diplomatic approach would be unwise and we must give our
nature free rein. Then I am prepared to sally forth arm in arm with you
and challenge the century."

The militaristic edge to Freud's voice had a purpose beyond that of
wowing Jung with his capacity for manly crudity. Freud also knew that the
divisions in the movement that had been seething subcutaneously since even
before Nuremberg were about to break into the open.

WITH RESENTMENT PROLIFERATING among Freud's European colleagues, Putnam's fidelity looked better and better. Omitting all mention
of the philosophical convolutions that had dominated Putnam's last letter,
Freud wrote to him as soon as he returned from Italy, "I have seldom been
as proud or as satisfied with myself, as when I read your essay of July 21st.
You convince me that I have not lived and worked in vain, for men such as
you will see to it that the ideas I have arrived at in so much pain and anguish will not be lost to humanity. What more can I desire?" As a crowning
proof of his admiration, he told Putnam that he himself was going to translate the essay for the *Zentralblatt*.

But Freud's esteem for Putnam had not translated into a larger embrace
of America. In fact, in praising Putnam to Jung, Freud contrasted Putnam's
work with "all the flat, sterile, insipid objections" that he and Jung were
accustomed to hearing "on the other side of the Great Water." He even
made his own foray into the great American energy debate as he mused on
what, exactly, constituted the source of New World dynamism. "In our
studies of America, have we ever looked into the source of the energies
they develop in practical life? I believe it is the early dissolution of family
ties, which prevents all the erotic components from coming to life and
banishes the Graces from the land."

For Putnam, Freud's words of praise were more meaningful than the
offer of the burdensome presidency of the new American Psychoanalytic
Association, as they came without a conditional clause. For this very reason,

they made him, also, more eager to serve. He had begun to identify what his ultimate role in the movement would be: "If I can do any service to the cause in which we are both so much concerned I think it is likely to be mainly through putting some of these questions in a clearer light before the medical profession, rather than by working out special points," he wrote to Freud. Putnam indeed proved himself the great communicator of psychoanalysis in the New World.

PUTNAM DID NOT seek to conceal his interest in Freud from Marian, but in the sheer administrative pressure of running their home it was easy to avoid talking with her about the extent of what was happening. In the autumn and winter of 1910 the prevailing family crisis was the illness of Putnam's cousin Lizzie, who was then living with the family at 106 Marlborough Street. In October she was told by her physician that she was fatally ill, upon which she took to her room upstairs and refused to come down again. She was dead by mid-January.

Lizzie had been a favorite with young children and Marian was haunted for many years by memories of the "peals of laughter" that often came from the rooms where she was playing "parchesi, or go-bang, backgammon or bezique." Before moving in with the Putnams, she had kept a little house of her own in High Street, where "waifs and strays and all of her family, no matter now distant the connection was, were welcomed by her and made at home by her fireside." The dismantling of her home after her death "filled to the roof-tree with family memorials of all sorts" made for both a sad and occupying time.

With Blow, the subject of analysis couldn't be skirted as it had been with Marian. Blow struggled between gratitude for his acknowledgment of dependency on her ability to bridge the worlds of Vienna and Boston and outbursts of frustrated passion at the limitations of his care. Putnam visited her in September to talk about his hopes for a new course of education at her hands. "It is a great pleasure to feel that the insights which make life 'tingle with tragic zest' for me have begun to exercise their compelling FORCE upon you," she wrote him after their get-together. "Eternity will not exhaust them and after some eons I hope to be more like what they tell me I ought to be . . . I hope your coat reached you safely. I was so sorry when I found you had left it. I hope you did not need it."

But there was an edge behind her solicitousness, as emerged later in the fall when, after another exchange on Freud, she belittled the significance of self-knowledge. Of course it was true that people needed to face themselves; however "double selfhood is inborn," she asserted, and "no matter how free from regrettable experiences our lives may be, no man or woman can escape the contrast of his finite with the infinite self." Whatever Freud said, it wasn't only the weight of the past but the burden of an unrealized future that shaped character.

As always, she was gauging Freud's insights against her own experience, and when Putnam sent her an essay by Jones, she responded in a agitated tone: "The former [Jones] has presented Freud's views with great clarity. It seems to me however that an obsession may arise out of a DEFECT of feeling of which we are conscious just as well as out of the positive feeling which expresses itself in a wish. Given a person of sensitive conscience, aware that he or she can only *see* what another person needs in so far as she loves that person—and aware also that she cannot summon at will the degree of love required—and this induces an anxiety or fear for the person which can be very tormenting and could easily result in an obsession." That "person" could be either Blow or Putnam, and either way it's a poignant portrait of their 20-odd-year relationship.

On the domestic front, Putnam's great hope was that everyone would still end up being friends. After Freud conveyed his hope that Putnam would attend the next congress of the psychoanalytic movement in September 1911, Putnam wrote that the invitation had "tempted" him so much that he had "already made plans to take my wife and children and a make a trip in Eastern Europe (England, France, and Switzerland) in the process." By showing them Europe in exchange for their letting him meet with Freud, Putnam was seeking to literally bring his world together with Freud's.

The gesture of inclusion extended to Blow as well. An oblique glimpse of her emerges near the end of January 1911, during a visit she paid the Putnams at 106 Marlborough Street. Putnam's sister wrote Elizabeth (who was on a cross-country sightseeing junket following her college graduation) how the family was "in a ferment of joyful plans." She noted that "Miss Blow came to tea, and I never have found her so cordially interested in each and every person and topic that came up. If you had been here you could have 'talked the language' better than I did. Somehow I am terribly practical, often to the exclusion of interesting lines of thought." There's no mention of Marian's presence at the little tea party, and my guess is that Blow visited on one of the many days when Marian had gone off to pay calls. The image of Blow gazing at each one of the Putnam children by turn and listening to all they had to say in the company of Putnam himself, while the Boston dusk scarred the windows with raw contusions of winter light, is haunting.

CHAPTER 18

Not Alms but a Friend

*As a power of example, evil may be as strong as virtue, but in
the individual soul I believe goodness has an infinitely more
unbounded career than evil; which is by its very nature
narrowing, can have. If this is so, the goodness that one
person, as a unit can add is more than one person can by evil
take away . . . Oh that anybody can be wicked or very sad in
such a beautiful world! If they could only see it as I see it—in
the glorious autumn sunlight, with the music of rushing waters
in the air and soft deep shadows on the everlasting hills, see it
with health and happiness for a medicine and have it made
alive and near to them by the companionship of good, great—
and loveable friends!*

Marian to Fannie Morse, Sept 12, 1883, from the Stoop

THE PUTNAMS' SILVER wedding anniversary fell in the winter of 1911.
On the day of their celebration, the 15th of February, the couple expected
that a handful of close relatives would come by the house to share a toast.
But in fact, the children had been planning a surprise party for weeks.
Marian donned "an old silvery gray summer dress" for the occasion. For
jewelry, she wore a Florentine silver chain that had been handed down from
her great-grandmother, who had made her own pilgrimage across the Continent in a horse-driven carriage.

As night descended, Putnam and Marian were asked to enter the parlor alone, whereupon the children hung a sheet across the doorway. Elizabeth had managed to gather almost everyone still living who had been at
their wedding twenty-five years before. Marian and "Jim" sat together in

the parlor hand in hand and watched a pageant of shadow figures pass across the sheet hung over the threshold. The couple had to guess the names of the dozens of guests who made their way forward in silhouette to honor them.

In the presentation of silver gifts that followed the ceremonial procession, Putnam's brother gave a Japanese monkey-tree twinkling with twenty-five silver dollars hung as fruit. And then there were poems—endless verses. Many of the lyrics seemed designed specifically to burden the pair with a sense of their own fated role as bearers of the weight of family tradition. The poem that accompanied an heirloom tea set celebrated the "high thoughts" and "living plain" that had marked the "good old times" of their forebears. Yet the survivors were not to lose heart. "The vision is no longer dim. It lives in Marian and Jim! Who gather round their genial board Find better times once more restored. So may the tea-set ever shine And keep the spell for auld lang syne—And aye, for their posterity."

After the reading of the poetry, a hush fell over the gathered crowd. No one was quite sure what to do next. But Putnam—at his spirited best— seized the moment. He leapt up onto a chair, took Marian's hand and helped her up next to him. As my great-grandmother reported, "He thanked everyone for their good wishes, and said that we would take it all as a tribute to the institution of marriage and home which we joined them in celebrating if everyone would stay for supper. This was done on faith, as we had not provided any supper!"

MARRIAGE WAS NOT a particularly popular pastime among the Cabots. Maiden aunts abounded. Marian's brother Frank, the Judge of Boston's Juvenile Court, was urged for many years to wed by his friends and professional circle—in part because bachelorhood was frowned upon in a job where one spent most of one's time working with wayward boys—but he resisted, remarking to one young married woman who criticized him for never showing any interest in her sex, "Well, this is what happens. You meet a girl and like her, and go to her house, where you find all her family assembled with her. You like them too, but one by one, they leave the room, and you find yourself alone with the girl—and you never visit that house again!"

For all the apparently settled New England existence of the Cabots, there was a picaresque, swashbuckling side to Marian's. Her father, Francis

Cabot, was expelled from Harvard for rakish conduct. After a period spent in the company of professional gamesters, he shipped on a New Bedford whaler for the South Pacific carrying with him, in a tiny leather trunk, as one family biographer noted, "the Bible, Shakespeare in two volumes, Southey, Shelley, and Keats in one volume, and Spinoza." Francis ended up being dismissed from the boat in Hawaii for reasons that are obscure. There, he somehow managed to receive the commission to tutor the King's daughter, a post that ended with the Hawaiian ruling family pressing him to take the girl's hand in marriage. Fleeing the call to found a Hawaiian dynasty, he returned to New England, where he worked as a treasurer in a series of textile mills, a vocation sufficiently undemanding that he could spend the bulk of his hours reading his beloved romantic poetry and philosophy.

Though the Cabots became "orthodox Unitarians," their reasons for being members of the church seem to have had more to do with avoiding religion in a non-heretical fashion than with a spiritual devotion to Boston's favorite post-Transcendentalist sect. "Religious emotion is an inexplicable thing to a person who is entirely without it," one of Marian's sisters wrote from Rome to the family. "What do you suppose we young people in America have which can do for us what religion does for others? . . . I feel as if love of humanity and sense of duty to one's fellow men was the kind of religion we tend toward."

As a child, Marian traveled with her parents and seven siblings to the Adirondacks to a retreat called the Ampersand Camp where, with cousins galore, she studied Latin, Greek, and German before going off for picnics and swims to locations where the children would read aloud Emerson, Stevenson, Carlyle, Schiller, George Eliot, and Browning. Their Sunday morning sermons were delivered by the philanthropist Phillips Brooks.

The lessons of speculative thought that Marian would later offer Putnam were primarily drawn from one of these figures: the Boston-American Moses, Ralph Waldo Emerson, and during the long period of their courtship Putnam and Marian's conversations and correspondence often revolved around philosophical topics. "You are very kind to remember my birthday and I shall enjoy the Emerson very much," Putnam wrote Elizabeth on the eve of their engagement in 1885. "It is like having the full organ in a cathedral to read a few pages after you have forgotten how fine they were."

Putnam's hopes seemed to center on the idea that marriage would be enlarging, both intellectually and emotionally. "The one thing that I ask for myself more than any other is to dare to trust my own desires and conclusions without too many hesitations, and that, as I said, I believe I am in a measure learning, both from you, and from the little volume of Emerson which you were inspired to give me on October 3rd," he wrote a few days after their betrothal. "Whatever they may be, the 'improvements' as well as the 'original property' are yours inalienably and heartily." One short, heartbreaking letter in this final phase of their premarital existence struck a note all too resonant with William James' comment on Putnam's choice ("a serious old maid, exactly like him"). "I never could quite understand," Putnam marveled, "the people who could not get on without their wives, yet looking forward, I see ourselves made by affection and good-natured habit into veritable Siamese twins. Well, I can imagine a worse future."

EARLIER IN THEIR courtship, however, their preoccupations were in a different key. In the winter of 1884, Marian had challenged Putnam on why he would not profess himself a Unitarian. Despite the fact that Christ was still the titular father of the flock, for her own family Boston Unitarianism signified a social covenant, made in terms palatable to society, in which one turned away from the cross to a community of dedicated service on behalf of one's fellow men.

"I cannot pretend to have studied these matters at all deeply," Putnam began, self-disparagingly, in a letter to her. "If I have not been to church for the past many years the reason has been indolence rather than principle." He maintained that it would never occur to him to "find fault with Unitarianism," partly because of laziness, "and partly because it seems to me of comparatively little importance in just what symbols a person clothes his ideas, so long as he keeps himself in a progressive spirit." It wouldn't be a good thing, in fact, if all the powerful associations with organized religion could be dropped "like an old glove at the bidding of reason itself." And yet, with these caveats, Putnam felt compelled to add that if forced "to take sides with either the Unitarian or the 'Ethical Culturists'" he would join the latter, "because I am inclined to think that a sober worship or religion of the highest morality can be made as inspiring, both for adults and children as any other form of worship, and it would have the advantage that we should not so often be at our wits' ends to find expressions which should satisfy the children by their picturesqueness and not dis-satisfy ourselves by their failure to express our meaning." In other words, just as he'd begun life as an ascetic materialist, Putnam adopted the guise of a purist in his spiritual praxis. Unitarianism itself, Marian had argued, was a "family habit" more than anything else, the purpose of which in Brookline had been, as a biographer of Marian's brother Fred wrote, "constant natural association with the superior men and women who gave the neighborhood its color." To be a Unitarian meant to avoid both extreme doubts and "mystical depths." But Putnam was not yet ready to see this position as anything but a compromise.

Furthermore, as would later be the case in his exchange with Freud, Putnam insisted that on the ultimate plane of ideals he and Marian must think alike. "I do not really see that there is much to choose between your position and this. . . . In your sense I hope we are all of us 'Christians,' but the term would rather lose its meaning if you were ready to call yourself a Buddhist also, and yet I think your definition would require this; for why should not one be a follower of every great man?" Putnam was hinting that Jesus himself could only be considered one of a host of great men. Marian herself, Putnam contended, had taught him the existence of a broader pantheon.

From this vantage point, Putnam made a statement diametrically opposed to the position he would espouse after coming to know Blow. He averred that the idea that an "ideal morality, besides being a possible possession of future men," might also enjoy "an actual existence outside of us, embodied or otherwise, seems to me not only something that we cannot assert but something which is not necessary to a lofty scheme of religion." The reality of this external Platonic realm was precisely what he would argue to Freud was a necessary axiom of human existence. Why did he reject this latter scheme as a not-so-young 38-year-old?

Putnam's indignation was directed at what he saw as the wishy-washiness of Unitarianism. Even Catholics were better, he maintained, because at least they canonized *all* their best men and women, "but our religion refuses any such place to everyone except Christ. I should like to change that radically, and have the reading of such lives as those in the Harvard Biographies considered a religious exercise in the highest and most technical sense."

It's droll to conceive of Bostonians kneeling at the pew over their crimson-bound biographies of great men, but Putnam had made a significant point. The world around them desperately needed reforming—needed, in truth, radical restructuring—but the Ethical Culturists were at least as likely as any church, even Unitarianism, to take up this task. Putnam believed that we should learn from the men and women who have acted in this world how to move the world we exist in into a higher ethical landscape. In fact, this was precisely the lesson that Marian had been teaching Putnam throughout the several years of their friendship.

The belief of a mutual acquaintance of theirs in the old figure of Satan was "quite as comprehensible, and more rational" than the simple faith in a world run solely by Christ, "for it relieves me from the dreadful necessity of supposing that a beneficent deity created the horrors of the North End." In 1884, this Boston neighborhood was a notorious haven of immigrant poverty, a cipher for abject suffering. The reference was also a pointed allusion to the charitable work that the couple engaged in together and separately throughout the 1880s. Putnam told Marian, in effect, that the moral imperative and scientific grounding of their work on behalf of the downtrodden compelled them to refuse cheap fairy tale explanations of the universe. There is real suffering going on outside, he said to her. This is why we must repudiate forms of easy solace, and support the efforts of the radical reformers.

Putnam knew that he'd "got" Marian on this point. Whatever the pollyannishness of her tone in later years, in the mid-1880s, Marian wasn't only a serious participant in the philanthropic whirl of late nineteenth-century Boston, she was a leader—a theoretician and tireless worker in the most significant New England charitable undertaking of the age. Putnam, in this capacity, was always her disciple, deferring to her superior experience, understanding, and powers. She was living out the key creed of her Unitarianism: active service to one's community, and for that very reason couldn't understand why Putnam was a stickler about terms. Putnam, on his side, felt that it was precisely her stature as an active do-gooder that compelled her to rigorously refuse the palliative of superstition: true immersion in the horrors of the North End left no room for Christ, in howsoever watered down a version. With his own crisis of faith years in the future, he could afford a pitiless atheism. "You had all the reins in your hand—except the reins of the chaise," he wrote of one charitable meeting they both attended shortly before their marriage, "and the rest of us had nothing to do but play the part of the chorus in the Greek plays." Elsewhere, Putnam worried about the labor that was being asked of her in the context of her appointment to the society's board of directors, yet felt that her abilities made these demands inevitable. "It seems to be a matter of sad destiny that a person who succeeds as a mortal, should have to submit to being translated and to wearing an uncomfortable crown in the circle of the Immortals," he wrote her. "We will admiringly watch you mount the ladder."

Where did Marian's authority come from? And why did the work they were doing together give Putnam a sense that they'd both transcended the need for formal religion?

THE IMAGE OF Boston in the years when Marian began to work that was painted by one leader of the Associated Charities in a pamphlet put out by the organization is more akin to something out of Bosch than the sphere of splendid, silent interiors glistening with ornamental porcelain and doe-eyed children we know from Sargent portraits: "Imagine a city of 250,000 people overwhelmed with social problems. Some were the aftermath of four years of civil war, some incident to the changes from a small homogeneous community to a large city with a teeming, foreign element. Unemployment was rife; armies of tramps infested both country and city. Business depression hung like a pall over the city and in 1872 a devastating fire wiped out the heart of the business district." Housing, sanitation, and general health conditions in the city were "menacing, and in spite of conscientious efforts to help, the work of amelioration was not coordinated and was totally inadequate."

This is a world dramatically at odds with the cultured, retentive stereotype of a city in which, rather than invading battalions of beggars, danger might be embodied by a pair of teetotalling feminist vegetarians in a row house somewhere in outer Cambridge dictating to each other tracts on communication with the dead. And yet, in a paradox that Putnam's contemporaries were obsessed with, this period of tremendous progress in industry, the arts, sciences, and, with the filling of Back Bay even ambitious urban renewal, went hand in hand with ravaging poverty. Once fashionable neighborhoods changed character with successive waves of new immigrants. Oscar Handlin, a Boston historian writing in the first part of the twentieth century, and himself the child of Jewish immigrants who lived through the era, described the process, "Enterprising land-owners utilized unremunerative yards, gardens, and courts to yield the maximum number of hovels that might pass as homes . . . the abundant grounds surrounding well-built early Boston residences, and the hitherto unusable sites created by the city's irregular streets, once guarantees of commodious living, now fostered the most vicious Boston slums." The national depression of 1873 hit Boston especially hard, devastating the garment industry and leaving the multitude of newly jobless men and women with little hope of being rehired elsewhere.

In this crisis, the inadequacies of the old charity delivery systems, both institutional and private, became apparent. Not only were the existing resources poorly integrated, the relief was simply unequal to the scale of need. Among Boston's educated elite there was growing awareness that a wholesale transformation of the system for fighting indigence was imperative. A worker from the Family Welfare Society wrote of how "a new concept of 'Charity'" was taking hold "in the hearts and minds of many serious men and women." One could go further and say that increasingly throughout the last quarter of the nineteenth century, the movement to reform the operation of reform itself superseded all others. Though these years of American history are often associated with the rise of the Gilded Age, they also mark the start of a fresh, idealistically rationalized approach to charity; they herald the arrival of what was dubbed "scientific philanthropy."

A PASSION FOR the theory behind philanthropy had, in fact, been part of the New England heritage since Puritan days. Though Putnam's ancestor Cotton Mather is now primarily associated with his nasty role in the Salem Witch Trials, he was better known while alive for his philanthropic advocacy. Of the more than four hundred and forty tracts he wrote, the most popular during his lifetime was *Bonifacus*, commonly known as *Essays to do Good*. Mather's argument was that people should be engaged voluntarily in "a perpetual endeavor to do good in the world." He promulgated a quasi-scientific approach to social welfare in which would-be do-gooders were entreated to make a roster of the needy in their neighborhoods and monitor their well-being as a prelude to actively helping them. Aid, moreover, was to go beyond material succor; indeed, "charity to the souls of men" was the true philanthropic mandate. In a section of the treatise that heavily influenced Benjamin Franklin, no natural ally of the Mathers, and continued to resonate down to Putnam's time, Mather charged his flock with the imperative of forming cooperative public societies to address the social ills of the age.

Mather's ambitious, visionary program was not indigenous to American soil. Rather, it marked an early instance of German influence in the New World. Much of his philanthropic philosophy was lifted straight from the works of the German Pietists. A number of ideas about charity that Mather adapted to the New World were revived by Putnam's contemporaries, remodeled for the industrial age.

THE BETTER OFF portion of the citizenry *did* rise up to meet the challenge of providing for those less fortunate to a striking degree during the last decades of the nineteenth century. In line with Mather's dictate from 1710, the help took many forms besides that of simple monetary donations or even donations of goods in kind. By the time of the depression of the 1890s Robert Treat Paine, the first president of the Associated Charities, was framing the spirit of charity in terms of demanding voluntary labor on behalf of the poor. "This last quarter of a century has witnessed a noble outburst of the energies of good men to help suffering brethren," he announced. There was a pervasive understanding that active charity work was a central element of everyday life.

Boston's initial response to the crisis of the 1870s took the predictable pattern of augmenting conventionally structured charity organizations and redoubling financial appeals from established groups. The failure of these amplified efforts called into question the value of knee-jerk generosity. As Annie Adam Fields, a future leader of the "new charity" whose husband had published *The Scarlet Letter*, wrote in response to one solicitation from the Boston Provident Association, it was true that financial contributions had to be made, for these were debts "of honor as well as charity," but once those had been paid, donors were obliged to ask whether their investment had been effective. "Does not an equal obligation rest upon the public of reflection upon the subject whether so large a sum as twenty-five or thirty thousand dollars may be better employed than in giving food and clothing to the healthy poor because they cannot get work?" she wrote in 1875. This kind of rethinking of the uses of charity became more pronounced as the century wore on.

Two of the most prominent men working with Marian Cabot and her like were Putnam's brother, Charles, and Putnam's close colleague and eventual cousin by marriage, Dr. Richard Cabot. But the reform of the reform movement was driven with a vengeance by women. Boston had a long tradition of middle-class female involvement in social reform, but in the years Putnam and Marian were working for the common cause, the role of the entrenched, patriarchal church and state were being challenged just as the figure of the social case worker was born.

The effort to create a new model of charity did not occur in a particularly warm, cooperative environment; indeed, competition between new groups and the established organizations could be savage. The founding of Boston's Associated Charities sparked particular controversy. "We fought as the Greek and Trojan heroes fought for the body of Patroclus," wrote Causten Brown, an early leader of Boston's Associated, Charities, of a meal at which the subject of the formation of that organization arose.

The creation of Associated Charities caused such an uproar in part because it was recognized as the future of philanthropy. The concept of the organization had been brewing for years before the group officially was launched in 1879. The first step was the founding of the Co-operative Society of Visitors among the Poor by Annie Fields and Mrs. James Lodge. Throughout the years that Putnam was setting himself up in Boston, efforts to refine the concept of what would become the Associated Charities were occupying the city's young idealists. Charles was actively involved in the founding of the organization and served as its president for the last seven years of his life. Putnam himself volunteered with his brother in the organizations that were working toward the "new Charity" and devoted huge amounts of time to volunteering with the Charities from the moment of its founding. Through his close relationship with his brother and other members of their social circle, Putnam was part of the dialogue in which the conceptual underpinnings of the Associated Charities were articulated.

The single most revolutionary element of the Charities' mission was its repudiation of responsibility for distributing material aid. This strategic decision was critical to the organization's eventual acceptance by other established Boston charities as the leaders of the Associated Charities not only didn't disturb but actively supported the continued dispensing of money, clothes, and so forth by traditional philanthropic groups. In the words of Paine, what the Associated Charities provided was "Not Alms, but a Friend." The organization offered empathy, rudimentary psychotherapy, assistance negotiating the ruling municipal and ecclesiastical authorities, other mundane forms of practical guidance, elevated solace, and peaceable legislative activism aimed at improving the quality of life for city residents. (Sometimes this lobbying could be conservative in nature, as was the case with the Charities' promotion of immigration restrictions.)

The type of demanding, intimate work required of volunteers employed by the Charities appealed directly to that self-sacrificing, occasionally self-mortifying quality stereotypical of Boston character. No sentiment better expresses this strain of attraction than the goal its predecessor organization, the Cooperative Society, carried forward from an early Unitarian minister: the ideal of "living the lives of the poor along with them." When Putnam made intellectual companionship with patients an aspect of psychological treatment, he was building on the model established by Boston's new philanthropy. In essence, the objective of the Associated Charities was to offer moral guidance and education to those in need and, for the first time on such a scale, at least on American soil, to offer such tutelage outside the context of organized religion. This approach held special appeal for Putnam and served as a basis for the mission he helped to shape: a framework for rigorous, self-abnegating, secular moralizing.

It's impossible to overstate the extent to which the Associated Charities seized the imagination of Boston society. When Henry James wanted to depict the psychology of his protagonist in *The Bostonians*, Olive Chancellor, he wrote, "She herself was nothing of a sybarite, and she had proved, visiting the alleys and slums of Boston in the service of the Associated Charities, that there was no foulness of disease or misery she feared to look in the face." Olive's employment with the Charities pinpointed her social niche. (Critically, in Olive's case, as with many members of Putnam's circle, involvement with Associated Charities often said as much about one's own proud taste for lenten fare as it did about any particular fondness for the poor.)

Charity work was seen, indeed, as a moral *right* of the volunteer. This premise is exemplified by the fascinating story of Boston's then longest-running divorce trial, the case of Lois Rantoul in the early 1900s, for which

Charles Putnam, her personal physician, served as a key testifying witness. A central argument by Rantoul's lawyers against her husband, Edward, was that proof of his abusive nature lay in his refusal to allow her to dedicate herself full time to charity work. Edward's unwillingness to permit Lois to find satisfaction through a staggering schedule of social work was even cited—sympathetically—in defense of her romantic liaison with another man. Charles Putnam's arguments supporting the charges of abuse against her husband echoed with the psychotherapeutic insights Putnam had dedicated himself to discovering.

IT'S DIFFICULT TO tell when, in their five years of working together, Putnam and Marian's shared engagement in philanthropic activism ripened into love. The process might have been almost too smooth to register. As Emerson wrote in "Fate," "Wonderful intricacy in the web, wonderful constancy in the design this vagabond life admits. We wonder how the fly finds its mate, and yet year after year, we find two men, two women, without legal or carnal tie, spend a great part of their best time within a few feet of each other. And the moral is that what we seek we shall find." Thus, one day, after an especially tender discussion about some inspiring charity case such as the boy Joe Scarlatti who, when taken by a friendly visitor into the Museum of Fine Arts, begged only for "More George Washingtons," Jim took Marian's hands and proposed marriage. Whenever it crystallized, however, Putnam's marriage was not just a surrender to the predominant model of local femininity, as I'd imagined before reading the courtship letters; it was also an act of commitment to the most visible form of idealism then being enacted in Boston.

Marian's own branch of the work was focused on the socialization of the poor. In several long essays written for the Associated Charities in the years immediately before and after her marriage, Marian expounded on the concept of "Friendly Visiting," sometimes also known as "Volunteer Visiting." Though the practice originated in England, it was given an American imprimatur in Boston, where Marian's version was an especially influential example of the model.

In her most important paper, written in the mid-1890s, she defined the Associated Charities' motto as signifying "that in the good offices and influence, the love and loyalty which we see exemplified in a true friendship, lies the power upon which we build our hope of helping others." Marian noted that the concept of "Friendly Visiting" is in fact "as old as human society itself." Her own definition of the term took the code of social manners she'd been raised on, grounded in the obligation to pay frequent regular calls on the network of one's social relationships, and applied that model to the challenge of charitable service. "'Friendly Visiting,'" she wrote, "meant seeing and knowing the people, whom we wish to help, in their own homes, and *after* we know them, taking hold with them to help them conquer their difficulties." One was to drop in, hear what the poor had to say over a cup of tea, commiserate, and make suggestions from one's own fund of knowledge as to what could be done to improve their lives.

By its nature, this was a politically static paradigm of reform. "The object of a visitor should be, first of all, to try to make the family better and happier where they are and with the resources they have. We come to realize after a time that the majority of poor families in a city must continue to live without any very striking change of circumstances." Marian contended that a prim attitude toward the work was inadmissible. A friendly visitor "must be prepared to see suffering and wrong-doing that he cannot prevent, and be willing to wait till he knows what the difficulties and troubles are, and then be ready to make the most of the opportunities that arise for meeting them." She held up the example of a woman with half a dozen dirty, half-nourished, half-clad children "fed on bake-shop pies" with a shiftless husband, a woman who "drinks a little herself" and idles away much of her time "talking with neighbors who are worse than she is." The future of such a family was "dreadful." Confirmed intemperance await the parents, while "crime and pauperism" become the inheritance of the children. The only hope, Marian argued, was a "direct influence that infuses a different spirit, new hopes and wishes, into their lives." Even though it was a difficult task, "little by little, the interest and dulled ambition of the mother may be awakened."

Marian's belief that friendly visitors were obliged to awaken a sense of higher purpose in their charges was not aimed, as Putnam's was when it came to psychotherapy, at the supernal realm. "The active sympathy of the visitor may rouse [the poor mother] to care for the little details of comfort and decency in the household, the total disregard of which is at the bottom of much misery and vice," Marian wrote. "The possibilities of making a room pretty, bright and habitable; the pleasant games at home and the parks and libraries abroad that are never resorted to…all these matters, trifling in themselves, may be made the means of reforming the home life, and consequently changing the whole future of the family."

However, even if the ultimate goals of these ministrations were closer to home than the ones Putnam referred to as the "higher views" of obligation that the physician was ethically bound to help his patient discover, one can see how the *process* of inculcating awareness of these views closely paralleled the one Marian enjoined. Much of the dynamic whereby Putnam's philosophically inspired psychology was to be communicated to patients was borrowed from his wife's theory of friendly visiting. "Our ability to help others depends on our belief that it can be done, and on our recognition of the common human or rather divine nature that belongs to us all and that can be appealed to," she wrote near the conclusion of her essay.

The influence of this labor on Putnam's own psychotherapeutic perspective extended further still. At the same time that he began to hit a wall with somatic therapy, Putnam's experience with the Associated Charities forced him to confront the role of environmental conflict in shaping character apart from any inherited physiological traits. Even the act of gathering basic background information from his objects of philanthropy encouraged a more complex perspective on the interplay of forces shaping the individual than he'd acquired from his anatomical studies in a basement laboratory with James. When Putnam began writing on psychoanalysis, and noted how therapeutically useful it was to have patients picture themselves acting in accord with the values of an imaginary "ideal community," his theory hearkened back to the field work of the Associated Charities and the hard evidence that the Charities aggregated on how the "network of family and community relationships" was a leading force in shaping individual character for good or evil.

More than anything, Putnam was influenced by the Associated Charities' highly personalized approach to casework. Tracts of the Charities at the turn of the century made the point that casework consisted of "the way in which I treat you and you treat me; not as a 'case' or a 'number' but as a human being; not as a man 'out of work' or a 'chronic heart,' but as John Smith, who besides being 'out of work' or 'sick' is perhaps a father, a stone mason, a resident of Blank Street, and so on. It is the humanizing of 'charity' and it is based on understanding." All of Putnam's initial moves away from materialism were based one way or another on the incommensurability of a purely somatic approach with the unique nature of the individual. Whether he was writing about the ways that a pathological report ignored aspects of the individual that could be crucial to the efficacy of treatment, or was discussing the intricacy of the network of influences that went into producing a person's psychology, the reference point was always, concurrently, the singular nature of each person and the "community" of elements that went into defining that individual.

What made Putnam's emphasis on the role of family and environment in shaping character so American was his faith that the forces behind this influence were intensely malleable. He found proof of the transformability of the individual in his experience on the ground with the Associated Charities. The tactics whereby volunteers built up their understanding of cases combined investigation into details of a person's family life with an empathetic, "golden-rule" style identification with the subjects of charity whereby the caseworker treated each individual as she herself would wish to be treated.

This was a very different form of preparation for the analytic dynamic than the one defined by spiritism, one that proved to have less popular resonance than that involving mediums and their efforts to beg friendly visits from the other world.

MARIAN ACKNOWLEDGED THAT objections could be raised to the approach she'd outlined, particularly that friendly visiting was an inefficient way of using charitable time and resources. Yet, she insisted, "Must not the best and surest way of helping people be to do it one by one?" Clearly anxious on this point, she returned to it repeatedly, insisting that the effects of friendly visiting were "far reaching," and putting forward the vague argument that even if one does not remain a "practical worker," friendly visiting contributes to the primary task of shaping public opinion—the basis of all reform efforts.

The new scientific approach to philanthropy served to bring under control the crisis of the 1870s and its aftershocks in the 1880s. But it depended on an army of dedicated citizen volunteers that was itself made obsolete by shifting social patterns of work and new, time-consuming opportunities for entertainment that arose near the turn of the century.

By the time Marian wrote "Friendly Visiting" in 1895, Putnam was hardly alone in recognizing that her ideas were being rendered obsolete by new shifts in social patterns. His sympathy for the Ethical Culturists was a sign of his craving for a platform for radical action. The Depression of 1893, triggered by a series of interlocked financial panics, was the worst America had ever known. Paine himself began militating for larger governmental policy reforms. "Pauperism cannot be wisely considered alone," he wrote, "but the problem of how to uplift the general level of life must be studied as *one whole problem*." The challenges were simply too vast to be solved by Marian's one-by-one approach, each sufferer marching hand in hand with a friendly visitor, as if onto Noah's ark. Putnam's critique of the somatic style paralleled the critiques he would ultimately make of Marian's philanthropic efforts as insufficiently contextualized. The purely materialist approach to the brain was no more adequate in itself than was the theoretically scientific, personalized approach to philanthropy. The problems were too great, involving not just the individual and the community, but the cosmos itself.

Susan Blow gave a cosmic amplitude to the moral faith Putnam had championed for years. Yet Blow's theories, profound though they were, were not easily applied to the details of real life.

Psychoanalysis seemed to hold the secret for synthesizing the disparate strands of Putnam's pre-Freudian existence. Here, in fresh guise, personalized, yet infinite, was the humanistic scientific approach he'd learned in the Associated Charities. Blow's old-fashioned speculative philosophy, along with Marian's friendly visitor social service and Putnam's somatic psychology, had all been overtaken by the great progressive movements that hit the American scene in the first decades of the twentieth century. Putnam saw Freud's methodology, and above all sublimation, as the way to recatalyze that triad.

Neither Susan Blow nor Marian quite got the way that Freud made everything fit together. In Marian's case, the consequences of this failure were lasting. However dubious she might have been about Blow, Marian had at least understood the drive behind Putnam's hunt for philosophical answers to the great questions of existence. The need to see everything through the lens of erotic hunger and the distortions that came of lust was another matter.

After their silver anniversary, as Putnam's work on behalf of analysis took on a more public face, she realized what had happened and felt betrayed. As Molly would later write, for all of Putnam's valuing of Marian's "intelligent common sense," and for all Marian's own devotion to his interests, nothing in "my father's background or hers prepared her for his interest in psychoanalysis." When Marian became aware of what had happened, "she reacted with tragic bitterness, feeling that he had been mistakenly lured into a false path which would ruin his professional standing."

On the latter score, Marian was all too prescient. As Boston finally registered the full Freudian tenor of Putnam's practice, his patient load began to drop off, and with each new slip, Marian placed herself at little further remove. Putnam was learning in his own person what it meant to embody the "pure and unselfish devotion" of his hero, St. Francis.

CHAPTER 19

The Universal Theater

It is everything at the same time—sexual, innocent, natural, and the rest. I scarcely dare believe it yet. It is as if Schliemann had once more excavated Troy, which had hiterto been deemed a fable.

Freud to Fliess, December 21, 1899

FREUD HAD HIS own project of synthesis. But its targets could not have been more dissimilar from the ones Putnam tried to unite. Freud's dream was not of integrating the various people who made up his world with each other and the cosmos, but of configuring a collection of historical fragments (cultural, psychological, and biological) to establish his work as the culmination of anthropomorphic science.

IT'S DIFFICULT TO go to Vienna today and not experience something like vertigo when confronting the density of museums that crowd the circumscribed city center. The monumental Kunthistorisches Museum, built in the era of the Ringstrasse to exhibit the masterpieces of the Habsburg monarchy, serves as a kind of axis between the two poles of display that dominate the city. On one side are endless halls of imperial and ecclesiastical loot occupying floors and flanks of the immense Hofburg complex, along with cathedrals and other palaces studding the winding streets of Vienna. Here, all that glitters is gold and the luster never subsides.

Though there are extraordinary secular riches in the State Apartments and Treasuries, the swag amassed under the auspices of the Holy Roman Empire and subsequent Catholic regimes is what takes the breath away.

Everything is encrusted with jewels, threaded with gold, and festooned with silk, rubies, emeralds, pearls and more gold—case after case after case. One wing of the State Apartments is devoted exclusively to opulently embroidered clerical vestments, each spread wide in its own glass case like the dream of a butterfly become an emperor. Elsewhere, a series of rooms displays reliquaries that create a kind of grand ball of dismembered splendor.

How was it that the Habsburgs became so well endowed? They didn't, after all, make anything. But the period in which the bulk of the imperial plunder was accrued corresponds with that of the discovery and despoliation of the Americas. So much gold flooded the European markets at the height of the conquistadorean enterprise that gold suffered perhaps its longest and most sustained depreciation in history.

Though Freud never expressed much interest in gilded Vienna, and despite the fact that much of the treasure was cordoned off from the public eye in his day, the volume was so great that it leaked and pressured the city's baroque stone walls, engendering a two-fold relation to fantasy. First, the objects are so spectacularly lavish that they partake of the fantastical. Second, the inaccessibility of Vienna's imperial treasures provoked a wealth of fantastical wishes on the part of those for whom the treasures were only mythological attributes.

The inaccessibility of this vast realm aligns it with the forces driving the creation of Freud's dream book. In a work that lays blame for the encoded character of dreams on the repression of erotic material, the actual subject of most of the dreams Freud reveals from his own self-analysis in fact concern ambition and the murderous drive to power.

The epigraph to *The Interpretation of Dreams* ("If I cannot move the heavens, I will raise hell"), like the famous *aliquis* incident from Freud's self-analysis recorded in *The Psychopathology of Everyday Life* (based on Freud forgetting a word in Dido's curse of Aeneas), is from *The Aeneid*. In both cases, Freud spoke from within an enraged female character. For *The Interpretation*, it was Juno who Freud "channeled." Juno's line expresses the fury by which she becomes possessed at the frustration of her ambition for power. Because she has been unable to destroy Aeneas, founder of Rome, she conjures the spirits of hell to enact her vengeance. Juno's promise of revenge includes the destruction of the erotic realm as collateral damage in the war for power. After summoning hell and acknowledging that she can neither stop Aeneas from one day taking his throne in Latium nor from eventually marrying Lavinia, Juno swears, "Maid, your dowry shall be blood, Trojan and Rutulian blood. War's Goddess." The idea of a dowry of blood would relate for Freud to the idea of supernatural male menstrual transmission of which Fleiss was persuaded and by which Freud was intermittently tantalized. It's the ultimate counterpoint fantasy to the one embodied in the dazzling collections of translapsarian Roman Catholic Vienna. Freud's act of interpretative violence to Habsburg psychology interrupted the process of hierarchical dissemination of power. Now what passes between father and son is stained with the universal blood of Oedipus which Freud, in the orphic capacity of interpreter, can dam. If I cannot stop the consolidation of higher powers, Juno says, yet I may prolong it "and cause delay in events so momentous; yes, and tear up by the roots the nations of both the kings. That is the price which they will have to pay in their subjects' blood before the bride's father and her lord can unite."

A narrative fascination with the power to shed blood, and a theoretical one with menstruation as a badge of fertility, are both examples of the ways Freud treated blood symbolically, as an archaic guarantor of transmission. Notwithstanding the limits to his Jewish education, Freud was certainly aware of the central biblical injunction to the Jewish people, "In thy blood thou shalt live." Against the empowering properties of blood he ranged the by-products of digestion. The waste that would not stay inside revealed a loss of control that signified, ultimately, impotence (burning ambition converted into an Icarus-style spill to earth).

The challenge Freud faced was one of self-control—of managing not to be dethroned by his own theories. Freud never himself constellated the scene in *The Interpretation* in which he "disregarded the rules which modesty lays down and obeyed the call of nature in my parents' bedroom while they were present," with the embarrassing moment by the side of Jung on the Palisades. Yet although, in America, Freud denied Jung's charge that there was a link between his enuresis and ambition, in narrating the incident of urination in his parents' bedroom ten years earlier Freud noted that his father, in reprimanding him, "let fall the words: 'The boy will come to nothing.' This must have been a frightful blow to my ambition, for references to this scene are still constantly recurring in my dreams." Further tying this scene to the story of Oedipus, Freud relates that in a dream based on the episode an old man must have represented his father because the former figure, like his father, was losing his sight.

AT THE OTHER antipode from the crypts of Imperial Vienna, with their representation and conjuration of straightforward desire for earthly power, lies the record of artistic endeavors associated with Viennese modernism. And here, as well, Vienna gives out with a frightening, lascivious prodigality. Within the Museum Quarter alone there are some 20 cultural institutions, including, in the most prominent of them, the Leopold Museum, 5,000 master works of the Jungendstidl and Secession movements. Klimt, Schiele, and Kokoschka dominate the space. If these works exist theoretically at the opposite pole from the ogle-inducing objects of Habsburg majesty, they're no less magnetic, and the physical placement of the museums housing newer art, as well as the masterpieces of Vienna's avant-garde architecture, relative to the old, is provocatively intimate. Wandering the streets of Vienna, passing between the different cultural exhibition spaces, one is caught in a magical revolving door between future and past. The abruptness of transitions seems itself of a piece with anti-naturalist elements of the modernist aesthetic.

The explosion of fine art, architecture, and applied art that took place in Vienna in the years when Freud was formulating his theories constituted a true renaissance. Though the Secessionists drew inspiration from new artistic movements in other countries such as, notably, the French Impressionists, Impressionism now appears as a period piece in ways that much Secessionist work does not. The extreme, self-involved sexuality of Schiele's work is only one vivid instance of this phenomenon. On a very different plane, Ikea would be inconceivable without the advent of functional aesthetics pioneered by leaders in the realm of *fin de siècle* applied art like Josef Hoffman. Architecturally, the foundations for Bauhaus were laid by Adolf Loos and his followers, whereas the unbelievable Secession Building, completed the year before Freud published *The Interpretation of Dreams*, looks like a climactic work of post-Modernism. It's as though, in this building by Joseph Olbrich, a gold-filigreed UFO designed by Frank Gehry has crashed into an art noveau-inflected mausoleum for Oscar Wilde.

In Freud's day, even more than was the case with the spoils of Habsburg Vienna, the aesthetic progeny of the city's modernist forces pressured the old façades and pervaded the visual field. Art wasn't neatly gathered as in the signature museums of today. Exhibitions in the Secessionist Building occurred simultaneously with displays in less formal settings. New paintings by artists like Klimt were unveiled in major public spaces. The sense of scandal surrounding the appearance of many of these works provoked front-page debates in the popular press.

The relationship of artistic modernism to the printed word exposed the complexity of fault lines scoring the culture sphere in Vienna. Though Karl Kraus in *Die Fackel* developed Habsburg journalism's most effective voice of opposition to the hypocritical, war-mongering, patriarchal Viennese bourgeois culture, he also aligned himself in opposition to the Secessionists, who had set themselves up as violent foes of the same enfranchised, conservative powers that Kraus devoted many essays to ridiculing. On the unveiling of Klimt's masterpieces "Philosophy" and "Medicine" for the University of Vienna, Kraus wrote that the new movement was "in danger of completely losing any sense of purpose." This was a notable contradiction to the old adage in which the enemy of one's enemy is one's friend.

Freud, in his circumambulations of Vienna, could not avoid coming up against the visual icons of the new aesthetic movement. Conversely, much of this work appears influenced by mature Freudian categories, even when the date of creation precedes the publication of *The Interpretation of Dreams*. This is most true in the realm of sexuality. Whereas Schiele's masterpieces were being painted contemporaneously with the composition of Freud's foundational essays in the first years of the twentieth century, many of Klimt's important erotic works predate Freud's annunciation of the primal role of sex in psychology. Turning to second-tier artists, one discovers a profusion of work concerned with the convergence among sex, fantasy, and the outside world—contemporary-feeling not just in being sexually explicit but in the candid fluency with which the realm of the perverse and the fundamental perversity of sex in society is rendered. What stares out at us like a billboard in Times Square in the work of the Secessionists concerned with sex is often an erotic vision that flashes the viewer a far more convoluted, socially self-conscious lewdness than anything genitals can promise in themselves. Where Manet's Olympia defiantly confronted society with the fact that sexuality exists, the Secessionists went one step further, confronting sexuality itself with the inescapability of mind—of trauma, imagination, and memory—in defining what constitutes the erotic.

However, it's not only in respect to the sphere of sex that this work evokes the father of psychoanalysis. Secessionist and Jugendstil art also relies heavily on the realm of dreams. This connection indicates the bedrock from which Viennese Modernism explicitly drew inspiration: the kingdom of the unconscious. The name of the Secessionist journal, the first edition of which was published in 1898, one year before the publication of *The Interpretation of Dreams*, a name also inscribed on the façade of the Secessionist Building, was *Ver Sacrum* (Sacred Spring). The source is primal nature: a wellspring located far back in time before the conservative generation controlling Vienna's cultural hierarchy ever appeared, back to humanity's origins, when art and life were conjoined in total harmony. In fact, the Secessionist slogan, "Back to the beginnings," referred specifically to a return to "the fertility of the subconscious." The unconscious was conceived as a feminine realm, largely defined by feminized eroticism. Hence the title page of the first edition of *Ver Sacrum* by the graphic artist, Alfred Roller, which depicts a tree planted in a container barrel in the process of splitting apart the pieces of wood to snake its thirsty roots into Mother Earth.

If the source of Secessionist energy was a feminine fertility, the primary object toward which this energy was directed was the overthrow of the rule of the fathers in the name of the new generation's right to self-determination. The rallying cry of the Secessionists, inscribed over the entrance door of Olbrich's building after a remodeling in 1901 was, "*Der Zeit ihre Kunst. Der Kunst ihre Freiheit.*" (To the Age its Art, to Art its Freedom.) At the core of the Secessionist endeavor was a bluntly oedipal aspiration: Liberate Us from the Older Generation; Liberate us to Liberation.

The particular division of male-female responsibility in the Secessionists' self-definition of truth came closer to the operative paradigm of psychoanalysis than Freud would acknowledge. From the very beginning of his work, in *Studies on Hysteria*, a significant aspect of the psychoanalyst's work involved a kind of ventriloquism from within the body of the female analysand. Major portions of the first case histories are literally narrated by women through the medium of Freud and Breuer's pens. Charitable feminist assessments of this process have suggested that the early female patients who were willing to give themselves over to the "talking cure" actually taught psychoanalysis to the analysts themselves. Less generous appraisals have charged that Freud simply stole the voices of these women and then reflected their words in the funhouse mirror of his own neurotic imperative.

Regardless, psychoanalysis used the verbally fertile, feminized state of hysteria as the grounds of inspiration in a manner evoking the Secessionist self-declared roots in a field of visually fertile feminized sensuality. Clearly, the subject realm of the Secessionists, dominated by fantastical dreams, invocations of myth, the unconscious, sexuality, and the embodiment of and nourishment by feminine principles, is akin on many levels to the one Freud explored. The artists were his natural allies. Yet, Freud had no more overt relationship with the individuals laboring in the contemporary visual arts than with the Habsburgs. Why did he refuse that connection?

IF FREUD WAS forbidden entry to the sphere of imperial power by exterior authorities, he denied any solidarity with the Secessionists and their cohorts out of his own internal fears. He knew perfectly well that his greatest challenge lay in convincing people that psychoanalysis was a science, not a speculative, art-style conjuring act of the imagination. Even though Freud clearly soaked up the representations of sex, dreams, and the unconscious, which played such an important role in Secessionist work—despite the fact that his own theories show every sign of having been stained with the imagery of the age—this was not an association he could afford to acknowledge. The whole psychoanalytic endeavor collapses once Freud gets grouped with the purveyors of fantasy, as opposed to the emancipators therefrom.

Freud was never searching for a Nietzschean balance of the Apollonian and Dionysian principles. He was concentrated on achieving the sublimated Apollonian ideal. On any number of cultural, ethnic, and personal professional levels, Freud would have been made uneasy then by artists who seemed to be valorizing the very forces in the unconscious his therapeutic practice was fashioned to tame. Where was he supposed to turn?

VASES, AMULETS, EROS figures, goddesses, mummy portraits, coffin masks, Buddhas and Bodhisattvas, steles, flasks, engraved mirrors, warrior figures, sphinxes and royal seals, jade lions, rings, scarabs, iridescent bottles and marble fragments from sarcophagi—Freud's collection of antiquities is astonishingly catholic. It's also enormous.

The compression of exotic display in Freud's study and consulting room evokes the cabinets of curiosity, or *Wunderkammern*, that became important mediums of display in the late renaissance. Often, the *Wunderkammern* would present both marvels of nature and of art, placing exotic specimens of plant and animal life alongside wondrous products of artisan workshops. There were also objects in which art and nature were fused, such as two famous pieces in the Kunthistorisches Museum with which Freud would have been familiar: an oil painting of *Phaeton's Fall* on a slice of alabaster in which the artist used the variegation of color and line occurring naturally on the stone to define the topography and sky of the scene, and a natural formation of precious ores that a Bohemian goldsmith transformed into Calvary by positioning tiny figures around the outcrop in a procession ending with the Crucifixion.

Both in the case where a single object merged natural and artificial elements, and in the overall constellation of articles within the cabinets of curiosity, the purpose was to provoke wonder that led to meditations, light hearted and grave, on the relationship between nature and art. In many instances, the ultimate purpose of this exercise was to suggest a reconciliation between the two, or at least to subvert viewers' understanding of what the distinction actually consisted in.

The exhibition of antiquities to the exclusion of almost all else in Freud's cabinets was not unprecedented in the tradition of *Wunderkammern*. But the range of *type* of antiquity and of provenance in his collection was unusual and suggests the complexity of what he was trying to unify. The aura of his exhibition rooms suggests that Freud may have had in mind the thesis of the sixteenth-century Flemish doctor, Samuel Quicchelberg, whose philosophy of the *Wunderkammern* and the art of collecting in general continued to hold sway in Freud's day. Quicchelberg had posited that the museum ought to function as a "universal theater."

Freud's consulting room does feel very much like a stage—and a profound microcosm. Freud's subject is history, but he traces it back so far, to a point at which humanity was so embedded in myth, that natural history and human history come close to merging. In Freud's ideal museum the realms that he seems determined to reconcile are the east and the west; the objects he collected graft memory and fantasy in the same way that a *Wunderkammern* display might conjoin nature and history. But wonder was also the emotion Freud intended to provoke. His retrospective play of the past, in which fragments and figurines of cultures, gods, desires, historical events, and ghosts were all confabulated in a universal drama, constituted a version of the sublime—the antithesis of Putnam's, which was directed piously toward an idealized future.

FREUD'S ANTIQUITIES ALSO convey the impression of an archeological dig from some fantasy civilization at a crossroads of east-west trade routes. His personal *bildung* occurred concurrently with the evolution of modern archaeology. The most striking instance of this development was the transformation of Troy from mythical icon in Freud's childhood to historical truth by the time of his university days. Freud was eighteen when Heinrich Schliemann was making his first breakthrough discoveries at Troy. The labyrinth of Minos on Crete was being excavated the same year that Freud published *The Interpretation of Dreams*. Freud bought *Ilos*, Schliemann's own book on the excavation at Troy, in 1899. The idea that the great legends of classical history had historical grounding and that, in effect, the antiquity of Western civilization's common cultural origins could be physically verified had massive interdisciplinary resonance.

Any number of remarks by Freud make explicit the ways in which heroic archeology served as his model for the psychoanalytic process. In the midst of his own self-analysis, and the confirmation of his theories provided by the case history of a young man, Freud wrote Fliess with an ecstatic comparison of his own work to that of Schliemann's discovery of Troy. Indeed, the core premise of psychoanalysis involves a deeply archaeological concept: the contours of our current psychologies are defined by the subterranean pressure of long-buried memories from our past. By digging at the site of memory one not only confirms the actual childhood roots of adult behaviors, one also dispossesses the artifacts of their purely mythological force.

This is not to discount the role of fantasy at the point of origin. The discovery of the maze at Minos was not the discovery of the Minotaur. Similarly, when Freud abandons the seduction theory he is still left with a palpable framework—the ruins of a family architecture—over which fantasies of seduction could be draped. Furthermore, the two-fold process whereby trauma becomes neurosis evokes the start of the archeological dig. In Freud's schema, a trauma suffered in childhood only flares up as an adult symptom when a second, contemporary event triggers a memory flash that penetrates (albeit unconsciously) the layers of personal history. In archaeology, at least in Schliemann's day, the process of reconstruction could only begin with the discovery of a visible fragment of the past in the here and now. This might be a chunk of marble from a ruin that the archaeologist stubs his toe on, or just a suggestive topographical distortion.

However, Freud's general fascination with archaeology and antiquity doesn't explain the specific ways in which the theater he fashioned resembles a polyglot cosmopolitan center. Why was it that Freud's display proffered almost equal time to Semitic objects and to objects of the Hellenic world?

IN 1908 FREUD wrote a brief essay entitled "Family Romances," which described the protoneurotic daydream of some children who imagine that their real parents are different, more exalted characters than the individuals who claim to be their progenitors. Eight years earlier, in the *Interpretation of Dreams*, he recounted a scene in which his father's cap was knocked off by a gentile shouting "Jew! Get off the pavement!" Freud's father told him that he responded to the insult by going and picking up his hat and getting off the pavement just as he was instructed. "This struck me as unheroic conduct of the big, strong man who was holding the little boy by his hand," Freud wrote. "I contrasted this situation with another which fitted my feelings better: the scene in which Hannibal's father, Hamilcar Barca, made his boy swear before the household altar to take vengeance on the Romans." This family romance involving the displacement of his father by a figure of Carthaginian ancestry also comprises Freud's embodiment of the voice of Dido in the aliquis incident. A clue to the special, catholic quality of his art collection can be found in the essay's mention of the "child's longing for the happy, vanished days" when his parents are the pinnacle of humanity. This golden age is one that predates, in fact, the division of ancestors into Jew and non-Jew.

Freud's doggedly heterogeneous collection of art works, in which Rome intermingles with Greece, which interbreeds with Egypt, Mesopotamia, Babylonia, and China, can be viewed as an objectified family romance. With these objects, Freud hearkens back to a point in time when the genetic division of west and east was not yet complete. The thematic cross-currents are so complex in these works that they express above all the shared ethnic and historical origins of mankind's foundational myths.

The Secessionists looked back before the dawn of civilization to the primal energy struggles out of which culture arose. That's a gesture to which an American could relate. The Habsburgs associated themselves with the start of civilization in Europe through the establishment of the Holy Roman Empire.

Freud rejected the idea of a return to a truly primal state; for him this was only to invoke the condition of mob power and of the terrible helplessness of childhood that was the womb of all trauma. Freud would surely have agreed with Kafka's aphorism about humanity in a letter to Brod: "They could not put the determining divine principle at sufficient distance from themselves; the whole pantheon was only a means by which the determining forces could be kept at a distance from man's earthly being, so that human lungs could have air."

However, if Freud rebuffed the call to return to a point before the beginning, he was equally unwilling to accept that the beginnings of European civilization stopped in Catholic Rome. All the myriad objects in Freud's collection can be seen on some level as a plea for the joint Semitic and Western legacy found in antiquity.

To walk into Freud's recreated rooms in London, with their dense exhibits of antiquities, is to enter a *Wunderkammern* of family romances. Everywhere one turns there's an object to which both the visitor and Freud are related in the primal past—the very past that it is the purpose of psychoanalysis to expose, even if the sight of it, as was the case with Oedipus once he'd bared his mother by removing the pins from her dress, would blind the gazer to the exterior world, leaving him unable to see anything but the cabinet of curiosities composed by his own interior fantasies.

CHAPTER 20

Self-Activity

The people I know who are threatened with collapse are either hiding their lesser self from the view of others and trying to seem better than they are or else, actually hiding from themselves and refusing to see something which is perpetually trying to make itself known in order to be outgrown.

Blow to Putnam, winter of 1911

PUTNAM GRADUALLY BEGAN to conceive of the Weimar Congress as the ultimate opportunity to make everything integrate. In so doing, he petitioned Blow's help more frequently and urgently than ever before. The Europeans were gratified that Putnam had agreed to attend. "It is astonishing what that old man is capable of accomplishing," Ferenczi wrote Freud. But at the start of 1911, none of Freud's inner circle had any idea what Putnam really had in mind.

He certainly wasn't mentioning the fact that Blow was providing him with his entire line of argument against Freud, supporting and amending his own position point by point as she saw fit. Putnam's silence on this count may have been due to his already feeling self-conscious about the apron strings that bound him, like a bathetic Laocoön, from the start. In proposing the Weimar address, he had to confess to Freud that his domestic responsibilities would follow him across the Atlantic: "It is uncertain just what time will be at my disposal," he wrote him, "for I shall probably be the only man in a party of ladies and children anxious to see something of Switzerland and Italy, and I may be obliged to act as escort."

Only after making full disclosure of this limitation was he able to solicit Freud's approval: "You are aware of my interest in certain aspects of philosophy and psychology, but I have not expressed as strongly as I feel that there are points of view which, I think, can be shown to be of distinctly practical importance as well as of theoretical interest." He was certain that if physicians helped patients understand why they ought to make an effort toward sublimation, this would increase the likelihood of their actually making the attempt. Psychoanalysis, he argued, had been guilty of an overly literal use of Darwin: "Mind, consciousness, reason, emotion, will are not merely *products* of evolution, but underlying *causes* of evolution."

This concept enabled Putnam to believe that with psychoanalysis he'd resumed work as a radical reformer. In helping individuals achieve sublimation, he wasn't just aiding the process of personal fruition, he was catalyzing the evolution of the species itself. "Would it be perfectly useless and ridiculous to bring *some portion* of this subject, that portion especially which relates to *practical motives* and the strengthening of *character*, before the Congress?" he asked; then, realizing that he was indulging in the kind of wishy-washy self-questioning that had been the bane of his life, he concluded, "I must sometime, in print, have the courage of my convictions and express just what I think." In his last sentence, he qualified himself yet again. "But perhaps the Congress is not the place to do this." Poor Putnam! He must sometimes have wondered whether he had any Emersonian self-reliance at all.

WHAT WAS THE nature of the belief system upon which Blow relied and Putnam depended? Although the story long beloved of German immigrants that German missed being the native tongue of America by only one vote in the Capitol may be apocryphal, the role played by German settlers and German intellectual currents in America remains one of the great repressed facts of U.S. history. The first idealist, utopian community to be established in America after the arrival of the Puritans was founded by a German-Protestant sect from Württemberg in Harmony, Pennsylvania. The leading Puritans themselves, such as Putnam's ancestors, the Mathers, were recognized scholars of German theology. Increase Mather's library contained more works in German than books by Dutch, French, and Italian writers combined. German pietism served as the great counterweight to the severity of Puritan dogma.

Surpassing the influence of German Pietist thought on the Mathers and their flock, Kant's Transcendentalism was *the* defining force in American intellectual history for decades. Emerson's version of Transcendentalism and the New England move away from the Unitarian church toward a private interior faith was, in part, enacted as a riff on the work of the Master of Königsberg.

Apart from the German influence on high thought, there was a sizable German presence in the composition of the American public. In the 1850s more than a million German immigrants came to America and 200-plus German newspapers plastered the language of Goethe, Schiller, and Kant across the nation's newsstands. The U.S. census of 1900 shows German immigrants trailing the English by only two million out of a total white population of approximately seventy million. From Henry Adams to James to Putnam, members of the New England elite invariably went to Germany to get their scientific education. G. Stanley Hall's first book was entitled *Aspects of German Culture.* Beyond providing for the *bildung* of much of the New England elite, after 1880, the entire approach to the teaching of philosophy in America was modeled on the German system. On top of the teaching of German philosophy itself, which had begun in the 1870s, a new reliance on elective studies in conjunction with seminars and support for research patterned on the German university took hold. In terms of philosophical trends, cultural sentiments, musical tastes, language, and education, the America that Freud discovered in 1909 was far less alien from the German-speaking empire to which he belonged than he wanted to believe.

Nowhere in America was the German influence upon intellectual life more pronounced than in St. Louis, where Blow grew up. Peppered through Putnam's letters to Freud are a series of phrases and concepts that sound abstract to the point of being nonsensical. "Self-activity," the "necessary presuppositions" (Putnam's theory of human motivation rooted in "a recognition of our responsibility as self-conscious beings"), his notion of an eternal scheme for the universe in which "mental life is the most real thing we know"—all these points and countless others may have had Freud glazing over. In truth, however, the perplexing obscurities referred to a specific body of logical thought with which Freud was at least somewhat familiar.

Almost every abstract idea that Putnam bruited before Freud had its origin in the workshop of one extraordinary school of thought: the St. Louis

Hegelians. Unbeknownst to him, when he dueled with Putnam, Freud was actually involved in a shoot-out with a gunslinger for Georg Wilhelm Friedrich Hegel, outfitted as sheriff-intellectual of the American Wild West. No town on earth was big enough for the two of them.

THE MAN BEHIND the movement behind Blow even *looked* like a cartoon cowboy. Described by one of his greatest admirers (his disciple, Denton Snider), Henry Brokmeyer was sinewy and whiskery with "the quick, almost wild eye of the hunter," along with "an enormous nose, somewhat crooked, which had the power of flattening and bulging and curveting and crooking in a variety of ways expressive of what was going on within him." While he cogitated on the infinitude of Hegelian insights, he sucked and blew on his "perpetual and vicious pipe."

Brokmeyer is a picaresque hero of monumental proportions. A German refugee from the failed revolutions of the 1840s whose father was a well-off Jewish businessman and whose mother claimed to be related to Bismarck, Brokmeyer landed in Manhattan at the age of 19 with twenty-five cents and three English words. He proved handy at every trade he took up, migrating slowly westward while working as a tanner and shoemaker. After making a tidy fortune launching a shoe factory, Brokmeyer turned back east and began passing in and out of universities, debating entire faculties and administrations to gain admission. At Brown, he was exposed to Emerson, Idealism, and Thoreau. Brokmeyer became seized with the desire to create a new Walden on purer principles than his eastern mentors dared attempt. He struck out for the west once again in 1854, squatting in a cabin in backwoods Mississippi. Most of his money vanished about this time in a failed banking venture. But this was also the moment when Brokmeyer discovered Hegel, and the compensation was prodigal.

Brokmeyer found in Hegel the answer to the question of the meaning of all life and his own purpose therein. In 1856, he moved to St. Louis, taking with him fishing tackle and an arsenal of firearms, as well as a compendious one-chest library featuring authors from Thucydides to Cervantes, from Shakespeare to Sterne, and Goethe to Hegel. When the Civil War broke out, Brokmeyer added to his library a volume on military strategy and enlisted as a Union soldier (notwithstanding the fact that slave labor had been crucial to his first fortune as a factory magnate). He returned to

Missouri a war hero, and speedily translated that success into a new career as a lawyer and general nabob of St. Louis. Bursting into politics, he was elected to the State Senate and in 1875 wrote the state constitution of his adopted city.

Before Brokmeyer went off to war, he had become friends with a New England transplant of more conventional credentials. After graduating from Andover, dropping out of Yale, and passing through a phase of obsession with mediums and mesmerists, William Torrey Harris moved to St. Louis to teach shorthand, where he soon bumped into Brokmeyer. Over the course of six or seven years of intense conversation, Harris arrived at the conclusion that the Hegelian wisdom Brokmeyer was touting was revelation itself. As he wrote with more than a touch of unselfconscious bombast in his own account of his intellectual education, "In 1866 I arrived at the first insight that is distinctively Hegelian and the most important apercu of Hegel's logic. I wrote this out in a letter to my friend Adolph E. Kroeger, an ardent Fichtean, whom I had discovered and was endeavoring to proselyte [sic] for Hegel."

But if Harris is guilty of a Casaubon-like desiccation of tone in articulating his own key to all mythologies, his discipleship, playing John the Baptist to Brokmeyer's Christ, was instrumental to the national success of the St. Louis Hegelians. Harris took the role of the movement's trustworthy communicator in a manner similar to the one Putnam enacted on behalf of Freud. In later years, Harris became a preeminent educator and was also, in this capacity, Susan Blow's mentor as she began to gravitate toward the movement. Harris helped Blow found the country's first kindergarten in 1873 (the same year in which, according to his intellectual autobiography, he "discovered the identity of all eastern philosophies") and remained a loyal supporter of hers through her various mental breakdowns. Harris' death in November 1909, just weeks after Putnam met Freud and announced his enthusiastic response to the Viennese doctor, caught Blow at a particularly vulnerable moment.

THOUGH HARRIS MAY not have felt qualified to announce his first Hegelian insight until 1866, even before the firing on Fort Sumter the prime importance of Hegel, and of Brokmeyer as Hegel's New World spokesperson, was manifest. In the dark hours before the Civil War broke out, the conviction grew in Harris and his immediate circle that America could be redeemed through a translation of Hegel's *Logic* into the vernacular. Only Brokmeyer was capable of such a work, and with the help of a couple of like-minded "respectable vagabonds" Harris put together a stipend for Brokmeyer to work on the first American Hegel. By the time the drums of war called him away, Brokmeyer had completed a first draft of the translation.

Using this book in manuscript form as his bible, Harris began to organize discussion groups on philosophy. With Brokmeyer's return at the end of the war, these meetings coalesced into a more formal association: the St. Louis Philosophical Society, predecessor to the St. Louis Movement. Snider described how, at the founding moment in January 1866, Both Brokmeyer and Harris described "with enthusiasm the prospects and purposes of the organization; both failed not to flash some prophetic lightning upon our unlit future."

Snider became, after Harris, the most prolific writer in the whole frighteningly prolific circle, writing thousands of pages that applied St. Louis Hegelian theory to subjects as diverse as Greece and Rome (treated in verse), Shakespeare (many plays received book-length Hegelian studies), feeling psychologically treated, Dante, the American State as a psychological phenomenon, Lincoln, Emerson, Goethe, Europe, and the act of writing as such. He was built like a beanpole with a ponderous brow, deep-set troubled eyes, a pitch black snort of a mustache, and a manner more commonly associated with prize fighters than philosophers. With the addition of Snider, the initial triad of the St. Louis Hegelians was complete.

ALONG WITH HIS translation of Hegel's *Logic*, Brokmeyer's most important work was *A Mechanic's Diary*. Written near the end of his life, the book purports to be an account of the seminal period of his association with Hegel and the founding of the movement that determined Blow's philosophical destiny. Yet it is so riddled with factual inaccuracies that it is now considered, charitably, more of a didactic autobiographical experiment— Brokmeyer's effort at a jauntier *Walden*—than an attempt at true historical record. Admittedly, many of the errors, such as his description of himself as the founding father of a major German colony in central Illinois at a time when his property consisted of a squatter's hut in the wilderness of Warren County, Missouri, redound suspiciously to his credit—as though his own life were simply a utopian fantasy concocted for his own self-idolizing gratification. Nonetheless, the effort to explain every conceivable event in Hegelian dialectical terms is a fascinating exercise. Even discussing a chance conversation about cannibals in the Caribbean that unfolded in a business office where he was working gave Brokmeyer the chance to distinguish between so-called natural freedom and Hegelian freedom. Missionaries had deprived the "cannibals of their 'natural freedom' . . . while some ten thousand of the same tribe are still enjoying their natural liberty, of eating their enemies, the Cabrees, or being eaten by them." In truth, we do not come into the world free at all: "The measure of freedom which I enjoy I have to achieve," he argued, "and this achieving is the task of my life."

When Brokmeyer mused on his choice of St. Louis as his home he singled out the energy and natural riches of the place. "Here if anywhere industry, economy and honest conduct must mean success—unless we have to believe that the world is but an annex of hell, as some people think. I heard this expression for the first time to-day, in a crowd that had gathered in front of the banking house of P.B. & Co.: 'The world is an annex of hell and St. Louis is located upon a choice quarter section.'"

Apart from the sheer axial dynamism of the place, Brokmeyer might well also have responded to the city's established Germanic character. A sizeable percentage of the city's huge German population had enjoyed the opportunity and alarm of intimate exposure to Prussian militarism, and when the Union levy struck Missouri, able regimens of refugees sprung up overnight to heed the patriotic call. Germans of all ages, from young bucks to stooped patriarchs with long white beards, organized in secret clubs throughout all but the richest neighborhoods of St. Louis to drill and whip up martial zeal.

In the first year of the War, an infantry brigade under the command of Colonel Blair that had been thrown together virtually overnight from local St. Louis German-Americans, succeeded in launching a surprise attack on Camp Jackson, achieving the first clear victory for the North. The event became known as "The First Great St. Louis Deed" and unleashed an ecstasy of Germanic pride in St. Louis exceeding even the scope of the population with actual ethnic roots in the Teutonic heartland. Further fed by events on the continent, including the Franco-Prussian war of 1870 and the annexation of Alsace-Lorraine, the St. Louis populace trembled with

awareness of what Snider describes as "the deep undercurrent of connection between German St. Louis and the old, or rather the New Fatherland
in Europe." The whole city was "borne along in the floodtide of German
spirit." Those who were not Germans, or German-Americans, were what
Snider called, "Germanizers" of which class he counted himself "a right
specimen. . . . Public manners and amusement . . . turned German; I joined
a German club in which English was tabooed and in some cases unknown.
The beer-house was then in its glory as a popular resort."

The availability of German literature was another key factor in the city's
Rhine-loving tendencies. There were three large and busy bookstores devoted entirely to German literature as well as a number of smaller shops
that Snider described as "ever ready to send orders to Leipzig and Berlin
for old and new volumes." Blow patronized these stores, all of which, Snider
wrote, were staffed by that incomparable figure, the "trained German book-
seller, known over the entire globe as the unparalleled of his kind, and
as the main pillar of the vast German book trade, being found in Asiatic
Tiflis and African Timbuctoo as well as in our Western cowboy town of
Hardscrapple."

By 1864, Germans filled the city council. The German language began
to be taught in the public schools and a strong movement for legislating
bilingual citizenship swelled over St. Louis. Germans, Snider declared, held
the reins of the "city's control, material and spiritual."

Over time, this fact came to seem a foreshadowing of the unique
millennial destiny of the city. "This upburst of domination of Germanism,"
wrote the irrepressible Snider, heralded "the uplift of a new strange spirit
. . . as the revelation of the peculiar racial consciousness of old Teutonia
welling forth just now on the banks of the Mississippi." A convergence of
factors led to an intoxicated, perhaps even hallucinogenic sense in the post-
War years that St. Louis was the "Future Great City of the World." This
faith extended well beyond the purviews of the St. Louis Movement. So
great was the certainty of St. Louis' citizenry that their city was destined to
surpass even Chicago, that "wicked Sodom" hanging over the top of the
state, that when the first census following the Great Fire in 1880 failed to
indicate that the Missouri Capital had overtaken Chicago, the city's leaders hired a top mathematician at Washington University to recalculate the
results of the entire census. Indeed, Chicago was but the first city St. Louis
was destined to outshine. Boston, New York, and Paris would successively

bow down in obsequious concession to that triumph. The faith in the city's divine soul was general, but the St. Louis Movement possessed an ability to articulate the grounds for the conviction that eluded most others.

The magic key to this interpretative potency was Hegel—Brokmeyer's translation of Hegel's *Larger Logic*. Publishers, however, found his earlier draft too clumsy and crude to print. On his return from the Civil War, Brokmeyer immediately set about retranslating parts of the book. He continued revising the manuscript for the next thirty years. In the last decade of his life, he once more retranslated the whole work. And yet, mysteriously, this book of books for the St. Louis Hegelians, translated by its charismatic founder himself who, Snider said, was on a par with Hegel himself "only more poetic," was never deemed worthy of publication. For decades, the manuscript circulated between members in ragged handwritten copies.

Everything that came into the sights of the St. Louis Movement was perceived through Hegelian lenses—beginning with St. Louis itself. The geographical position of the city, in the middle of the country, on the edge of the frontier, was seen as proof of its embodiment of the final, most advanced, resolutional stage of the Hegelian triad. In an even more localized sense, Hegel's system was applied to the contest for supremacy between St. Louis and Chicago. Chicago was the antithesis of St. Louis. The Great Fire was seen as the close of its phase of dominance, after which St. Louis would enter its rightful stage of synthetic leadership. Within St. Louis itself, "the great real estate boom, or 'illusion' in St. Louis was the 'thesis,' the founding of the Philosophical Society the 'antithesis,' and the building of the great Eads Bridge the 'synthesis.'"

Some of this dialectical frenzy may, of course, have been triggered by the confusion and tragedy of the Civil War. Hegel, as Marx knew well, was nothing if not a master of fitting negative events into a larger, necessary scheme en route to inevitable, progressive fruition. Predictably, therefore, the War itself was Hegelianized by the Movement. But Harris later recalled that the passion for dialectical contextualization grew so acute that "even the hunting of turkeys and squirrels was the occasion for the use of philosophy."

In all these instances, and countless more, conflict was ultimately a positive phenomenon, serving as the creative engine to growth. Despite Putnam's embrace of Freud's views on how conflict sparked neurosis, he was never comfortable ascribing a purely negative function to so pervasive a phenomenon. Putnam welcomed the St. Louis Hegelian idea that even the most primary conflicts, such as that between the individual and society, were preliminary stages to the recognition of the higher self. For Freud, of course, this was never the case. Freud saw such dissonance as an interminable flaw in the order of being. Although the elite could sometimes rise above these oppositions, they remained lurking in the depths of the mind waiting to erupt and drag one back to the perpetually yawning abyss of primal savagery.

CHAPTER 21

Making Hegel Talk English

*Dear Mr. Alcott — Here I have before me the programme of the
Concord School, the bill of fare a banquet of the gods.*
                Elizabeth Peabody to Bronson Alcott, summer of 1881

JUST AS HEGEL'S philosophy developed as a dialectical response to Kant's
Transcendentalism, Brokmeyer's movement emerged as the Hegelian synthesis between New England Transcendentalism and the new American
materialism. Transcendentalism was not rejected by the St. Louis Hegelians
but it was seen as too fuzzy minded in and of itself to provide a sufficiently
forceful response to the late nineteenth-century American embrace of
purely material values.

It is, of course, an irony that many of the figures behind America's
materialism were themselves German. Much of contemporary science in
Putnam's time evolved from the great German leaders in geography, chemistry, astronomy, and physics. Textual criticism of the Bible itself, as well
as of Christianity, which had helped people like Putnam develop a pluralistic
viewpoint of the standards for canonization, was a German innovation.

Hegel rejected what he saw as the overly mystical tendencies in transcendentalism and sought to create a philosophy based on real-world process, the unfolding of the mind of God in tangible history rather than
supernal abstractions, through a dialectical movement. In his psychotherapeutic philosophy, Putnam adopted Hegel's idea of the "concrete
universal," the notion that recognition of personal incompleteness propelled
progressive movement in history. It was to this that Putnam was referring
when he wrote Freud in the summer of 1910 that "if the universal is eternal and in some sense perfect, and if the 'mental' is the real, then the

imperfection and evolution which we see around us must have some meaning compatible with the perfection of the general scheme."

The St. Louis Hegelians put an idiosyncratic American slant on Hegel's
theories. The most important, as far as Putnam was concerned, was their idea
that individual existence was a factor of communal being. This idea was central to Putnam's psychotherapy as it was by helping patients recognize the
circles radiating out from themselves to an ever greater series of communal
obligations that the physician paved the way to sublimation. *This* indeed was
the great mission that Putnam believed analysts needed to incorporate into
treatment. When he spoke to Freud about the imperative of making patients
aware of "higher views of their obligations" he referred to the ever-expanding
groups that ultimately create the individual's own existence. Freud's idea of
sublimation and the larger psychoanalytic process gave Putnam what he
believed to be a scientific armature for the philosophical mission of therapy
he'd already conceived in conversation with Blow. Freud's libido would provide the natural energy resources to execute that mission.

THOUGH BROKMEYER DID not succeed in his self-appointed calling to
make "Hegel talk English," this failure in no way retarded the rush into
publication of innumerable other works by members of the Movement: the
eleven members who made up the innermost circle authored a combined
total of 229 books—and this leaves out entirely the 479 works single-
handedly composed by Harris. Indeed, despite Brokmeyer's own failure
to get his manuscript into print, he enjoined his followers to both write and
publish. Publishing one's thoughts was, in tandem with pedagogical activity, the approved means whereby individuals affiliated with the Movement
could promulgate the ever-expanding ripples of consciousness that Hegel
had identified as the route to universal freedom.

Of the vast, logorrheic body of writing that the Movement gave birth
to, far and away the most important vehicle for disseminating the Hegelian
gospel was the journal founded by Harris two years after the end of the
Civil War. Begun in a pique on the rejection of an article he'd written for
an established magazine, Harris' journal became the "primal creative act
of self-publication of the St. Louis Movement," according to Snider. *The
Journal of Speculative Philosophy* was the first periodical in the English-
speaking world devoted to speculative thought not in the service of any

specific theological creed. In twenty-two volumes published over twenty-six years, the *Journal* presented an extraordinarily diverse array of ponderous essays. However, abstruse and gummed-up the writing sometimes became—however few people actually read it—Harris and the gang in St. Louis basked in the awareness that everyone they cared about, from Emerson in Concord to a stunning array of prominent philosophers in England, Scotland, and on the Continent were followers.

Indeed, in one of the most mind-boggling transatlantic zigzags of influence, Ludwig Feurbach and J. H. Fichte became auxiliary members of the St. Louis Movement, inspired to do so by Harris' journal. When we consider the centrality of these two figures in the evolution of a German philosophical cast critical to Freud's own project, we can see why, encountering Putnam's philosophy, Freud would have experienced an actualization of his maxim that the finding of an object is always a refinding.

IN HIS PREFACE to the first issue of the *Journal*, Harris laid out the mission of the St. Louis Hegelians. He described the "immense religious movements" sweeping America and England, and the body of mystics "beginning to spring up who prefer to ignore utterly all historical wrappages and cleave only to the speculative kernel itself." And yet, "the vortex between the traditional faith and the intellectual conviction cannot be closed by renouncing the latter, but only be deepening it to speculative insight." In other words, mysticism does not offer a genuine escape hatch from the strictures of reason and science.

The attraction to mysticism was especially powerful because, Harris argued, "the idea underlying our form of government [has] hitherto developed only one of its essential phases—that of brittle individualism—in which national unity seemed an external mechanism, soon to be entirely dispensed with, and the enterprise of the private man, or of the corporation substituted for it."

However, he added, consciousness of the other "essential phase" has now at last arrived, the phase in which the individual recognizes his most profound self to be identified with the State as such. This "new phase of national life demands to be digested and comprehended, is a further occasion for the cultivation of the Speculative."

Science was not to be rejected but somehow incorporated within the greater philosophical scheme, just as, for Putnam, philosophy was to be inscribed within the scientific template. The purpose of the *Journal* was to demonstrate what this synthesis would look like. Harris introduced an article on "The Speculative" with a manifesto from the "Orphic Sayings" of the other great wise man of Concord, Bronson Alcott: "We need what Genius is unconsciously seeking and by some daring generalization of the universe, shall assuredly discover, a spiritual calculus . . . omniscient, omnipotent, self-subsisting, uncontained, yet containing all things in the unbroken synthesis of its being."

No less grandiose was the epigraph taken from Novalis: "Philosophy can bake no bread, but she can procure for us God, Freedom, and Immortality." Harris was announcing that the philosophy he promoted would have an application in daily life as fundamental as that of bread. By doing so, he hoped to nurture the creation of a "true 'American' type of speculative philosophy." This was to be the antithesis of professionalized philosophy conducted in the cloister by academics. Harris sought to translate the zenith of Occidental Idealism into the commerce-soaked dirt and minerals of American soil.

His mission captured the imagination of a striking cross-section of thinkers. Essays in the *Journal* were composed by intellectuals living far beyond the literal purviews of St. Louis and her "electrifying city-soul," in Snider's phrase. William James published essays in the *Journal*, as did Royce (whose first printed work was in the periodical). More surprising, given his later move away from Hegel, is the fact that John Dewey also published his first paper in the *Journal*. A single volume taken up at random might contain almost three dozen essays, including a paper on anti-materialism by G. Stanley Hall, essays on the *Merchant of Venice* and *Julius Caesar* by Snider, a translation of "Hegel's Philosophy of Art Chivalry" by one Sue A. Longwell, an article on the philosophy of law, a study of philosophy in Europe, a treatise on the Parmenides of Plato, as well a foray by Harris himself into the hot, controversial question, "Do the Correlationists Believe in Self Movement?"

SUSAN BLOW ALSO published in the *Journal*. And it was within this ferment of high-on-the-hog Hegelian hopes and a Germanizing, universe-swallowing conviction of St. Louis' manifest destiny that she came of age. Though Hegel had little faith in woman's capacity for freedom, and Snider struggled with misogynist tendencies peculiar to himself, the New World Hegelians had resolved to take an open-minded approach to the question of female aptitude for philosophizing. Snider was soon compelled to grant that Blow made the fourth corner of the eternal square that he, Brokmeyer, and Harris had begun to formulate in triadic fashion. A friend of Blow's, Anna Brackett, soon became another star of the Movement. These two women were followed by numerous others. Indeed, in 1880, when John Albee, an out-of-towner Hegelian, came to visit St. Louis, he noted that he had never seen a city in which women played so prominent an intellectual role. "I have not talked with any woman here who has not philosophized me beyond my depth," he marveled. As for Blow, he told Snider, "A day or two ago I went with Miss Blow to one of her kindergartens to see the children play, and she so overwhelmed me with her ponderous Hegelian nomenclature in explaining a little game of the babies that I heard my brain-pan crack like a pistol shot."

The context of Albee's mind-splattering encounter with Blow hints at one reason so many women were to play at least a peripheral role in the St. Louis Movement, and also points to its second great arena of action: pedagogy. Along with writing and publishing, the other sphere in which the ideals of the St. Louis Hegelians could be enacted was the American education system. As schoolteaching was a field dominated by women, it was natural that the Hegelians experienced an inrush of females into their ranks. Blow's first inspiration to become a teacher was the Holy Scripture (her first job was as a Sunday School teacher in Carondelet). After the Bible came exposure to Froebel. But it was contact with Harris and the consequent immersion in Hegel that crystallized her theories of education and stimulated the dialectical didacticism of all her future work.

However dull Harris may seem to the contemporary reader, Blow's account of her discovery of Hegel in the course of a talk Harris delivered demonstrates that as a teacher of the philosophy for which he cared most, Harris was a figure of Pentecostal-style charisma: "The open secret was revealed and I knew that I stood upon the delectable mountains and discerned from afar the shining pinnacles of the Eternal City." Blow wrote of the encounter almost fifty years later, "That afternoon was a solemn crisis in my life. I beheld eternal Reality. I was a novice admitted to a sacred

fellowship." If she were capable of injecting even a fraction of the lightning she'd gleaned from Harris in her own verandah talks with Putnam,
it's no wonder that he felt forcefully converted by her to a new faith.

EVEN BEFORE PUTNAM met Blow, however, Hegel had begun circling
closer to Boston and even the Adirondacks. The suspicion among some of
the St. Louis Hegelians that Harris had always been a New Englander at
his core was borne out when he became involved with a long-standing
scheme first conceived by Bronson Alcott to form a School of Philosophy
in Concord modeled after the School of Athens.

A certain tension between the soft-focus cerebral world of New England
Transcendentalism from which Brokmeyer took his first inspiration and the
muscular philosophical movement launched on the Missouri frontier was
present from the start. Harris was generally cast in the role of peacemaker
between the two camps. When Alcott appeared in St. Louis on a speaking
tour visit and began treating the Hegelians to one of his rambling disquisi-
tions, Snider and Brokmeyer at once communicated a laconic contempt
for the self-styled seer from Concord with his "dark, torturous, and
riddlesome" oracles. After listening with snorting impatience for as long as
he could bear, Brokmeyer, Snider wrote, seized on one of Alcott's orphic
pronouncements and "at the fiery touch of his dialectics, set off with his
Mephistophelean chuckle, he simply exploded it into mist with a sort of
detonation, as if it were a soap bubble filled with explosive gas." Alcott tried
to recover his composure and even to challenge Brokmeyer, which led to
his making the unfortunate pronouncement, "It requires a Christ to interpret a Christ." At this, Snider, who had remained, if one discounts grunts
and mutters, silent all evening, rose to his feet and commented, "Gentlemen, if I may be permitted to state my interpretation of this last saying: its
hidden meaning is, in my judgment, that only an Alcott can rightly interpret an Alcott. That being the case, we all had better now go home."

However hurt he might have felt, Alcott knew that he'd found a formidable potency in St. Louis and would not abandon the notion that a conversation between the two sides was valuable enough to suffer for. "If wanting
in the courtesies of conversation, these western minds take every freedom
of tart debate and drive home the argument at a fearful rate," he wrote of
the encounter in his journal. "Customs, traditions, which we call deference

to authorities, they hold as embarrassing and set them rudely aside, ignore them altogether. 'Tis refreshing to see, and worth the journey."

The dialogue between Alcott and Harris continued, made easier by the fact that Emerson, though now in his dotage, remained a figure of reverence for the Hegelians. The two men together concocted a scheme to found a school of philosophy that would mark a new era in American intellectual history. For Alcott, such an institution had the potential to become the vehicle for transmission of his theories, as he had never counted himself a writer of books. For Harris, the school could serve both to provide the anti-academic educational framework he believed was essential to the promulgation of the new philosophy and, even more importantly, could become the final movement in the Hegelian triad of America's cultural progress toward true freedom. Emerson's Concord had been the Thesis against which the St. Louis Movement was the Antithesis. Though it is doubtful he would have made his intentions explicit to Alcott, Harris hoped that by creating the school in Concord and filling it with teachers from the West he would achieve Synthesis.

The School opened in the summer of 1879 in Alcott's home, Orchard House, with a six-week session including eleven lessons per week. Though it lacked both operating budget, and endowment, Harris and Alcott managed to tap into the Boston area's lecture thirst sufficiently that the School funded itself by ticket sales in its very first year. Alcott delivered ten lectures on the power of personality. Harris gave another ten-part series of talks on "Philosophic Knowing." Emerson, half senile, lectured on "Memory."

For the following year, donations from a New York philanthropist enabled the construction of a new building on the Orchard House grounds, dubbed the Hillside Chapel. It was kept purposefully rustic, in the Platonic manner, with gaps between the wall boards through which, as Lillian Whiting, a turn-of-the-century Boston historian, wrote, "vines and greenery found hospitable entrance and twined their way in with a decorative effect." Busts of figures as diverse as Plato, Pestalozzi, Emerson, and Alcott himself ornamented the room, while an engraving of The School of Athens hung over the mantle. Lecturers spoke from behind a table in an alcove while pupils absorbed their words from a cluster of camp chairs.

The dense subject matter of the lectures neither deterred audiences from attending nor guaranteed that once having arrived they would remain glued to their seats. The proximity of an actual hillside cooled by shady trees to Hillside Chapel in which the temperature, notwithstanding the spaces between the wall boards, had a tendency to become sweltering, was viewed by many of the listeners as an invitation it would be folly, not piety, to forego. As Whiting recounted, "During a five hours' discourse upon the 'Genesis of the Maya,' or of 'Reminiscence as Related to the Pre-existence of the Soul,' there was, to the unregenerate mind not fully initiated, a certain mundane joy in a brief vacation from these high themes, and it was found that on returning it was possible to recognize the point to which the lecturer had conducted his hearers with no perceptible loss of its deep significance."

The Concord School grew in reputation and ambition for a number of years. James ended up lecturing there and Putnam wandered in and out of at least one session. Blow was also an occasional speaker in the pastoral purviews, but, more importantly, Harris had made her his deputy in St. Louis upon his resettlement in the East. Harris, Snider wrote, "probably proposed to hitch the two horses, Concord and St. Louis, to his philosophic chariot, and to keep them in the race from his Eastern home. This he succeeded in doing for a time. Then he had here able and devoted lieutenants, especially one cleverest woman, who would obey him to the letter."

Although Blow may have obeyed Harris, her relationship with Snider grew increasingly confrontational in the 1880s, and the larger Movement lapsed into a downward spiral. Brokmeyer himself, disappointed by the limited scope of the Hegelian revolution he'd struggle to effect, and by the continued failure of his book to find a publisher, had largely abandoned St. Louis, making cyclical migrations to points farther and farther west.

Ultimately, he left his family altogether to live among the Creek Indians, whom he strove to instruct in speculative thought. Brokmeyer invited Snider to help him found a kindergarten for the Creeks and when Snider went to visit him, he discovered Brokmeyer "explaining the deeper philosophy of deer-stalking in a pow-wow with some Creek Indians." The Creeks named him "Great White Father," and tried to get him to take a bride among the maidens of the tribe. His Hegelian philosophy compelled him to forego this pleasure.

The last ten years of his life (he died in 1906) were spent quietly in St. Louis where he occupied himself by whittling mahogany walking sticks and fancy toothpicks for his friends. On his deathbed, Brokmeyer's son Eugene asked his father what ought to be done with his translation of Hegel.

Brokmeyer made the tragic reply, "Just leave it in the attic for the vermin; I have enjoyed every minute of my life devoted to it, in the hope that I might justify my existence by leaving something to posterity worth while, but apparently there is no demand for anything like that at this time."

AS FOR THE Movement itself, for all of Blow's devotion to Harris and her pride at having been passed the mantle of the St. Louis kingdom, she seems not to have had the administrative gifts or the nervous health necessary to keep the Hegelians unified under the banner of the *Journal*. On coming back to St. Louis after stints in Chicago and Concord, Snider balked at the fact that while he was the teacher "she was the ruler." After having initially seen in Snider an ally, Blow found him increasingly "too heathenish." He had assigned himself the mission of converting her "Calvinist Regeneration" into a "Classical Renaissance." Their competition became ferocious. Snider claimed that Blow's entire involvement with Dante only began when she set up a course to offer the public a lesson in the Divine Comedy unsullied by the "perversion" that Snider brought to his own instruction on the subject.

Abandoned by Brokmeyer, out of favor with Blow, Snider still never surrendered his skepticism about the Concord School, which was really his doubt about the New England spirit as such. He concluded an account of his own experience lecturing there with the observation, "Here I may remark concerning the conversational frequency of Sleepy Hollow in Concord, that this beautiful cemetery seems to be interwoven into the very life and speech of the citizenry. I never knew an American town whose graveyard was such a vital, intimate, even artistic part of its daily existence. Dead Concord in a way appears more alive than living Concord. I suppose that Egypt with its mummied cities must have been somewhat similar, and perhaps China is, with its worship of ancestors. At times there came over me in certain places of Concord, the uncanny feeling with which I wandered through the old Etruscan tombs of Italy—all that is at present left of a great people, of its glory and its civilization. Concord's own folks are now saying, as I have been told, in grim self-criticism, that Sleepy Hollow has become their chief civic asset."

Yet the influence of the St. Louis Movement was not buried at Sleepy Hollow. In 1889, Harris was elected U.S. Commissioner of Education, a post he held for seventeen years. In this capacity, he actually reorganized the entire American public education system in accord with the precepts of Hegel. On the eve of the great depression, Nicholas Butler, President of Columbia University, founder of the *Educational Review*, and one of the preeminent forces shaping American education policy for many years, said of Harris that his work was so well accomplished "as to be already almost forgotten." Although the ascent of Dewey eclipsed Harris, even Dewey began as a Hegelian—as a philosopher on the roster of Harris' *Journal*.

THERE WAS YET one more channel beyond Blow and the Concord School through which Putnam was imbued with the St. Louis Hegelian vision.

One of the most idiosyncratic followers of the St. Louis Movement was the Scottish émigré-scholar Thomas Davidson. After a stint in Boston in the mid-1870s, Davidson became a close friend of James, and even introduced James to his future wife, Alice Howe Gibbons. In a eulogy after Davidson's untimely death in 1903 James called him a "knight-errant of the intellectual-life."

Not long after the closing of the Concord School at the end of the 1880s, Davidson founded his own philosophical retreat a few minutes away from Putnam Camp in Keene Valley. Davidson sought to construct a more formal environment for intellectual exchange at Glenmore (named after Davidson's ancestral Scottish home) than the one Putnam, James, and Bowditch had founded in the woods next door. He oversaw the construction of an actual campus, complete with a refectory and numerous guest buildings. Aspects of the communal space may have been based on Putnam Camp itself, such as the central gathering place, Hilltop Cottage, which was a more elaborate version of the Stoop. In addition to James, Davidson brought in none other than Harris to discuss the curriculum for Glenmore. Harris became so involved that he built a home on the property, and the prospectus for Glenmore also ended up looking very much like the masthead of his *Journal*, though with a Follensby Pond inflection.

Thus, the invasion of the St. Louis Hegelians came to color even the utopian communities of the North Country where Putnam and James felt most free. Of course one could say that because Transcendentalism as a Movement itself had origins in the Adirondacks at Emerson's Philosopher's

Camp, this was in fact a homecoming. Blow's tutelage of Putnam consummated a process of education in American Hegelian concepts that Putnam had begun in informal, outdoorsy fashion years earlier.

One of the Shakespeare courses that Snider taught at the Concord School focused on *Love's Labour's Lost* as the exemplary instance of a cluster of Shakespeare plays in which "flight from civilized life to the woods and to a primitive existence" was followed inevitably by "return of the fugitive to civilization and its institutions." Snider was astute enough to recognize that Concord had actually lived through a version of the "great human comedy of the Shakespearean model." Alcott had taken his flight to Brook Farm, Thoreau to Walden. Emerson intermittently longed to flee to anywhere beyond the reaches of Boston, though he could never quite muster the necessary funds or will to abandon his family.

Snider characterizes this movement as diastolic, away from civilization and back again; but he points to one key aspect of *Love's Labour's Lost* that in fact suggests a more complex movement. In the play, the retirement of the King and three Lords away from the world was specifically "for the purpose of studying philosophy" and transforming the court "into a little Academe, named and patterned after the Athenian home of Plato."

For Putnam, as for Brokmeyer, James, Alcott, Emerson, Davidson, and a host of others, the American wilderness represented a space in which civilization could be perfected—not simply abandoned. The highest arts of culture could thrive in the wilderness. The Americans of Putnam's generation were not trying to get back to primeval nature, as Freud might have at first believed; rather, they were trying to fulfill civilization's potential in the greater freedom a natural existence afforded the mind. Rather than being perceived as an admonition, as the symbolic antithesis of Boston and New York, Putnam's Adirondacks foreshadowed the ultimate cosmic synthesis.

The definition of the wilderness as a place where one could do as one wished without the same moral consequences that exist within civilization would have been seen by James and Putnam as the epitome of false freedom.

CHAPTER 22

———

Struggles of the People

*Travelling as we do it is hard to get hold of the real life and
inner history of the places we see, but if we could get this it
would [sic] outway all the rest in richness and significance.*

Putnam to Molly, summer of 1911

AS SPRING SOFTENED the Viennese air and brought out the seasonal
dresses like hothouse blossoms along the Ringstrasse, Freud withdrew into
a cocoon of deeper, darker enmities and paranoias. Bleuer, he wrote Jung,
was a prudish *"nuisance."* Gross was a "complete nut" and "parasite." Freud
kicked out a Dutch female patient because she had grown unbearable to
him. Brill certainly had his "resistances." Jones' marriage was "utter nonsense." Adler's behavior was "simply puerile." Stekel was a "strange son of
chaos."

It must have been hard just keeping track of all the different occasions
for bilious expostulations among his immediate circle, let alone in the larger
world. But after months of Jones and Ferenczi exerting pressure, the
American Psychoanalytic Association had finally come into being in Baltimore, with Putnam as its president. The flowering of a new shoot of the
movement across the Atlantic made Freud feel more confident about pruning the plant back at home on the Continent. Freud didn't know that
Putnam's acceptance of the leadership role had been predicated on his
personal decision to use all his powers of persuasion to steer the movement
toward the shores of higher philosophy where, he believed, humanity's true
destiny lay in shimmering wait.

———

HAVING SLAVED OVER his paper for three months in constant communication with Blow, Putnam girded himself for what he believed would be
his most important effort on behalf of the psychoanalytic movement to date.
And at this climactic moment of his career, he had to entertain a retinue of
overstimulated, voluble daughters, a melancholy, worrisome son, and a wife
whose skepticism about her husband's professional judgment was matched
by an invincible dedication to the principle of domestic responsibility.

In the compendium of family letters, journal entries, and essays on the
European tour of 1911 that Marian assembled, the motivating purpose of
the entire trip was mentioned exactly once and in passing. At the end of a
long account of the family's sojourn in Italy, Marian wrote: "We passed two
delightful days at Gossensass, a charming village in the Austrian Tyrol,
where we took a long breath after the heat of Venice. We wanted Louisa
and Elizabeth to start on their journey to England refreshed and cool. They
were to leave us at Innsbruck and, with Jamie, were going home, while Jim
and I with the three younger girls stayed on for another month. Jim was
going off for two weeks, first to Zurich, to see Drs. Jung and Freud, and do
some work with them, and then to Weimar to read a paper at a medical
meeting; and I was planning to join Mrs. Eliot in the mountains somewhere
until I should meet him again, later, in Germany." It's as though once they
got over there, Putnam had the happy inspiration of dropping in on the
leading figures of psychoanalysis to lend a hand in their labors before going
on with the real business of escorting his relations around the sights of the
Continent.

ON THE 23RD of June, after a day spent rather incongruously touring
Harvard Yard and the Lampoon, followed by a sleepless night, the family
boarded the "Numidian" for Glasgow. The girls wore matching suits of dark
blue serge with checked collars and cuffs and straw hats adorned with sprays
of bright flowers. Marian inspected the ensemble and pronounced their
appearance "very nice."

The ship was one of the austere "North German Lloyds" on which Freud
had sailed in the opposite direction two years before. Putnam saw didactic
advantages even in the asceticism of their vessel. He commented in a letter
to cousins at home that the absence of luxuries meant their fellow passages

formed a "company of distinct intelligents," questors after culture traveling for enlightenment like themselves, rather than sybarites seeking the indulgence of ennui. Still, the scene on board was hardly dour. Shuffleboard tournaments and races allowed the children to display their prowess at leisure pastimes. Against a forlorn Newfoundland background of cold sea pocked with a few fishing schooners, a lighthouse, and monumental icebergs, Putnams came out on top in every contest "except when Putnam came against Putnam." Late in the voyage, a concert was staged by a male quintet Putnam had joined. In the midst of all his anxieties about Weimar, he found time to compose a comic ditty entitled "From Boston to Glasgow," with a chorus that ran, *"There were school-girls, and teachers, and preachers, Professors and athletes galore; But—my!—what a wild lot of creatures, They showed up when once off from shore."* Marian entered into friendly relations with many of the passengers, and soon the family was engaged in a series of social calls not unlike the daily rounds in Boston. The contrast with Freud's male-on-male-on-male trip in 1909, in which even the interlude of travel was dedicated to the game of psychoanalysis, could not have been more acute.

After docking in Glasgow, the Putnams commenced their grand tour, riding through driving rain in a horse-pulled carriage to the "beautiful ruin" of Dunstaffnage Castle, where the Stone of Scone had once been kept. In Gairloch they tasted scones of a more fluffy variety while enjoying a symphony of pinks: walking a strip of pink beach where they collected pink sunset shells before a dinner of pink salmon and more scones served with strawberries in the roseate glow of the long solstice dusk.

In Edinburgh, the family marveled at the fact that all the moors as far as they could see belonged to one person, "the Duke of something or other." Fourteen-year-old Frances wrote in her journal, finding it "too killing to hear them talking about dukes and kings and everything we have in history." As they toured one sight after the other in an irrepressible entourage, she noted, "Our family are a good deal like the family who went to see a moose that was on show; they were a family of ten children and the father and mother, and when they got there the man who owned the moose opened the gates and said, 'You can come in free for it's just as much of a treat for my moose to see your family as for your family to see my moose.'"

From Scotland, the Putnams went on to tour castles, lakes, and cathedrals around the British Isles before spending ten days in London and then crossing the channel to Dieppe. There, the family wondered at the filth of

Rouen with its "picturesque little streets" running with "sewer gutters"; yet even Marian acknowledged that this did not stop the "extraordinary Frenchwomen from being exceedingly clean." Their inn in Rouen was something out of a storybook, where they could eat outside under vines of roses, geraniums, and clematis, from the bounty of a kitchen in which copper pots and pans hung "like so many mirrors" and a dozen chickens slowly revolved on spits over an open fireplace.

After a brief stay in Paris, the family mobbed the top of a double-decker tour bus to Versailles and then went on to Switzerland, "the most wonderful place," where they rode up a funicular to the top of Mt. Pelerin. At the summit they suddenly heard "violent screams" and watched two boys rush past on bicycles: Armory and William Goddard, two frequent habitués of Putnam Camp. The boys were in high spirits because they were about to embark for New York "and thence straight to the Shanty."

The family stayed five days in Grindelwald in a "rough little chalet" from where they hiked a steep hill to an inn at the foot of the glacier for meals of bread, greasy soup, and leathery meat. On a night when storms made lingering at the inn hazardous, the innkeepers were persuaded to give the family "bread and butter and eggs and chocolate to take home" with which they cooked a supper that "tasted like nectar and ambrosia."

To climb along the Jungfrau, the family roped themselves in a line with Putnam in a full suit at the head, followed by his wife looking like a formidable aunt misplaced from a Wilde drama. Marian stayed behind when the more intrepid members of their party climbed the Wetterhorn. They were caught en route in a hurricane and trapped as huge stones dislodged by the storm began crashing down around them. Molly was struck a glancing blow by one rock, but was not injured. The girls, unfazed, began trying to "bank coast" their way down, but the rainfall made that method too long and slippery. Frances rolled down over her hand which worried their "corking guide." After they made it back, Jamie "was loud in his praises of the girls' pluck and powers of climbing, their Adirondack training having stood them in good stead."

The final stop of the tour with all the family in tow was Venice, where they stayed only a week because Putnam feared the heat along with whispers of cholera. The family resided at Casa Frollo and rode enough gondolas for the girls to sigh at the "dark handsome" gondoliers crooning, "O sole mio" and "Santa Lucia." They shopped for leather pillows and portfolios and in one shop to which they'd been sent by an acquaintance they succumbed completely to the American passion. "To see and possibly get one or two things was our intention when we started out," wrote Frances, "to buy, buy, buy was more a necessity than an intention when we got upstairs." At each new object the Putnams purchased their hosts "hopped up and down and giggled violently."

Replete at last, they rode back over the Alps in a long journey in an open landau pulled by four horses. At Paretenkirchen, Putnam finally detached himself from his family and turned in the direction of Zurich. He was on his way to the Jungs.

LONG BEFORE THEIR physical separation, Putnam had been consumed by thoughts of the impending Congress. While escorting his loved ones up each famous high place and into every hallowed, stingily lit gallery, while sharing their variable meals and fighting for better rooms in their various *pensiones*, his soul was elsewhere. In the throes of violent anxiety, there was only one person to whom he felt he could entrust his unmediated thoughts. It was not his wife, not Edward Emerson, not even Susan Blow. In his hour of greatest need, Putnam turned to his 18-year-old daughter, Molly.

At one-thirty in the morning one night in France, before they turned their train toward the Alps, Putnam wrote Molly an astonishing letter made all the more poignant by the fact she was right next door in an adjoining suite the whole time. In his ardor, Putnam sounds like Lambert Strether in *The Ambassadors*, recovering a sense of youth and beauty's glories on a long delayed return visit to the French capital. But unlike Lambert, who regained primarily a sense of how much he had lost, Putnam seemed to feel infused by the nacreous Parisian atmosphere with a conviction of how full the golden vessel remained, beckoning his lips to the draught. He saw himself still absolutely in the thick of the fray.

Putnam told his daughter that he was buzzing with too much cafe au Pre Catelain, with things that she had said to him, with parts of a letter by a cousin, and by his own "tendency to think over my paper forever and ever." Molly had remarked that "London and Paris make Boston seem tiny," an observation Putnam agreed with, adding that the revelation of this dispro-portion concerned more than physical size. Putnam's entire letter carries the tone of a man breaking out of some cramped, dark dwelling into the rush of world-historical radiance. "Real history," he wrote, "whether of individuals or nations, means the series of efforts through which men have, half blindly, tried to find freedom and express love." But he tacked on a romantic spirit that always guided his philosophy. He instructed Molly to read Victor Hugo's *Les Misérables* and study Hugo's accounts of the "'gamins' of Paris, homeless boys who used to eat what they could get and sleep under the arches of the bridge, but who nevertheless had a real spirit of freedom and courage." Putnam's Hegel was always half Hugo, and the exuberant empathy he felt for the revolutionary spirit makes his philosophical abstractions more touching than pedantic. Putnam staunchly defended the French Revolution despite its excesses, for the way it did bring about a "Government of the people," and fostered "many good institutions of reform." He took Cousin Fannie Morse to task for her distaste for "the particular efforts of particular men" to further the essential course of history in the direction of freedom and love. As for himself, Putnam wrote, "I feel strongly that one can't stay on both sides of the fence, and for my part I throw in my lot with the radicals and reformers." In the peroration of the letter he wrote, "I shall try, above all, to see that I do not let personal comfort and prejudice stand in the way of *the people's* progress. . . . The most important movements in history have been and will be the (unpicturesque) *people's movements* and the history of the King-fellars is of little significance except as seen against the background of the history of *the people* and as bearing on the people's life. *Institutions* and the evidences of the *struggles of the people*; those are what we really want to see—whether at Versailles or Chartres. Now I must go to bed."

Given its tone, one might picture the letter being scrawled by a feverish, radical student to his heartthrob—a letter of the young Camille Desmoulins to an actress, perhaps. How remarkable that in fact it represents the "midnight reflections" of a nervous, self-torturing, ascetic 65-year-old blueblood Boston doctor and family man to his adolescent daughter.

But if Putnam's tone is unexpected for an elderly patriarch, we must bear in mind that the sentiments, above all his revolutionary faith in the common man, form the underskeleton to both his metaphysics and his great gripe with Freud. The idealism had been hard won in years of selfless service to the poor. Putnam's direct participation in Boston's philanthropic reform movement complemented decades of work in the city's chief public hospital and at the clinic in his own home where he never begrudged a

patient treatment out of financial considerations. Even though his speculative thought had a tendency to dissolve in mist-shrouded vagaries, his work
was always grounded in the most basic tenet of the physician's task: the
imperative to heal those in pain. Thus, in the best American fashion, he
could not accept that psychoanalysis—and indeed the highest form of analytic accomplishment, sublimation—would fail to become *the* people's
psychological heritage. Beneath Putnam's plea for philosophy we must see
the picture he carried around with him, the way others might carry "French
postcards," of ragged street urchins beneath the bridges of Paris where today
only Bateaux-Mouches ply their trade.

REGARDLESS OF WHAT would become of his paper, the trip was clearly
proving a success in terms of mollifying Marian. After the couple went their
separate ways, she wrote him a long, cheery letter from a hotel in the
Dolomites where she had rendezvoused with the children. "Dearest Jim—
I suppose you are all established in Zurich by this time (8:30 P.M.). I hope
you had a good journey and found your trunk at the other end." Despite
the beauty of their location, a traveling companion thought "the charges
high and the food poor and dislikes all the servants." As for herself, "I should
not think of minding it—The expense is about $2.50 a day a piece. . . . Please
be very good and send me a daily bulletin, just a card would satisfy me—
How is Dr. Jung? I hope you got your paper safely to Zurich—If Mrs. Eliot
can be induced to stay here we shall be very well and happy here for ten
days I am sure." Either Putnam was shielding her, or she was unwilling to
engage with the angst he was experiencing.

The postcards that Putnam dutifully wrote Marian once he got to Zurich
no longer made a pretense of concealing the mounting drumbeat of his
nervous excitement. "Very interesting morning with Jung and Mrs. Jung
who helped me nicely with the paper," he wrote in one. After lunch he'd
gone over to the Burghölzli where Bleuler himself ("very nice, a real gentleman, as the Swiss all tend to be") showed him around. A spark of personal
vanity crept in, indicating, perhaps, an effort to displace attention from his
paper. "Then I was so rash as to buy a suit of clothes; good stuff I think but
bright blue so that I shall look frightfully young."

As Freud approached Zurich, the Jungs seem to have made a point of
deflating Putnam's professional hopes. "This afternoon I am going to

afternoon tea at Dr. J's and shall then have a chance to talk alone with Freud," he wrote Marian. "From all accounts I think it will prove impossible for me to become a thoroughly successful practitioner in these new lines without a kind and amount of special training which it now seems impossible for me to get." Perhaps this gloomy assessment was meant to reassure Marian as to the venial nature of his involvement with Freud. He jotted one last optimistic note on the front of the card: "My new suit, which is warmer than the old one, feels very comfortable."

Freud analyzed Putnam for about six hours over the course of his stay in Switzerland, a duration that was acceptable for the brief, intense analyses of the era. Short though it might have been, the encounter proved sufficient to deliver a shock that destabilized Putnam's self-image at its core. He later wrote of the experience, "I remember that Dr. Freud pointed out to me, in the very first of our few conferences in Zurich, that I was a murderer! . . . I was to be healthier-minded from then on, and happier, and better able to stop being a murderer."

Freud had also begun to pry open the Pandora's box of Putnam's feelings for Molly. Perhaps the kindred currents of Freud's own relationship with Anna gave him special insight into Putnam's feelings. Something in Freud's technique enabled Putnam to confess to an array of convoluted emotions with respect to his daughter that he'd never spoken of to anyone before. Freud swiftly intuited that Putnam's aggression against himself was a blade that could cut both ways: today's masochist is tomorrow's killer. In the immediate wake of the sessions, Putnam was reeling.

Even if there was a slight vindictive twist to Freud's labeling Putnam a killer given his occasional resentment of Putnam's reputation as an exemplar of ethical saintliness, it's doubtful that Freud would have sought to disorient him before the Congress. No one would benefit from the exposure of weakness in the movement's American pillar. But when Freud left Zurich for a few days before the opening of the event, he abandoned his patient at a point of terrible vulnerability.

FREUD DOESN'T SEEM to have explained to his colleagues why he needed to part from them. Between analyzing Putnam and inaugurating the third international conference of analysts, he stopped back in Vienna to celebrate his own silver wedding anniversary on September 14th. It was not an event he shared with a wide circle of friends and loved ones the way Putnam had done. The Weimar Congress had initially been scheduled to overlap with his anniversary. Even to his intimate friend, Karl Abraham, Freud wouldn't reveal the reason he needed the date changed: "For private family reasons September 16th is a very inconvenient, practically impossible, date, though I am loathe [*sic*] to arrange the date of the congress according to my personal requirements," he wrote evasively.

On the 14th, Freud met up with his immediate family in the Tyrol hamlet of Klobenstein. A photograph taken at the event shows Oliver, Ernest, Anna, Sigmund and Martha, Mathilde, Minna Bernays, Martin, and Sophie gathered in stiff dark suits and long light dresses around a neat white table with an ornate floral centerpiece. The family members all gaze morosely into the camera. Freud himself injects an extra furrow into his signature scowl. It's hard to imagine the family party snapping into festive gaiety once the picture had been shot. The mood in the image is sober and dutiful, less silver than leaden.

Martha seemed to take little more pride in her husband's career than Marian did at Putnam's work on Freud's behalf. She thought it frankly absurd to use psychoanalysis on children, and long after Freud's death told the French analyst, Rene Laforgue, "I should think psychoanalysis is a form of pornography!"

CHAPTER 23

The Dark Wood of Introspection

*Now I must just run and take a look at Goethe's house before
the session opens.*

Putnam to Marian in the last hour before he
delivered his Weimar address

THE NIGHT BEFORE the Congress began, Putnam stayed up till after one
in the morning to work on his paper, "making needed changes and considerable improvements," as he wrote to Marian. He knew that he couldn't
keep insisting on the imperative of philosophy without saying what philosophy, as he understood it, was, but his desperate last-second emendations
to the essay indicate irksome doubts as to whether what he'd written actually answered the call. As the hour of destiny arrived, Putnam resorted to
the only self-calming strategy he possessed: he tried to convince himself
that the people he was going to be addressing were awfully smart and nice.
The members of the Psychoanalytic Association, he wrote his wife just
before delivering his talk, were "intelligent, interesting men," in addition
to which there were "about a dozen intelligent women guests, including
Mrs. Jung." As the Congress opened, Putnam repeated to Freud how impressed he was by the high caliber of his followers. "They have learned to
tolerate a piece of reality," Freud tersely remarked.

The German, Austrian, Swiss, Swedish, and Dutch doctors in attendance
at Weimar had been primed to anticipate Putnam's paper as the *pièce de
résistance* of the Congress. Everyone knew of the invaluable contributions
Putnam was making to the Movement in the crucial proving ground of
America. Many members already understood that the New World would
become the central propagation point for analysis as a whole. The guests

were eager to hear what Putnam's vision of the higher purpose of psychoanalysis actually consisted in.

Putnam had been sleeping poorly for weeks; the psychoanalytic sessions
had left him wobbly and scared, and he was cut off from the support system of his family. It may have only made things worse that back in Cazenovia
Susan Blow was glued to her mailbox, expecting news of something close
to a miracle. She had convinced him—he had convinced her—they had
convinced each other—that at Weimar a mass conversion could take place
in which the entire fold of psychoanalysts would rise to their feet from the
rude Teutonic benches, raise their arms to the fourteenth-century rafters,
and cry, "St. Louis Hegelianism is my Salvation! Hegel is Thesis. Freud is
Antithesis. Putnam is Synthesis."

He stood stiff and gaunt before the large audience in his dapper blue
Swiss suit, with his white beard neatly barbered and his spectacles polished.
He tried to feel his vigor. He glanced down at the mound of pages before
him and up at the audience again, greeting his judges with a crisp, anxious,
hopeful smile. And then, speaking in German, he began.

PUTNAM'S PAPER, LATER published under the sprightly English title,
"A Plea for the Study of Philosophic Methods in Preparation for Psychoanalytic Work," began on a note the audience must have found promising,
with an extended paean to Freud. Putnam disclaimed any intent to criticize Freud, insisting that his purpose was only "the suggestion of a supplement." Putnam had enjoyed an unmitigatedly positive experience in regard
to the analytic process itself. In typical conscientious fashion, he went so
far as to acknowledge that even in cases where he thought he'd found an
exception to Freud's rules, "a still deeper probing of the patient's consciousness and buried memories have shown me that I was wrong." After review-
ing in broad strokes the main achievements of psychoanalysis to date,
Putnam noted that far beyond the clinic, analysts had demonstrated the
ways that "great pieces of imaginative and creative literature of the world"
as well as the operation of "wit and humor" along with "other modes of
native expression" were all "permeated by the same tendencies" characteristic of hysteria. The symbolisms of creative expression, "like the symbolisms of language, of dreams and of life itself" were all, as Freud had
declared, "to a considerable extent a sex symbolism."

Then, subtly, he crafted a bridge to the real argument of his paper. Not surprisingly, the transition point concerned the American fixation on personal energy. In broaching the subject, Putnam put Freud on his own side: "I believe, also, that one may admit, with Freud, that the principle of the 'conservation of energy' can be applied as profitably with reference to mental phenomena as it has been with reference to physical phenomena." Thus, he explained, "An experience [in the mind] is a fact to be reckoned with just as much as is a quantity of heat." Freud had shown that the energy associated with thoughts, if it seems to disappear at one point, will pop up elsewhere, "like Proteus under the grasp of Hercules, in the great fable."

However, the principle of the conservation of energy whereby "no energy is lost" only told part of the story. In fact, Putnam contended, the theory of the conservation of energy was actually so incomplete that it was "dangerous as a working principle in applied psychology." Because, as the Freudian unconscious demonstrated, there was more going on the mind than we are aware of, how was it possible to categorize mental dynamics along the traditional lines of an energy storehouse and dispenser? Putnam took a further leap: "The main service," he wrote "of the psychoanalytic investigations which have been made thus far, under the impulse of Freud's genius, has been that of forcing us to recognize the repressed devils that lurk within us." It is obvious, however, that we should never have felt these tendencies as "devils" and repressed them unless we had a standard of good. We can't be possessed by demons unless we also harbor angels within us, he argued.

With this thesis, Putnam turned the theory of the conservation of energy on its head. In so doing, he brought the notion of mental energy in line with that of James, the Hegelians, and, indeed, self-help gurus down to our own time. Culminating in a rather lovely analogy, he averred that the principle of the conservation of energy did not bestow the right to assume "that as no energy is ever lost, so no energy is ever gained, and that we live in a world of determinism, where the same old forces, coming no one knows from where, are shuffled to and fro, like the bits of glass in a kaleidoscope." Without fresh influxes of energy Putnam insisted, the ability to create anything new would be forestalled, while evolutionary adaptation would become a "simple moulding of man on the world of nature, as wax is moulded on a stamp." This couldn't be the case. "No one really accepts such a world as this." The true student of physics and chemistry know that ideas like the conservation of energy were "but modes of speech" and that underneath them lay "real, self-active energy"—that is, the natural resource discovered by the St. Louis Hegelians.

As psychologists, Putnam pleaded, it was wrong to countenance the "complacent habit of neglecting the study of the 'real,' 'needful'" inner truths. Putnam crystallized the various strands of American energy theory then circulating into a single Hegelian proposition. Whatever approach might be tolerable when studying inanimate matter, "when the object to be studied is a human being, thrilling with hopes and fears, dimly conscious of a destiny, dimly aware of the fact that in so far as he is intelligent, in so far as he possesses the gift of intuition and a will, in so far, in short, as he is 'real,' he is a participant in the primal energy of the universe and must be studied as such." Not only do people have to be analyzed in their bodies and minds, they have to be psychoanalyzed body, mind, *and soul*—which is to say, as creatures coextensive with the cosmos. "The mind contains a real, permanently abiding energy, of which the life of the universe itself is made." Just because this other, profound facet of the mind was unpicturable didn't detract from its reality.

How exactly this other, deeper facet, what Putnam calls *psyche genera-trix*, was to be investigated remained fuzzy. Putnam never got much beyond saying that psychoanalysts must come to feel "wholly sympathetic toward all, even the crudest, subconscious leanings of the patient in the direction of the truths that we hold to be important and philosophically sound." In this spirit of sympathy, the physician was to somehow help the patient "unravel that portion of his unconscious yearnings" that pointed toward "his spiritual genesis."

Citing Blow's touchstone literary work, Putnam likened the process of psychoanalysis to Dante's journey under Virgil's leadership. It is not a good idea, Putnam maintained, to go into the "'dark wood' of introspection, unless there is a good prospect of continuing it until the logical end of it is within sight. The physician, at least, should have a clear vision of the best outcome." The physician must keep his sights on Paradise itself.

Near the conclusion of his paper, Putnam invoked as justification for his plea the "biblical sentiment that 'the people who do not see visions shall perish from the face of the earth.'" How we actually nurture a society in which people see visions—ones that are creative rather than destructive—

was, of course, another problem and one with regard to which Putnam remained disappointingly abstract: "If I am right in my belief that every man has a dim intuition that there is something in him which makes him akin to the creative energy of the universe, and that his sense of obligation is one element in that something, and if this intuition can be deepened by a process of self-analysis, then, surely, we can do him a service if we help him to make such an analysis."

Putnam could not communicate the means to implement the policy he felt to be so urgent. The end of his talk was a garble of Hegelianism, mythology, and still more opaque abstractions. "In each act the mind goes out, as it were, from itself, only to return to itself and rediscover itself. The dim realizing of this outgoing and returning finds its symbolic expression in the constant phenomenon of recurrence in the sun myths, and of endeavor and failure and re-endeavor in many myths of gods and heroes . . . we who practice psychoanalysis learn well to know what symbolism means. We should, then, more than any others, succeed in realizing that these primal fundamentals, the inevitable constituents of every mental act, must have symbols which are bound to be deeper than any others." He pleads, he tangles, he peters out.

THE APPLAUSE AND rustle of expectation that had greeted Putnam's appearance gave way to a hush, to a frozen quiet—and then, more slowly still, to the stirrings of restlessness, the tugging of beards, a peppering of coughs, the shifting of rear ends. His audience was nonplussed. Stumped.

In the immediate aftermath of his address, Putnam would neither have had the means of knowing that things had gone horribly wrong, nor the self-delusion necessary to believe that things had gone well. In the note he penned to Marian just after having resigned the lectern, he tried hard to put a brave face on matters: "Well the paper is read and done for and when one thinks that *of course* most of the folks (including Freud) have no head for philosophy, I think it went quite well. I had talked it over at some length beforehand with Jung and others." Then a trace of anguish seeped through. "I am glad on the whole to have done it, though when I think of the thousands of hours that I have spent on it . . . not so much on the matter, which I ought to have studied more, but on the words, I feel at moments rather sore." Incorrigible optimist that he was, he couldn't help finding a positive result of the experience. "I learned a good deal of German by the way, and have got on well in talking and *possibly* the agonies of thinking just what to say have borne some fruit. I hope so for I could have read a dozen books in the same period. Some of the audience were much interested."

Pfister—himself invested in finding a way to fuse psychoanalysis with religious consciousness and hence a natural ally of Putnam's—later recorded his own impressions of the scene during Putnam's talk. With perhaps a hint of irony, he wrote, "The audience, under the spell of a profound spiritual achievement, was glowing with the noblest sentiments, but the copious rush of thoughts left behind a certain bewilderment." Jones took Putnam to task for the fact that his "burning plea" of philosophy acknowledged only the Hegelian strain of philosophical truth. Freud's assessment was more blunt. He told Jones, "Putnam's philosophy is like a decorative centerpiece, everyone admires it but no one touches it."

Jung was the one person who later expressed admiration for Putnam's talk. Given the amount of input he seems to have had in the final shaping of the essay this is not surprising. As tensions escalated with Freud, Jung seized on Putnam's charge that the realm of ultimate meaning was missing from psychoanalysis. Putnam's insistence on the urgent importance of metaphysics, if not Putnam's metaphysics themselves, became part of Jung's arsenal as he constructed his own, more deadly, indictment of Freud.

IN PUTNAM'S ABSENCE, his family had been having a jolly time. The children danced with Tyrolese peasants in Garmisch, and everyone laughed when a tall, distinguished-looking German youth clicked his heels before Marian, making a deep bow while asking for permission to dance with one of the Eliot daughters. Marian, thinking the invitation was directed at her, rose to her feet, extending her hand to the young man. So ebullient was her mood that when the family reunited in Munich, she even generously urged Putnam to go back and take another week in Weimar. But given the paper's reception he was not in the mood. He told her that Jung would be off on military duty and it was not worthwhile.

And so the family resumed its arduous sightseeing itinerary, escaping the endless storms pounding Munich by spending hours at the "German Museum." The children marveled at the experience of going down a fake coal mine "with very real-looking men working here and there"; they saw "electricity and radium, which were terribly interesting."

In the midst of his private mourning for the future of his philosophy, Putnam remembered his wife's birthday, which everyone else had forgotten. To celebrate, he took the family to a concert at Cologne Cathedral. On the eve of their return to Boston, the family all sat together on the church's hard benches, while outside the rain trickled down the ancient gargoyles and stained glass, listening to a splendid recital of the old Putnam Camp favorite, Wagner's *Tannhäuser*.

CHAPTER 24

The Sediment of Experiences

*I hope that although it will not be the last time that I write, it
will be the last time that I trouble you with my private affairs.
Just now, however, when I am started on a Selbst-analyse, I
want as much help as I can have, to enable me to do justice to
my patients and to get the satisfaction out of life which everyone ought to get, without needless and hampering sense of
apprehension and anxiety.*

Putnam to Freud, September 30, 1911

THE PUTNAM FAMILY'S ability to isolate themselves from the larger political vectors of the time was not an option available to Freud. Just four
days before the Weimar Congress opened, on Sunday the 17th of September, a mass gathering of workers marched on City Hall and through the
main districts of Vienna to protest the rise in meat prices. The authorities
mustered a huge phalanx of police, along with infantry soldiers and cavalry
divisions, to cordon off the area where speeches were being delivered,
punctuated by cries for revolution. Hitler, who was probably among the
audience watching the protest, referred to the event in *Mein Kampf* as a
"gigantic human dragon slowly winding by." Some protesters went on a
rampage, smashing windows, storefronts, and gaslights. The Imperial forces,
composed—in a move that the predominantly ethnically German march-
ers found particularly affronting—of Hungarians and Bosnians, were ordered to advance. The workers threw rocks and set up barricades. Enraged
matrons hurled kitchenware out the windows at the militias. After first
confronting the rioters with bayonets and sabers, the police then drew their
firearms. Several workers died. Scores were severely injured.

If Putnam had witnessed this scene, it might have challenged his romantic adulation of the "struggles of the people." Would he at last, like Freud, have recoiled in bitter disgust from the bloodthirsty passions of the mob?

FOLLOWING WEIMAR, FREUD allowed the quarrel with Adler and his supporters to erupt into the public forum. It's extraordinary, given the degree of theoretical division and personal animosity existing between the two men, that the relationship had rattled on as long as it had.

Although his views on psychology were more nuanced than Freud's disciples would concede after Adler's departure (Jones liked to cite a remark by Freud that in Adler's system the ego was like a clown who claimed credit for every act in the circus), Adler's system was concentrated on the theory of an ego-based will to power with roots in his political vision of the struggle against capitalism. With this came an admirable devotion to education and principles of democratic entitlement. "My psychology belongs to everyone," he remarked on more than one occasion. Putnam was sympathetic to Adler, precisely on account of this liberal political strand in his thinking. But ultimately, in a long, self-questioning, even tormented essay he wrote during the First World War, Putnam repudiated Adler's work. His rejection stemmed simultaneously from what he characterized as the easier route it opened for patients to shirk the most painful, sexual revelations about the self and from the failure of Adler's "Individual Psychology" to take metaphysical account of humanity's innate drive toward perfection. "I believe that I, myself, appreciate, for instance, as thoroughly as any psychologist in the land, that feelings and motives and tendencies such as one may classify as 'normal' or 'the best' are mingled in some measure with others of a very different sort," Putnam wrote. "There is, I think, no real 'normal' short of absolute perfection." But that didn't change the fact that every man remained at once "drawn toward a better or the absolute best goal" while also "by virtue of his evolutional history" being attracted to the infantile. The urge to realize more primitive goals might be what Adler called, the "masculine protest" against feminine aspects of mental life, but it was yet a false feeling or false 'protest,'" one that Putnam viewed as a "'resistance' to be recognized and removed."

Freud was more blunt in his response to Adler's defection. In August 1911 he wrote to Jones of Adler's break: "It is the revolt of an abnormal individual driven mad by ambition, his influence upon others depending on his strong terrorism and sadismus." But by October the strain of the dissension was beginning to tell. "Rather tired after battle and victory," he wrote Jung on the 12th. "I hereby inform you that yesterday I forced the whole Adler gang (six of them) to resign from the society. I was harsh but I don't think unfair." Amidst health complaints of various magnitudes—colds, toothaches, and the interminable American colitis—Freud's disgust with his enemies and despair at the prospect of having to shoulder the essential labors not being performed by others grew livid. As was typically the case in these moods, the ghosts began to close in around him.

In the midst of his autumn squabbles he took time to write a long letter to a female member of the Viennese circle, Else Voigtlander, in which he began to outline what amounts to a psychology of ghosts. Voigtlander had criticized Freud for paying insufficient attention to constitutional disposition in character relative to "accidental influences" on character formation. Freud responded that he was in agreement with her except for one "minor modification." In psychoanalysis, one discovered that one was "dealing not with *one* disposition but with an infinite number of dispositions which are developed and fixed by accidental fate," he wrote to her. "Constitution after all is nothing but the sediment of experiences from a long line of ancestors." Less than two weeks after writing Voigtlander, Freud made the surprising admission to Jung, "If there is such a thing as a phylogenetic memory in the individual, which unfortunately will soon be undeniable, this is also the source of the *uncanny* aspect of the doppelganger." For Putnam and Jung, the potential for phylogenetic memory would point toward archetypes of an ideal community—a sort of numinous circle. For Freud it referred to a chain of metempsychotic ancestral spirits through which individual consciousness was constructed, totem-style.

By the start of 1912, Freud had begun work on his first systematic exploration of the religious impulse from a psychoanalytic perspective. The tone of *Totem and Taboo* oscillates between what one might call a colonialist perspective on the indigenous peoples under study and a fascination suggesting an urge to incorporate the primeval powers of the natives into the cosmopolitan self.

Though Freud claimed to be working out the psycho-anthropological premise that one could learn about present-day neuroses by studying the actions of tribal peoples stuck at an earlier stage of cultural development, in fact the intricate network of parallels and divergences he charted took him in other, necromantic directions. This was especially the case in his analysis of sorcery, where he focused on telepathy (the paranormal practice Freud flirted with his whole life) and the idea of the "omnipotence of thought."

Freud posited that "the primary obsessive actions" of all neurotics were "really altogether of a magic nature. If not magic they are at least anti-magic and are destined to ward off the expectation of evil with which the neurosis is wont to begin." The secret behind the idea of evil, Freud proposed, was death itself. Schopenhauer had stated that in the problem of death lay the origins of every philosophy. Long before his speculations on the death drive, Freud incorporated the problem of death into his theories in two ways. Parts of the neurotic's mind were seen as dead by virtue of a dedication to endless repetition of the past; analysis itself could also be said to contradict conventional notions of mortality by postulating that one's psychological constitution is simply an accretion of residue from psychologies of the deceased.

Freud struggled long and with little satisfaction on *Totem and Taboo*. He complained to all his correspondents on the slow, painful progress of the book. In his New Year's greeting to Karl Abraham, Freud juxtaposed the problem of the book directly with the question of transmission. Recognition would come only to the next generation, despite the pleasure they gained at knowing they'd had the first insights. "My work on the psychology of religion is proceeding very slowly, and I would prefer to drop it altogether," he added. To Jones he described the book as "an unborn, I hope not a stillborn infant."

In mid November 1911, Freud characterized the book to Putnam as the fruit of his meditations on Putnam's own Weimar address; that paper had impressed Freud "deeply—although in a very strange way." Thus, while Freud's work may have delved into areas Jung was exploring, Putnam also helped inspire Freud's arduous trek into the wilderness of theology. Indeed it's likely that Jung's massive charisma, complex intellect, and intimidating persona had hitherto warded off Freud's urge to make a foray into the religious realm. Putnam was a manageable foil. It wasn't then so much that Putnam influenced Freud's ideas about theology by transmitting his own beliefs to Vienna, but rather, as was so often the case, that Putnam embodied a position that needled Freud, inspiring him to articulate his own response, and leaving Freud feeling sufficiently unthreatened that he could do so with poise and panache. In this instance, the fact that a man as rational and intellectually open-minded as Putnam could still evince a religious need was part of what stimulated Freud to "prove" that the analytic perspective encompassed the metaphysical one, not the other way around. Freud intuited that, with Putnam, went the United States.

But if Putnam's talk inspired Freud to attempt some definitive ultra-materialist response, the deeper Freud went into the subject, the more he found himself in a quagmire. In trying to sniff out religion at its source, he entered the realm of archaic majesty, the sphere of ghosts where he himself, without always acknowledging the fact, felt most at home.

In the midst of composing *Totem and Taboo*, Freud made the surprising declaration to Ferenczi that none of the deeper, more ancient psychic remnants *ought* to be overcome. Aligning himself with the "primitives" he was writing about, Freud warned Ferenczi against a "fear of complexes" and said, "Man should not want to eradicate his complexes but rather live in harmony with them; they are the legitimate directors of his behavior in the world."

Where Blow and Putnam saw humanity's mission as a constant struggle to transcend and sublimate the demonic complexes, Freud claimed that we must learn to cohabitate with our ghosts, rather than trying to stifle them. Indeed, if we learn to cooperate with them, our dark spirits, born of the netherworld, are our best guides. At one point in *Totem and Taboo*, Freud said that a "spirit" is nothing other than the representation of a remembered person or thing when it is absent from conscious perception.

THE QUESTION OF how to respond to Weimar became a preoccupation with Putnam even before the family left Europe. His attribution of blame did not linger long on the audience and their inadequate philosophical training. Nor would it have occurred to him to fault the contents of the philosophy he'd been flogging. Whatever the fate of his paper, Putnam felt the pulse of Blowian conviction still coursing through him. With the obvious objects of potential resentment cleared of culpability, only one suspect remained. Hardly more than a week after Weimar, Putnam fixed the fault for failure squarely on himself.

Sitting up late in Paris, where just a month earlier he'd composed his delirious rhapsody to his daughter, Putnam scrawled another long, manic epistle, this one to Freud. And in this letter, rather than reflecting on the *people's struggles*, Putnam described the psychic struggles within himself. The barricades, the Government, and above all the struggle to "find freedom and show love" were all internal now.

Though Putnam had begun his self-analysis immediately after Freud left Putnam Camp, the experience of analysis with Freud in Zurich convinced him that he needed to resume the process from scratch. Even when embedded in the great ganglia of his family as they migrated between German galleries and cathedrals and then back to the City of Love, he hadn't let a day go by without dutifully recording and dissecting every dream he had. Having decided that his own complexes were responsible for the defeat at Weimar, a re-energized self-analysis was the only hope he had.

He described to Freud one of the dreams that he'd had the night before leaving Weimar. In its central scene, Putnam rode a dog-cart up an increasingly steep hill; the horse eventually pulled off the "safe road" to try to take a short cut over the grass. Putnam tried to stop the horse by pulling back on the reins but the horse plodded steadily forward, taking no notice of Putnam's efforts.

The horse, Putnam proposed, stood for his sexual drive, "which I would wish to regulate but I cannot check." His choice of symbols hid a reference to Freud's final lecture at Clark, in which Freud related the folk tale of peasants feeding a horse fewer and fewer oats as a way of saving money until the horse simply starved to death. Freud used the story to allegorize the problem of providing insufficient direct nourishment to the sexual drive.

Concurrently, Putnam's solo ride on the increasingly steep hill represented his "wish to be independent," constantly defeated by an overreliance on his wife and brother. "Possibly this feeling about my wife and my brother (dependence, yet 'protest,' and sometimes irritation—really, at myself) may refer both to father and/mother or homosexual vs. heterosexual." There's a sad circumscription even to Putnam's grand internal dramas. At the very moment when he confesses to Freud that the driving rule of his brother and wife inspires a sense of "protest" he still feels obligated to add that this protest is really aimed at himself.

Considering that in the hundreds of pages of *The Interpretation of Dreams*, Freud consistently avoided the question of his own sexual drive as it found or didn't find release in his life, the fact that in Putnam's first dream after Freud jump-started his self-analysis he led the horse straight to water is remarkable. But he traveled still further along the confessional route. He informed Freud that in order to understand what he'd written so far it was important for Freud to know that "my sexual relations with my wife have been rather infrequent for many years, of late years exceedingly infrequent, and that I have 'dreaded' them—partly because I believed that many of my friends did not continue such relations at my age, but mainly because although the first effect was one of great relief from a very unpleasant state of tension (erythrism, Angst, etc.) yet for a number of days afterwards I always felt abeschlagen (exhausted), sleepy, depressed etc."

With this confession, Putnam flaked off the last bits of decorous molding from the façade of his perfect family. If his wife begrudged him his enthusiasm for Freud, he begrudged her sexual intimacy. Yet, notwithstanding the real anguish in Putnam's tone, reading this revelation as the final indictment of an unsatisfying marriage would be an instance of twenty-first-century hindsight. If Putnam dreaded intercourse in part because he thought that many of his contemporaries had seen it as their moral obligation to give up sex, the pressure to restrain himself may just be the obverse face of the pressure now exerted to constantly rekindle the libido. How many sexagenarians today worry that most of their friends *are* having sex with their wives and girlfriends all the time?

And still, Putnam could not reconcile himself Central European–style to a permanent deficit of fulfillment. As he stated at the outset of his letter, he wanted to get his self-analysis right both for his patients and for himself. "At the time of Weimar," he wrote Freud, "I had had no such relations for a good many months, but the 'tension' was I think coming on partly as a result of the fact that I was expecting to meet my wife after a two weeks absence, partly as a 'reaction' from the intellectual excitement of the congress. . . . I was not aware of any sexual excitement yet it may have been present 'in the unconscious.'" And then Putnam issued a kind of cry, "It is certainly true that the sexual Trieb [drive] *has* always been like a horse that I could not satisfactorily drive or restrain, though I have never been, in any sense, a 'pervert,' and never experienced the Abgeschlagenheit (exhaution) after sexual intercourse until a good many years after being first married." In the final passage of his letter, Putnam flagellated himself into a paroxysm of self-denigration. He described a youthful "Phantasie" in which he longed for a cozy married life with his own home in which he would see himself "sitting before an open fire in an otherwise unlighted room, with wife and young children . . . playing about and receiving caresses" and asked for Freud's interpretation of the scene. Putnam's own view was that, with its idealization of personal memories, the picture symbolized the fact that "affection, readiness to be caressed, narcissism, 'protest,' [in the Adlerian sense] autoeroticism, homosexuality, heterosexuality—all played large parts in my early life, as also sense of Minder-wertigkeit (too small sexual organs, etc.) and desire for recognition as a means of escape from Minderwertigkeit." Nor was this all. Along with being a needy, narcissistic, bisexual, angry masturbator with a tiny penis, Putnam added that he was a cravenly show-off. He tried to compensate for "assumed internal lacks by external aids—things that I could *buy*, influential friends, etc." He has always "been fond of *trifling* means" of self-adornment. But, at the same time, he was a cheapskate. He liked looking in shop windows, "though without any real intention of buying, as I am 'sparsam' [frugal], even in es-sentials, though occasionally, as contrast or through 'protest,' extravagant." He liked "courageous people" but was himself "timid." His crowning self-criticism doesn't exactly come as a surprise. Along with everything else, Putnam noted that he was not at harmony with himself.

Putnam's willingness to denude himself before Freud stems from his faith that the obligation to bare one's mind before the analyst was the same as the need to bare one's body before a physician. He apologized for writ-ing so long a letter but pleaded, "You can help me very much by even a few words, and I *must* get myself *free* and able to use my powers." That was the essential justification of his appeal and the link to Weimar. At the end of his day, he was not begging for help in order to increase his own measure of personal happiness. He was soliciting Freud because he yearned for an access of potency with which to carry out his larger world mission. He was looking to better himself so as to be a more effective comrade in the *struggles of the people.*

Freud responded with the most generous, empathetic letter he ever sent Putnam. "You certainly describe yourself as a very bad character," he began. "But a far worse man would be uncovered were I to lay myself bare in an analysis as you have done. And you overlook the fact that your sincerity itself indicates greatness of soul." Referring to a question Putnam had asked earlier about symptoms exhibited by his daughter, Louisa, Freud assured Putnam that nine chances out of ten hysteria was the correct diagnosis (Freud was wrong and Louisa suffered from epilepsy her whole life).

Freud confirmed Putnam's own interpretation of his dream, adding just that the "safe road" described in the dream from which the horse departs also referred to his former "safe" therapeutic style relative to the psycho-analytic method "of which you seem very much afraid." Foreshadowing the letter he would write Ferenczi in November where he warned about "fear of complexes," Freud told Putnam that he was "much too frightened" by his fantasies. These fantasies couldn't be transformed into reality. "As soon as you give up that fear, you will learn more about your fantasies, find them interesting, and experience relief."

This brings the role of analysis closer to that of Aristotelian *katharsis* and Freud and Breuer had indeed nicknamed their technique the "cathar-tic method" at the very genesis of analysis. Aristotle's vision of the working of catharsis is often viewed as homeopathic (we watch on the stage an ex-cess of pity and fear-inspiring scenes that work to cancel our own). The Greek philosopher expresses the purpose of catharsis as intellectual plea-sure through mimesis. We take an educational pleasure in actively imitat-ing (and witnessing the imitation) of objects and beings that in reality would cause us pain. Applying this model to the analytic situation one can pic-ture the scene as one in which memories are "imitated" more than they are reconjured (as when Freud wrote Fliess that everything depended on the "reproduction of scenes").

But did Freud really believe, as he wrote Putnam, that such memory fantasies "cannot possibly be transformed into reality"? Perhaps the aes-thetic pleasure Freud took in exercising authorial control over the memo-ries of patients and colleagues was partially a factor of insecurity regarding the actual dormancy of his own past. He did not trust the solidity of the ground on which he walked over the dead. His own self-analysis, at least as recorded in *The Interpretation of Dreams*, is less the brutally honest exercise in self-exposure that his followers like Jones claimed it was, than a mimesis of a self-analysis.

If Putnam was haunted by the ethical rigor and self-denial of his Cal-vinist forebears, Vienna was haunted by the impending madness of the future. Kraus called the city an experimental laboratory for the end of the world. Freud's association with a series of fatal scenes—the near death of Emma Eckstein, the death of Fleischl-Marxow by cocaine, the suicides of Paula Silburstein and Victor Tausk—position him before the bubbling test tubes as, to cite Kraus' vision of Freud, Goethe's sorcerer with his apprentices. 1911 was the year in which Austria committed what has been called the greatest mistake of its history: the invasion of Serbia, initiating a conflict that helped to usher in both world wars.

Perhaps the reason Freud could pooh-pooh the problem of Putnam's fantasy materializing in the real world was just because it was so unbelievably mild. Next to the acid drooling from the leprous green dragon maw of the Viennese fantastic, Putnam's little daydream home scene reads like a description of a painting by Greuze, a hearth-lit orgy of cooey, rosy cherubs lapped in familial caresses. Outside of poking out an eye on mother's knitting needles, what danger conceivably lurks in this picture? The deepest, darkest, self-damning fantasy of which Putnam is capable is as harrowing as the death scene in Dickens of which Oscar Wilde famously quipped, "One must have a heart of stone to be able to read the death of Little Nell without laughing."

Indeed, Freud was put in so generous a mood by Putnam's nursery nightmares that, after cheerily diagnosing Putnam as "suffering from a too early and too strongly repressed sadism expressed in over-goodness and self-torture," and pointing out that were Putnam to strip away his "fantasy of a home life" he would find the "normal fantasies of rich sexual fulfillment," Freud reminded him of their intimate conversation before Weimar. "It is the influence of these fantasies which causes the sense of physical dissatisfaction with one's wife," Freud acknowledged. "These are symptoms of aging which I am beginning to experience myself, as I told you in Zurich."

Freud didn't feel he was giving up an essential secret in disclosing the desexualized nature of his relationship with his wife. As the core of his own fantasy life lay elsewhere, the fantasy others might have of his sex life with his wife was one he could cede without great psychic cost.

It was also at Zurich that Freud told Emma Jung his marriage "had long been 'amortized' [and] now there was nothing more to do—except die." As Jung represented the future of the movement in Europe, Putnam was now the face of its American fate.

CHAPTER 25

Atavistic Nonsense

*It matters not how strait the gate, How charged with punish-
ments the scroll; I am the master of my fate; I am the captain
of my soul.*
 Lines quoted from "Invictus," by William Ernest Henley,
 by Putnam in a letter to Fanny Bowditch Katz, spring 1912

DESPITE THE MORTIFICATION it involved, Putnam sensed for some
time that he was making progress in his renewed self-analysis. The pace of
his correspondence with Freud was accordingly heated. From on board
the R.M.S. *Oceanic* on the way home, Putnam reported that he was "carefully reading the last edition of the *Traumdeutung* and hope to finish it tomorrow. *I read it in a new light.*" A few weeks later, in the midst of an
unusually stormy New England autumn, he proudly informed Freud of his
successful interpretation of a "'baby-diapers' dream of comfortably lying
in excretions (warm water and mud turning into a bed—a long dream evi-
dently taking place during waking)."

So confident was Putnam of the pure-minded higher purpose of his
analytic effort that he felt no compunction about telling Freud of a revenge
dream he had regarding Freud himself. This was a degree of openness that
Freud himself might have dissuaded his intimates from practicing. But if
Putnam was told that a successful analysis demanded absolute candor, then,
to the best of his ability he would offer nothing less. He wrote Freud in
late October that he had recognized an *Uebertragung* [transference] toward himself, "and a 'revenge' in which I took you through a church (my
philosophic ideas) and then made you (indignantly) confess that you had

symptoms of depression (as I, *formerly*, and slightly of late) which psycho-analysis could not remove."

Notwithstanding the naive form in which Putnam was able to concep-tualize vengeance taking, the dream expresses what he might not have completely confessed to himself: he was beginning to feel genuinely frus-trated with Freud's philosophical recalcitrance. It thus came as both a sat-isfaction and a source of apprehension to Putnam when Freud in his next letter made mention of the fact that he had begun his effort to understand religion from the psychoanalytic point of view. Putnam begged of Freud that instead of the books he'd informed Putnam he was reading to prepare for his essay, Freud would, instead, "read certain ones *which I will send you.*" In the list he proceeded to tender to Freud, he described as "the best book of all" *Hegel's Logic* by Dr. W. T. Harris.

In the burst of energy following his captivation by self-analysis, between the late fall and spring, Putnam wrote five more essays that were published in prestigious American medical journals. One of these papers was devoted to a description of a "staircase dream" taken from his self-analysis. The central scene could have come straight from an obscene Mack Sennett film. Putnam described how a man who, 24 hours before the dream, had "per-formed a coitus, and was feeling excited during the following day," dreamed about seeing a man "in whom he thought he recognized himself, climbing up a steep ladder" against an indistinct background. "On the very top of this ladder there was a strange object, something like a vessel, hollow, dark, with a thick round brim—perhaps a pail made of papier mâché—which was inverted over the top of the ladder, though its outlines disappeared in the dark, indistinct background. It seemed to the dreamer that the climb-ing man at last pushed his head against the pail, and that his head seemed to fit well in the cavity of the bucket." The man then discovered that he was holding a pail and brush, whereupon he began painting the ladder with "a yellow liquid."

Putnam's gratification at the idea that Freud had entered his "church" was quickly dissipated by Freud's approach to the house of worship. On Christmas day, as Putnam and his wife made rhyming place-cards for their guests, and scenes from *Heidi* were rehearsed along with a "procession of the months," in which Louisa played the month of November dressed as Diana the huntress, Freud mused with cavalier irony about his own absorption in the study of religion. It wasn't going quickly, he told Putnam, but all he needed was a long life to make it work. "On the whole," Freud wrote Putnam, "doing this [taking up the study of religion] makes me feel like an elderly gentleman who contracts a second marriage late in life. *L'Amour coute cher aux vieillards* [Love is expensive for old men]." Comparing the exploration of religion to the taking of a mistress was the most offensive metaphor Freud could have chosen in the eyes of someone who saw the study of philosophical religion as the great exception to the dominance of sexual instincts in mental life.

Putnam didn't write Freud back for more than two months.

DAY AFTER DAY, alone in his dim, austere study after long nights of hard dreams, Putnam grappled with his self-analysis like Jacob with the angel, struggling to thrash above waves of self-loathing, self-discovery, and self-torture like a drowning man. He would sacrifice the last remaining tatter of privacy if doing so would liberate him to push up through the surface of his being and reach in the star-filled heavens. At times, Putnam felt certain he was getting closer; at times he knew he was drifting deep back into opaque depths.

And always, in the midst of everything, there was the family, surrounding him like a ring of dogcarts. On top of Louisa's confirmed diagnosis of epilepsy, Frances, the most cheerful, socially adept of the children had begun showing signs of frailty. Such worries took time away from the imperative of self-examination.

Putnam turned to Blow at once in his distress over his children's illnesses, and the difference between her response to the bitter news of Louisa's malady and Freud's cool conviction that the problem would ultimately fall within the purviews of his own theories must have struck Putnam. "I couldn't half tell you yesterday what I felt," Blow wrote to him after he'd visited her in New York in late January 1912. "You have been so good to all nervous sufferers that it seems too hard you should have to have children you love so tenderly suffer. And then you know so much more what it means that your pain must be greater. I hope you won't feel I am entering into regions of your personal life I have no right to invade for I can't care for you as much as I do and feel all the gratitude I do without wanting you to know how deeply I sympathize." She talked about the need for religion as well as philosophy in times of trouble and added that philosophy itself was "nothing more than the vindication of the Conscious Reason of truths which religion presents through concrete symbols to the heart and imagination." Whereas all religions attempted to deal with pain, only Christianity had "boldly based itself on the fact that God suffers." The "deepest conviction" of her soul was Cordelier's vision of the cross as "the ground plan of the universe."

For Blow, God's suffering was a prerequisite to human growth. For Freud, although God (or the superego projection thereof) might suffer, that suffering was primarily an earnest of God's rage. The pain and fury signified, not an opportunity for human progress, but a sign that humanity was damned.

Freud was anyway less interested in the notion of God the One and Only suffering as with that of *gods* suffering—and causing suffering. In the classical hierarchy, Freud himself, in company with his band of disciples, was not so different from the fickle ringleader of the Grecian divines. For many years Freud wore a Greek-Roman intaglio on a ring inscribed with the head of Jupiter. Hanns Sachs reported that Freud "never tired of examining every detail by look and touch" of the "delicately carved bearded head." For all his fascination with Moses, Freud's own behavior was more akin to that of the lightning-commander and moody chief of a flighty pantheon than to the self-denying leader of the Jewish exodus.

As SPRING AT last reached Boston, Putnam began to despair at the limited results of his self-analysis. He wrote a letter to Ferenczi beseeching him for information about the "standing and intelligence" of one Dr. Jeno Kollaritis, a Hungarian neurologist who'd written a cogent book on nervous disease challenging Freud as to whether most patients could stand the "brutal shock" of a full analysis. He asserted that everyone knew of patients who became "victims of the method," departing analysis "without being healed and with increased nervousness." Putnam admitted that he himself had witnessed the "bad effects" that could come from "an imperfect treatment by psychoanalysis." Might the whole effort simply be too harrowing?

Ferenczi's response was a nasty piece of work, full of personal attacks on both Kollaritis and his mentor, Professor Jendrassik. Neither of them,

Ferenczi claimed, had any real knowledge of psychoanalytic literature, nor had they ever even "done *analysis*." Kollaritis was so naive as to believe everything his patients told him to be true. Jendrassik was "struggling with a sexual complex" and hence was always doing his best "to ferret out immorality in analysis." Ferenczi added that Jendrassik had recently married the mistress of an aristocrat "in spite of the fact that he thereby lost all his social respectability." Kollaritis suffered from "a limited intellect" and was tubercular. If such a thing were possible he was "still vainer than Jendrassik, and without a grain of independence in his make-up."

Though this gleeful savaging may have seemed to Ferenczi just the thing to boost Putnam's morale, the tactic backfired. Just days before he'd written Ferenczi, Putnam had defended Freud from scurrilous attacks by Dr. Moses Allen Starr, a colleague at the New York Academy of Medicine. Putnam could not countenance Ferenczi and Jones' eagerness to reciprocate with gutter attacks on Freud's detractors. Instead, Putnam became increasingly concerned about the potential harm that the character flaws of the analysts could inflict on patients. "So far as I can see, a psychoanalyst ought, theoretically, to have reached the millennium of perfection before he begins his work," he wrote to Freud in June 1912. The problem Putnam identified continues to be a basis for criticizing analysis to this day: How does the imperfect analyst keep from projecting his or her own neuroses onto the patient's vulnerable mind? For Putnam, this structural problem was only further proof of the need to supplement analysis with aspirations of a higher order. Because neither analysts nor analysands would ever be able to rid themselves of every neurosis, at a certain point both patient and doctor needed to turn their gazes outward, toward the stars.

In the most polite, deferential manner possible, Putnam was saying to Freud: Hasn't the time come to acknowledge that your own personal flaws may shade your conception of psychoanalysis?

THE EXPERIENCE OF Fanny Bowditch Katz with Jung was another factor behind Putnam's newly critical stance.

Putnam had dandled Fanny on his lap as a baby and enjoyed countless hours in her company in the mountains and at social gatherings in Boston where Henry Bowditch, a prominent physiologist, insisted on Fanny's regular attendance, despite—or perhaps because of—her natural tendency to bashful introversion. Bowditch genuinely wanted to help his daughter come out of her shell, even when he wasn't quite sure of the best way to proceed. The pressures he placed on Fanny did not make him an especially dour patriarch. Putnam wrote of his friend of thirty-plus years that whenever his "hearty laugh had an excuse for making itself heard, as kite-flyer, mountain-climber, inventor, photographer, furniture-maker and repairer— in all these capacities and many more, he showed a humor, kindliness and charm which made him a delightful and most genial friend." Bowditch was also a close friend of Richard Hodgson's, an avid researcher into paranormal phenomena, and a cofounder of the American Society for Psychical Research. In her youth, Fanny's home played host to numerous mediums and séances; she grew up in an atmosphere steeped in occult references and expectations.

Bowditch was everything to Fanny, who developed into an ungainly, stout young woman who, in her late thirties, had still never enjoyed a romantic courtship. Rather than socializing with her peers, Fanny served as her father's nurse throughout the last years of his life. On his death, in the winter of 1911, she plunged into a depression so acute that her mother, Selma Bowditch (the ringleader in the German flag-making party for Freud's visit to Putnam Camp), appealed to Putnam out of fear that Fanny would take her life. After a consultation with Fanny, Putnam recommended that she go into analysis with Jung. She left for Switzerland almost immediately.

In choosing Jung above Freud as the doctor for the daughter of one of his oldest friends, Putnam was partly motivated by his experience at Weimar. Jung had been the only member of Freud's inner circle to accept Putnam's argument that psychoanalysis needed to encompass a spiritual-philosophical perspective. Though Jung had leveled criticisms at Putnam's paper, he'd also lent a hand in its composition and Putnam could not but feel that they were on the same side of this most vital debate. Given Fanny's lifelong confinement within the metaphysical hub of Boston, it probably seemed to Putnam that Jung would offer a more sympathetic strain of analysis than Freud could provide. Putnam's suggestion made him feel doubly responsible for Fanny. Not only had he recommended that she go into analysis, he'd even pushed her to a specific practitioner.

When Fanny went off to Europe Putnam stayed in close contact with her, striving to serve as her father figure back by the hearth. He reminded her that whatever was happening with Jung in Europe, her heart was still fixed in the familiar world of cousinly compassion that defined the topography of Boston. But by the end of 1912, Fanny's analysis seemed to have taken a dark turn, and she was writing Putnam letters that sounded disoriented and starved for approbation. Jung had begun supplementing his own analysis of Fanny with that of a partner, the former nurse Maria Moltzer. Between them, the pair swiftly managed to make Fanny feel stripped bare in ways that further eroded her fragile stability. Still, Putnam defended the "bitter medicines" of Dr. Jung as a necessary purgative to enable Fanny to begin her life afresh. Painful confrontation with the truth was, after all, a New England tonic of unimpeachable pedigree, and she'd been in grave danger when she departed Boston.

"This is a cold Sunday morning," Putnam wrote her in February 1913, "with a blue sky and bright sun, and we are all scratching round after breakfast into our various employments, . . . This is just a bit of a picture of New England life, the interior of an American family, as it were, to make you feel as if you were at home. Louisa, who is indulged nowadays in being lazy, has just come down and is conspicuously engaged in trying to do without her dress behind, with her own hands—an acrobatic feat of no mean difficulty, I should suppose. The rest of the family is busied in cleaning off the table, except poor Molly, who is upstairs with an acute cold, without which no self-respecting New England family can long get on. 'Uncle Charley' has just been in and has given her bitter medicines, of course. And now dear Fanny, for yourself. I can well imagine, even without the reminder of your letters . . . that you have been through fire and water with Dr. Jung. But think of the alternative. Here you were, putting on a good face, but feeling poorly, and although gaining a little and losing a little, never getting far ahead. *The conditions had to be changed.* If a clearer insight into human nature—your own and the world's—could be counted on to give you a new start, it was right you should have it. You may have difficulties enough of mind and body and external problems to overcome after you get home, but you will meet them in a new spirit and with new hopes. That at least is my belief. *If I had the chance I would put myself in your place.*"

Putnam's depiction of that winter morning at 106 Marlborough Street appears also to be invoking the "fantasy" of married home life he'd described to Freud in the letter on his self-analysis. Was Putnam idealizing the home scene for Fanny in order to strengthen her sense of connection, or, rather, was he beginning to realize that the life he'd achieved was not so very different from the one he'd daydreamed about as a young man? If the latter were the case, he must have experienced an access of self-confidence. It had been in relation to this very fantasy, after all, that Freud had diagnosed Putnam's "strongly repressed sadism expressed in over-goodness and self-torture." Putnam might have seen Freud's impugnment of idealism challenged by this proof in his own life that a certain register of ideals could be actually realized. Perhaps self-analysis had taught Putnam to appreciate more fully what he'd already succeeded in bringing to fruition.

Though Putnam wanted to believe that Jung was in harmony with his and Fanny's New England spiritual values ("I consider him as religious without realizing it," he wrote Fanny at one point. "At any rate, he is a 'constructive idealist' to some extent."), from the outset he also recognized Fanny's vulnerability to the cannibalistic tendencies of the Zurichers. Two months before sending her the epistolary portrait of the family at home, he'd admonished her that psychoanalysis was making her feel "far too much of a fly on sticking paper." But though he clearly fretted about Jung's domineering ways with patients, Putnam had no inkling of the direction Fanny's Swiss adventure was actually taking her.

Jung and a colleague were in the process of establishing a new form of psychoanalytic society in Zurich. A core mission of Jung's splinter group was the encouragement of dialogue on the release of primal drives, a premise dramatically at odds with Freud's program. Given Fanny's virgin status, it's not hard to imagine the effects of this atmosphere. Over the next several years, Jung indulged a mounting fascination with alchemy, Wagnerian mysticism, and a host of pagan experiments that culminated in the impressive fantasy of his own Mithraic rebirth as the "Aryan Christ." In the midst of this, Jung began degrading Fanny in ever more humiliating ways. He called her weak, cowardly, dull, and hopeless. What was a poor, awkward, virginal girl from the pent-up brick blocks of Boston to make of this Alpine polytheistic orgiastic megalomania?

Eventually, Fanny underwent a conversion to Jung's symbolic universe, filling journals with alarming streams of consciousness and mystical paintings of her own fantasies based on a host of Teutonic gods. Analyzing one set of drawings she mused that they contained "the very archaic and the very high" and that she was required to learn how to enact them in the real world.

One of the ironies of Fanny's situation was that in its early stages the mystical faith that Jung was reveling in might have seemed to her just a bolder fulfillment of her father's decorous, indeed delicate, Boston variety, philosophical pantheism. What chance did Putnam's admonition to her that "you cannot and should not change the dear Fanny Bowditch whom we all love," stand against Jung's declaration that her dreams were prophetic of her potential for achieving cosmic rapture?

IN JULY, FED up with his followers and their endless struggles in Vienna and Zurich, Freud left the frenetic Austrian capital with his wife for the stately walks of Karlsbad.

Although Freud strove to be reassuring to Jung, he'd been terrified by Jung's reaction to an event earlier that summer that Jung insisted on calling the "Kreuzlingen gesture" (the name of the town not far from Zurich where Freud had visited their colleague, Binswanger). According to Jung, Freud had not only not bothered to stop over in Zurich to visit, but had even omitted to tell him that he'd be in the area. Jung insisted that this had been an intentional slight, motivated by Freud's disapproval of Jung's new libido theory, notwithstanding Freud's own assertions that he *had* written Jung and that the visit had been both last-minute and brief, undertaken for a special purpose. In truth Freud, perhaps to his credit, knowing that Binswanger was a vulnerable rival of Jung's, did not share the news that Binswanger had just undergone surgery for a malignant tumor.

Jung continued lashing out. "Now I can only say: I understand the Kreuzlingen gesture," he wrote in response to Freud's efforts to explain his side of the story. "Whether your policy is the right one will become apparent from the success or failure of my future work."

On learning of the contretemps, Jones leapt to Freud's defense with a move straight out of *Totem and Taboo*. The prince's crown was to be splintered and the shards parsed out among his most intimate courtiers.

Whereas on one hand the formation of "The Committee" suggests a dark, cultic act of secretive power mongering, on the other it's so childish and zany as to be almost endearing. Claiming to be bemused by the "complete puzzle" of Jung's behavior, Jones managed to call into question the loyalty of Putnam and Stekel as well by reminding Freud of how he'd once tried to defend Stekel to Putnam (even when Stekel's behavior was indefensible), prompting Putnam to respond (according to Jones): "It makes me a little uncomfortable to find any virtues lacking in any prominent psycho-analyst. I feel as if we ought to be something superhuman, to justify our doctrines." This quote—ostensibly meant to point out that the real problem with Jung was not his inevitable imperfections but his failure to identify sufficiently with the movement—could only feed Freud's apprehensions that *Putnam's* idealism would ultimately doom his devotion to analysis. The absurd standards to which he wished to hold analysts ensured that he would eventually become fatally disillusioned with the movement's real life members. In the one extant letter Putnam wrote Jones on his discomfort with Stekel, no such sentiment as Jones ascribes to Putnam can be found. Rather than criticizing Stekel for not being a superman, Putnam objected to the relish Stekel took in exposing the dark, weak sides of others, "if we must, *as we must*, publish the facts as they are, we are also under obligation to do this reverently and not to roll the unpleasant morsels (unpleasant at least to others) under the tongue as Stekel does." This is a very different argument from the one Jones cited to Freud at a moment when Freud's fears of mutiny were riled up.

"I get a little pessimistic at times when I look around at the men who must lead for the next thirty years," Jones continued, in a wistful, corrosive vein. "Jung abdicates from his throne, Stekel is obviously impossible, even Rank may be hindered by material considerations unless something can be done for him . . . and so on. Perhaps I am wrong to talk like this, but I can't help wishing that things at the top, gathered around you, were more satisfactory." And then, cautiously, Jones introduced his plan.

Noting that he'd already had a talk with Ferenczi and Rank in Vienna in which the two expressed dissatisfaction "with the whole Zurich attitude," Jones, paradoxically echoing Putnam, proposed that the only hope was for all of them to carry their self analyses "to the farthest possible limit, thus purging *personal* reactions away so far as can be done." In Vienna Ferenczi had pointed out how desirable it would be for a small group of men to be comprehensively analyzed by Freud "so that they could represent the pure theory unadulterated by personal complexes, and thus build an unofficial inner circle in the Verein and serve as centres where others (beginners) could come and learn the work." Freud was now to be formally invested with infallible authority as the only doctor capable of performing a scrupulous analysis and thus ensuring the dissemination of "pure theory."

Jones was forthright about the roots of the scheme: "The whole idea of such a group had of course its prehistory in my mind: stories of Charlemagne's paladins from boyhood, and many secret societies from literature," he wrote in his biography of Freud. Fellow Committee member, Hanns Sachs, observed that this "practical" plan had "the spice of a schoolboys' secret society."

Freud seized on the plan as salvational. At last he'd been offered a solution to the interminable problem of transmission. "What took hold of my imagination immediately is your idea of a secret council composed of the best and most trustworthy among our men to take care of the further development of psychoanalysis and defend the cause against personalities and accidents when I am no more," he answered Jones by return post. Freud was so excited that he felt the need to claim priority on the plan. "You say it was Ferenczi who expressed this idea, yet it may be mine own shaped in better times, when I hoped Jung would collect such as a circle around himself." He mused, "I dare say it would make living and dying easier for me if I knew of such an association existing to watch over my creation. I know there is a boyish perhaps a romantic element too in this conception, but perhaps it could be adopted to meet the necessities of reality." He remarked that the committee would have to be kept *strictly secret.*

Freud's hopes of parsing out his kingdom before his death to those who loved him best suggests a still more poignant allusion to King Lear than that of his plan to carve up the kingdom with Jung two years earlier at Nuremberg. In the spring of 1912, shortly before Jones' suggestion, Freud had written an essay exploring the symbolic links between Portia's three caskets in *The Merchant of Venice* and Lear's premature division of his kingdom. Freud's interpretation of the two plays centers around the idea that in each case an encounter with fatal necessity is transformed through the operations of wish fulfillment into a game with echoes of the Judgment of Paris. Proposing that the selection facing suitors in *The Merchant of Venice* is really a choice among three women, Freud developed a haunting allegory whereby the selection being made was actually between the three phrases of woman a man encounters in life: mother, lover, and the Goddess of Death. Ultimately, this choice is also an illusion because "the silent Goddess of Death will always take him in her arms." On its surface *King Lear* imparts the "wise lessons that one should not give up one's possessions and rights during one's lifetime, and that one must guard against accepting flattery at its face value," but the deep inner truth of the fable is that we must learn to love our mortality. The "doomed man" Lear is "not willing to renounce the love of women; he insists on hearing how much he is loved." At the climax of the play, "Lear carries Cordelia's dead body on the stage. Cordelia is death. If we reverse the situation it becomes intelligible and familiar to us. She is the Death-goddess who, like Valkryie in German mythology, carries away the dead hero from the battlefield. Eternal wisdom, clothed in the primeval myth, bids the old man renounce love, choose death and make friends with the necessity of dying."

THE COMMITTEE SERVED as a benign, funhouse mirror version of Freud's primal band of brothers in *Totem and Taboo*. In Freud's essay, the brothers distributed the father's body among them in order to incorporate his strength. To nourish and bind together the Committee, Father Freud took it upon himself to distribute antique Greek intaglios (icons of his spiritual body) among the five pre-war participants. Each tribe member had his intaglio mounted on a gold ring, the way Freud had already fixed his Jupiter head.

Given Freud's obsession with the idea of revenants, another moment in *Totem and Taboo* invoked by the passing out of the rings is that in which Freud describes those left behind after a loved one's death "handing over some of their omnipotence to the spirits," sacrificing some of their freedom in the process. "These cultural products would constitute a first acknowledgement of *Anake* (Necessity) which opposes human narcissism," Freud wrote. "Primitive man would thus be submitted to the supremacy of death with the same gesture with which he seemed to be denying it."

One final element may have underlain Freud's ebullience at the idea of the Committee: despair over his failure to have effected a marriage between the Hellenic and Semitic strands of his cultural heritage. Anti-Semitism in Vienna was increasingly flagrant as the ethnic antagonisms that climaxed in the First World War gathered force. "My intention of amalgamating Jews and *goyim* in the service of psychoanalysis seems now to have gone awry," Freud sighed to Ferenczi. In words that could have been applied to the larger situation in Vienna, he concluded, "they are separating like oil and water." The sequence envisioned by the poet Grillparzer was already unfolding: "From humanity via nationality to bestiality."

Ferenczi went into a kind of hysterical jig on learning of the formation of the Committee, recalling his posturing at the Nuremberg Congress two years earlier. Just as on that occasion he hadn't bothered to temper his indictment of the worthless Viennese, this time around he crowed that the Swiss were "all a bunch of anti-Semites." Indeed, he marveled, "it has never been so clear to me as now what a psychic advantage there is in having been born a Jew and having remained protected in childhood from this atavistic nonsense." His anti-Christian revelation just kept mushrooming. "Even *Putnam* can easily relapse; you must always keep an eye on *Jones* and cut off his line of retreat."

Freud seems to have been a bit taken aback by the scope of what Ferenczi was prepared to purge. In his response, he made no reference to Ferenczi's admonitions and even commented that Jung (on his way to America once again) had finally written him something "that made it possible for me to reply." However, there was no way to retreat from the course he'd set. As long as he could keep himself from being implicated in the "conditions and pledges" of the Committee, Freud was not altogether displeased that his "Paladins" had drawn their blades.

ON LEARNING THAT Jung was to lecture in Fordham in December 1912, Putnam dropped everything to travel to New York and try to find out firsthand what was going on with Fanny, as well as to do what he could to smooth over the widening division between Jung and Freud.

In addition to delivering nine talks to a large gathering of medical professionals at Fordham, Jung gave a two-hour seminar every day for the entire fourteen days he was in New York, in the course of which he laid out the theory of the libido that Freud had begged Jung to clarify for him before leaving Europe. Essentially, Jung argued that Freud was wrong to confine the definition of the libido to the realm of sex. As humanity's most fundamental source of primal energy, libido encompassed far more than the biological drives.

There were clear affinities between Jung's new concept of the libido and elements of Putnam's theories, such as the *psyche generatrix*. Only in his fascination with pagan mythology did Jung diverge from Putnam, and he continued to be cautious about citing those forces outside the circumference of his immediate circle in Zurich.

Though Jung was in New York more than a fortnight, and Putnam made repeated attempts to see him, including attending at least one lecture, Jung barely found time to exchange a moment's talk with him. When he did so, he dismissed the notion that there were any problems with Fanny's analysis and reported that all was proceeding just as it should.

In many ways, Jung was simply monstrous. Yet, his insights about individuals and cultures were often charismatic and occasionally brilliant. Near the end of his 1912 visit to America, Jung was interviewed by *The New York Times*, and the article indicated how far psychoanalysis had come in the New World in the three years since Freud's visit: "Together these two men stand at the head of a school of thought which is considered by many students of the subject to give the most radical explanation of the human mind, and the most fundamental, since the beginning of its study," wrote the interviewer. Where Jung focused on the idea that "if a man can understand his hidden motives and impulses, he comes into a new power," Freud had made discoveries that rendered American psychology obsolete by showing that "a mental effect might well have a mental cause in combination with a physical rather than just the latter." Of course the truth was that Putnam and his colleagues had been working with variants of the notion for years before Freud's visit.

"When I see so much refinement and sentiment as I see in America, I look always for an equal amount of brutality," Jung told the interviewer in a vein somewhere between Oscar Wilde and Barbara Kruger. Jung blamed American brutality on American prudery. Giving this notion a more idiosyncratic, Nietzschean stamp than Freud would have done, Jung suggested that America was about to discover itself, and that once the country accepted its own brutality that brutality would prove a good thing. "It will be transformed into great emotions which shall give impetus to your National development far beyond what you now hope for."

As for Libido, Jung declared, "I would say that the Libido of the American man is focused almost entirely upon his business, so that as a husband he is glad to have no responsibilities. He gives the complete direction of his family life over to his wife. This is what you call giving independence to the American woman. It is what I call the laziness of the American man. That is why he is so kind and polite in his home, and why he can fight so hard in his business. His real life is where his fight is. The lazy part of his life is where his family is." On the subject of marriage, Jung was at his most strident: "You believe that American marriages are the happiest in the world. I say they are the most tragic. . . . I find that men and women are giving their vital energy to everything except to the relation between themselves. In that relation all is confusion."

If Putnam heard similar comments in the lecture he attended, he would probably have been unmoved, for all the force of Jung's insights. Even when the businessmen he saw in his clinic contradicted the principles of breadth and egalitarianism he struggled to uphold in his life, Putnam neither accepted that the American male capitalist animal was the harbinger of the future, nor believed that his own model of the gentleman intellectual was a thing of the past. "He seems to me a strong but egoistic man (if I may say this in complete confidence)," Putnam wrote in unusually blunt language to Jones following the brief conversation he did eke out of Jung after one lecture, "and to be under the necessity of accentuating any peculiarity of his own position for his own personal satisfaction." Nonetheless, Putnam added, "I cannot think that any serious breach would be occasioned by this present movement on his part." Even if Jung were mistakenly deemphasizing sexuality, doing so would still "go far (although possibly in an unfortunate way, in some respects) toward gaining adherents for the psychoanalytic method." Perhaps thinking of his own quarrel with Freud, he concluded, "whatever ideas are really the most sound will *in the end*, far away, come most strongly to the front."

But though he reassured Fanny about her analysis after speaking with Jung as Jung had wished, he did not scruple to add that "it is a fault in D. Jung (*entre nous*) that he is too self assertive, and I suspect that he is lacking in some needful kinds of imagination and that he is, indeed, a strong but vain person, who might and does do much good but might also tend to crush a patient." He beseeched her to recall their shared Emersonian faith. "Life is or should be an affair of each person, each one of us, getting in touch with the elemental forces of the universe (which is throughout a *personal* universe) and feeling his own dignity and power at their full measure."

WHILE JUNG ALTERNATELY flattered and flabbergasted the Americans, setting aflutter the hearts of untold numbers of bored New York females in the process, Freud decamped to his beloved Rome. Addressing Anna from the Hotel Eden as "my future traveling companion," Freud wrote, "The weather was sunny, the situation splendid." "Rome was certainly the best choice for me." To Martha he wrote that he enjoyed Rome more than ever. "My plan for old age is made: not Cottage [a suburb of Vienna], but Rome." Indeed, he informed her, he'd never before "lived so idly, giving in to every wish and whim." As his crowning indulgence after an evening of light theater, he'd become inspired to search for a gardenia, the eventual acquisition of which put him in "the best of moods."

Every day, in "somewhat melancholy solitude," he would set off on long walks. Often, he made his way up the Palatine hill and meandered through the endless, labyrinthine ruins of the palaces that had belonged to Augustus and Nero and the temples where they made offerings to forestall the fate to which the site now bears testimony. He wound through the orange trees and fountains of the four-hundred-year-old Farnese Gardens, and stepped down into the Cryptoporticus. This gloomy, half-submerged tunnel constructed by Nero to connect outlying buildings on the Palatine and the Domus Aurea was probably a more important influence on Freud's archaeological model of the mind than was the sublime Forum with which his topography of the psyche is usually associated.

Day after day, Freud walked over shattered bricks, through the faint, skeletal geometries of gargantuan structures, to the edge of prospects revealing columns without buildings, the overgrown, grassy oval of the Circus Maximus and the gaping jaw of the Coliseum, in which all the gladiators who were to fall had long ago breathed their last to the roars of the bloodthirsty horde. He walked and thought and paused to rest while scavenger birds croaked overhead and the principle of timelessness, like Roman sunlight, at once scorching and muted, seeped into his veins.

Freud had come to Rome to console himself for the crown prince's rebellion. The cure administered by history's relics proved far more efficacious for that disease than the Karlsbad waters had been for the illness of his digestive system. "After all kinds of relapses," he wrote Binswanger, he was now healing. With respect to Jung, Freud declared himself "willing to take any step leading to an outward reconciliation, but inwardly nothing will change any more."

Almost every day, also, he wandered up from the ruins of the axis of the ancient Roman capital to "pay a visit to Moses in St. Pietro in Vincoli, on whom I may perhaps write a few words."

To follow Freud's route today uphill to the neighborhood above the Forum on which St. Pietro in Vincoli is perched, one must follow a perilous narrow road, rubbed by speeding cars peeling around hairpin bends to an ugly, slanted, cobble-front piazza where tour buses endlessly idle, awaiting the return or fresh disgorging of primal tourist mobs.

All day long, the niche encaging Michelangelo's statue is surrounded by a crowd holding up cameras, endlessly firing their flashes over the marble. Moses turns away, like a celebrity avoiding the paparazzi's relentless, raping gaze. The flashes never stop; the marble never ceases to be washed by burns of white light. Indeed, what the statue really looks like is an object on an altar with flames dancing before it. It's as though, in St. Pietro in Vincoli, the image of Moses has itself become the golden calf.

Freud's essay interpreted Michelangelo's figure as a different kind of hero from that of Exodus, one who, at the final instant, sublimated his rage at his people's slavish response to independence. Freud envisioned Michelangelo's Moses clutching the tablets at a fulcrum of absolute tension. The statue's gaze evinced wrath and understanding in equal measure: this was his people, whom he'd sacrificed himself to save. Moses could not relinquish his dream of their higher purpose. If Freud climbed up the Tridente to Moses now, he might judge Moses mistaken in not having smashed the second set of tablets and abandoning the Israelites. Today, Freud would confront a defeated leader, himself buried and lost in the blind clamor of the idolatrous mob.

CHAPTER 26

Déjà Vu

For sheer obsequiousness nobody dares to pluck the prophet
by the beard and inquire for once what you say to a patient
with a tendency to analyse the analyst instead of himself. You
would certainly ask him: "Who's got the neurosis?"

Jung to Freud, December 18, 1912

FOR ALL OF Putnam's optimism about the benefits that would accrue to him as a philosophical missionary through his self-analysis, it was nine months before he could bring himself to raise the subject to Blow of the paper on which the two had collaborated. "I am longing to see you and have some talks," he at last wrote her. "You will be interested to know that the Weimar paper, in which I set forth as well as I could in a brief space, the ideas that you have so ably represented, made some real impression, so that it was discussed at a meeting in Vienna, and received both favorable, and of course antagonistic comments. Dr. Ferenczi of Budapest, one of the best of the psychoanalysts, is to write a rejoinder, to which I shall have the opportunity of replying. I will send you a reprint of the paper as soon as I receive one." So much for the debacle. Even on the last point Putnam was deluded. In the event, Ferenczi "forgot" to mail Putnam a copy of his harshly critical essay in time for Putnam to make a response.

Putnam's reasons for placing this rosy lens over the fiasco were, however, pressing: "Now I have been advised, and feel inspired, to attempt this same statement on a larger scale. I need not tell you what the scope of the attempt will be, because you can imagine it already. But one part will occupy itself with something of an analysis of Dr. Harris's books, as well as of the views of Bergson, James and Royce. It is needless to say that I shall positively need your sympathy and assistance, and that I hope you will send me a copy of your report if it is in any shape to send."

The fall of 1912 was a logical time for Putnam to commence his opus, the book *Human Motives*. America's passion for pragmatic idealism was reaching its zenith and he was desperate to be on the front lines of the battle for radical change. Whereas it's true that the era was also marked by jingoism, racism, imperialism and evangelicalism, the tide of the country was running hard the other way. The presidential election of 1912 was viewed by many contemporaries as the climactic, synthesizing act of the disparate reform initiatives launched over the previous twenty years that had been aimed at countering the tendencies toward the *laissez-faire* individualism of the industrial revolution. The most striking evidence of this new American spirit was the explosive growth of the Progressive Party. Though the Party began as a result of Republican infighting between Roosevelt and Taft, it became a force for social amelioration far exceeding in influence any previous major party effort, even that of the Populists in the 1892 election.

Roosevelt's candidacy for the Progressive Party made for a genuine three-cornered election—the first since before the Civil War. His platform included reform initiatives on issues ranging from child labor to minimum wage, to workmen's compensation, and the regulation of business and industry. Surpassing the responsibility to ensure the health of free markets, domestic security, or even the well-being of the church, the Progressivists declared at the opening of their Party platform: "The supreme duty of the Nation is the conservation of human resources through an enlightened measure of social and industrial justice."

The roster of Progressive Party positions proved so popular that key tenets were lifted by the other two parties and Woodrow Wilson's campaign rhetoric was almost identical to Roosevelt's on most key issues. Between them, Roosevelt and Wilson took 70% of the vote. Even Taft, in the conservative slot on the triangle, adopted many of his policy positions from the reformist agenda. While muckrakers unmasked corruption in town halls and slaughterhouses, plans were made to restore power to the democratic civic institutions able to address pressing problems of social and economic reform, in addition to tackling race relations, child labor, and general human rights. Redistribution of wealth was a sufficiently viable notion that Taft could accuse both Wilson and Roosevelt of promoting a shift whereby the "rich are to be made reasonably poor and the poor reasonably rich by law."

Americans viewed their country's credibility as a model of enlightened democracy to be contingent on an internal house cleaning of corrupt political and business practices. The idea of patriotism was concordant with that of civic responsibility. In the midst of so much idealism there was a pervasive sense that America's greatness lay in its utopian potential, not in its God-guaranteed superiority. The natural consequence of the former sense was an impulse toward international solidarity rather than provincial condescension.

Putnam's letter to Molly at midnight in Paris is wonderfully idiosyncratic, but in many places it could also be quoting directly from the works of dozens of progressive thinkers of the time. For all his elite European education, Putnam's interest as a mature established doctor in the Continent lay in the *people's struggles.* Even his personal pleasure in drinking, he wrote Molly, counted for less than the possibility that by abstention he would become part of a solidarity movement to save the poor from the ravages of alcoholism. One might disagree with the desirability of promoting a teetotaling society, but this was still ethics by the golden rule.

The pressure exerted by the principle of international community on American politics was also apparent in the ascendancy of the American Socialist party, which in 1912 witnessed its greatest victory in U.S. history. The Socialist party candidate, Eugene Victor Debs, named by his Alsatian-born father after Eugene Sue and Victor Hugo, reread *Les Misérables,* Putnam's touchstone work of political romanticism, almost every year of his life in the original French.

When Debs arrived at Madison Square Garden for a campaign rally shortly before election day, more than 15,000 people inside the arena along with another 3,000 outside, applauded, as the *Times* reported, for an unbroken 29 minutes. "It matters not where the slaves of the earth lift their bowed bodies from the dust and seek to shake off their fetters, or lighten the burden that oppresses them, the Socialist party is pledged to encourage and support them to the full extent of Its power," he declared. Although the Socialists won only 6% of the national total, the major parties conceded that the success of Debs' campaign influenced their own programs.

Nonetheless, Woodrow Wilson, the victor of the campaign, shifted in the space of a very few years from the reformist platform he'd run on to an agenda based on a millennial Christian conviction of America's right to dictate world affairs. Seven years after that euphoric election, in a tide of anti-Bolshevism and general xenophobia following the Great War, Wilson had Debs arrested on trumped-up charges of anti-Americanism. After his conviction, Debs addressed the court with a speech calling for precisely the sort of broad, humanitarian empathy that was fast becoming alien to the White House: "Your Honor, years ago I recognized my kinship with all living beings," Debs proclaimed, "and I made up my mind that I was not one bit better than the meanest on earth. I said then, and I say now, that while there is a lower class, I am in it, and while there is a criminal element I am of it, and while there is a soul in prison, I am not free." Putnam's position was identical.

BLOW WAS BEGINNING to experience an onset of new, unsettling symptoms, but at this crucial juncture of his latest definitive effort at composition, Putnam was loath to let go of her hand. "I am very sorry that you have had these troublesome noises in your head," he wrote her, "and sincerely hope that you may find some relief from them. I am now sending you a typewritten manuscript which is an answer to a criticism of my paper published in the 'Imago.' I beg you, positively, not to read it if it troubles your head, or if you have not time. I must learn to stand on my own feet in philosophical matters, and feel that I am gradually acquiring a better right to do so, although my knowledge of the subject is still exceedingly imperfect."

Of course Blow could not resist the urge to try to help him, whatever her condition. "I have read your paper with great interest," she wrote, and then proceeded to issue a series of criticisms. "I think you would be accused of making a rash claim if you said one could have positive knowledge of mental origin and final destiny." She had given him his faith, but had not been able to impart to him the intellectual foundations for that elaborate belief system that could keep him from sounding foolish when he tried to articulate it on his own.

Putnam couldn't know that the mounting violence of Freud's quarrel with Jung left Freud too distracted to pay attention to Putnam's higher aspirations, no matter how eloquently phrased. The agitated letter Jung wrote Freud after his return from America that same fall lurched between wild accusations and upbeat news of the movement's progress, signaling everywhere the end of their partnership. Announcing that he had just returned from America and though he ought to have written Freud weeks ago from the U.S. had been so occupied that he'd had "neither the inclination nor the leisure to write," Jung gloated over the success of his lectures and added that by making room to express his own views of libido, he'd managed to "win over many people who until now had been put off by the problem of sexuality in neurosis." He blasted Freud for thinking that the modifications he had made to analytic theory reflected personal resistances. This had not been a matter of whim, "but of fighting for what I hold to be true. In this matter no personal regard for you can restrain me."

In response, Freud did his best to project high-minded detachment. But it was hard to suppress his sense of injustice: "I greet you on your return from America, no longer as affectionately as on the last occasion in Nuremberg—you have successfully broken me of that habit—but still with considerable sympathy, interest, and satisfaction in your personal success." He pointed out that Jung's success in winning advocates to analysis by softening the sexual message could be intensified by leaving out sex altogether. Jung answered Freud imperiously, demanding an immediate conference in Munich of the presidents of the different branch societies. "Kindly inform me *by return* whether you accept this invitation in principle." With respect to the problem of who controlled the different journals currently circulating under the aegis of the movement Jung wrote, "I dare not offer you my name for your journal since you have disavowed me so thoroughly, my collaboration can hardly be acceptable."

However, when the conference was actually staged, Jung surprised everyone by behaving reasonably and insisting that he'd only wanted to figure out the best way of handling the switch of power from the discredited Stekel to a new journal that would now become the movement's official mouthpiece.

After the formal session was over (it was still only eleven in the morning), Freud and Jung went off on a walk together to talk over their quarrels. In Freud's account, he asked Jung why was he continually harping on the Kreuzlingen gesture. Jung sniffed about how mean it had been of Freud to go visit his "enemies" Binswanger and Haberlin without paying a call on him. How would Freud like it, he asked, if Jung had informed *him* after the event that he'd been in Wiener Neustadt? Freud patiently repeated that although he wouldn't like it one bit, in fact he had written Jung in advance of the visit on the very same day that he'd written Binswanger. Hadn't Jung received the card? No, Jung pouted, he hadn't. Freud continued to assert his innocence, whereupon "something quite unbelievable and unexpected happened." Jung suddenly, "meekly," revealed that he'd been out of town over the weekend on a sailing expedition, from which he'd not returned until Monday morning. Freud now took the dominant position. Hadn't Jung even bothered to look at the postmark of his card? Didn't he see that basing his suspicions on such a thin thread of evidence was absurd? Jung "was absolutely crushed, ashamed and then admitted everything;" Freud recounted. The former Crown Prince went on to divulge that he had long been frightened by the thought that intimacy with Freud could harm his independence, and acknowledged that this fear had been his motivation in pulling back from their relationship. Moreover, he had "certainly construed" Freud through the lenses of his father complex and had been frightened about what Freud would make of this. Jung finished by declaring that it wounded him "to be judged a complex fool, etc."

In describing the peculiar scene to Ferenczi, Freud commented that Jung began talking about his sad experiences with a colleague who had committed suicide (Honegger), reminding Freud "of homosexuals or anti-Semites who become manifest after a disappointment with a woman or a Jew."

But the day was not done yet. Freud, now flush with power, went on to a victory luncheon at Munich's Park Hotel with Jung and a few other members of their circle. The men drank wine. They became jolly. It was 5 o'clock by the time the festivities wound down. As Jung was saying goodbye, Freud recounted to Ferenczi, he remarked, "You will find me completely with the cause." Freud wanted to rise to his feet but felt faint. According to Freud, when he did manage to stand up, he felt nauseous, and that was the end of the incident. The reality, as attested to by other accounts, was far weirder.

At some point in their meal, the conversation turned to a recent paper by Abraham on the Egyptian monarch, Amenhotep. Abraham argued in the essay that the rebellion sparked by Amenhotep, which culminated in the invention of monotheism, was born out of Amenhotep's feelings

*S*igmund Freud, his mother, and three sisters at his father Jacob's grave in 1897. Freud's gaze into his father's place of burial in the capacity of the ascendant male patriarch is also a stare into the womb of psychoanalysis, an image of totem and taboo.

The Vienna General Hospital in 1895 where Freud began working in 1882, having left his research work for financial reasons to become a clinician. He wrote Martha of his anguish at this compulsory "separation from science," speculating that it might not prove permanent.

"The Universal Theater." Freud's study with the plush, oriental-draped couch on which patients reclined surrounded by displays of evocative antiquities.

A note on the back of the original photograph reads: "Party of Eight." The Putnam family mountain climbing at Grindelwald before the Weimar conference.

*P*articipants in the Weimar Congress, September 1911. Freud stands augustly near the center left of the image, flanked by Ferenczi on the left and Jung on the right. He towers over Jung because he is standing on a box. Jones stands in the second row on the far right. Putnam is to his immediate left. Lou Andreas-Salome sits in the front row, mantled in a boa.

*E*mperor Karl and Empress Zita at the funeral of Franz Joseph I, 1916. High ritual mourning near the grand finale of the Habsburg era.

*C*over of the inaugural issue of the Secessionist journal, *Ver Sacrum* (Sacred Spring), by Alfred Roller with the roots of a thirsty tree splitting its container to regain contact with the earth.

*V*iennese design extravagance. A cover program from the *Cabaret Fledermaus* ("The Bat"), where the interior décor and props were all productions of the Wiener Werkstätte (Vienna Workshop), a world of aesthetical spectacle antipodal to Putnam's Boston.

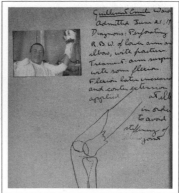

T op Left: Elizabeth Cabot Putnam and James Jackson Putnam, Jr. in France shortly after Elizabeth's arrival to begin volunteer service as a nurse in the spring of 1917. *Top Right:* A page from the album James Jackson Putnam, Jr. compiled of his medical experience in France, with descriptions of wounds and treatments opposite the soldiers' own accounts of how they were wounded.

E lizabeth's note on the back of the original photograph reads: "Fourth of July 1917—My patients from Neuilly on our trip to Cimetière de Picpus." (This small cemetery in Paris is where many victims of the revolution's guillotine are buried—along with Lafayette.)

James Jackson Putnam stands before the Putnam Camp farmhouse in "solitude of the soul" one year before he met Freud.

op: Molly Putnam tending her Little Compton garden in the early 1970s, near the end of her life. She grew to look more and more like her father even as she became ever more devoted to the art of gardening from which her father drew such deep sustenance.

Bottom: The author and Molly Putnam in 1961.

*G*ravity sublimated. The enchanting Putnam Camp farewell to departing guests in a photograph from around 1900.

—

We'll dance like a fairy and sing like a bird,
Sing like a bird, sing like a bird.
We'll dance like a fairy and sing like a bird,
And while the hours away!

of aggression against his father. This was the explanation for why he'd erased his father's cartouches on numerous steles. Jung began objecting that Abraham placed too great an emphasis on Amenhotep's removal of his father's name. As Jung later described the scene in his autobiography, he'd found the reduction of Amenhotep's religious creativity to a father complex irritating. Other pharaohs had also erased the names of their fathers on their accession, as they were all supposed to be incarnations of the same God, but other pharaohs had not, as Amenhotep had done, founded a new faith.

During Jung's challenge to Abraham, Freud grew increasingly distraught. He interrupted Jung and asked why it was that he and Riklin, the other chief Swiss analyst, were busy writing articles in Swiss journals without ever mentioning Freud. Forget Amenhotep's father, why was his own name being eliminated? Jung replied that it seemed unnecessary to cite Freud's name because he was already so well known. Freud refused to accept this explanation. He became more and more distraught until suddenly he collapsed to the ground in a dead faint. Jung lifted him up and carried him over to a couch. Jung claimed that in this position, as Freud slowly regained consciousness in Jung's arms, he stared up at him "as if I were his father." The first words out of Freud's mouth, as he gazed weakly up into Jung's eyes were, "*Ess muss suss sein zu sterben,*" how sweet it must be to die.

So, for a second time in a public space surrounded by people, Freud had become so emotionally overwhelmed in Jung's presence that he lost consciousness.

Because Jones, unlike Ferenczi, had actually been present at the scene Freud couldn't expect to dismiss the event quite so summarily as he had done before. To Jones, Freud mentioned that he'd visited Fliess in Munich on more than one occasion. "I cannot forget that 6 and 4 years ago I have suffered from very similar though not so intense symptoms in the same room of the Parkhotel," he wrote. Are we even to believe Freud here in a literal sense? Was he invoking the haunting of the space to soften its homoerotic resonance? Was he trying to limit the operative range of his homosexuality to Munich and people who reminded him of Fliess? Whatever the particular contours of Freud's proclivities, he confessed to Jones: "There is some piece of unruly homosexual feeling at the root of this matter." Jones responded that he had "suspected a homosexual element, this being the reason of my remark in saying goodbye at the station that you would find it difficult to give up your feeling for Jung."

FREUD'S LETTER ABOUT Munich to Putnam contained no mention of these events. Instead, he put rose-colored lenses over the conference in exactly the same way that Putnam had done with regard to Weimar in communications with Blow. "Last Sunday there was a meeting in Munich of Jung, Riklin, Seif, Abraham, Jones, myself and the Zurich secretary representing Maeder which was most satisfactory," Freud wrote him. "Everybody was charming to me, including Jung. A talk between us swept away a number of unnecessary personal irritations."

Yet in retrospect, how could Freud have believed that Munich signaled the dawn of new relations with Jung?

After Freud's faint, Jung wrote him a brief note expressing concern about Freud's health. Freud took the bait. "Many thanks for your friendly letter, which shows me that you have dispelled various misconceptions about my conduct and encourages me to entertain the best of hopes for our future collaboration," Freud wrote. The incident in Munich had been no more grave than the attack in Bremen before embarking for America. In fact, the real culprit was the Park Hotel dining room, which seemed, Freud mused, to hold "a fatality" for him. "Six years ago I had a first attack of the same kind there, and four years ago a second. A bit of neurosis that I ought really to look into." He signed off, fatally, "Your untransformed Freud."

Jung sneered back at Freud: "This 'bit' should, in my opinion be taken very seriously indeed because, as experience shows, it leads 'to the semblance of a voluntary death.'" He then went into a tirade about Freud's failure to appreciate his work. Everything swiftly unraveled. In the five weeks between Jung's first letter following their meeting in Munich and New Year's of 1913, they descended into open hostilities. "If you doubt my words, so much the worse for you," Jung lunged. "I would, however, point out that your technique of treating your pupils like patients is a *blunder*. In this way you produce either slavish sons or impudent puppies . . . Meanwhile you remain on top as the father, sitting pretty."

One month after telling Putnam that the Munich pow-wow had been a success, Freud was compelled to write him an exhausted confession of defeat. The loss of Stekel, he noted, "was really a gain." But Jung, in whom he "had invested much personal feeling" was another matter. When Freud expressed a feeling of "déjà vu," in connection with the way that "half-analysts" like Jung reproduced the objections made by non-analysts, it's plain that the sensation was more complex than Freud was ready to acknowledge.

In his vulnerability, Freud even tried to flatter Putnam's metaphysical side. "Don't let our lack of understanding of philosophy interfere with the formulation of your ideas. We are not competent in these matters because we work in other fields; but nevertheless we listen to you attentively, and after us will come other, less limited analysts for whom your stimulus may prove fruitful."

While America floated up in a balloon of delirious national optimism, Vienna descended on a reverse course. Freud's fainting, what Jung called his "voluntary death" act, was as culturally symptomatic as Putnam's personal decision to give up alcohol in the name of the people's progress was of the American atmosphere. During the winter of 1913, Trotsky, Lenin, Hitler, and Freud were all living a walkable distance from each other inside tiny, grandiose Vienna. A bomb dropped on the center of the city in January of that year would have wiped out twentieth-century history.

Perhaps, as some scholarship suggests, the First World War really began because of interlocked violations of antiquated notions of national honor. The slap in the face from Serbia compelled Austria to challenge the Balkans and, by extension, Russia, to a dual. Regardless, it doesn't require Freud to suggest that the need to privilege an abstract idea of honor over the survival of the entire Habsburg Empire betokens a surrender to some desire beyond the pleasure principle. Housing shortages, inflation, inadequate workers' rights, inadequate social service delivery systems (and no great movement to reform them as was the case in America), protests and riots by immigrant groups in defense of their traditional languages and of their rights—all of these problems, as well as the intensifying mess in the Balkans, played a part in the destabilization of life in Freud's Vienna. To the extent that a utopian impulse existed, it did so not as a unifying principle in the contemporaneous America style, but as the birth of what we now call identity politics among the ethnic groups patchworking the empire. Whereas there was no common Austrian aspiration, among Zionists, Hungarians, and Czechs, for example, there was a sense that national self-realization might engender profound communal transcendence—for their people alone. This divisive panoply of utopian fantasies has its own relationship to the central myth of *Totem and Taboo* in which men band together only to murder their creator.

THE CLIMACTIC SCENE of the drama with Jung took place at the Hotel Bayerischer Hof in Nuremberg during the Fourth Congress. For all the dissension, the Congress, with 87 members and guests, was almost double the size of the last one, held in Weimar two years before. The addresses were not particularly distinguished and at one point in a presentation by a member of Jung's camp, Freud leaned over to Jones and commented, "All sorts of criticisms have been brought against psychoanalysis, but this is the first time anyone could have called it boring."

Freud had decided to oust Jung by default, rather than by an act of open aggression. It was to be, in other words, an overthrow in accordance with his interpretation of Michelangelo's sublimated Moses. At the moment when Jung's name came up for re-election as president of the Association, 22 out of the 74 members abstained from voting. This was a sufficient margin for Jung, fuming mad, to take the nomination. Nonetheless, he felt thoroughly betrayed. After the tally, he went up to Jones (who'd voted against him) and, in one of his ridiculously ugly expostulations, remarked, "I thought you were a Christian."

Freud decamped, wasting no time in boarding the train that would deposit him, once again, in Rome. While continuing to ponder the figure of Moses, he wrote the first draft of the essay "On Narcissism."

CHAPTER 27

JJP Complex

*I am more than a little thankful to note that the children seem
free from my besetting weakness, which has cost such acute
misery and so many nights of sleep.*

Putnam to Marian, spring 1913

As PUTNAM APPROACHED his seventh decade, some combination of age,
the quietistic influence of Blow's philosophy, and, perhaps, a more subtle
access of self-knowledge inspired by Freud, moved the bar for revolution
from the political to the psychological realm. The first step to communal
paradise demanded climbing out from one's own interior hell, batting the
demons back down where they belonged. "Remarks on a Case with Griselda
Phantasies" is considered Putnam's most successful description of an analysis; Putnam himself is its subject. Even if self-analysis had not brought him
full liberation, Putnam understood the importance of publishing his experience for others who might take his revelations as a catalyst to realize their
own higher potential.

Because of the intensely personal nature of this essay, it was here, if
anywhere, that I expected to find evidence of the true nature of Putnam's
passions—to discover, for example, whether he entertained extramarital
fantasies related to his intimacy with Blow. And indeed the "Griselda" *is*
all about a man riven with illicit sexual fantasies. However, their object is
not one of the man's friends; the "Griselda" character Putnam writes about
is the patient's own daughter. It was Molly, not Susan Blow, who inspired
excruciating lust in Putnam.

The study's title refers to a fairy tale in which a farm girl is elevated to
become the wife of a king. The king proceeds to test her loyalty by stealing

her children at birth and telling her they have died; he also asks that she perform a series of increasingly humiliating labors. Through all this abuse, Griselda refuses to complain.

The sadomasochist fantasy life of Putnam's subject is commensurately harrowing. He characterized the man as "belonging to the best of society . . . very well-educated, altruistic and strong . . . with exceptionally refined family traditions." However, the man suffered from periodic depression. It's revealed that he has been a chronic masturbator all his life. Over time, desire has become entirely concentrated on his daughter. The complex dance of need, succor, and hostility between father and daughter reached a crescendo, Putnam discloses, when the father went abroad with the daughter, expecting her to nurse him back from a mild bout of depression. In addition, he had hoped that the trip would end the "curious estrangement" that had arisen between them over the past year," despite the fact that "they were very attached to each other." This voyage was Putnam's Weimar expedition.

The daughter, Putnam wrote, "played her part gladly," but the longed-for recovery did not take place. They returned "without having got any pleasure from their travel. Each felt an indescribable sensitiveness toward the other, which they found impossible to discuss." A "fairly strong love-hate complex emerged." Pondering the further deterioration of their relations, Putnam observed that "forcibly suppressed feeling for his daughter now dominated him perhaps to a greater extent than he imagined." As recently, then, as the eve of the recommencement of his self-analysis, Putnam's passions were at a pitch of convolution.

There's a haunting novelistic quality to Putnam's description of the chamber of emotional violence and longing in which he was locked. He related how even the rustling of the daughter's dress "when she chanced to touch the door in passing, or the casual sight of the light in her room, made his heart beat faster." Putnam reviewed the loneliness of the man's austere, overdisciplined childhood, remarking how he began to live more and more in dreams, many of them involving "dramatic situations in which imaginary people, mostly women, had to endure lasting pain or grief."

On entering into "a very happy marriage," the subject experienced complete impotence. Consultations with a physician were of no use. Only by teaching himself to tap into the sadomasochistic fantasies he'd constructed as a young man was the subject able to have sex. He discovered that he could "immediately produce an erection and emission by thinking of painful occurrences," and "he began to use this means as an indispensable aid to normal coitus, a custom he had retained up to the present time."

Sometimes the fantasy scenarios impinged on real life. On one occasion, "he had been with her to a matinee which they had both enjoyed. They then joined the other children at a meal, where he noticed how his youngest son, a very lively boy, played with his daughter, poking his nose through the back of her chair and making her press back with some force. The father, watching this game, could not refrain from wanting to replace the child's nose by some sharp or pointed object, as for instance a pen-knife 'though with the blade closed,' so that the daughter would in the course of the game be compelled to feel real pain. From this time these imaginings remained the only means used by him to practice masturbation."

There's something both heartbreaking and helplessly absurd about the fact that even in his darkest, most vicious fantasy life, when Putnam is thinking about pushing a pen-knife into his daughter's spine, the blade is closed. He described a dream in which he and his daughter were on stage. Putnam had taken off a ring of his daughter's and stamped on it for no reason, after which, he wrote, "I had a small pistol in my hand which I handed to the girl whose ring I had torn off, with these words, 'They cannot marry me with this. Take it!' At this moment the pistol went off and shot her."

Though the individual Putnam describes has supposedly made great progress in controlling his autoerotic urges of late, he still finds himself in peril when he reads about particularly evocative cruelties, such as those practiced by the Chinese. "He dared not expose himself to the temptation of glancing through the book [of Chinese tortures] only looking for accounts of cruelties." The image of Putnam as a snowy-haired, upstanding New Englander staying awake late at night in the study of his narrow Marlborough Street Boston townhouse, furtively and feverishly paging through a book of Chinese cruelties is vivid indeed.

Given the incestual focus of his passion, it's tempting to see the Griselda as evidence of Putnam's sense of family imploding on him *à la* Poe's "Fall of the House of Usher." However, this was Putnam, and the very act of recording the case history corresponded with the revitalization of his philosophical impulse. Putnam insisted that the recognition of the sexual inferno teeming inside be viewed as an opportunity for learning how to convert the fires to purposeful ends. Just as his Puritan ancestors were driven by the code of their faith to plumb the depths of their own wickedness as a prelude to the reception of divine grace, Putnam accepted his own uglier desires as the stuff best suited for conversion to a higher plane: "one could regard the masochistic feeling of inferiority as the lever with which one can . . . arrive at sublimation."

From picturing the depraved bliss of Chinese torture methods, Putnam advanced to the optimistic declaration that "the first real step in the solution of these difficult riddles of the How and Whence of the universe, of existence, of life etc., would certainly be taken if we could get accustomed to reducing all phenomena to a single principle, to one single form of activity." The question of how, exactly, recognition of one's sadomasochistic feelings was to be converted into transcendence was where Putnam faltered. It could only have annoyed Freud that Putnam ended up citing Jung to buttress his speculations about how the "libido, just as other forms of energy" can be regarded as "self-creative and life-giving." By the end of the paper he'd spun into a sort of philosophic rhapsody devoid of the narrative force marking his earlier descriptions. The purpose of everything, he now suggested, lay in discovering the "reality underlying the symbolism of our life." He had floated into the heavy clouds of Brokmeyer's Hegelianism.

And yet, in some sense with this essay Putnam *did* free himself. At least as a fantasy (and fantasy after all is as psychologically real in Freudian terms as actual memory) the study charts the course of an ideal sublimation. Having undergone a version of that process through a steadfast unveiling of his own mind, Putnam was ready to tackle the subjects for which his heart pined without the need to look so far back or inward again.

Still, it must have been frightening to write the Griselda analysis. Doing so revealed Putnam's isolation even in the bosom of his family. "The whole life story of this man," he observed at one point, "was characterized and pervaded by masochistic mortifications leading to a feeling of inferiority."

Molly herself was by now away in college in Berkeley, California. She'd begun to show an interest in her father's profession, which her mother was doing everything possible to quench, but Molly still diligently read Putnam's books and journals. When Putnam sent Freud the essay, he noted that "for special reasons I do *not want* it published in the 'Imago,' since my patient reads it." But if Putnam was really concerned about his daughter discover-

ing the paper, it's hard to imagine that he would have permitted its publication at all. There's something of the classic case of the criminal wanting
to be caught in his surrender of the paper to Freud's discretion.

Freud quickly surmised (and shared with others) the fact that the
paper reflected Putnam's self-analysis. An incest dream that Putnam acknowledged as his own and later sent Jones sufficiently corresponded with
remarks in the "*Griselda*" that Jones was able to confirm Freud's suspicion. By the end of 1913 one begins to find scattered through letters between Freud, Jones and Ferenczi references to other people's "JJP complex"
as code for incestual desire.

BUT EVEN AS Putnam bounced up and down the east coast to psychoanalytic conferences in Washington, Baltimore, and New York, a new tone
crept into his communications with his wife. At the same time as he became more confident in demanding recognition for his views from Freud,
he sounded a more affectionate note with Marian. Perhaps the experience
of self-analysis had not liberated him to become a prominent philosophical missionary of cosmic mysteries, but the self-knowledge he attained may
have made him a fonder, more emotionally engaged husband.

The ongoing crisis in Louisa and Frances' health made a recovered intimacy essential. Putnam's letters to Marian were filled with reminders of
how blessed they'd been with both girls, intermingled with words of praise
for her mothering. "If I cannot guide her," he wrote with respect to Frances
and the diabetes she'd recently been diagnosed with, "I can at least learn
from her. . . . They are good children and I will try to do my share, here-
after, in keeping them also well, so far as that may be. You do nobly."

Nonetheless, by the summer of 1913, Putnam was on the verge of despair about Louisa. It increasingly appeared that even if she were to survive her epileptic attacks she would have to be institutionalized. "I wish I
could help more," he lamented to Marian, "but, whatever happens, we will
make it true, what Edward Emerson said, that we draw closer together
through these troubles. Certain it is that the whole history, even of happiness, is not written in any easily read set of terms." It's a strange, poignant
observation. As though the book of happiness itself were a work as obscure
as the metaphysical tomes he paged through with Blow. "Fortunately, happiness goes more by essence and quality than by quantity and as long as

you can keep well we can surround Louisa with affection for almost every deprivation," he wrote Molly a few weeks later, remarking on the same day to Marian, "Your letter makes me feel . . . dumb and heavy, but the time of seeing compensations and of finding reasons and means of enduring and helping is, fortunately, bound to come . . . There must be something better than another to do, but the sacrifice cannot be more drastic than Louisa wishes to make it."

In the saddest letter of all, in mid-July 1913, Putnam tried to convince himself and Marian of the joys Louisa would still be able to take from life even if she were never again able to be an active participant: "I have thought a lot about Louisa and carried on imaginary talks with her, but realize that your actual talks are better. I suppose the hope is that she will learn the great pleasure of living and watching the great pageant, and sympathizing, and contributing what she can, without demanding the personal satisfaction of over-much recognition. Everyone's real circle is a small one, but everyone's *interest* may be unlimited." For Putnam, the whole of whose idealist philosophy was based on the imperative of action, whether to apply the stuff of philosophy in the real world or to devote one's full being to the practical causes of the "people's movement," the need to accept that one of his daughters was knocked out of the fray at so young an age must have been the hardest of all blows. If there is anything his life was not, it was not based on taking spectatorial pleasure in the pageant of the world.

FAR FROM THE burning rivalries of the European circle, Putnam's world was being literally engulfed in flames. In his letters to Freud from Camp, Putnam made no mention of the fact that in the late summer of 1913 he was caught in the middle of three weeks of unprecedented forest fires that were transforming the Adirondack landscape. Instead, he continued, as he said, "pushing my philosophical ideas a little hard." Over and over, he argued that in trying to answer the question of what constituted the true wellsprings of personality, the most satisfying answer was bound to be "one which best stimulates to sublimation."

President Wilson called up the National Guard to fight the Adirondack fires in its first ever peacetime deployment, and a division stationed itself just across the river from Putnam Camp. Putnam worried that the conflagration was an omen; the wilderness in which he'd spent many of the happiest moments of his adult life was going up in smoke. Nonetheless, with more than two dozen guests in attendance, Putnam Camp remained full to capacity. As always, evenings were marked by ambitious sing-alongs around the Stoop bonfire. Yet the blaze consuming the surroundings was never far from anyone's thoughts. Each morning, they woke to the sight of a dull, smoky mist. Despite his age, Putnam joined the other male guests and residents of the valley below Camp in spending nights on the surrounding mountainsides, digging ditches to block the fire's progress.

With her condition clearly worsening, Frances wrote a feverish account of the fires for her class at "Miss Winsor's school" in which she described the mountains dotted with flames as "brilliant cities," and noted the handsome guardsmen stationed nearby. "Their encampment was so near us that we could hear all the thrilling bugle calls," she recalled. "They had all been stationed in the Philippines . . . and the tales they told of the barbarisms of the natives made our hair stand on end." The division major himself was so taken with Frances that he arranged for reveille to be set forward an hour so that she wouldn't have to be woken before six in the morning. He told Marian as he left with his soldiers, "I don't know when I have been so taken with any one as I was with your little girl. She had a way with her that made me want to tell her things." He laughed at the fact that the men didn't know why things were starting an hour late. "They'll make a joke of how I changed the orders just to please the little girl, whenever they want to tease me!"

On one of the last days in September, the family walked to Chapel Pond, a little over a mile from Putnam Camp. Frances described the experience of being near enough to the conflagration to actually see the trees snap into flame: "Tree after tree toppled down the slope, and the burning branches were shattered into thousands of pieces that ricocheted off the rocks, casting sparks as they plunged. . . . Every blaze was reflected in the dark water below." The roar of the fire was terrifying and the family stood close together, staring at the devastation in helpless silence.

The question of whether the primeval forests and their Adirondack Camps would survive was uncertain. Federal units from Plattsburgh had failed to douse the fires. But in the fourth week of September, heavy dark rains began to fall in torrents, finally extinguishing the blaze. In the midst of one of these cold downpours, the family returned to Boston.

BLOW'S SUMMER HAD also been a trial. Her niece and companion, Nelka, had fallen into a depression. "If you or Freud or anybody can find a way of meeting the problems created by the kind of original nature which both Nelka and I have you will be great benefactors," she wrote Putnam. "I have just had my 70th birthday. It had not occurred to me that it was different from any other until letters, telegrams and presents began to arrive." But the accolade conferred no joy. "I realized that I had reached the term of life and that if by reason of strength I still lingered I must expect labor and weariness. I hope I shall keep some measure of mental youth. For youth means that we are still able to learn. I dread nothing more than the weakening of the eyes . . . and the confinement of effort to already beaten paths."

CHAPTER 28

To See God

I also note carefully your statement that psychoanalysis may,
by unmasking a man's most vital tendencies, make him, at last,
healthier (and honester?) yet viler? I can well believe that this
might happen, for several patients have said to me, "I cannot
help admitting the conclusions toward which the analysis
points, but I feel that you are robbing me of all that makes life
attractive."

Putnam to Freud, December 25, 1913

EVEN AMONG THE suicide-obsessed Viennese, 1913 was a banner year, with 600 successful acts and almost three times that many serious attempts, among them a child of 7. While Franz Josef mustered the byzantine Noah's ark of the empire's 97 different ethnic platoons on the Schwarzenbergplatz, each with its own nationalist costume, from the leopard hide-mantled Hungarian hussars to the Tyrolean Imperial rifles crowned by a spray of white cockfeathers, to the Levantine Balkan infantry soldiers sporting fezzes and broad scarlet sashes, the metastasized bureaucratic economy teetered ever closer to collapse. The underemployed and out of work made use of Vienna's overcrowded homeless shelters (little more than concrete bunkers lined with straw mattresses) 500,000 times over the course of 1913—this when the total population of the city was under two million. Other indigents slept in the foul sewer system, by compost piles attached to nurseries, and in the mud and filth of any anonymous dark corner. Hospitals were overwhelmed by individuals and families hunting for shelter, and sensationalist press reports described emergency accident victims, as well as mothers with sick infants being turned away. The cotton and metal industries were largely shut down. Construction of new buildings had more or less stopped. In the elaborate parade to the Centralfriedhof that took place on All Soul's Day, Karl Lueger's grave continued to receive the most ostentatious of the hundreds of flower displays, despite the fact that he'd been dead for three years.

IN LATE NOVEMBER, Freud held a séance at his own home in the company of various analysts and their wives, along with his own brother and children. An effective invocation of the dead, as Freud knew, could never be so self-consciously staged. It had all gone wretchedly, he wrote Ferenczi: "hardly any indication of success. . . . I handed Professor Roth [the medium] an envelope [money] to put him in a favorable mood, but the contents were wasted." Freud complained that Roth's idiocy outweighed even his craftiness, so that the mention of his experiments might end up humiliating the psychoanalytic movement. Freud never suggested that the paranormal itself might be no more than a daydream.

The fascination he felt for the occult was matched by fear and repulsion with respect to mysticism. Ferenczi nursed Freud's worries that Putnam's strain of spirituality made him a natural ally of the Swiss. "I just read Putnam's 'Griselda-Fantasy,'" he wrote Freud in the spring. "It reminds me of Jung's work on libido, both are incomprehensible and mystical." After the battle fever of Munich, Freud saw the Jungian vulnerability of Putnam with new vividness. Even when Jones passed along one of Putnam's letters to Freud that showed, as Jones said, how Putnam's "tough stomach unhesitatingly rejects Jung's mish-mash in spite of the sprinkling of philosophy and ethics," Freud responded unconfidently. "Putnam's letter was very amusing. Yet I fear, if he keeps away from Jung on account of his mysticism and denial of incest, he will shrink back from us (on the other side) for our defending sexual liberty."

Putnam never once questioned the merits of Freud's views on sex. The note of sorrow that had crept into his recent correspondence, rather than indicating that he was contemplating a rupture, testified to Putnam's lingering conviction that if only they could share the sorts of long, uninterrupted talks he enjoyed with Blow, it would come out that there was actually no difference between them at all. "Would that I might have the chance of talking with you, not for a few minutes only but for a long enough time to reach conclusions," he wrote. In an atypical sigh of resignation he added, "That chance may never come, but, at any rate, we shall remain friends and at least occasional correspondents."

Putnam rightly intuited that many of the hostilities cropping up in the movement were motivated as much by personal vengefulness as by theoretical differences. Early in the year, when the division with Stekel was widening, he'd written Freud: "If Dr. Stekel was only a *little* different, and a little less *personal* in his reactions, he would be admirable, for he certainly has much talent and much vigor and productiveness." To Fanny, after Munich, he confessed his grief at the unfolding schism in Europe: "Altogether it puts a strain on my philosophy to keep from getting blueish. Why can't everybody be good!"

Whereas Freud wrote Putnam that he regretted Putnam's not having been in Munich as his "presence would have helped to mitigate the tone in which this conflict was expressed," to Jones Freud communicated only skepticism: "There is no doubt all these men incline strongly to Jung," he wrote, "or to put it correctly, they tend away from psychoanalysis; it is only your personal influence which may keep them back, doubtful for how long a time. They all seek gratification, not science, perhaps *Erlosung* [deliverance] from their own erotic charges."

Flattered by Freud's ascription to him of the authority to keep the mystics in check, Jones wrote back, "I was impressed by your remark about Putnam, etc., seeking gratification rather than science, and the episode shows how novel and insecure the scientific attitude still is in the world. Your own rigid adherence to it has always called forth my admiration. Progress in culture has always meant renunciation of wish-phantasies . . . and mankind is for the most part nothing if not timid." Four days after Jones wrote this letter Freud was holding a séance in his house. Not so many months earlier, Jones had been accused of sexual manipulation of two children on different occasions. His wife was in the throes of a morphine addiction for which he bore some responsibility. Cold reality left an unpleasant taste on everyone's palate.

PUTNAM SPENT MUCH of the autumn on Cape Cod, where the family celebrated Frances' sixteenth birthday, with a white cake covered with a bouquet of confectionery violets, roses, and chrysanthemums as brilliant

as fresh-cut blossoms from the Cotuit garden. When Frances cut beneath
the frosting, she discovered a series of tiny packages filled with poems from
various family members. Jamie gave her a silver snuffbox. Molly and Elizabeth presented her with a silver pendant that opened to reveal a store of
saccharine. When she returned to Boston, Frances sounded like her old
self: "My gracious, but this is a busy place! I feel as if I were in one huge
whirl all the time," she wrote a friend. "I enjoy the whole whirl tho! I'm
just crowded with invitations for Sat's, Sun's, and Frid's. . . . I had a wonderful time at Cohasset. Played tennis at the Thackers in the A.M. and shot
the wave since the P.M. It was delicious."

But Putnam and Marian were conscious of how often she looked pale.
The doctors allowed Frances to continue with school and attend the Friday dance to which she referred in her letter, but she left an hour before it
finished, and the doctors, Marian wrote in her journal, "did not give us hope
of further improvement. The look of compassionate sympathy in Dr. Joslin's
face when we talked over the details of her treatment was only too clearly
to be read, and I knew that the day was not far off when she would have to
give up her active life."

FANNY CAME HOME for a visit to Boston near the end of autumn and
poured her heart out to Putnam about the increasingly vicious course her
treatment was taking with Jung. Putnam was horrified, but decided that
telling her straight out to drop analysis would risk provoking a complete
breakdown.

On returning to Zurich, in a misguided act of candor, Fanny disclosed
her conversations with Putnam to Jung. Jung became frightened that Fanny's
revelations would goad Putnam to speak out against him. He turned all his
powers to convincing Fanny that what she believed to be frankness actually
amounted to pathological lying. Fanny's sense of reality stood no chance
against Jung's magnetism. She was manipulated into writing a pathetic letter to Putnam in which she retracted every negative thing she'd ever said
about Jung. "I am fearfully dishonest, Cousin Jim, I have lied in analysis both
unconsciously and consciously; I have deceived Dr. Jung and sister and now
you too—O Cousin Jim I've been dishonest all my life because I am too much
of a coward to do anything else. Dr Jung says he is willing to go on with me
if I care to come to him, but he has no more interest in my case—he says his

only motive in taking me back is his duty to humanity." Conceding the desperation of her situation, she yet insisted that "the feeling that at last you know me as I really am, that I've had the courage to tell you the fearful truth will be a help in going on, and I mean to go on at all costs—finishing analysis means more to me than my life—far more."

Richard Noll has suggested that Putnam's vote on whether analysis in America would take a Freudian or Jungian direction made Fanny "a critically important pawn in a larger political game for the future of psychoanalysis and Jung's own career." Putnam, by this point, guilty though he was of having sent Fanny to Jung, was hardly less of a tool in the power machinations over whose theories would direct the future of analysis in the New World.

Fanny showed Jung the multi-page letter she'd written Putnam and he convinced her to write Putnam again to broadcast the astonishing latest results of her analysis. "It all came over me then that instead of hating Dr. Jung I felt a deep and overpowering love for him," she dutifully confessed in a heartbreaking follow-up letter. She now saw that her "fear of him had been a distorted love, and that for the first time in my life I was capable of a disinterested love." Though it was all terribly confusing she maintained, "I *have* taken a step in being able to show my soul to Dr. Jung as it really is and I firmly believe that in time I can overcome my faults even though they are so fearfully serious. . . . I've read all this to Dr. Jung and he says it is right. I *am* sending it gladly, Cousin Jim, and I am ready to take the consequences whatever they be."

The first consequence was Putnam's overdue termination of his relations with Jung and a newly minted resolve to defend Freud's camp, whatever the theoretical differences between them. On the tenth of December he wrote Fanny a desperate letter of his own in which he did everything in his power to make her realize that Jung's sorcerer-like spell was leading her to destruction. "You owe it to yourself to preserve a self respect which should override and outlive even the discovery in yourself of more or less falseness. Who is not false? Not one of us, not Dr. Jung either. . . . Perhaps I am wrong, but there will be no harm in realizing that he is also no god but a blind man trying to lead the blind, and that you are as much at liberty to criticize him as he is to criticize you."

But it was too late to draw her back into the cozy world of Back Bay. In the course of her analysis, Fanny met a young Dutch psychiatrist who'd also gone into treatment with Jung. She fell in love with him and they became engaged, leading to a sexual awakening and a bout of extraordinary hallucinations on Fanny's part involving the Tree of Life, Wotan, and Mother Earth. "The creation of the Personal God," she wrote in one journal, "the alpha and the omega—and all and everything—my drawing is embryonic, as it should be, it is the embryo of this God—my own consciousness of religion—bringing with it the four degrees."

At the end of her analysis, Fanny moved with her new husband to the Netherlands. He proved an inveterate philanderer and a cruel partner to his susceptible bride. When he died in 1938, she came back to America, moving to New Hampshire and creating a kind of mystical den for herself from where, in a final twist of the blade, she sang the joys of her time with Jung as the acme of her existence. Fanny never settled in Boston again.

THE MOUNTING DISTRESS in Putnam's letters to Freud from the end of November through early December, in which he struggled to prove that the two men were on the same side, and that Jung's heresy would not draw him in its wake, fell on deaf ears. The smart of the wound Jung had given Freud overpowered his diplomatic savvy. Putnam wrote Freud at the end of November: "You and I might differ on these points, but I am sure we shall never differ in any way that will prevent us from working side by side, although in most respects it will always be as teacher on your part and learner on mine." Shortly thereafter, he added, "I only wish I could be of some service in these uncomfortable times." But Freud's only response to these hand-wringing assurances was increasing impatience with Putnam's willingness to entertain the possibility that any aspect of the Zurichers' work might be worthwhile. To Jones, Freud groused: "I am tired of leniency and kindness. The motives are too clear and the innovations too stupid."

Freud could not know that it wasn't only genuine loyalty on top of horror at what Jung had done to Fanny that was motivating Putnam, it was also the brimming sense of tragedy in his own life that made him desperate to clutch onto the professional realm in which he could still find hope.

On Saturday, the 4th of December, the family rode out to Milton to watch a hockey game between Milton Academy and the Winsor School. Frances led her Winsor classmates in cheering. Sunday the 5th, the weather was cold and rainy, and Putnam and Marian went to Concord to have lunch with the Emersons. All four girls were left behind painting cards and engaging in other Christmas preparations.

When the senior Putnams returned at dusk, they noticed Frances' pallor. But her mood was upbeat. Hattie Shaw, the apparently immortal Putnam Camp cook, was coming to dinner and Frances put on one of her dance school dresses to show her. That night was restless. Frances woke on Monday, Marian wrote in her journal, "feeling ill, and from then on she grew rapidly worse until Friday, December 12, when she fell asleep soon after midnight and died peacefully about eight o' clock."

As an epigraph to her memoir of her daughter, Marian quoted a letter written by a cousin to describe Frances' character. "To live a perfectly happy life, making all about her happy—never to fear—never to dislike—never to think of one's self either for praise or blame—to feel that what is right can be done—that there are no unconquerable obstacles—no perversities of nature—is indeed to see God."

All the evidence about Frances suggests that she really was a creature of joy, able to communicate her delight to those around her. Molly may have been the daughter who conjured Putnam's dark, incestual passions. This was due to a significant extent to the ways in which their personalities were akin. Frances was Putnam's inspiration. She embodied the upward-aiming forces in the mind that countered neurotic demons, and so constituted the proof that Freud's etiology was incomplete. Frances was the living, surging form of Putnam's idealism.

There's a grim resonance in the fact that his youngest daughter, his Ariel and Phoebe, the personification of high, cheerful optimism, passed away on the eve of the World War.

WHY WAS IT that Putnam couldn't bring himself to tell Freud directly of Frances' death? His reticence may have reflected a misplaced unwillingness to trouble Freud. It also indicates, however, the growing difficulty Putnam experienced in exposing his deeper feelings before Freud.

To Jones, Putnam wrote a simple factual account of what had happened. Yet in its faint note of bewilderment, one can feel the hairline cracks through which anguish threatened to break. He told Jones that one of his daughters, "a very promising, vigorous-minded girl, of rather rare balance, and exceedingly healthy up to within a couple of years has just died, after a short illness." He asked Jones to pass the note "to our friend, Dr. Freud," adding that Freud "would remember her, because she was at the Adirondacks when he was there, and I well recall a pleasant picture of her sitting next to him at the table and chatting happily, as it seemed to me, with him. She was singularly free from self-consciousness, and met every one, including strangers, with a natural simplicity and appreciation of their good qualities. . . . Strangely enough she seemed, up to the time when this trouble was discovered, to be the strongest member of our family."

Instead of telling Freud of his loss, less than two weeks later, on Christmas day itself, Putnam locked himself in his study to write Freud a detailed, multi-page letter agonizing about his relationship to psychoanalysis. He told Freud that he wanted it "perfectly understood" that "I *desire* to practice this branch of medicine (psychoanalysis) in accordance with the very best principles, and if I fail to do so it will be because I cannot rise to my own standards, on account of resistances which I realize to exist but find it hard to master." And yet Putnam begged Freud wasn't it the case that when it came out in the course of analytic conversation that the patient felt "a certain debt to his family, his state, his 'team,' etc. in short, that he acknowledges the calls of loyalty," this sense could be safely encouraged? Having lost the most hopeful of his children, it was only by clinging to the sense of duty and responsibility in ever-widening circles that he could hold onto his own sanity. He closed with a stark challenge. If it were the case that a man felt his scientific ability contingent on accepting notions like those mentioned in his Weimar address, was that person "to be regarded as unfitted for psychoanalytic work?" For the first time, Putnam asked whether the theoretical divergences between them made him hypocritical in calling himself an analyst.

BUT FREUD BLOCKED out everything Putnam was saying except what was salient to his own power struggles. "Even in theory he is making more concessions than we could expect," he wrote to Jones after Putnam's letter and Jones' own note on Frances' death, "although to be sure the repressed is coming back by a '*Hinterthur*' [back door]. Please return his letter for answerings sake. I regret the loss of his child but it is not the beloved one, the Griselda." Freud's crassness is stunning. He seems to be implying that because Frances wasn't the object of her father's incestual longing, Putnam's grief must be mitigated.

Putnam must have managed to tell Blow the news of Frances' death immediately after she passed away, because the next day Blow wrote him a long passionate letter of condolence in which psychology and the mystical truths by which they had tried to live their lives merge in a kind of rapture. "Your letter shows me how thoughtfully you accept suffering which means that your dear Frances shall escape suffering," Blow wrote. "Our griefs are often a selfish plea, born from personal pain which is really lack of love. You have loved so well that you can forget self and there will be no sting in your sorrow. You made your dear child happy while she lived, you prepared her for larger happiness and you will always have the direct message of the happiness she brought to you. For the rest we can none of us do more than try to realize that because God *is* all must be well."

Over and over, she wrote Putnam to empathize with his pain and express her faith that his character and goodness were so elevated that he would survive the loss despite his inestimable pain. In one letter she reassured him, "Your dear Frances left such a vivid impression upon me even in her early childhood that I can understand how strongly she must have made herself felt as she matured. A young life may be a very complete life."

THE ICINESS IN Freud's response to Putnam at last thawed as his rage at Jung's betrayal cooled. In late February, in regard to Putnam's continued insistence on the place of philosophy in analysis, Jones snarled to Freud, "Putnam is incorrigible, he is a woman not a man." Freud seemed taken aback by the charge and began questioning Jones' anger. "Perhaps you are too hard on him," Freud countered. "He is over 60 and a doubter by constitution, he is brave for all this." Jones at once backed down when Freud dropped his own bullying tone: "My impatience with Putnam was of course only momentary, for I recognize how much there is to admire and to love in him."

Putnam wrote another four major addresses for the analytic movement between the beginning of 1914 and early summer. Of the first of these papers, "On Some of the Broader Issues of the Psychoanalytic Movement," with its description of psychoanalysis as "a phase of education," Freud declared to Putnam, "I like it exceedingly, perhaps best of all those excellent, eloquent and significant papers you have sent me. . . . There is no part of it that concerns psychoanalysis with which I could not identify myself."

In June, Putnam's spirit was dashed again with his brother Charles' death and he decided not to hold back the news from Freud. "The group which you met at the Adirondacks four years ago, is [thus] broken into for the second time, this winter, by the death of very dear and important members," he wrote. "The first was my daughter, then a gay and self-forgetting child of 12, by whose friendly prattle at table I remember that you were amused; the second my brother with whom you walked home from an excursion beyond the Ausable river. Without his energy and devotion the enterprise which has given great pleasure and brought much real 'sublimation' to a large number of people in the course of the past thirty years would never have come into existence."

This time, Freud rose to the occasion and wrote Putnam a moving note in which he expressed "great regret" at the news of Charles' death. Reading the newspaper obituary that Putnam had enclosed, in which Charles was glowingly eulogized as "he who made the soil in which medical-social co-operation could sprout," Freud added, "I understood better why I remembered so clearly his friendly kindness to me." To Putnam's news that he was not coming to the Congress, Freud responded with heartfelt sorrow.

But on an intellectual level, Freud's efforts to reconcile himself with Putnam were not entirely successful. They came too late, after Putnam had turned afresh to Blow's inspiration. "I came from Cazenovia last night, arriving here early this morning and have been sitting ever since—after taking a cup of coffee and the remainder of Miss Blow's nice and ample lunch—reading the *whole* of the NY Times, which was entirely given up to the exciting news from overseas," he wrote Marian after one visit to his mentor. "Very different was Miss B.'s quiet 'Academy Porch' and the discussion of 'first principles.' Yet these are after all even more endurably important, and one wishes that all the European rulers and generals might have been assembled there." It's a lovely picture: all the crowned heads and military powers of the Continent gathered on Susan Blow's veranda in Cazenovia, New York. Putnam concluded, "Miss B. grows more interesting every time I see her and seemed younger and stronger than last year." When one considers that as of 1914 Putnam had been "seeing" Blow for about a quarter of a century, this is a remarkable piece of praise. Even the experience of a motion picture show becomes an occasion for extolling the virtues of Blow. Putnam recounted the experience of going to the movies with Edward Emerson "not as being the best thing in the world but as about the only thing available. These shows get somewhat tiresome toward the end but they are extraordinary to the last point and certainly engrossing. This was an absurdly melodramatic story of the wars of Rome and Carthage, but how they can work the lifelike scenes up beats me. However that is trivial enough as compared with the wonder of Miss Blow's grasp of life."

One can't help wondering what it was like for Marian to have so much of Putnam's mind, if possible only more so in later years, constantly percolating with thoughts of this extraordinary character. In an interview Molly gave near the end of her life she was asked about Putnam's relationship with Blow and after discussing what a "serious friendship" the two had enjoyed and commenting on the mysterious disappearance of her father's letters to Blow, she noted, "I've wondered since I grew up whether her relationship with my father was anything of a trial to my mother. I certainly never felt it at the time, but I think the conversations were largely between my father and Miss Blow and I don't know to what degree my mother went in on it. She wasn't too much interested in the philosophical approach, but in the practical child rearing approach." Marian wouldn't have had much opportunity to go in on it even had she been more interested, as most of the conversation occurred when Blow and Putnam were off elsewhere. Her view of their relationship was always partially obscured. Emblematic of her position is a note from Putnam regarding a letter of Blow's that he'd forwarded to Marian. Parts of Blow's missive were blacked out. To Marian, Putnam wrote, "I thought you would be interested in a part of a letter from Miss Blow. Whatever else she is, she's a good woman. I have scratched out portions simply because they need explanation."

CHAPTER 29

The Great Unknown

I am not willing to assume that the entire trend of history has been in a wrong direction.

Blow to Putnam, April 19, 1914

FREUD'S FIRST REACTION to the onset of World War I was typical of his countrymen. The flare-up of open hostilities in the summer of 1914 produced a sense of relief; a vague sense of injured honor and general indignation was converted overnight into an energetic muster against a common Balkan foe.

Freud was unabashed about the personalized inflection of his own experience. "Simultaneously with the declaration of war, which transformed our peaceful spa, your letter arrived, at last bringing the liberating news," he wrote Abraham of Jung's withdrawal from the movement. "So we are at last rid of them, the brutal sanctimonious Jung and his disciples. . . . For the first time in thirty years I feel myself to be an Austrian and feel like giving this not very hopeful Empire another chance. Morale everywhere is excellent."

Reports of Germany's triple declaration of war only topped off his elation. Freud leapt to his feet with boyish enthusiasm, hurrahing the great "release of tension through a bold-spirited deed." For days, he could do no work at all and spent his time pacing up and down the Berggasse devouring every available war report. "All my libido is given to Austro-Hungary," he announced.

But within a month, as the gravity of the debacle pressed home, Freud's jingoism fizzled. Describing how he returned to his true character, he recounted an old joke about a Jew who lived in Germany for many years, gradually taking on German manners and fashions until he appeared indistinguishable from the natives of his adopted homeland. One day the man returns home to his family. Even they are convinced of his transformation—everyone except the grandfather. In the course of preparing for bed, the man begins removing his clothes. The old patriarch takes one look at his denuded grandson and cries out triumphantly, "*Juden!*"

Part of what brought Freud back to his familiar pessimism was his fear of losing Anna. Anna had gone to England in July of 1914 for an apprenticeship as an elementary school teacher. When war broke out, she was in danger of being interned as an enemy alien for the four years of the war, as were many of her compatriots who remained after Germany's invasion of Belgium.

Freud's fear of being separated from Anna by war coincided with his anxieties about her leaving him to marry Jones. The letters he wrote in this period betray evidence of Freud's own version of the "Griselda" complex—something closer to an Oedipus at Colonnus complex—and may help explain why he was feeling more generous toward Putnam. "I have no thought of robbing you of the freedom your two sisters have enjoyed [to marry]," he assured her. "But it has been the case that you have lived more intimately with us than they and I comfort myself with the hope that it will be more difficult for you than for them to make a decision about your life without assuring yourself first of all of our (in this case, my) consent."

When Anna was eventually analyzed herself (by Freud), she revealed complexes that were the mirror reverse of the ones Putnam exposed in his self-analysis. She later wrote up her own case history under the title, "A Child is Being Beaten." Where Putnam's masturbatory fixations had involved fantasies about sadism toward his beloved daughter, Anna's autoerotic reveries consisted of masochistic fantasies of being beaten—apparently by her father.

Adding to Freud's disillusionment was the sight of his sons marching off to join the army. Both Martin and Ernest were dispatched to fight on the front lines in Galicia and Italy. Martin, who in his cavalier hero-worship of his father rarely acknowledged any sign of weakness in Freud, wrote that during their farewell visit his father seemed "deeply depressed and far from well."

"I know for certain that I and my contemporaries will never again see a joyous world," Freud wrote to Lou Andreas-Salome in November. "And the saddest thing about it is that it is exactly the way we should have expected people to behave from our knowledge of psychoanalysis. . . . We have to abdicate, and the Great Unknown, he or it, lurking behind Fate, will one day repeat such an experiment with another race." As the conflict wore on, he retreated into an increasingly isolated existence composed of essay writing and cataloging his antiquities.

PUTNAM QUICKLY TURNED the war into fodder for his own form of philosophical rumination. Disappointment at the failure of the European leaders to make nice was at first a stronger emotion than a sense that his own optimistic faith was threatened. Yet the seeds of a greater despair were present. Everyone in Boston, he wrote Jones, could "hardly think or talk of anything but war and everyone feels at liberty to become a war critic if not a Napoleon or a Moltke, or a Cassandra. It is horribly interesting to glance at the whole situation from the standpoint of a psychologist, but heart-rending to think of it from most other standpoints." At last, Putnam cried from the depths of his spirit, "Think of men who might have rendered incalculable service in the cause of sublimation, going down before a stray bullet or a bayonet, fired or used presumably by no unfriendly hand!" He mused with horror, "Suppose it had all happened twenty five years ago, and Freud had been the victim." And yet, the foundation of his belief system remained intact. "Well, the only consolation is that sublimation does *on the whole* gain (doesn't it?) as the centuries roll on; and perchance some future German if really in fear of some Slav power will conciliate a future France instead of furiously dashing itself against her!"

From distress at specific German policy positions (particularly in regard to the right of Slav self-determination), Putnam moved toward an increasingly encompassing disenchantment with the culture from which he'd absorbed both his philosophical and medical education. By November, the "events of the war, with all their collaterals" had begun to take a toll on his ability to sleep and even to work on *Human Motives*. He acknowledged to Jones that in addition to the fact that he found the war "immensely engrossing," it was also "exceedingly depressing." He reported having gone to a lecture by a German specialist at Harvard who had given an eloquent talk on the country's ideals. Yet, "impressive though it was to hear the apotheosis of the German strivings for the success of their national ideals . . . the ultimate effect was to make me feel all the more (as I used to feel with reference to Nietzsche's superman idea) the intolerability and the tragedy of the situation," Putnam wrote. The pro-German professor, while resisting the idea that Germany had sought the war or planned a pan-Germanic state, admitted that "the ideals of the military part did involve, almost necessarily, the crowding out of 'uncomfortable' neighbors." To counter this, Putnam avouched, "the world cannot stop at nationalism but must pass on to cosmopolitanism, in the best sense."

Later in the war, after a bombardment of hospitals in Boulogne, Putnam's disillusionment was more severe. "It is hard not to believe that they—the Germans—knew what they were doing," he grieved to Elizabeth, "for besides the fact that the hospitals are plainly marked (which might not count for much in the hit-or-misfiring of an avion (?) Boulogne is not, I presume, of much military consequence except as a hospital station. Moreover this is said to be the fifth or sixth time the same thing has been attempted. Human development seems by no means symmetrical and in that of the Germans some of the best fruits of evolution seem to have been strangely omitted, on a large scale. I suppose their success on certain lines has been partly due to the fact that some of them were out and out cads and large numbers of them more or less caddish. But fortunately in that non-human ideal and perfected world of which we love to dream, excess is not needed, and diverse good qualities can develop side by side." Even at this pitch of disappointment, Putnam resisted jingoism: "Meantime, some plan of peace must be formed which will afford the best Germans their best chance. And, then, what of ourselves? How shall we get our best chance, and learn to be decently cooperative?"

Before the end of the first year of war, the primary question became that of how, under the circumstances, his personal duty to the larger community could best be enacted. "I will not try to swell the list of adjectives or to apportion blame," he wrote Jones after the sinking of the Lusitania. "The whole situation makes one too dizzy to contemplate it with justice. But the pressing question is What can we *do* to help?" His son had already arranged to work as an orderly in the American Hospital in Paris. Elizabeth was beginning to shape plans to serve as a nurse in France. As for Putnam himself, a newspaper clipping stuck in his correspondence for 1915 notes, "Dr James J. Putnam of Marlboro street is collecting surgical instruments for Servia."

Whatever gloom Putnam himself might have experienced in consequence of the war, Susan Blow's anguish was incalculably greater. She lacked his recourse to professional service as a physician, and her philosophy, on which she depended for all her strength, held no place for what was happening. If for Freud, the tragedy of World War I confirmed his view of the world as, essentially, a sewer, for St. Louis Hegelians, the war utterly repudiated their essential theories. They had staked their intellectual and spiritual lives on the irreversible course of human progress. Not only did the War destroy the specifics of their faith; it shut down the mainstream effort by educated intellectuals to blend a sophisticated spirituality with a rigorously scientific outlook. Those optimists who did manage to hold onto the upbeat American vision generally did so by channeling it into a new nationalism that was anathema to Blow.

WITH RESPECT TO Freud, Putnam fell back on the grace of simple human friendship. As the carnage of early 1915 continued to mount (the German effort to dislodge the Russians from the crests of the Carpathian mountains in the so-called "winter war" alone resulted in over 190,000 Russian deaths) Putnam sent Freud a card with a line drawing of two joined hands. This physical clasp of support and friendship was Putnam's trademark gesture until his dying day. Above the picture, he wrote, "I hasten to assure you that neither war nor differences in opinion can change the estimate which I formed long ago. I trust it may be the same with you, and feel sure of it."

Freud was uncharacteristically unguarded in his gratitude for what he referred to as Putnam's "handclasp across the wide ocean." He assured Putnam that "not even the postal disruptions of this war will estrange us." He would, he said, write more often, only "the idea that there is a censor paralyzes the desire to write." War had externalized the everyday Freudian mental topography with its checks and balances of desire and ego.

Another factor prompting Freud's increasingly benevolent tone in letters to Putnam was associated with Anna. After having managed to reenter Austria, she had turned to Putnam's work as an especially satisfying expression of the analytic mission. Anna believed sufficiently in Putnam's vision that she made one of his essays the object of her first foray into print. At the same time as Putnam was finishing *Human Motives*, Anna set about translating his essay "On Some Broader Issues of the Psychoanalytic Movement." For all of the work's endorsement of Freud, this essay is equally concerned with the inability of analysis to address the essence of the self. Putnam argued that if the movement focused too much on biogenetic methods, it would be "liable to turn aside the attention from others, of still greater value, which refer mind, instincts, and chemical processes alike, to the influence of a self-renewing, self-active energy, seeking fuller and fuller opportunities for self-expression." The fact that Anna would choose as her maiden publication one of Putnam's works integrating analysis with philosophy—and that she would still have found meaning in the sublime hope of his metaphysics in the midst of war—may have given Freud cause for reflection.

WHAT, FINALLY, IS one to say about *Human Motives*? In this little, forest green volume embossed with gilt deco lettering, Putnam attempted to synthesize *all* the beliefs and systems of knowledge that went into constituting his own self-conceived best intelligence—post self-analysis. The book explicated Putnam's theories of education and psychoanalysis and the ways these practices could be integrated, buttressed by thinkers like Froebel, Freud, Blow, Bergson, and Helen Keller. One philosopher, however, lurked in the background of ideas appearing on almost every page, the man whose work Marian had reminded Putnam of decades earlier: Emerson. In making the final, consummate statement of his metaphysical perspective, Putnam returned to a figure from an earlier generation and used his work to suggest an update of New England Transcendentalism.

The epigraph of *Human Motives* is taken from Emerson's "Self-Reliance," and the closing passage of the book is a citation from an Emerson's poem. The body of the small-format 175-page book contains more than a dozen additional direct references to Emerson and countless other invocations of his ideas. Though Freud himself, of course, never accepted the contextualization of his thought that Putnam wanted to impose, even while devoting one respectful chapter solely to Freud's work and discussing psychoanalysis throughout, *Human Motives* always fit Freud into the larger landscape in which Putnam felt the Great Truths abided: "psycho-analytic doctrines, like all scientific doctrines," he wrote "are valid only within certain definite limits."

There's no indication that Freud had read Emerson or would have known what it meant to be categorized as an Emersonian thinker. And yet, no single thinker influenced Nietzsche the way Emerson did, and Nietzsche's influence on Freud was immense. One of the uncanny aspects for Freud of the experience of reading Putnam's exposition of his work in which his thought was juxtaposed and larded with Emerson's must have been that of seeing—to cite Emerson's "Self-Reliance"—his own thoughts returned to him "with a certain alienated majesty." That Putnam was at least dimly conscious of this tie is borne out by the fact that—very unusually for his era—he saw the link between Emerson and Nietzsche. He raised the connection in a manner significant for his understanding of Freud and the future of psychoanalysis in America.

Putnam took up the problem of individualism in the book's penultimate chapter, entitled "Instincts and Ideals." "Individualism and self-assertion have at times been lauded as so valuable that to attack them seems almost a ground for criticism," he wrote. "Indeed it is true that the willingness to go forward and bear one's burdens and if possible one's neighbors, to say 'No,' to espouse a cause which is unpopular, to cast aside the tendency to seek excuses for one's existence, to expose oneself to risk of life or reputation indicates a possible line of progress of a fine sort." For Putnam, individualism and self-assertion signified, equally, the idea of acting independently—sometimes on behalf one's neighbor. Yet, even this noble form of individualism contained inherent dangers: "Such willingness means progress," he went on, "if it leads onward to something better still; but if this does not happen, it indicates a real arrest." Combating what he saw as a misinterpretation of Emerson (in favor of one that many recent interpreters of Emerson's work also espouse), Putnam noted, "The individualism which plays so large a part in the poems and essays of Emerson, for example, and which was quietly but firmly exemplified by him in life, constitutes a noble trait. But all readers of Emerson must be aware that this doctrine was preached by him as a stepping-stone toward the same recognition of dependence on duties and ideals that I have endeavored in this essay to emphasize as important [i.e., community oriented ones]."

Putnam used this idea to segue to the creator of the Superman: "One cannot read Nietzsche's fiery lines without feeling that his individualism also had much to recommend it, based, as it was, on the doctrine of the voluntary endorsement of that which each person finds genuinely present in himself. What was in Nietzsche's mind, when he did not go too far, was like that which was in Emerson's mind when he said, 'If I am the Devil's child, I will live from the Devil.' But, unfortunately, this self-assertiveness can be terribly overdone, with the result that the person subject to it becomes an advocate of criticism gone mad, instead of a center of helpfulness to his neighbors and his community." Putnam was certainly thinking here both of the overreaching that had come to characterize German culture as a whole and of Freud's own system when he concluded, "The moment individualism ceases to be a stepping-stone to something better and gets itself ranked as a goal to be pursued in and for itself alone, it unmasks itself as a sign that the development of the individual received a check at an earlier stage, and that we have before us a situation of immaturity." Where Freud's focal act of unmasking was to peel back the façade of civilization and reveal a brutish, nasty maelstrom of drives, Putnam's was directed toward the irresponsibility of individualism—taking exaggerated individualism as proof that a person had failed in the imperative task of becoming an adult.

Human beings are born into conflict, subject to the impulse of two opposing sets of motives. One of these Putnam called "motives of constructiveness"; the other he described as "motives of adaptation." In this culminative statement of his philosophy, Putnam returned to the metaphysics of energy. Motives, he writes, "like the individual himself, may be said to stand at the point of intersection of numerous lines of energy, each of which 'Hath had elsewhere its set, And cometh from afar.' The main lines of energy with which a man must reckon represent, on the one hand, his evolutionary, biologic history, with all that implies in the way of half-blind self-assertion, temptation, struggle, victory and defeat; and, on the other hand, his spiritual history—that is, his relationship to the life of the universe as a whole." This agon could be described as a conflict not between Eros and Thanatos but between Eros and Super-Eros—between libido and loyalty. Humanity's spiritual history is entirely a factor of relational—*communal*—consciousness. "The fiend that man harries is love of the best," Putnam quoted, approvingly, from Emerson. It's tempting to read *Human Motives* as a defense of the essential goodness of human nature against the theory of innate depravity.

PUTNAM'S BOOK WAS taken up in Boston with the level of excitement that might welcome a slab of cold cod. Just as *Human Motives* represented a major amplification of his Weimar address, its failure represented a defeat on a far greater stage than that of the continental congress of misfit analysts.

The book found few readers and among those who did take it up few advocates. The *Dial* deemed Putnam's book "consoling when not convincing." Putnam's cousin and former colleague at the Emmanuel Movement, Richard Cabot, wrote it off as a hopeless mish-mash of ideas transplanted from Putnam's heroes like Emerson and Freud. Even Putnam Camp blinked. A note in the Camp log written shortly after the publication of *Human Motives* relates how a young woman was taken into the Stoop by a chaperone who proceeded to read her a page of Putnam's book "and then talked to her so long and in such an interesting manner by way of illustration that she presently fell asleep and almost rolled into the fire." Behind many of the criticisms lay the suggestion that Putnam's book was, on top of being obscure and mystical, obsolete. What was he doing beating the drum in defense of communal bonds at a moment when America's increasing mobility rendered them increasingly irrelevant? Wasn't loyalty itself a uselessly abstract quality? When Putnam's beloved cousin, Frances Morse, expressed uncertainty as to whether she really got his meaning, Putnam moaned, "I am very much in doubt whether anyone outside of a small group will take the slightest interest. You speak with doubt of your understanding it. But Goodness me!!!, if that were or is so, then the small group becomes vanishingly smaller."

Even Susan Blow, in her own discreet way, signaled that the book had been a disappointment. Though it could only have been gratifying to her that Putnam's book focused on education in general, and her own pedagogical theories in particular (his closing argument was that human motives depended on the "standards" arrived at through education), her regrets were more a matter of what was not said than of what was expressed. "I have read your book with much interest and I am going to read it again so that I may write you more intelligently than I can do today," she wrote him about a month after its publication. "One needs to be in a more alert mental state than I yet find myself to say anything about a book so provocative of thought as yours is, you may expect another letter from me when the wings of my mind are a little stronger." Putnam knew perfectly well that the wings of Blow's mind at their weakest were still far more powerful than those available to almost any other reader. If they were failing her, the ground around his little volume would be littered with feathers.

Her one explicit critique was directed at Putnam's treatment of psycho-analysis. "I should like very much to have more illustration of Freud's point of view and doubtless it would be a great thing for the Freudians could they assimilate your philosophy," she observed. Given that Freud's name and ideas were scattered through the entire book, and that an entire chap-ter of almost 40 pages was devoted exclusively to the psychoanalytic move-ment, Putnam could only have seen Blow's request for more Freud as evidence that he had not made his case to his most loyal fan. When she stated that "it would be a great thing for the Freudians" to accept Putnam's philosophy she gave no indication of believing that this could actually hap-pen. Blow's cool reaction to Putnam's book may reflect the fact that, with the First World War, she had come to see the divorce between religion and science as final.

INITIALLY, MY OWN response to the book was on a par with the harsh-ness of Putnam's contemporary critics. The book was so fusty and quaint! So unpleasantly certain of its optimistic conclusions about human nature. How *could* Putnam believe a set of propositions for which he offered next to no hard historical evidence, and which known history seems to stead-fastly contradict? I understood why the book provoked something more than ordinary frustration, triggering a reaction more akin to aggravated ire.

A number of Putnam's terms, beginning with "creative energy," seem opaque and deficient in resonance. They've been plucked out of the dense, massive volumes of the St. Louis Hegelianism he learned from Blow, and fall flat without that universe-encompassing frame of reference. And yet, picking up the book off and on over the course of several years, I've begun to think that I was wrong in dismissing it out of hand. There is a simpler, more timely argument at work in the pages as well.

Although Putnam's vision of human character is, based on the classic American model, always open to transformation, unlike the blithely perni-cious dispensers of self-help promises in our own time, there's no built-in guarantee that if we follow any particular path we will achieve the desired results. The work involves not self-aggrandizement or self-empowerment, but self-effacement and sacrifice. In order for one to assert the relation-ship between the self and the larger universe, one must enact a species of what Putnam calls "noblesse oblige." In the best democratic tradition, he was defending the community we construct out of a voluntarily accepted sense of responsibility toward the universe into which we're born. In the final pages of his book, he riffed off another Emerson quote, this time from "Compensation": "God offers to every mind its choice between truth and repose. Take which you please—you can never have both." But his use of the line went against the grain. Putnam argued that even if one did reject repose, the choice of truth was not something that came of its own accord to the chooser (unlike, say, the vision of a savior who enters the believer's life upon the believer's decision to accept that savior). "Let it not be sup-posed," Putnam wrote, "that the outcomes proposed by Emerson, in the form of the richer meanings which the universe offers to all who will seek for them, are to be had only for the asking. To assert this would be to over-look a number of important facts. When he says that evil will bless, and (as in 'Compensation') that our own best selves rush, in spite of all obstacles to meet us, he announces what may be, not what must be. The determina-tion of the actual outcome rests with us." What we're called upon to achieve, "when pain, adversity, sorrow, or temptation make their challenge to the human soul" is nothing less than sublimation. Like Beethoven, overcom-ing his deafness with "his power of inward hearing," or Helen Keller dis-covering "a world of beauty and music richer than that in which she otherwise would have lived," we must actively convert the dross of our selves into something sublime. The way to achieve conversion is the construc-tion of community.

In the final movement of the book, Putnam proffered his most dramatic reinterpretation of a Freudian concept: "Our real world, think of it in what-ever terms we may, is a world modified and adorned by fancy, and the problem for each individual is to make it correspond to the expression of his best self and the best selves of other men." In other words, Putnam accepted Freud's sweeping implication of fantasy in the operation of human psychology, but then argued that this sway of imagination provided even greater opportunity for injecting the ethical imperative into the world. Freud presented America with a fantasy realm in which the most primal urges of the individual were running wild and could only be tamed by being caught in the analytic sights, then willfully fettered like rabid beasts. Putnam took that same realm and insisted that our powers of fantasy were to be nourished because they defined the space in which transindividual morality was most free, able to evolve new strains more resistant to the corrosions of the real world.

In the last paragraphs, Putnam justified the focus he'd placed on motives as a malleable substance: "The choice of motives, whether voluntarily or instinctively made, must depend in the final analysis on the standards arrived at through education, the true function of which consists in leading to the discovery of deeper and deeper relationships between the outside world and the inner life." The system of education Putnam was championing was in fact identical to the one supported by the former American commission of education, Blow's mentor, William T. Harris. In 1915, it was still conceivable that America would take upon itself the immense challenge of concentrating its pedagogical mandate on teaching students community obligation and self-sacrifice for others as the course to personal accomplishment.

There's one way in which Putnam's work does seem profoundly outdated. When he wrote *Human Motives*, he believed wholeheartedly that if people were made aware of their larger network of social obligations it was inconceivable that they wouldn't embrace that responsibility. Freud's understanding of our primal urge to individualism has been vindicated— in part by the failure of our society to hold up an ethically higher standard of social education.

WHAT HOPE FOR Putnam's great American dream of absolute synthesis could survive the slaughter of more than half a million men in 1915 along the Western Front? What angels could be said to remain in the depths of humanity's motivational maelstrom when day after day after day the killing waxed to new heights of brutality? By the time *Human Motives* was published, Blow was becoming resigned to utter defeat. "If I do not urge your coming beyond saying what a pleasure it would be to see you it is only because I know what important things keep you at home," she wrote him near the end of the year in a singular instance of her refraining from pressing him to visit. Beyond his domestic obligations, she wrote, "I realize that

I might not be able to talk as much or as much to the point as I wish I could." Her response to the darkening picture of the war was to fall into deeper and deeper silence. Blow was left, at the last, speechless in horror at the new world she'd survived against her will to witness. An undated note in her commonplace book captures her state in the summer of 1915 with icy accuracy: "We are always praying for vision but there are times when we should pray to be blind."

CHAPTER 30

The Reality of the Unseen

My friend Putnam maintained in a recent book which is based
on psychoanalysis that perfection has not only a psychic but
also a material reality. That man can't be helped, he must
become a pessimist!

Freud to Lou Andreas-Salome, July 30, 1915

THE HARSH DEPRIVATIONS war brought Freud in Vienna, from the increasing scarcity of cigars, food, and heating fuel, to his anxious separation from his two sons at the front, could not, at first, entirely erase the acid satisfaction of seeing his analysis of human nature vindicated. At the very moment when Putnam was petitioning for a radically increased sense of communal responsibility and lamenting the dwindling circle of people who understood this summons, Freud was contemplating with mixed emotions the return of his splendid isolation. "The *Verein* is as doomed as everything else that is called international," he wrote Jones. No doubt all their journals would soon cease publication. "Everything we wanted to cultivate and care for, we now have to let run wild." What turncoats like Jung had permitted to survive was "perishing in the strife among the nations."

Yet it was with some relief, also, that Freud contemplated a retreat into the anchoritic cell from where he would do what he could to keep civilization alive. He'd already begun writing essays at the most productive clip of his entire life. These are eloquent and disturbing works. In "Thoughts for the Times on War and Death," he wrote of how war would sweep away the "conventional treatment" of morality whereby each individual imagined himself to be the solitary stalk spared the reaper's scythe. "Death will no longer be denied; we are forced to believe in it. People really die: and

no longer one by one, but many, often tens of thousands, in a single day
. . . and the accumulation of deaths puts an end to the impression of chance."
And then Freud delivered the *coup de grace*. "Life has, indeed, become
interesting again; it has recovered its full content."

Implicit in his analysis of what still remained extant in wartime was the
notion that whereas hysterics might have suffered on account of reminiscences, the same sensitivity made them part of the caste that kept the dead
alive. Unlike his biblical prototypes, whose prophecies were filled with
admonitions to mend one's ways in the here and now because "the end is
near," Freud preached that the end was happening at every instant.
Whereas Putnam's self-effacement was intended to foster the continued
development of the larger social body, Freud's was meant to hasten the
process of wiping the slate clean so that, as had happened once before following the great flood, "the Great Unknown" could begin its work afresh.
Though some of Freud's ideas at this time carry a taint of nihilism, allowing them the didactic purpose he did not quite own up to, one finds a moral
argument at work: When we allow ourselves to give up all hope of saving
anything in this world, we give up the basis for adopting an ideology that
insists that saving the world is possible, if only everyone would cooperate.
Freud understood that the urge to eradicate immorality from the face of
the earth easily transformed into the propagation of further evil by the
crusaders themselves.

One of the strangest mysteries in the history of Freud's written legacy
concerns the fate of his missing papers on metapsychology. Between mid-
March 1915 and early August of the same year, Freud wrote *twelve* essays
on metapsychology. References to the papers crop up throughout his correspondence to Jones, to Andreas-Salome, to Binswanger, and to Putnam.
As late as the end of 1917 Freud was writing Abraham that the book of
essays was ready for publication. Yet only five of the papers survive. The
usual explanation for the other papers' fate is that Freud felt dissatisfied
with their quality and burned them. Jones posits that the lost essays on
metapsychology was a "summing up of his life's work" to date and so had
no place in the new ideas that were to emerge post war. Apart from the
fact that there's no clear reason Freud would have felt it desirable to destroy a summation of the work he'd done so far, Jones' thesis would seem
to be contradicted by the fact that Freud told Andreas-Salome that his first
effort at reconstituting the incomplete works of metapsychology would be

"Beyond the Pleasure Principle"—an essay that could be said to anticipate Freud's final phase.

The solution to the mystery may lie rather in the fact that Freud destroyed the papers on metapsychology because they pointed to a *new* direction of thought that he decided to shut down. Freud's correspondence in this period and the two essays, "Thoughts for the Times on War and Death" and "On Transience," suggest that he'd become fixated on the possibility that after the purge of war it might be possible to re-create civilization along lines laid out by psychoanalysis. This is not exactly an optimistic proposition, but it is a philosophical one, and one based moreover on the potential for progress—so long as analysis was made a kind of state religion. Intriguingly, one of the two final papers in the absent metaphysical series was devoted entirely to Putnam's own obsession: sublimation.

Early in the summer of 1915, in response to a letter from Putnam announcing the impending arrival of *Human Motives*, Freud wrote good humoredly, "My chief impression [however] is that I am far more primitive, more modest and more unsublimated than my dear friend in Boston. I see his noble ambition, his profound curiosity. I compare them with my own way of restricting myself to what lies nearest, is most tangible, and yet is actually petty, and with my tendency to be satisfied with whatever is attainable." Yet a month later, after Putnam's book had made it to Vienna and Freud had actually started to read *Human Motives*, he began to communicate in a different key.

Though *Human Motives* failed to set the world of psychologists, philosophers, educators, and theologians on fire back home in America, the book succeeded in accomplishing what Putnam had tried so long and failed to do: he engaged Freud's imagination on the questions nearest his heart. Moreover, Putnam's book drew from Freud a rare sustained meditation on the deeper ethical motivations informing his own character.

"I am in no way in awe of the Almighty," Freud announced in his blustering opening sally. "If we ever met one another, it is rather I who should reproach Him, than he me. I would ask him why he had not provided me with a better intellectual equipment; he could not accuse me of not having made the best use of my alleged freedom." But after noting his cosmic dissatisfaction, Freud added an important qualification: "I consider myself a very moral being . . . I believe that in a sense of justice and consideration for one's fellow men, in discomfort at making others suffer or taking advantage of them, I can compete with the best men I have ever known." Freud clarified that he was discussing morality in a social not a sexual sense, and proclaimed, "Sexual morality as society—and at its most extreme, American society—defines it, seems very despicable to me. I stand for a much freer sexual life. However, I have made little use of such freedom, except in so far as I was convinced of what was permissible for me in this area."

Whereas it's the first part of Freud's statement, in which he noted his failure to act on his belief that sexual existence ought to be more liberated that's usually cited, the provocative second half of his statement has been neglected: Freud's cryptic admission that he in fact *has* made use of this freedom in areas where he was convinced it was acceptable to do so. Freud must be referring to something more than his tepid conjugal relations encompassed. He may well have been hinting at his indulgence in sexual fantasies, which were quite possibly homoerotic in nature and grandiose in their trappings.

Jumping from this observation to a denunciation of Jung (the subject of his last powerful homosexual attraction), Freud justified his own resistance to religion. The sting of betrayal throbs from the page, and suggests that the disappointment of desire, fantasy, and fantasized desire were responsible for Freud's unwillingness to indulge mysticism: "What I have seen of religious-ethical conversation has not been inviting," Freud wrote Putnam. "Jung, for example, I found sympathetic so long as he lived blindly, as I did. Then came his religious-ethical crisis with higher morality, 'rebirth,' Bergson and at the very same time lies, brutality and anti-Semitic condescension toward me." Metaphors of blindness crop up repeatedly in Jung's accusations against Freud. The growth of Jung's sense of independence from Freud was coupled with the idea that he'd regained his own freedom of vision from Freud's occluded gaze. Freud's remarks regarding the desirability of blindness and the cave of illusion, even if tongue-in-cheek, form the antipode to Putnam's veneration of Helen Keller's struggle for light.

At last Freud dropped the note of bile and allowed himself to draw closer to Putnam than he'd come before. "When I ask myself why I always have striven honestly to be considerate of others and if possible kind to them and why I did not give this up when I noticed that one is harmed by such behavior and is victimized because others are brutal and unreliable, I really have no answer." Freud related to Putnam that he took no pleasure in his ethical superiority and then extended the olive branch. Prompted in part, no doubt, by bitterness at Jung and wonder at his own character, he wrote, "You might almost cite my case as a proof of your assertion that such ideal impulses form an essential part of our nature." In concluding his combination of peace offering to Putnam and vindication of himself against the siren-betrayers of his love, Freud noted: "If knowledge of the human soul is still so incomplete that my poor talents could succeed in making such important discoveries, it seems likely that it is too early to decide for or against hypotheses such as yours."

This admission may seem mild, or even self-serving, but it's virtually everything Putnam had been asking for all along. Putnam's pleading had been directed toward eliciting Freud's acknowledgment of the *possibility* that there might be truth in his metaphysics—not an orthodox embrace of them.

Yet in Freud's religious imagination there was no realm of transcendent sublimation. Opening to the unknown meant erasing the boundaries between one's self and the underworld. This subterranean sphere was a Faustian, spellbound theater of darkness in which the omnipotence of thoughts contested with magical potencies of a nameless, demonic pantheon. Freud had the diplomatic sense not to share this context with Putnam.

Nor did he broach the subject of the haunting dreams that accompanied his reading of *Human Motives*. On the same night that he wrote Putnam, Freud recorded a dream in which "Martha comes toward me, I am supposed to write something down for her—write into a notebook, I take out my pencil. . . . It becomes very indistinct." The day before writing the letter and having the dream, Freud had noted in his journal "successful coitus." The inability to use his pencil as Martha dictated is suggestive within Freud's schema as an allegory of impotence—at least when it came to Martha. A further clue to the dream's meaning may lie in Freud's unconscious meditation on themes he'd written Putnam about before going to sleep. The image of everything becoming "very indistinct" is also one of the subject going blind. Blindness is linked with the inability to fulfill Martha's wishes—to fulfill Martha herself. Blindness was what he'd shared with Jung, when the two had enjoyed perfect intimacy. Oedipus blinded himself with the pins holding up his mother's dress; she became naked at the instant he lost his vision. The "higher morality" that Putnam invoked threatened to pull away the mantle of blindness which, as Mother Thanatos, cloaked and nurtured Freud's fantasy life.

A still darker manifestation hovered on the edge of Freud's reading of *Human Motives*. Two days after writing his letter to Putnam, Freud wrote Ferenczi about a dream that creates a kind of *mise en abyme* of his relation to the occult. It had been some time since Freud had heard word from Martin, whose unit was fighting at the front in Galicia. The busy night on which he had the dream of going blind in relation to intercourse with Martha, a night on which Freud had fallen asleep reading Putnam's book, Freud had a terrible nightmare. He awoke having dreamt vividly of Martin's death. So real was the nightmare that Freud was afraid that the dream was actually a clairvoyant message from beyond indicating that his son had been killed in battle.

Given the open hostility Freud sometimes felt toward Martin as a ne'er-do-well adventurer, one might suspect that a Freudian lexicon could be successfully employed to elucidate the dream—that the dream hid an unconscious death wish against Martin. Indeed, in the case of other dreams in which his sons met with disaster, Freud acknowledged that the nightmares symbolized jealousy for their youth. In his letter to Ferenczi, however, Freud interpreted the dream, instead, as a supernatural test related to *Human Motives*: "I had a prophetic dream, which very clearly had as its content the deaths of my sons, Martin first," he explained. "I was able to clarify very well the mechanism and occasion for the dream; it was a bold challenge to the occult powers after reading a book that demanded piety from me, of all people." Though just 48 hours earlier Freud had expressed appreciation to Putnam for the ideas he put forward in *Human Motives*, to Ferenczi he confessed resentment at what he viewed as Putnam's baiting him to be good. By refusing to accept Putnam's faith, Freud felt that he was taunting the forces of the underworld, tempting them to do their worst by murdering his first-born son. Because he would not accept Putnam's heaven, he was opening the doors to his own hell. He paraded his success in the duel by telling Ferenczi that the dream was not accompanied by feelings of mourning, "and I hope now to be right in the face of all evil spirits."

It was at best an archaic angst, one that indicated just how far Freud really stood from Putnam's, de-anthropomorphized, disembodied, dull, philosophical Olympus. Freud's faith, to the extent that he had one, reads at times like an anti-Semitic version of the Old Testament, dominated by a

God that can't save, but might still damn and kill. If Martin survived, Freud and his idiosyncratic vision of science were stronger than the black powers. If not, hell and chaos had come again. It's impressive that Freud could read Putnam's opus—a book which, if anything, suffers from being too dainty-minded—and see that work as triggering a visitation from the infernal regions to warn him that his son had been killed in revenge for his faithlessness.

The note of triumph in his letter to Ferenczi swiftly dissipated. After proclaiming his apotropaic hope, Freud admitted that he'd learned on the day after his dream that the "good boy" who'd saved Martin following his skiing accident "has now been killed himself." The furies were circling awfully close. So far from really believing he'd put the demons to rest, Freud now waited desperately for word from Martin himself to prove the oracular dream false. Ten days later, the silence still had not been broken. Finally, on the 21st of July, Freud told Ferenczi that he'd just received a card from Martin dated the 7th, showing that the "clear death dream about Martin" he'd had after reading *Human Motives* could not be correct. "So, we are certainly not dealing with such crude things," Freud announced with relief. And yet, in the very next sentence, he reported that they'd just received news from the front line indicating that Martin *had* been lightly wounded by a Russian bullet. "He doesn't indicate a date." Freud vowed to find out the time that the injury had happened. Perhaps, he mused, as "one can be far more sensitive at night," what had been registered as a death on the tablet of dreams had actually been an injury. The results of the contest were tantalizingly borderline. Though Freud badgered Martin to tell him the exact date on which he'd received the wound, Martin never answered his question.

How frustrating and painful it must have been for Freud to have come so close to a definitive answer to the question of the truth of the occult, and then to again find himself cast in the liminal space where both possibilities remained alive. This supernatural ambivalence was, itself, an instance of the uncanny.

THE DIFFICULTY OF communicating during wartime cut off the exchange between Putnam and Freud on the questions of ultimate meaning and purpose at the very moment when they both became fully engaged.

Not that Putnam was willing to give up. In response to Freud's remarks on his book, Putnam composed the longest letter he'd ever written Freud, an epistle summarizing his entire philosophical position, along with the application of that position to the history of the psychoanalytic movement and Freud himself. In fact, the letter was so verbose that Putnam opted not to send it, waiting a month to write an abridged version about half the original length. He also tried to soften the stridency of what he'd initially written, but the core of his argument remained intact. "It is you who have helped to teach me to be 'religious' and to believe in the reality of the unseen, and in 'free will,'" Putnam charged. The notion that truth and justice exist simultaneously within and outside the individual and that we are to "make *voluntary* sacrifices for them," an idea Putnam ascribes to Freud, "is religion and the worship of the unseen." This is the essence of what could be called either the great American analytic revelation or sleight of hand.

Putnam's vision of that unconscious as a place where hope of personal fruition could amplify to infinity was predictive of what became of psychoanalysis in the New World. In this sense, Putnam's book, *Human Motives*, in fact did signify the murder of Freud's most beloved "son."

CHAPTER 31

Solitudes of the Soul

I must hold however that the double selfhood is inborn and
that no matter how free from regrettable experiences our lives
may be, no man or woman can escape the contrast of his finite
with the infinite self. Old Homer knew this when he made the
eidolon of Herakles appear to Odysseus in Hades and yet
declared that he himself was enjoying on Olympus the banquet
of the blessed Gods.

Blow to Putnam, October 23, 1910

THE OPTIMISTIC VISION Putnam hailed in *Human Motives* jarred too
harshly with Blow's experience of the world for her to gloss over the dissonance. Paradoxically, on a number of points, Blow began to sound closer
to Freud than to her Boston doctor and disciple. To begin with, she was
not, to put it mildly, of a naturally cheerful disposition. Even intellectually, though her philosophy can sound idealistic to contemporary ears, she
considered herself a brand of realist. "Dr. Harris always held to realism
and I have long realized that much of the defect of contemporary thought
was its purely subjective idealism," she wrote Putnam a year before the
outbreak of war. Long before that, she had repeatedly expressed her conviction that evil was a part of the world and human nature. The only com-
pensating factor was the way that guilt could fuel the drive to redemption.
In her commonplace book she once wrote, "Pessimism is the sense of evil
without the sense of sin."

Blow was not without loved ones who depended on her, most notably
the orphaned children of a deceased sister whom Blow supported and

helped to care for her whole life. Yet for whatever reason, the calls upon her sense of duty were not vivid enough to distract her from her demons.

It might not have been the start of gas warfare at Ypres, or the 400,000 allied troops killed at Somme or the proliferating insanity of trench warfare across Europe that tipped the scales. But at a certain point in 1915 the World War overwhelmed Blow. In autumn, Putnam learned that she was on the edge of a breakdown. "You have always been the best and kindest of physicians and friends," she informed him. "I am greatly touched by your note which has just come. But I can't even think of having you come to New York just to see me. If you happen to be here anytime for other reasons I shall be glad and grateful if you can come to see me. I was very tired when I got to New York and when one is physically used up one has less self control. I suppose Miss Fisher felt I had gone to pieces. I don't mean to deny that I have—but I am more rested now and have myself a little more under control. I suppose that these breakings up of equilibrium will beset some of us always. When they come they must be faced. That many others are facing them as well as myself I know. How can it be otherwise when everything we thought we thought is challenged by the great world-tragedy and when the depths of sin revealed by that tragedy find so much like themselves in our own hearts? 'If thou gaze into an abyss, the abyss also will gaze into thee.'"

Soon after this she wrote him again to prop up his faith that she—and their philosophy—would survive the crisis. "What we have seen is true and no weakness in me can change that truth." The demons, she tried to tell him, were her own: "I was born when my mother was in an unstable state and I have always had lapses into unstability. The philosophy whose truth we know has done more than anything else to cure my congenital defect. It is acting now as an organizing and remedial force. So do not fear that through emotional disturbance I shall do something you would regret. . . . As I have said the real question concerns our relation to the Divine First Principle. You are occupied with that question in so far as it relates to personal immortality. I am occupied with it in its relation to sin and the deliverance from sin. Must I not face my problem as you face yours and may it not be that through facing it I shall see further implications in the one great insight?"

At the end, she turned Freud against Putnam to argue that she had to be trusted as she directed her gaze toward the vertiginous depths. "Nothing is more conducive to unhealthy states of mind than refusing to look a difficulty in the face. Surely as you have so often said it is the suppressed evaded problem which is dangerous. . . . This letter needs no answer. It is really only to say you must feel perfectly easy in your mind about me and must not *further overtax yourself.* You see what has happened. You have cured me by 'the expulsive power of a new feeling.'" How could Putnam have felt his anxiety assuaged?

When he finally found time to visit her at the start of the New Year in 1916 the two talked a great deal about Freud. "The Psychoanalytic method seems to me (perhaps because I do not understand it) to be too exclusively concerned with man himself whereas so far as I can see what is really involved in sin is the breaking of a tie between the soul and god," she wrote him afterwards. "That tie cannot be restored by the kindest and best of physicians." The real problem with analysis, Blow hinted, was that its view of human nature wasn't intractable and dark *enough.* "I fear we shall have to be wholly free from sloth, lust, gluttony, avarice, anger, envy and pride before either introspection or retrospection can be free from agony. I do not say more of the thoughts which are occupying my own mind for several reasons. . . . I hope it does not seem ungrateful that for the moment I cannot talk. There are solitudes of the soul as well as deserts and seas in the world. When I get to an oasis or find a harbor I shall tell you."

In February, as the Germans advanced victoriously on the garrison town of Verdun, launching a battle that would ultimately be the longest in the war and claim above three quarters of a million lives, Blow wrote the last surviving letter in her correspondence with Putnam. She began by talking of Putnam's wife, praising her strength and steadiness and remarking that Marian was "so altogether woman at her best that it is a comfort to think of her," then she moved on to Putnam himself. "Your letter is very very kind and I read all it says between the lines," she wrote. Whatever Putnam had explicitly expressed, recognizing the desperation of her state he may have finally, delicately, conveyed his love for her in the midst of gratitude for all the faith and knowledge she'd given him over the years. "I shall not say anything about the war," she concluded. "I realize I am not in a state to form calm and equable judgments. I wish someone with clear and piercing vision might arise to show us what we ought to do. The absence of such vision makes one realize as never before the greatness of the heroes of vision, faith and courage who in past crises have seen what should be done and done it."

A month later, while visiting friends in New York City, Blow died. The Cathedral of St. John the Divine held a memorial service in her honor. Hymns and readings from the New Testament were followed by a series of eulogies offering personal reminiscences about her first kindergarten and the impact her life had on generations of educators and students. In the quarter century between the time Blow opened America's first kindergarten and 1898, when Harris gave his ninth annual report as U.S. Commission of Education, 189 cities founded public kindergartens. In 1910, when Blow went back to St. Louis to attend a meeting of the International Kindergarten Union, upward of 600 kindergarten teachers, steeped in her Froebelian cum Hegelian vision of early childhood education, applauded Blow's appearance. Her work unfolded both on a macro scale, with the development of overarching principles designed to inform all aspects of kindergarten teaching, and on a detailed practical level. With regard to the latter, for example, at the same time as she was immersed in the study of Hegel's *Larger Logic*, she designed what the Director of the St. Louis Public Schools characterized as "20 Gifts of Learning" to assist children in mastering drafting and the properties of lines, solids, and surfaces. The first gift was "six soft balls of various colors" intended to teach color. Gift number fifteen consisted of "plaiting material . . . to form geometrical and fancy figures." The nineteenth gift was described as "peas work" meant to "develop the eye for perspective drawing," and so on. At St. John the Divine, one former student remembered the good common sense that led Blow to replace the original, regular-size desks in classrooms with desks and chairs scaled to the size of children, and another extolled her powers of imaginative empathy, recalling her skill at handling bouts of homesickness. Blow, he reminisced, "took me on her lap and told me a little story about two small buckets, one behind each eye, that turned over and spilled out water for tears when I wanted to cry," until wonder at the mechanics of it quelled his sorrow.

In the *Times* obituary, which reaffirmed her status as America's "Mother of the Kindergarten," Blow's death was attributed to depression brought on by the Great War. Just as members of apocalyptic millenarian sects who predict the end of the world on specific dates have been known to commit suicide when destruction and the rapture did not ensue, Blow, perhaps the last of the doctrinaire St. Louis Hegelians, could not survive Verdun, mustard gas, and the destruction of a generation that was supposed to have been advancing on a steady forward march to God.

Yet in at least one respect, she surpassed both Putnam and Freud. Blow knew, better than either of the two men, how to make of a grand, unrequited love something noble and generous. At the end of one long, dense, philosophical passage in a letter she wrote Putnam in 1910, she summed up both her philosophy and her spirit in a single sentence: "To put it as simply as I can, I believe God is so full of love that he actually needs you and me."

Putnam composed his own obituary of Blow for the *Boston Transcript*. After going through the roster of her professional achievements, he broke into a reverie in the final paragraph about the enchantment of their friendship. For all that Blow was a gifted writer, Putnam wrote, "her speech and manner carried a conviction that the printed characters could not equal, and in the give and take of conversation, still more in the intimate talk of a congenial friendship, she showed a force of discrimination, a richness of memory, a power of definition that seemed truly marvelous. I heard her once describe 'humility' as the quality which induces one to share with others all that one has. This quality she possessed in full measure. The door to her splendid intelligence, her keen, unbiased insight, her generous heart, stood ever open, and a summer's day spent in 'the porch' of her hospitable cottage at Cazenovia was a day never to be forgotten."

The only written evidence of Marian's response to the news of Blow's death suggests that it was not her finest hour. During the war years Molly had begun her medical studies. Though Putnam made a valiant effort to convince Harvard to reconsider its refusal to admit women into the Medical School, the policy of exclusion remained in place and Molly ended up studying at Johns Hopkins. It's not surprising, given the complexities of his own relationship with Molly, that Putnam would have been too cut up to write Molly himself with news of Blow's death. And so, squeezed into the margin of one of Marian's standard long chatty epistles ("Today is the great day for Margie and Ken, where you and Lue ought to be here arranging flowers and pouring tea") filled with trivial news of visitors come and gone ("Elizabeth has been staying at Ellen Forbeses and is coming home today to go over tomorrow to Betty Wiggenses") and scheduling logistics ("I am not sending you a birthday present because I have to count your journey in as that. By the way, Mrs. Geo. Blake of Weston wants you to give her children sailing lessons next July"), scribbled just above the salutation and before the farewell one reads: "Jamie is very happy at the City Hosp—Miss Blow died last week, it is a very great loss to Papa. Much love to You Your Mother."

Marian's relegation of Blow to the status of an apparent afterthought in the margins is made more poignant by an unsigned fragment of a letter dated less than a month after Blow's death in the Blow-Putnam file at the Countway Library. The note appears to come from an administrator at the institution where Blow passed away. "Dear Dr. Putnam—I have been meaning to write to you for a very long time . . . and now our dear Miss Blow's death brings you very near to my thoughts and heart, for I know how much you will feel it. Still I know, too, that you will rejoice for her to be free—It was very sudden at the end—She has had a hard winter—and bore it very bravely—the war cut very deep—for Hegel failed her there and it seemed as if so many things one had counted as truth were falsified. I believe she agonized over it, but underneath was always her great intellectual honesty and fine courage. . . . We talked of you dear Dr. Putnam when she first came and she was so interested to hear of your visit to us last summer and of the help you had given us. . . . She said she thought Mrs. Putnam was the type of real and *ideal* woman (forgive me for being personal) because she entirely fulfilled [illegible word here] her work in life—the work a woman should do—and with sureness and poise."

As Susan Blow was settling into the place where she would die, her conversation turned from Putnam to Marian. Some of her last words were devoted to praising the wife of the man she loved. Blow had lived in the great world, from Europe to South America. She'd helped to transform American education, written exhaustively on a host of intellectual subjects, lectured, and been an active proselytizer for one of the most important American philosophical movements of the nineteenth century, and in her final hours her thoughts concerned Marian Putnam. It was *she* (and by inference not Blow) who was the archetype of the real and ideal woman. It was Marian's work, raising a family, supporting and engaging with their home life in all minutiae, and not her own work as a Hegelian educator that was the real "work a woman should do." Perhaps this fervent devotion to Marian's example was the only way Blow could reconcile her grief for the life she did not live with the man she could not help loving.

CHAPTER 32

A Species of New Birth

This is not a propitious time for physical well being, nor does it matter.

Freud to Putnam, January 26, 1916

AS THE SCOPE and fury of the First World War became apparent, America's young—alternately educated, privileged, patriotic, idle, hapless, and heroic—began flooding into Europe.

"When I left Father on the dock I thought I should certainly burst; I never felt so awfully in my life," Elizabeth Putnam wrote in her diary as she left New York in 1916 to begin two years of work in France as a volunteer nurse. "I looked everywhere for him on the wharf until the boat sailed, but it is just as well I didn't see him, for I should probably have gone on shore again for good if I had." However, her tone quickly grew more chipper as she described her French actress cabinmates: "I am delighted to be with them, for I learn how to apply white-washes, lip and cheek rouge, eyebrow pencils, curling irons and fake curls—as well as some French." She even enjoyed a mild, romantic moment, sitting out on deck after hours to hear a group of talented singers. "One evening a man came along and sat with me, in the pitch dark (no lights allowed, all windows covered), and we had a long and pleasant talk (he was a travelling man from Oklahoma), but I have no idea what he looks like and he probably doesn't realize that and thinks I cut him dead next day. You see he saw me when he opened the door to let me in, but I didn't like to turn around and stare at him." A few days later, as the boat approached land she wrote, "This curious adventure called 'going to France' is about to begin. I feel rather swamped."

IT SEEMED LIKELY that Marian, at least, would have been anxious about the idea of her daughter traveling into the theater of war. Instead, even after Elizabeth had been overseas for a year when she asked her parents what she ought to do about renewing her tour of duty, both Marian and Putnam, separately, strongly encouraged her to remain in service, unless, Putnam conscientiously added, she felt she was in danger of "shell shock." Rather than worrying about her coming home, Putnam's main concern seemed to be that she not squander the chance to soak up as much of the French atmosphere and real life of the people as possible by trading in her living arrangement with a family in Paris to set up quarters with a friend who'd arrived from Boston.

During the initial weeks of her adventure, Elizabeth's letters swung between intoxicated elation and awed compassion for the injured men she encountered. She could be at once condescending and effusive, reporting for example how "one gets awfully fond of the men almost at once, they are so very friendly, and so childlike in their capacity for enjoyment. It gives them the most exquisite pleasure to say 'Good morning, Mees Petnam,' in English." One night, she went to hear a service at Notre Dame ("It really was the most beautiful singing I almost ever heard . . . it seemed to be born and not made") then on "with Mr. Sedgwick to a very gay restaurant called the 'Café de Paris' where we had the most delicious—and *far* the most expensive, thank Heaven—meal I have ever eaten."

She described snake dancing in the streets of Rouen and the permeating, debilitating stench of wounds. During the bombing of Paris she wrote her mother: "Just back from 'Tosca.' When we got out everyone was running, and behold there was a raid on. You don't know how pretty the French planes are—great yellow 'flying stars' . . . We went for the Metro and stood at the entrance, in the Place de l'Opera, watching the planes and the silvery flashes of shrapnel from the anti-aircraft guns, and listening to words of comfort from strange Australians. The Australians are certainly attractive—so very big and clean-cut and often handsome—they are about the most attractive set here."

Though she never entirely lost the hopeful bubble of her tone, Elizabeth's view matured over time. She talked less about her own pleasures and more about the plans she'd developed to "treat" her *blessés* (wounded) in small ways—distributing money when she could to those in need, assembling little gifts. Despite her increasing exhaustion and sadness, she wrote, "I couldn't bear to leave everything still going on here." Her notes on the men in her care gradually devoted less time to their good looks and more to knowledgeable descriptions of their wounds.

Both her parents were writing her voluminous epistles every few days. A number of them carried a didactic philosophical purpose, and though she strove to reassure them about the happiness all the correspondence brought her ("I adore Father's 'rambling letters,' so don't ever let him make them any different," she wrote to her mother), as her exposure to France deepened she felt obligated to tell him that she was not able to serve as his philosophical missionary by proxy. In the late winter of 1917, she wrote her father half-humorously and half in earnest the principal lesson she took from the war, one concerning herself and her own limitations, addressed directly to Putnam's world-historical metaphysical calling. "My poor Father, I want to break it to you gently that I shall never do the glorious deeds you would like me to. I shall be fond of my family and friends and try to make life pleasant for them, but as to reforming or even informing the world, I'm afraid I haven't it in me . . . I know I'm an awful disappointment to you, but I can't be helped. I really can't come back and rehabilitate France."

Though Elizabeth was no doubt correct in her surmise of how Putnam would respond to news of her contracted horizons, the awareness of the boundaries of her self that she'd arrived at was both rare and salutary for an American abroad. Even when a note of silliness crept into her remarks about the foreigners, she grew to genuinely savor the Gallic way of life. After a time, her letters became filled with observations on "enchanting" days spent wandering the streets of Paris. She had developed no aspiration to Americanize the place in response to any inadequacies she witnessed. Rather, serving in France had taken away whatever impulse to convert others to the New England ethos she may have arrived with. In the last of her reports from France, Elizabeth described having so many gifts to dispense in Boston she would have to open her own "Home Service" office. "And only two short months before I am back in France!" She was writing in September, and the armistice came before she could return.

JAMIE BEGAN SERVING in an ambulance corps in France two years before Elizabeth. He wrote at least one long letter home recounting the routine of his new life. (The day began at 6:45 AM, whereupon "for fifteen
minutes we wave our arms in the air, breathe deep, and hop on one leg—
same new wrinkle every day. Dr. Nichols says he sees no sense in it, but
for all that it certainly gets up your appetite. . . . This life is certainly conducive to the fat and rosy physique!") But the major record of Jamie's experience of the War is a small, haunting scrapbook bound in maroon leather
that he kept in 1915. It evokes a work by Sebald or, more accurately, one
created by a character in one of Sebald's books. Following introductory
pages devoted to photographs of two handsome doctors leaning back against
a wall with a black dog at their feet, a map of France, and a roster of the
arrondisements, Jamie pasted a series of photographs of different soldiers
he'd cared for alongside strangely lyric descriptions and diagrams of their
wounds. The most poignant aspect of the book is the way in which, along
with his photographs and depictions of injuries, Jamie has allowed each
soldier to write in his own hand a statement of *"Comment je fus blessé"*—
how I was wounded. Sometimes in a painfully shaky scrawl, at others in
lovely script, the soldiers have carefully, often at length, inscribed the history of events surrounding their fall on the battlefield. In its grace and
deference before the narratives of these poor men, the book ends up being
a portrait of Jamie himself as well.

THE ATMOSPHERE ON the home front was not especially bleak. Notwithstanding the death of Blow and Marian's unflinching resistance to psychoanalysis, Putnam clearly took more joy in his home life, in Marian herself,
and in their vicarious exposure to the adventures of their offspring than it
had been possible for him to take in the past. The daily routine of life, writing
essays on analysis, participating in congresses, celebrating family gatherings, visiting friends and tending their garden on Cape Cod demanded as
much time and gave as great a reward as ever. Though, throughout the War,
the trees were "swarming with gypsies," Putnam wrote Elizabeth that
"Cotuit was never more lovely, and the veg. garden is in most respects a
dream." Nor did the family ever stop traveling to Camp. One summer
during the War, the Camp log reported that Dr. Putnam was "Popsy Wopsy
today at Forky for the first time in history." But he had not slowed down

much. Though he was in his seventies, he scaled the exhausting peak of Giant without a trail over the north shoulder and "after some exciting experiences in rock climbing, climbing to the sense of touch," camped out on the mountain face in the frigid Adirondack fall.

The family's social life, now often combined with war-relief projects, was unusually busy. At the beginning of 1917, Putnam confessed to Elizabeth that he'd been to a philanthropic event at which he'd even found himself *dancing* with one "Mrs. Hocking," having been "tempted thereto by the pretty music and her evident readiness. She danced like a fairy and I enjoyed it though we both got out of breath. My last dance, I guess!" This too became fodder for metaphysical speculation as Putnam, recounting that he certainly did like Mrs. Hocking "as company," mused why it was that we like some people and don't like others. He concluded that it was fortunate that there were people we *did* like, "but it's hard on the unliked and the whole thing gives one a queer *compulsive* feeling."

Though Putnam still peppered his letters to the children overseas with philosophical ruminations, he struck a new note, if not of moderation, anyway of surrender to life's hopeless ambiguity. "The fact is *everything* without exception has to be looked at from two standpoints, of which the scientific and the emotional are examples," he wrote his daughter not long after she'd admitted her inability to rehabilitate France. "You can't find a middle course, or true mixture, and the best man is the one who learns to pass quickly and instinctively, from the one attitude to the other, realizing that he does so, and not letting himself be bothered by the apparent paradoxicality."

Homely occupations were not just an integument sheathing the organ of metaphysics; the two were so interlarded as to be immune to disentanglement. "This morning before breakfast, the shadows are still cool and blackish and the birds are singing just as if there was no war," he wrote Elizabeth in the summer of 1917, and proceeded to describe how he and Aunt Amy had "passed a long day yesterday in weeding and weeding and—on my part at least—trying to invent new positions for getting more or less parallel with the earth's surface that should be a little less uncomfortable than the one just left. It's curious how the inherent optimism of man carries him through experiments like this. With each new shift one says to oneself, 'why this is just the needed thing' but before many minutes and seconds have elapsed the sense that we are not four-footed animals makes itself painfully felt.

To picture us as at this moment we are, the hot but breezy afternoon, imagine the cool-looking Aunt Amy sitting by the table, reading, and M. [Molly] (refreshed by some 15 hours in bed) looking up insect-pests and poisons. Mamma, also looking cool in a muslin dress spotted with lilac-colored flowers, saunters in with a pair of J.'s trousers which she had been mending, and then comes J. himself looking quite superior in his khaki with Lieutenant's shoulder pieces and tall boots—fairly handsome if his hair was a little thicker—and in good shape. Louisa is playing the piano in the back room, and I am sitting at the desk by the open window."

On Bastille Day, before Elizabeth's homecoming, Putnam reported that the garden was displaying "the exact French and American flag colors and nothing else: long spikes of larkspur above, then the pure white of the Madonna lilies (pretty nice, this year) and below a strip of quite superb red poppies." He went on to marvel at the day's symbolic import. "Isn't it wonderful to have the times so changed that the storming of a government prison becomes a cause of rejoicing even to the government itself. Would that poor Russia might be celebrating that day. But even that will come. And do tell me, by the way, just what you had in mind when you said that the war didn't seem to you to bring out people's best qualities but rather the reverse? Of course both statements are justifiable; but it is, surely, *both*. And the same is true of churches, which seem to get on the nerves of you and Mary. They are surely 'very, very good' and likewise 'horrid'; and sometimes music seems the only thing that fits the bill."

The stirrings that great music elicits from the soul were coextensive with the sense of elevated hopefulness that Putnam derived from his larger philosophy. The impossibility of articulating the nature of these feelings and beliefs as well as one would like did not justify abandoning the effort. The endless aspiration to say the impossible was, indeed, Putnam's form of religious praxis. Even in the darkest hour of war there were sufficient indications that the holy as well as the evil continued to flourish side by side, not as a sign of reality's ambivalence, but of the opportunity and call to choose God.

ANY SATISFACTION FREUD took at the confirmation of the analytic view of human nature brought by war gradually paled before the deprivations of life on the losing side. His sons were at risk every day in a conflict that he did not view as redemptive service the way that Putnam saw the volunteer labors of his children in France. A deficit of flour in Vienna resulted in bread being baked out of coarse cornmeal. Meat, which Freud loved dearly, was increasingly difficult to find. Patients paid him in potatoes. Jam was made out of turnips. As the war drew near its end, food and coal shortages became severe enough that they jeopardized Freud's physical survival. The poorer classes were eating their pets, and the worst off were hunting down the cats and dogs of others to feed on. Freud's study was so poorly heated that the ink in his fountain pen congealed. Quoting Heine in a letter to Abraham, Freud wrote, in reference to the Entente and Quadruple Alliance, "*Doch es will mich schier bedünken.*" "I rather suspect that both the rabbi and the monk stink alike."

Near the end of 1917, the ultimate indignity occurred as his cigar stock was almost cut off. "Yesterday I smoked my last cigar and since then have been bad-tempered and tired," he wrote Ferenczi. He experienced palpitation and a new flare-up of a painful inflammation on his palate. "Then a patient brought me fifty cigars, I lit one, became cheerful, and the affection of the palate rapidly went down."

On the occasion of his sixtieth birthday wartime conditions and thoughts of absent friends led Freud to dissuade his loved ones from carrying out the celebratory fete they'd planned. Yet he was nonetheless lionized by the press, overwhelmed with flowers on a celebratory drive through the streets of Vienna, and—wartime economy notwithstanding—feted with everything short of a marching band. For all of his crotchety resistance, one suspects he was immensely gratified by this long-awaited evidence that Vienna had recognized his stature. It was only to be regretted that these marks of valorization came on the verge of the Empire's destruction.

IF NOT THE metaphysics, yet something of Putnam's communal mission unexpectedly seemed to impress itself on Freud's outlook at war's end. The first meeting of the International Congress held since the start of the war was staged in Budapest in September 1916. It was a modest gathering, with only forty-two representatives in attendance, almost all of them, to Freud's unease, Jews from the collapsing Austro-Hungarian Empire. Much of the Congress was devoted to a discussion of shell-shock and related traumatic injuries that were then overwhelming hospitals. The sheer volume of psychiatric cases arising from the war presented an opportunity for the psychoanalysts to prove their utility. Freud's own focus was not, however, on the returning soldiers. The paper he delivered in Budapest contained an unexpected homage to Putnam's position on the larger social purpose of analysis.

Where Putnam always argued for the right of all men to strive to elevate themselves, in part through analysis, Freud insisted for most of his career that the masses were, basically, unfit for the benefits analysis had to offer. At the 1916 Congress, however, Freud altered his position. He spoke of extending the opportunity of psychoanalysis to much "wider social strata" in order that "men who would otherwise give way to drink, women who have nearly succumbed under their burden of privations, children for whom there is no choice between running wild or neurosis, may be made capable, by analysis, of resistance and of efficient work." This was still a long way from suggesting that the potential for sublimation could be offered to the multitude like a communion wafer. But it was, nonetheless, an admission that analysis might have an obligatory role to play in promoting the larger public good.

In the handful of letters that passed back and forth between Freud and Putnam in the months following Putnam's response to Freud's comments on *Human Motives*, a shift occurred. Whereas, throughout the first seven years of their exchange, it was Putnam who communicated an urgent need for dialogue, in the final letters, Freud was the one who longed for a resumption of their correspondence, and who sounded dependent on their friendship. He even altered his handwriting for Putnam into a script that he hoped would enable him to read the letters unassisted. "I may have suffered the loss of many a letter from you which would have delighted me had it come," he lamented to Putnam in late January 1916, and expressed happiness at the thought that Putnam's feeling for him was still a welcoming one. "I deeply feel the loneliness which surrounds me," he wrote Putnam, closing on a note that was almost effusive. "You know what my wishes are for you—a long *Otium cum dignitate et studio* [dignified and scholarly leisure] and added to this, the well-being of your family. Do remember me from time to time." In the last extant piece of their correspondence, Freud ended with the cry, "Let us hope for better times!"

It's clear from Putnam's correspondence with Jones that there were three letters he wrote Freud that never arrived in Vienna. However, there's no evidence that any of these missing letters were written after the winter of 1916. A certain poetic justice attends the thought that with Blow's death,

Putnam, who'd never acknowledged the role her voice played in his conversation with Freud, lost his power to communicate with the father of psychoanalysis.

The end of Putnam's side of the exchange may also reflect his resignation to the fact that Freud's deeply personal letter on *Human Motives* marked the bedrock of Freud's metaphysics. Putnam's apparent silence with respect to Freud in the last two years of his life can be understood as a sign that he'd reached the terminus of his own analysis. Having reconciled himself to the limits of the transference, Putnam was able—as an analysand at the end of the journey should be—to dispense with his analyst. This is to suggest, also, in Freud's defense, that in Putnam's case psychoanalysis may have succeeded.

Not only was he happier in his marriage and easier on his children (with the possible exception of Jamie), Putnam no longer sounded quite so torturously hard on himself or so anguished at the failures of his metaphysics to save the world. Putnam knew that his book hadn't made a dent in the materialist tendencies of America, but he kept trying to say the impossible. He accepted the fact that, even if he was never properly heard, crying in the wilderness was his destiny as a philosophical missionary. He began to sound as much amused as harrowed by this fate.

In the simplest terms, it's as though some tension finally snapped and Putnam was able to—well—*relax*. This may be because in strictly Freudian terms he was able to face aspects of himself that he'd long repressed and in so doing became a healthier, more integrated human being. Or perhaps, he really had absorbed the lessons he put forward in the "Griselda" essay in which he wrote of how the effort to discover the sources of feelings of inferiority led also to the discovery of "opposite ones" tying the subject to the "deep primordial forces of the universe." In other words, it may really be that in exploring the roots of his incestual, infantile desires, Putnam not only completed the Freudian terms of analysis, he also took, in his own person, the philosophical next step.

IN THE SPRING of 1918, Freud published one of Putnam's final essays, "The Interpretation of Certain Symbolisms," a complement to a case history entitled "Sketch for a Study of a New England Character" that he'd written the previous year. Evidence strongly suggests that the essay, although primarily about Susan Blow, is a composite portrait that interpolates elements of Putnam's own psychological history. In the earlier essay, Putnam had used Freud's techniques to compose a kind of eulogy for the woman who had transformed his life. In doing so, he wedded his identity with hers in the ideal manner he was prevented from effecting in the real world. Ultimately, the study serves as a kind of summary portrait of Blow, Putnam, and the ideas they joined together in their shared dream of a better world. In concluding the first half of the essay, Putnam had written that with treatment, his patient came to feel she'd experienced "a species of new birth."

But just months before his own death, with war still raging on the Western Front, Putnam tackled the subject again, adding another theoretical layer that disclosed his anxiety on the question of whether he'd done justice to Blow's soul, or to the larger forces at work inside every human being. This second "Interpretation," expressed his fears that *by definition* his own efforts to guide his patient in his capacity as her physician, along with the patient's own wish to "make her experience, even if painful, of use to others, and to the cause of science," led to distortions of her psychology. Fealty to the cause of analysis had prompted them both to stress "the erotic, pleasure-loving, individualistic side of her character, which had grown luxuriantly in the dark" in the absence of actual stimulus. He noted that as time went on he "came to regard her readiness to adopt the purely erotic or 'infantile-fixation' explanation itself as a symptom." If the willingness to identify a sexual etiology as the true interpretation of our symbolic fixations is, itself, symptomatic what, really, has Putnam left Freud?

To make his point, Putnam explored the topic of symbolism associated with the number three "(or the idea of triplification, or triangulation)" so important to the patient's unconscious life. For the next *twenty pages* Putnam dedicated himself to showing why the sexual implications of the number, though real, tell an incomplete story. Given Blow's triangulated place in Putnam's own life, the idea that the number three would have borne fruit in the depths of her unconscious is as striking as is Putnam's determination to show that erotic desire is not the only force that lies behind the number's interest.

By the end of his paper, Putnam had swerved around to highlight the obligation of the *analyst* to heal his own psychological state so that the physician's mind could accommodate philosophy. "All that I have said applies rather to the edification of the physician than—directly—to the edification of the patient," he acknowledged. Until analysts understood the larger ethical implications of their task, they would do well to make their ambitions modest indeed. "It may be necessary," he continued, "or desirable, to confine the psychoanalytic inquiry to a certain group of repressions of which—it should be said—the physician can more or less accurately prophesy the nature, and which the patient—reversing, as all patients are prone to do, the path of the repression—will sooner or later bring to light."

Putnam knew in his own person the potential damage of sexual repression. Freud may, on that count, have solved the riddle of the sphinx. He had not solved the mystery of the triangular, heaven-aimed pyramid at the sphinx's back. "The patient's mind contains also a variety of other data which he is not likely to bring to light, yet which it is vitally important for him to recognize, if this can be brought about without detriment to his progress, as significant sources of motive," Putnam wrote. At the core of this other data is the notion of human connectedness and the tonic corrective that consciousness of community offered to the operations of narcissism. The physician must at least be aware of the "inherent 'moral obligations,' which every one who listens to his own conscience will find that he feels, first, as a member of the 'community,' in a widening sense; next as a virtual member of an ideal community, or—if one will—of the universe." These principles must be present inside every analyst, operating as a purer undercurrent, a second, truer voice within the individual, in precisely the same way that Susan Blow herself now existed inside Putnam.

AT THE MOMENT that "The Interpretation of Certain Symbolisms" appeared in print, Putnam was diagnosed with a mild angina condition. Marian wrote Elizabeth the news in France in May 1918 as Elizabeth was weighing whether or not it was time to come home. Putnam followed Marian's note with a letter suggesting that it would be better for Elizabeth to stay in service for the present and that concern for his health should on no occasion be made a reason to return. "You would all be off if you imagined that because the mysterious word 'heart' was used, that means something, or anything, mysterious and somber. That is absolutely not so, and I want you to understand it," he insisted to Elizabeth. "I simply cannot play the youthful quite so freely as I would still like. But, in the first place, I am going on 72; and in the next place, even youth is still mine (to be used discretely [sic]) and you will soon hear of me as chopping big trees at Canaurnet. That's the last word on that subject." He went on to describe their latest round of family visiting, and his own volunteer work stuffing envelopes with circulars for the French wounded. He'd spent, he informed her, a "pleasant couple of sunny hours" at the Public Library getting back "into a literary atmosphere and into the streams of other people's thoughts." He was reading essays on topics ranging from the "Romantic Vein in Ethics," to "Scientific Management of the Railroads," to "Thomas Hardy," to "The Russian Reform Movement," to "County Government in Massachusetts." "Just note the subjects and think about how much I ought to know when I have digested the entire menu," he marveled, adding with a wink, "It takes a good lot of psychoanalytic estimating of motives—your own and t'other man's—to mark these essays fairly, and the question of before or after dinner has to be considered, among the rest."

In Putnam's last surviving letter to the Freudian camp, a note to Jones written in December 1917, he announced that he was planning a new round of volunteer hospital work as there was much "indirect war-work" that needed to be done "and indeed I greatly wish to be of service." Reflecting on the course of world events and his long argument with Freud, he concluded, "The way out, I think, and one which does not necessarily bring in metaphysics, is to keep alive the feeling that, *theoretically* a psychoanalytic treatment should not be regarded as complete until it had seen the patient landed (I will not say 'how,' for there trouble begins) on the shores of a somewhat advanced sublimation. I will write again soon."

AFTER WORKING LATE one night on a new essay, Putnam awoke in some physical discomfort. His doctor was called. The family gathered around him, though Putnam assured them that there was no cause for concern. The doctor approached. Putnam reached up to shake his physician's hand and, in the process of clasping on to him, died. As Putnam extended the hand of human fellowship one last time, he passed away. One could say his good manners killed him, or that he departed this world making the sort of tangible gesture of solidarity that symbolized the continuity of the human spirit beyond physical life. Like his old friend, William James, Putnam had requested that his body be cremated. The funeral ceremony took place at Mt. Auburn Cemetery, after which his ashes were transported for burial to an old family plot in Walnut Hill Cemetery near Newburyport.

Putnam died on November 4th, the same day that the armistice was declared in Austria, exactly nineteen years after the publication of *The Interpretation of Dreams* and one week before the general armistice. Though he lasted almost two years longer than Blow did, neither he nor his peculiarly self-effacing strain of American optimism quite survived the Great War.

Two weeks after his death, in the midst of a flood of condolence visits and letters (in more than one of which, Marian reported to her children that "Papa" had been deemed a saint, and was recalled by one cousin as the man he'd "revered" more than "any other man—no one was ever more beloved by all who knew him"), Marian had already found someone to "let Papa's rooms." The lodger would pay a thousand dollars and Marian told her children that this rent "would make a good deal of difference." With all the fullness and variegated pleasures of the family's existence, in the course of his rich life Putnam had accumulated virtually no monetary savings whatsoever.

Just a month later, Jones sent Freud the news that "dear old Putnam" had died; the news of Putnam's death was one of the first reports from America to reach Freud following the armistice. Freud's response was a rare cry of lamentation. "I had no news from America these two years and I feel the loss of dear old Putnam grievously," he wrote Jones. Freud contrasted Putnam favorably with "the whimsical, unreliable G. Stanley Hall," who by this time openly sided with Adler in opposition to the analytic movement. Freud's overall mood was black. The conditions of life in recent months had been the harshest of the entire war. Martin was being held prisoner in Italy." We are all of us slowly failing in health and bulk," Freud wrote, "not alone so in this town I assure you."

For all of Freud's mourning the loss of Putnam, he made a curious slip of the pen in his letter to Jones regretting Putnam's death. Freud writes (in English), "He [Putnam] was a pillar of psychoanalysis in his country and behaved most truly and gallantly *against* me" [emphasis added]. This "Freudian" miswording perfectly expresses the larger ambivalence of their nine-year friendship.

WHEN JONES' OBITUARY turned to the subject of Putnam's spiritual philosophy, he added an important qualification. Putnam, wrote Jones, saw his plea for metaphysics "not as a criticism of psycho-analysis, but as a proposed enrichment of it; indeed it was rather a quarrel with science as a whole than with psycho-analysis." Jones marveled at Putnam's ability to keep his own ego detached from this mission. "I do not know of any other example in which philosophical views have not become placed in the service of some or other unconscious resistance, manifesting themselves in the guise of a skeptical opposition to some aspect of psycho-analysis." So intense was Putnam's modesty that "it bordered on a slightly morbid self-depreciation. He always regarded himself as a beginner, a learner, as primarily a student, an attitude much fortified by a restless striving for knowledge."

In the preface Freud wrote to Putnam's collected addresses (published in 1921), he described Putnam as "not only the first American to interest himself in psycho-analysis," but also as someone who "soon became its most decided supporter and its most influential representative in America." Because of the reputation Putnam had built through his work "as a teacher, as well as through his important work in the domain of organic nervous disease, and thanks to the universal respect which his personality enjoyed, he was able to do perhaps more than anyone for the spread of psycho-analysis in his own country." Along with this, however, Freud wrote that Putnam at last "began to extend beyond the limits of analysis, demanding that as a science it should be linked on to a particular philosophical system, and that its practice should be openly associated with a particular set of ethical doctrines." Of course, in truth, the metaphysical strain in Putnam had been there all along, only made more virulent by Freud's protracted resistance.

Freud couldn't keep from adding that despite Putnam's own conviction of the essential truths of philosophy, "his enthusiasm, so admirable in a man of his advanced age, did not succeed in carrying others along with him. Younger people remained cooler." To the last, Freud needed to broadcast the youthfulness of his own spirit.

The preface ends with a surprising acknowledgment: "It is our duty to express our thanks to the author's widow, Mrs. Putnam, for her assistance with the manuscripts, with the copyrights, and with financial support, without all of which the publication of this volume would have been impossible." For all of Marian's unrelenting opposition to Putnam's engagement with analysis, she saw it as her duty to selflessly assist Freud when she was called upon to help honor the memory of her husband's labors for the psychoanalytic movement, and his quixotic dream of transforming the universe through a metaphysical application of Freud's theories.

CHAPTER 33

The Torso

I am ready to confess, that fate has not shown injustice and that a German victory might have proved a harder blow to the interests of mankind in general. But it is no relief to have his sympathy placed on the winning side if one's wellbeing is staked on the losing one.

Freud to Jones, January 15, 1918

MARTIN DESCRIBED IN his memoir the near-anarchy into which Vienna had descended by the time he was finally released from his Italian prisoner of war camp in August of 1919. Not only had inflation reduced the value of the several thousand kronen Martin had saved over the course of his military service to a sum insufficient "for the re-soling of one pair of civilian shoes," the former middle classes watched discipline deteriorate to where bullying mobs roamed the once fashionable city center mocking and even attacking their erstwhile social superiors. Bands of hooligans marched along Vienna's cobblestones, singing, "Who will now sweep the streets? The noble gentlemen with the golden stars will now sweep the streets." Janitorial staff at hospitals received three times the salary of surgeons. "You might set apart enough money in the morning to pay for a suit," wrote Martin, "only to find that by the afternoon it would only meet the cost of a waistcoat. The cost of a *Schinkensemmel* [ham sandwich] in Vienna would also meet the year's rent of a luxury flat or a first-class railway journey from one end of Austria to the other." Passengers stripped the interior of railway carriages of every leather strap and curtain, pocketing the removable articles without even attempting to conceal the theft.

The whole of Freud's fortune, the equivalent today of several hundred thousand dollars, had been in Austrian national bonds. After the armistice, his savings were wiped away to nothing. At the end of November 1918, he granted an interview to a student of psychoanalysis who hoped Freud could comfort him for the destruction of the empire. Yet despite everything, Freud responded that though he knew Vienna's "abysses," he shared the young man's "unrestrained affection" for the city. Freud showed him a note he'd written on the day of the general armistice: "Austria-Hungary is no more. I do not want to live anywhere else. For me emigration is out of the question. I shall live on with the torso and imagine that it is the whole." His world had at last become coincident with the fragmented classical objects he'd devoted so many hours to collecting.

FREUD WAS PRESCIENT about the fact that with the shattering of the Austro-Hungarian empire would come a new dependence on America, and specifically on what he had always seen as the New World's own strain of communicable plague, "the almighty dollar." There was something cruel in the fact of his becoming reliant on money from a nation he believed to be consumed by its own worship of the greenback.

Yet in itself, material greed was not the most dangerous aspect of American character. As the peace negotiations unfolded, Woodrow Wilson proved to be a kind of nightmare caricature of Putnam, yoking Putnam's sense of necessary human spiritual progress to a larger American global mandate, and subsuming both beneath a sense of his own personal God-given license to direct world fate. In Wilson's part at the armistice, the worst of American faith-based arrogant politics was coupled with the most egregious American capitalist bullying.

One of the oddest, least-read works in Freud's canon is a psychological biography of Woodrow Wilson that he wrote with a prominent American diplomat, William C. Bullitt. Bullitt grew friendly with Freud during forays into Vienna for aesthetic pleasure and political business. On one occasion, Bullitt visited Freud after he'd had an operation and found him depressed. Freud announced that he didn't have long to live, and that his death would be irrelevant to him and everyone else "because he had written everything he wished to write and his mind was empty." Bullitt, who'd been part of the American Peace Commission in Paris but resigned his post to protest the injustice of the terms of the armistice, broached his idea for a book on the Treaty of Versailles. "Freud's eyes brightened," Bullitt reported, "and he became very much alive. . . . Then he astonished me by saying he would like to collaborate with me in writing the Wilson chapter of my book. I laughed and remarked that the idea was delightful but bizarre."

It is, indeed, a strange incident. Though the work presents a psychological biography of Wilson going far beyond the War years, its focus is a compelling indictment of the American part in the peace negotiations, and thus, by implication in the settlement that fed the rise of fascism. Wilson wielded almost unimaginable influence over events in Versailles, and he systematically betrayed his own ideals as well as the basic diplomatic principles through which an equitable peace might have been forged. Most galling, he did so wearing the mantle of world savior.

The case made by Bullitt and Freud for how Wilson allowed his various complexes to cloud his judgment is intricate, resting on a detailed analytic study of his development from early childhood onward. Most alarmingly, however, the combination of Wilson's popularity, his idealized vision of the League of Nations, and the resistance he encountered to this body from a number of important figures, led Wilson to intensify a long-standing identification with Jesus Christ.

When England and France steadfastly opposed his famous "Fourteen Points," and larger vision of global harmony, Wilson did what other "subjective idealists" in his shoes have done: he surrendered everything. Instead of trying to at least eke out a compromise from Lloyd George and Clemenceau, he withdrew the entire utopian platform. In their reconstruction of events, Bullitt and Freud imagined Wilson picturing to himself the consequences of holding to his principles, seeing himself "reviled from one end of the capitalist world to the other, and that was his only world."

The introduction to the book, which Freud wrote alone, makes clear why he found Wilson a perfect subject: "It was reported that Wilson, as President-elect, shook off one of the politicians who called attention to his services during the presidential campaign with the words: 'God ordained that I should be the next President of the United States. Neither you nor any other mortal or mortals could have prevented it.'" Freud commented, "I do not know how to avoid the conclusion that a man who is capable of taking the illusions of religion so literally and is so sure of a special personal intimacy with the Almighty is unfitted for relations with ordinary children of men. As everyone knows, the hostile camp during the war also sheltered a chosen darling of Providence: the German Kaiser. It was most regrettable that later on the other side a second appeared. No one gained thereby; respect for God was not increased." Indeed, Freud concluded, Wilson "repeatedly declared that mere facts had no significance for him, that he esteemed highly nothing but human motives and opinions. As a result of this attitude it was natural for him in his thinking to ignore the facts of the real outer world, even to deny they existed if they conflicted with his hopes and wishes. [But] when, like Wilson, a man achieves almost the exact opposite of that which he wished to accomplish, when he has shown himself to be the true antithesis of the power which 'always desires evil and always creates good,' when a pretension to free the world from evil ends only in a new proof of the danger of a fanatic to the commonweal, then it is not to be marveled at that a distrust is aroused in the observer which makes sympathy impossible."

FREUD'S WARTIME FANTASY of monkish retreat and self-occlusion quickly gave way to the more congenial role of a general marshaling his troops after a rout. In his communiqués to members of the secret ring in the months succeeding the armistice, Freud deliberated a grab-bag of schemes for regenerating the movement, from launching a publishing house, to starting a new psychoanalytic journal for Britain and America, to resuscitating the *Jahrbuch*, to planning a reunion congress, to endlessly strategizing on how to augment their political strength as individuals and a confederated body. "There is already something dream-like about the times behind us," Freud wrote Abraham in March, 1919. "The dreadful conditions in this city, the impossibility of feeding and keeping oneself, the presence of Jones, Ferenczi and Freund (a colleague, no relation to Freud), the necessary conferences and decision-making, and the hesitant beginnings of analytic work (five sessions = 500 crowns) result in a vivid present in the face of which memories quickly fade." Further preoccupying Freud and distracting him from the lingering hardships of post-imperial life was the geographical shift in the movement's center of power that had been accelerated by the First World War. "In other words," he declared to Abraham, "the orientation toward the west proclaimed by our Chancellor!"

The labor that went into reactivating the engine of the psychoanalytic movement was accompanied by a flurry of domestic excitement. Martin and Ernest both married, and Sophie gave birth to Freud's second grandchild, Heinz. These happy events were savored still more when Freud's nephew by marriage, Edward Bernays, succeeded in transferring a box of Havana cigars to Freud through the offices of a diplomat who'd been assigned the task of investigating postwar quality of life in Vienna. (Edward went on to become known as the "father of public relations" in America. Given that today we focus on the essential obligation to heal the image as opposed to the inner psychological state, there are parallels between the social valuation assigned to visiting one's publicist now and that of going to an analyst thirty years ago. Edward may be a more authentic inheritor of Freud's mantle than the typical psychotherapist.)

The string of happy tidings at home ended cruelly with the death of Freud's daughter Sophie from influenzal pneumonia in 1919. Twenty-three years old, pregnant with her third child, Sophie had fallen ill suddenly, and the absence of trains between Vienna and Germany made it impossible for Freud to reach her before she died. He tried to reconcile himself to the anguish but slipped at times toward incoherence. To Pfister, Freud described how Sophie had been "snatched away in the midst of glowing health, from a full and active life as a competent mother and loving wife, all in four or five days, as though she had never existed. . . . The undisguised brutality of our time is weighing heavily upon us. To-morrow she is to be cremated, our poor Sunday child!" Perhaps his most lonely lamentation was written to Ferenczi. "As a confirmed unbeliever I have no one to accuse and realize that there is no place where I could lodge a complaint. 'The unvaried, still returning hour of duty' and 'the dear lovely habit of living' will do their bit toward letting everything go on as before. Deep down I sense a bitter irreparable narcissistic injury. My wife and Annerl are profoundly affected in a more human way." One tragic consequence of the radical individualism at the heart of Freud's theories was an inability to experience even the death of his own child as anything but hurt to self-image. This sentiment resonates eerily with one Emerson articulated in "Experience" regarding the death of his own son. "People grieve and bemoan themselves, but it is not half so bad with them as they say. There are moods in which we court suffering, in the hope that here at least we shall find reality, sharp peaks and edges of truth.

But it turns out to be scene-painting and counterfeit. The only thing grief has taught me is to know how shallow it is. . . . In the death of my son, now more than two years ago, I seem to have lost a beautiful estate—no more. I cannot get it nearer to me." Emerson realized that a narcissistic injury will always be healed, because the narcissistic subject is always intact, even and perhaps especially with the subject's own death. He continued: "Something which I fancied was a part of me, which could not be torn away without tearing me nor enlarged without enriching me falls off from me and leaves no scar."

FREUD TOOK FROM Sophie's death further validation of his orphic powers. Many people assumed that *Beyond the Pleasure Principle* must have been inspired by the loss of his daughter. In fact, as Freud insisted on pointing out, the long essay was finished while Sophie was still in excellent health. "Probability is not always the truth," he declared to Franz Wittel. Efforts to explain what did prompt Freud to write the strange, relentlessly pessimistic paper in which he outlined the theory of the death instinct often turn toward the experience of war and a resumption of interest in ideas Sabina Spielrein, a one-time patient of Jung's who went on to become a provocative member of Freud's fledgling psychoanalytic association in Vienna, and, long before her, Schopenhauer, had explored. Undoubtedly, these were important sources for Freud. However, Putnam's *Human Motives* may well have been another crucial stimulus for the work. Just as *Totem and Taboo* can be viewed as a rebuttal to the argument Putnam put forward in his "Plea" for philosophy at Weimar, Freud's essay on Thanatos, begun just a few months after Putnam's death, can be viewed as a response to Putnam's magnum opus—as the great *Anti-Human Motives*.

Whatever else, *Beyond the Pleasure Principle* is certainly no less speculative, metaphysical, and scientifically implausible than Putnam's book. Freud, to be sure, expressed less confidence about his conclusions than Putnam appeared to allow for, but the inscription of skepticism in the tone of the work seems itself part of his philosophical message: everything, even theory and rhetoric, ultimately disintegrates. Freud's essay can be seen as the dark side of the moon to Putnam's spiritual luminescence. Where Putnam wrote that underlying all human behavior was an original ideal truth that men could learn to perceive and so raise themselves closer to the fulfillment of their sacred communal destiny, Freud suggested that underlying human behavior was a yearning for individual annihilation.

Like Putnam's book, Freud's essay also presents a narrative of two warring sets of motives that together and in opposition constitute our psychological being. In Freud's case, also, "constructive" motives make up one half of the equation. Only for Freud, the opposing set of motives are those of Thanatos. In his scheme, the *higher* set of motives are the same ones Putnam describes as lower and "evolutionary." In what amounts to a direct slap at Putnam's position, it is Eros, the *sexual drive* that comes closest to mimicking his "instinct to perfection."

But the most flagrant reversal of Putnam's position is Freud's explanation for why it is that as *"the aim of all life is death,"* humanity and the organic universe don't immediately self-destruct. The reason for "the organism's puzzling determination . . . to maintain its own existence in the face of every obstacle" is that "the organism wishes to die only in its own fashion." Putnam, we remember, saw the course of individual progress toward the divine as a process of bonding into ever greater systems of unity. Not only does Freud say that the individual is advancing in the opposite direction from immortality, he argues that the only way this trip can be consummated is by isolating oneself absolutely from others and finding in the attainment of perfect individualism the secret path to death. An ever greater process of fragmentation—of entropy—was the road to the utter monad of mortality. Not by fire, not by water, not by human hands—ahh by esophageal cancer. Now at last I can expire.

If Putnam learned from Freud that psychological therapy could foster the drive to sublimation and hence serve as a catalyst to the sort of philosophical growth that linked people in an ideal community, Putnam succeeded in convincing Freud that community was only a factor of the (relatively) short-lived sexual instinct and that in the depths of man's being there nested a yearning to become absolutely atomized; isolation was the portal to the grave. One could say that contemporary American individualism enacts Freud's metaphysics just as the European welfare state comes at least closer to Putnam's turn-of-the-century American ideal body politic, another surprising reversal given that Freud's position was at least in part formulated as a response to *America's* social idealism.

However, there's another key aspect of Freud's essay, one that transcends the urge for defiance. Freud's death drive sanctifies the principle of repetition, apotheosizing the instinct *"to restore an earlier state of things."* The psychoanalytic task of reharvesting memories evokes Proust's notion that the recovery of lost time is a subversion of temporal ephemerality. By restoring the analysand's past state of mind, the analytic process, en route to death, chisels history into relief. Implicit in this notion is Freud's prescience about American apathy for the earlier state of things—for previous stages of civilization and life as such.

The final speculation of *Beyond the Pleasure Principle* concerns a myth from Plato and a parallel story found in the eastern Upanishads scripture. Both myths concern the idea that originally there was a third sex combining both male and female genitalia. In Plato's version, this third gender was split apart by Zeus; the sexual instinct reflects the effort of those two halves to find each other again. In alluding to these myths Freud was returning to the notion of structural bisexuality, only here the principle was coupled with a polemic concerning the moment when East and West shared a common, cosmic sensibility. The instinct to restore an earlier state of things in organic being as such is consistent with Freud's profound drive, reflected vividly in his art collection, to restore the moment when the Hellenic and the Semitic were conjoined. The third sex, signifying the ideal melding of male and female principles, was a third cultural path. Bisexuality, on an ultimate substrate, was equated with primeval East–West integration.

Buried under the nihilistic philosophy that suggests that the true purpose of life is the end of life lies an idealistic dream no less vivid than Putnam's in which the opposition between Judaism and Christianity, along with that between Freud's masculine and feminine sides, and even between his dead models, such as Hannibal and Napoleon, could be sublimated. Not coincidentally, a footnote in the essay mentioned that one theory Plato was likely to have taken over from the oriental tradition was that of the transmigration of souls.

Freud seems to have been ambivalent as to whether the grave meant the void or entry into a sort of eternal Platonic symposium from which different guests arose now and then to wander off and take possession of another mortal's soul. Freud's own quest for ultimate unity was a search for marriage with time past, rather than with the abstract, perhaps eviscerated, community of the future. On this subject, Freud was willing to suspend the injunction he repeated to Putnam of remaining in the realm where definitive answers were possible. The final words of *Beyond the Pleasure*

Principle, a citation from the German translation of the *Maqamat* by al-Hariri, which also figured in Emerson's library as a key work of New England's fascination with the East, could have served as the inscription on Putnam's gravestone: "What we cannot reach flying we must reach limping. . . . The Book tells us it is no sin to limp." While Freud tried to embrace the reorientation of his movement Westward, his heart was left behind on the shores not just of the old, but of the most ancient world.

CHAPTER 34

Music of the Quills

The earth is a small planet, not suited to be a "heaven." We cannot promise those willing to follow us full compensation for what they give up. A painful piece of renunciation is inevitable.

Freud to Richard S. Dyer-Bennet, December 9, 1928

ALL OF FREUD'S works from the fall of 1923 on were written in the shadow of his cancer of the jaw. An operation on the 26th of September of that year to remove a malignant ulcer in the upper part of the palate, which had already metastasized into surrounding tissues and the cheek, was the first of more than thirty operations he would undergo over the last sixteen years of his life. From the outset of this ordeal, Freud exhibited sangfroid. Shortly after the initial operation, he wrote Abraham, "Dear Incurable Optimist, Today the tampon was removed, I got up, and put what is left of me into my clothes. Thank you for all the news, letters, greetings, and newspaper cuttings. If I can sleep without an injection I shall soon go home." Two years before that event, in early 1921, Freud had noted in a letter to Eitingon that he had taken a "step into real old age." From that point on, "the thought of death has not left me and sometimes I have the impression that seven of my internal organs are fighting to have the honor of bringing my life to an end."

In fact, Freud had been consumed by the idea of his own mortality since early middle age. His letters to Fliess were riddled with attempts to deduce the date of his mortal term, and his resentment of Putnam's reference to the fact that he was "no longer a young man" carried with it a supernatural fear that mention of his age endangered his youth. Even the epigraph of *The Interpretation of Dreams*, Freud's "prayer" to the powers of the underworld, bespoke a special sort of intimacy with the realm of death. The whole of *Beyond the Pleasure Principle* can be read as a long riff on the sigh Freud emitted after being revived in the arms of Jung in Munich, "How sweet it must be to die!"

Whatever philosophical validation the approach of mortality might have tendered, Freud's stoicism in the face of a prolonged, excruciating process of dying was extraordinary. One of his operations trigged an infection in the Eustachian tubes that led to deafness in his right ear. The cannibalization of his mouth by the cancer and consequent operations to excise it eventually necessitated the installation of a prosthetic palate and jaw. The prosthesis never properly fit; it chafed at the sores on his mouth, lacerating his bleeding ulcers even as it distorted his speech. It was a punishment worthy of Freud's beloved Greek myths for the original analyst to be losing both his powers of hearing and of utterance. Near the end, the cancer consumed the inside of his cheek and kept on spreading, protruding through to the surface of his face.

And still Freud did not betray an urge to valorize or sentimentalize his suffering. His tone in referring to his sickness was alternately sardonic (he described the cancer as "my dear old carcinoma") and analytic (in the last months of his life he wrote Marie Bonaparte to record the psychological sensations associated with the action of radium in his body).

Yet, there was one arena in which the advent of mortality may have pushed Freud's perspective away from the Lethe-lapped bank of classical disdain: the realm of the spirit. On his 75th birthday, in 1931, he told the Chief Rabbi of Vienna, "In some place in my soul, in a very hidden corner, I am a fanatical Jew." In 1933, in a letter to a friend, Freud confessed, "It may be that I too have a secret inclination toward the miraculous." The fact that he devoted his last years to a study of religion, *Moses and Monotheism*, even in a subversive sense, indicates the degree to which the metaphysical subjects that Putnam had pressed on him had come to occupy Freud in his final years. Nothing would have moved Putnam more than Freud's twilight concern with the unknown, which he'd ostensibly avoided for so much of his life. Putnam would have felt their friendship at last opening to the eternal universe in which the men could find their true, common home.

With regard to the occult realm, Freud's latter declarations were still more extreme. The most puzzling statement of all was one made in 1921 in a letter to Hereward Carrington, the publisher of a journal of occultism in New York who'd invited Freud to serve as a co-editor of the periodical. Though Freud turned down the offer, he told Carrington, "If I had my life to live over again I should devote myself to psychical research rather than to psychoanalysis." Freud relished telling the inveterately skeptical Jones of clairvoyant experiences he'd had with patients, in particular ones involving a foreknowledge of death. These conversations, Jones wrote, often took place after midnight, when Freud seemed to become especially attuned to the possibility of a true basis for supernatural experience. After one such scene, Jones remarked on Freud's tendency to accept the truth of paranormal experiences even when there was little evidence. "I don't like it at all myself," Freud replied, "but there is some truth in it." Jones asked Freud why, if one could believe in "mental processes floating in the air," one shouldn't go on to believe in angels. To this, Freud responded, as Jones wrote in a "jocular tone" but with "something searching in his glance, 'Quite so, even *der liebe Gott.*'"

SOMEONE MUST HAVE told Sam Goldwyn of Freud's passion for antiquity, explaining why, when Hollywood tried to enlist Freud as a consultant on a movie about the greatest love stories of all time, Freud was told that the initial episode would concern Anthony and Cleopatra. This story, indeed, had, in theory, the added bonus for Freud of directly portraying the reciprocal desire of the Hellenic world for the Semitic in the person of the Roman emperor's longing for the Egyptian queen. Seven years after the end of the war, Goldwyn offered Freud $100,000 to help with the drafting of the script, a sum that could have catapulted Freud's whole family into a position of undreamed of wealth.

America was already proving crucial to Freud's economic recovery. First, there was a large monetary gift to Freud by a much-resented cousin in New York (about whom Freud felt only more bitterly after the donative). Second, there was an influx of American patients who paid in hard U.S. currency at a time when the exchange rate had ballooned to where a trillion kronen purchased a single dollar.

Yet Freud refused the siren call of the City of Angels. He declined that offer just as, in 1920, when his family's access to even the most basic goods was tenuous, he turned down an offer from *Cosmopolitan* to write a series of articles, the first of which alone would have brought him $1,000. Women's magazines at the end of the nineteenth century and start of the twentieth were regular outlets for publication by America's foremost psychologists, including both Putnam and James. By 1920, however, the terms of the contract between popular magazines and America's intellectual elite were changing. Freud had written Edward Bernays to propose composing a group of popular essays on analysis for a prominent New York magazine. The first, he suggested, would be entitled, "Don't Use Psychoanalysis in Polemics." Bernays seized on the scheme and arranged contact between Freud and *Cosmopolitan*. The magazine bought Freud's plan for four articles but suggested, instead of Freud's proposed topic, that he wrote on, as Jones reports, "The Wife's Mental Place in the Home," or "The Husband's Mental Place in the Home." Freud was horrified at the idea that the articles would have to be shaped to the palate of *Cosmopolitan*'s demographic and backed out.

To his credit, Freud refused to let material need cloud his judgment about the fact that psychoanalysis in debased, mob-entertainment form was no longer psychoanalysis. This was not a matter of anti-democratic European preciousness, but rather a recognition of fundamental incompatibility. For all of the moments when Freud appears vindictive, consumed by magical beliefs and riddled with terrors, he did not surrender a gravitas of purpose. He created a framework of exchange in which each analysand became Oedipus before the mythical near-silent oracle, and understood that this was a sacral dialogue—not between analyst and analysand, but between each patient and a version of his or her own ultimate self in potentia. To make light of that dialogue, to mock the analytic situation, was to jeer at the human aspiration to self-knowledge.

We don't have to accept Freud's answers, but in a world where religion has lost its hold for many people, certain questions still need to be asked. A framework has to be fashioned with sufficient gravity to interrogate the self even when there is no longer any hope of a divine voice from the clouds trumpeting the answer. With all the present-day hostility and, worse, neglect —despite the manifold disappointments that must follow on a longer gaze at Freud's life and work—one comes away no less and perhaps still more convinced of this solemnity over time. Entering the reconstructed rooms where Freud wrote and saw patients, one is overwhelmed with the sense, between the thousand figurines and fragments of fallen civilizations, that this was a serious place in which serious work transpired. Here, as the poet Phillip Larkin wrote in "Churchgoing," is a house "in whose blent air all our compulsions meet," a place where some deep knowledge seems to await the visitor, "if only that so many dead lie round."

All the years of Freud's illness, Anna served as his principal nurse. The first time Freud suffered oral hemorrhaging, it was Anna, not Martha, who remained the whole night at his bedside. She, not Martha, changed his prosthesis when he could not manage alone. Of Anna's role, Freud wrote to one friend, "She is wife and mother to me during the day, though only the latter at night." To Lou Andreas-Salome, speaking in Mephistopheles' voice, he positioned Anna in terms at once more narcissistic and self-damning: "In the end we all depend on creatures we ourselves have made."

When the pain of his cancer at last become unbearable, Freud asked his physician, Dr. Max Schur, to give him a lethal dose of morphine. In making the request, Freud was drawing on an agreement they had made years earlier. According to Schur's memoirs, at the end of his life, Freud seized his doctor's hand and said, "My dear Schur, you certainly remember our first talk. You promised not to forsake me when my time comes. Now it's nothing but torture and makes no sense any more." The gesture of grasping Schur's hand to announce the imperative of ending his life is, as it were, the perfect negative to the image of Putnam shaking his physician's hand in a gesture of greeting at his own last moment. Freud's contract with Schur is still cited by advocates of assisted suicide as an argument for the humanity of allowing terminally ill patients to choose euthanasia.

Regardless of whether or not this is valid, it's striking that Freud refused to burden his family at the end. Though he instructed Schur to "tell Anna about our talk," even she was not allowed to be present in his last hours. Freud died alone.

AFTER FREUD'S DEPARTURE from Vienna in June of 1938, his apartment came to serve as communal lodging for Jews who'd been evicted from their real homes. It was a way station to the official Jewish ghetto in the 2nd district, which was, itself, a transit point en route to the camps. It made for a neat ecology. Jews who, through whatever combination of money, connections, and fortune were able to flee Austria in the final months when escape was possible, had their apartments repossessed by the Nazis to house other Jews who had not been able to flee but whose apartments had nonetheless been repossessed by the Nazis. The number of Jews in the latter category far exceeding that of those in the former, the size of households tended to balloon until the point when the inhabitants were slaughtered. Thus, for instance, there were at least 15 people living in Freud's apartment before the numbers began to dive.

By 1942, everyone was gone. The Nazis assigned Freud's apartment *Reichsmietwohnung z. b.V.* status, signifying that it was unoccupied and available to the families of soldiers serving in the Wehrmacht. The apartment was broken up into several flats. In the late 1980s, one of the new inhabitants described her situation with wonder. "We got the apartment number 5 on Berggasse 19 in 1942, the Freud apartment. . . . My God, the apartment was available. . . . The apartment was available. Completely empty. There was absolutely nobody in it. That's the way it was then. It was so simple. There was no problem."

Following the defeat of the Nazis, the Freud apartment continued to be inhabited by random Viennese until the 1970s. There was no great movement by the post-war government of the Austrian republic to salvage the relics of Freud's Viennese life. In 1968, with the founding of the Sigmund Freud Society, Anna Freud began spearheading an effort to found a museum in Freud's memory inside the apartment. In conjunction with the Society's president, she began a slow process of negotiation with the tenants. After three years, in just three rooms of the former apartment, a fledgling version of the Museum opened with a few pieces of Freud's furniture, several objects from his art collection, and the beginnings of a library. Five years later, the city of Vienna formerly acquired the apartment. It's evocative of Freud's own Viennese experience that during the long years following the city's belated intervention in 1976, the minimal elements of a shrine languished in a state of malignant neglect. This was a time when the government's overt anti-Semitism made it unnecessary to find excuses for failing to support the development of the Museum. It wasn't until 1996 that the last tenants agreed to vacate Freud's former living spaces, completing what the director described as a twenty-year process of reconquest.

The vast majority of Freud's possessions emigrated with him to London, and the Museum in Vienna has been pinched for funds since its founding. If the explanation for the lack of governmental assistance in the first decades of the Museum's existence was its dedication to a Jewish subject, today, when overt anti-Semitism is no longer fashionable, the criticism of the Museum by the keepers of the cultural purse is that Freud is no longer relevant. Under the circumstances, Vienna's historic indifference, limited budget, few actual artifacts to be reclaimed, and the status quo of analysis today, it's logical that the Museum at Berggasse would become a caretaker for interstitial material, the objects forgotten through the psychopathology of both everyday life and history, overlooked in a special kind of Freudian slip. I suspect Freud might have been amused by this use of the apartment, in which what has been collected are the "curiosities" more than the big-ticket prizes; it's restored 19 Berggasse to a kind of *Wunderkammern*.

One of the stranger stories in this regard concerns the papers of Freud's sisters. After the elderly sisters themselves were all deported to be gassed at Theresienstadt, the papers came, in a roundabout manner, into the possession of a dealer with a history of shady transactions with the Nazis. After the dealer died, his lawyer held them in a kind of trust that forbade any further action with respect to the papers for fifty years. On the death of his client, he was the only person alive aware of the survival of the letters, so there was nothing to prevent him from burning them at any time. Or, alternately, of selling them on the black market.

Instead, one day the museum director received a phone call from this man telling her that if she wanted the papers she had exactly one hour to come and collect them. In one hour, if she hadn't arrived, the lawyer would destroy them all. The director was alone in the Museum at the time, so she raced down to her car and sped off to (successfully) save the papers.

The story is inscrutable. If this man loathed the papers, the lives they represented, or some other factor associated with the record so intensely that after waiting fifty years, he refused to wait another month or week or day before obliterating them, why did he make that phone call? Why did he allow the documents to be rescued only in a single hour?

When I asked these questions to the Museum's director at an old Austrian restaurant serving a slightly upscale version of Freud's much loved strips of boiled beef, she smiled in that knowing way I'd seen before when the Viennese raise points germane to a spectrum of traits that defined inhabitants of the last city of the west and the first of the east: "He was ambivalent," she said.

———

IT WAS COMMON practice in the formative years of psychoanalysis to arrange the couch in such a way that the analyst himself was not in the patient's line of vision. This was intended to encourage patients to free associate without the self-consciousness consequent on the analyst's presence. In Freud's consulting room, if patients glanced in one direction, they would confront his desk top, arrayed with an army of ancient statuettes; turning the opposite way they confronted a wall with a projecting shelf on which different ancient stone and bronze heads were arranged; if the patient was fully reclining on the couch, above and behind his own head lay a second horizontal face, this one set in a glass case. Freud sat Janus-like between the patient's own upturned face and a painted Egyptian death mask.

This room in which patients attempted to probe the depths of their individual selves is eerily depersonalizing; it contextualizes the countenance of the analysand with ones from antiquity, just as the individual's history is submerged in the immensity of time contained in the room. It's a place for the conjuration of fantasy in a very particular idiom: the mythological, the religious, the classical antique, the undead revenant.

The last time I visited Maresfield garden, I went behind the velvet rope to briefly lie on the old couch swathed in a rich oriental rug dominated by maroon and amber shades. It was much softer than I'd imagined—infinitely soft, like a waterbed. Perhaps a spring or two has broken over the past hundred years. But it seems unlikely that it could ever have been as hard as the archetypal, rigid, black leather New York analytical couch, which then may prove to have been just another American spin on Freud's foundational vision. In Freud's couch as it is today one sinks down so far it's as though one's descending into an underworld—the very space Juno in the epigraph to *The Interpretation* promises to invoke when the higher powers won't respond to her.

While there, I finally lived out my dream of seeing up close and taking into my own hands the porcupine that my great-grandfather gave Sigmund Freud. Before my visit to London, I had imagined it to be a cute little cozy metal creature such as Putnam might have lifted from his children's toybox. But this porcupine is huge and heavy, ferocious and frightening, snarling, with a horribly wrinkled snout. Most startling are the quills, which are incredibly long and pointed and stick out into space like a shower of arrows shot by pygmies. On closer inspection, it no longer seemed strange that Freud would give the object a prominent place in his collection. The dramatic spines reminded me of the dense and intimidating style of exhibition Freud adopted for his antiquities.

Amidst the ancient bibelots congregated on his desk top, Putnam's porcupine bristles savage and complete—an apparition from the ever new and always timeless actual and manufactured wilderness: America glowers on Freud's desk, like a beast about to spray its spines and kill. Whether to protect its master or to destroy an interloper is unclear.

Before releasing the metal beast, I ran my fingers over the quills. The plucked, xylophone-like chords sounded sweet and haunting in the deep silence of the rooms, but it *hurts* to pass one's fingers back and forth across the sharp tips. The music of the quills is painful to make.

CHAPTER 35

Productive Work and Women's Love

Very pleasant people, 2 children, bath, balcony, garden,
profusion of own fruit and vegetables. Analysis begun—
Odd process.

Molly to Elizabeth, Bastille Day, 1933

MARTHA LIVED ON another thirteen years after Freud's death in 1938. She became a familiar figure around Hampstead Heath, an independent, diminutive woman who insisted on doing her own shopping and taking her solitary constitutionals up and down the neighborhood's streets, many of them as steep as Freud's section of the Berggasse, but offering a manner of shelter that the hard, baroque thoroughfares of Vienna were not designed to tender.

If, as Freud once said, psychoanalysis is the science of the heart, the formula thereto proved difficult to transmit to the next generation. In his awkward hagiography of his father, Freud's eldest son, Martin, described the control Freud exercised over the organization of family mushroom-hunting expeditions. First, Freud would go off in the woods on his own and scout out a "fruitful area." Having identified a likely foraging ground, "father was ready to lead his small band of troops, each young soldier taking up a position and beginning the skirmish at proper intervals, like a well-trained infantry platoon attacking through a forest." Freud's troop, it appears, was battling primarily against itself. "There was always a competition to decide on the best hunter," Martin says. "Father always won." Lighthearted and admiring though the comment might be, it poses the question of what kind of father would feel it necessary to beat his children every time in a competition that all involved clearly cared about.

Anna, of course, never married. Martin (whose career highlights were a failed toothpaste manufacturing company and his memoir of his father) married, had a string of affairs, and was finally left by his wife after nearly two decades of conjugal unhappiness. Oliver, always a worry for his father on account of his various neuroses, married and divorced, then married again. Sophie fared better with her marriage, but then died tragically young. Mathilde seems to have had the best love relationship of Freud's daughters, but chronic invalidism and a fumbled operation prevented her from ever having children. Ernest, an architect and the father of the painter Lucian Freud, probably had the best time of it.

As for Putnam's children, his idealistic desire to promote their ability to love in a healthy, sexually unafraid fashion that would at last bury the family's Calvinist ghosts, was largely thwarted. Between the operations of fate and certain recalcitrant New England character traits, even had Putnam lived another twenty years he would have enjoyed little chance to see the lessons he'd learned from Freud bear fruit in his children's relationships.

Only one of his five offspring, my grandmother Elizabeth, succeeded in creating a reasonably fulfilled marriage with children. Her relationship with my southern grandfather, Monroe McIver, was a deeply formal union. Even when they dined alone, the two never failed to dress for dinner or to observe stringent manners in each other's company, a mode of conduct that appeared as respectfully deferential as it was firmly distancing. With all their gentleness, the couple rarely broke through their proper comportment even so far as to call each other by their first names. They were almost always in my presence Dr. and Mrs. McIver to each other. Indeed, the most remarkable violation of this reserve occurred at my grandfather's deathbed when my grandmother cried out, "Oh Monroe, Monroe, don't you know a gentleman always lets the lady go first?"

Though Frances died at 16 and Louisa remained an unmarried invalid all her life, James Putnam Junior may have had, on the face of it, the saddest life. A sweet, not especially ambitious man, his happiest hours were spent on small, intricate woodwork projects. He had dreamed of becoming a carpenter, but this was so contrary to Putnam's ethos of vocational service, a code based finally on the need to aspire to nothing short of saving the world (a law particularly inescapable for the family's one male heir) that my great-uncle was neither strong nor stubborn enough to resist. James submitted to Putnam's will that he attend medical school and embark on a medical career he never wanted. For many years, he served as an obstetrician in Foxboro, a small hamlet just south of Boston.

He eventually married a woman who, soon after they began living together, started showing symptoms of lunacy. For decades, he served as her caretaker. In what seems, on the face of it, to be a rare instance of family mean-spiritedness, the larger Putnam clan eventually forbade Jamie to bring Willa to family gatherings at Cotuit and Camp. One of Willa's symptoms was a tendency to break into loud, maniacal laughs, and adults worried that these howls would frighten the children. Jamie resigned himself to the group wish. He was more firm against their mounting insistence that he have Willa institutionalized. At last, however, he surrendered on this point as well. Not long after her institutionalization, doctors discovered that Willa's supposed symptoms of mental illness were attributable to Lupus disease, which had gone undiagnosed for years. The family members, all of whom had been trained by their father to be acutely psychologically attuned, had projected the syndromes they were familiar with onto a foreign physiological plane. Willa was released but soon hospitalized again because of her fast-deteriorating physical condition. She died less than a year after being correctly diagnosed. "You may be interested to know that you gave Willa three books for Christmas—Robert the Quail—a story about a fox and another animal story," began one of the handful of touching letters Jamie wrote to Molly in the 1960s. "Reading aloud is one of our chief amusements. Our other amusement is eating ice cream. . . . Willa's appetite is A. 1. We have been reading Joe Lincoln books—about 15 or 29 at a year but when they run out I know that Willa will enjoy the new books and thank you for the scarf. It is the softest thing I ever felt." By this time Molly was spending her winters on Captiva Island birding and gardening and Jamie added with a touch of wryness, "You may not know it in the sunny south but we have winter up here in the North." In 1969, they celebrated the holiday in the hospital. "Louisa came and we had a tree (2ft) as well as an icecream cake and candy. Willa had quantities of packages but we rationed them out until New Years day so as not to get her too tired. We didn't try to bring her home. She remains cheerful and happy. Of course she is very thin and gets tired easily but she rarely complains." By this time, my great-uncle had retired. He spent his remaining years in the woodshop of his home in Foxboro and at Putnam Camp constructing elaborate, beautiful doll's houses. Molly remarked in her interview with Gifford in the 1970s that Jamie was the most silent man she'd ever known.

My own memories of him—all from Putnam Camp—are not, however, of an especially sad man. I don't remember him ever saying a word, but my image of Uncle Jamie, a little plump, puffing on his invariable pipe, sitting in the afternoon radiance on the dark bench beneath the sundial on the red and brown farmhouse building, are of a mild, almost beatifically benign presence. He had a way of catching children's eyes that was conspiratorial and even quietly jubilant. When I sat next to him at the long green dining table, stealing glances at the tobacco-stained pockets at the corners of his lips, he would wink and direct my gaze to a place beneath the table where he held coins and a matchbox, which he would proceed to make vanish and reappear in deft acts of sleight of hand that always felt like a pleasing secret just between ourselves.

It was a far cry perhaps from Putnam's vision of his children's contract to revolutionize society. But it was a peaceful and enlivening form of charity all the same—one that made us children believe that the enchantments of storybook realms we read about and played within were not entirely exiled from the province of adulthood.

INDEED, ONE MUST be cautious not to extrapolate too far from the melancholy that tinges the image of Putnam and Freud's children, lest the nuances of their defeats and achievements elude us. Even Louisa, on her limited canvas, continued her mother's tradition of philanthropy, actively participating in the work of numerous social service organizations, some direct descendents of Boston's Associated Charities.

This obverse face of the posthumous story is most obvious when we turn to the two favored daughters of the men. Though Anna and Molly certainly suffered their own sadnesses, there is a haunting symmetry and generosity of accomplishment to their lives that deflects any interpretation that contains their experience to the shadows cast by their fathers, or suggests that their existences were stunted, even in terms of love.

For all Anna's inability to find marital bliss or create a body of work that many people outside the profession are familiar with, by specializing in the treatment of children, Anna did break out on her own. Her career as a lay analyst and as a prolific theoretical writer in her own right was productive and rewarding. As Lisa Appignanesi and John Forrester note, the novel that Lou Andreas-Salome (who resumed the analysis of Anna her father had begun) dedicated to her was centered on the idea that "a quiet receptivity to everything that life brings is a more fruitful way of being than any frantic, desirous striving, however purposeful." Anna trained as a teacher, and during the First World War divided her time between working at a day care center and serving with an organization that found homes for orphaned children.

Though there were a number of influences on Anna's approach to child analysis, most notably that of Hermione Hug-Hellmuth, the field was almost nonexistent before her entry. Anna's work was always more focused on practicalities than her father's was. She once wrote to Lou Andreas-Salome of how other analysts "understand things better when they distance themselves from the human beings and put things in coldly theoretical terms. And with me my understanding just disappears very easily when it is detached from the human being." For this very reason, aspects of her work may have more clinical relevance today than much of analysis can claim to possess.

At the core of Anna's theories was a belief that the child's superego was almost completely malleable and that the overall structure of children's psychology was porous and in flux. This conviction led her to endorse the centrality of education in molding human psychology in a manner bearing affinities with core tenets of Blow's and Putnam's philosophy. Like the two Americans (and in a manner that put her at extreme odds with Melanie Klein), Anna resisted the idea that innate factors could be determinative in shaping character. There was an implicit idealism, perhaps even the residual glow of a Putnamesque American perfectionism, in her belief that because environment played so central a role in psychological development, the amelioration of a child's living and learning conditions, along with the right educational strategy, could repair almost any distortion of character. Perhaps this same attribute was what led Alix Strachey to describe Anna as "that open or secret sentimentalist."

Anna's unmarried state did not signal the absence of intense intimacies. The most important of these was with another woman, Dorothy Burlingham, the youngest of Louis Tiffany's eight daughters, with whom Anna lived and traveled for many years. The two women successfully established a home together—by all accounts a richly loving one—with Dorothy's children from her own failed marriage. In another foreshadowing of Molly's life, in 1930 Dorothy and Anna bought a farm less than an hour from Vienna where they raised a menagerie of animals and maintained both vegetable and flower gardens. Dorothy remembered Anna telling her, "I like it about farm life that it brings down to a simple formula even psychic things."

IN OLD AGE, Molly recalled the fact that out of deference to her mother's opposition to psychoanalysis she did not enter analytic training while Marian was alive. Molly always wanted to work with children, however, and after completing her medical studies at Johns Hopkins she worked for a number of years as a general pediatrician at Boston's Children's Hospital. This experience only confirmed her decision to eventually follow in her father's footsteps. The backward, almost nonexistent state of child psychiatry in America in the 1920s appalled her. True also in this sense to her father's spirit, Molly saw this deficiency as a call to service.

She'd been on another expedition to the continent with Louisa in 1923, ten years before her mother's death, during which she began to make contacts for an ambitious career in the field of child psychiatry. The two young women even stopped in Zurich to visit Jung, to whom, as she reported to her mother, she was "very much attracted." Molly praised Jung's "nice smile," and the fact that along with "a good sense of humor" he seemed "unusually sane and well-balanced." She would never have heard details of Fanny's misadventures with Jung from her father, and Jung was no doubt the best choice of mentor from her mother's point of view precisely because he'd chosen to sever his ties with the analytic movement. Molly asked Jung questions about the "best mode of procedure in preparing to understand the psychiatric aspect of children's work," and found his advice "very good."

For all the restraint she showed in avoiding the Freudian camp as long as Marian was around, just months after her mother's death in the winter of 1933, Molly had packed her bags and was recrossing the Atlantic: this time with the intention of plunging straight into her own psychoanalysis. "I can hardly believe I am myself on this boat," she wrote Louisa in July from on board the *Europa*, one of the invariable "Norddeutscher Lloyds." "I was not sick *at all*." Some of the buoyancy in her tone probably derived from the fact that she was now literally leaving the sphere of her mother to enter that of her father.

Helene Deutsch had been singled out to serve as Molly's analyst before Molly set sail, probably by Freud himself, who wanted to make a connection between the rising female star of his movement and the daughter of his old, helplessly optimistic friend. Deutsch (who oversaw the induction of most analysts in training in the 1930s) was thus the first person to greet Molly in Vienna, and assisted her in the process of arranging lodgings with a sympathetic local family.

For a period of 27 months, excepting one hiatus back in Boston, Molly was analyzed twice a day every day of the week, except Sundays, on which her analysis lasted only a single hour. Even by the standards of the time, this was an unusually concentrated experience. The cost was $10 per hour, which was considered substantial.

Deutsch's reputation, not just among detractors of analysis, but also among many feminists, is mixed. She's been accused of upholding some of Freud's more regressive viewpoints on women's anatomically designated role. Like Freud, she was also obsessed with the possibility of telepathy, and her analytic sessions in certain cases were strained with occult fascination and the desire to understand how analysis could work without the intervention of the analyst's consciousness. She may have been building on hints Freud left of a psychoanalytic theory of thought transference in his essay, "The Unconscious" (one of the surviving metaphysical papers). "It's a very remarkable thing," Freud wrote there, "that the *Ucs.* of one human being can react upon that of another, without passing through the *Cs.* This deserves closer investigation."

Deutsch was also, however, the first analyst to make a concerted effort to study the nature (and implicitly thereby validate the reality) of female libido. Her sophisticated advocacy of ideas of universal human bisexuality took some of Freud's most progressive thoughts on the masculine and feminine capacities of every human being further than Freud had gone. Deutsch's research into female erotic masochism, and the conflict between eroticism and motherhood, remains pertinent to different contemporary debates. The dated aspects of her work, particularly those associated with notions of female passivity, should not obscure the fact that Deutsch also endorsed women's ability to find professional fulfillment that could substitute—effectively—for the sacrifice of active motherhood.

Many aspects of Deutsch's theories had special resonance for Molly, none more so than the idea that a daughter's absorption in her father ideal could actually be a positive step toward propelling the self into a larger extra-domestic social existence. Related to this was Deutsch's idea that, in certain cases, the analyst could help women renounce sexual gratification to pursue fulfillment on a canvas larger than the family home could supply. "Observation teaches us that a strongly sublimated father–daughter tie does not necessarily involve neurosis or feelings of frustration and privation, even if it impairs the girl's erotic life," she wrote in the *Psychology of Women*. "Fulfillment of the positive goal of life is not necessarily connected with normal sexuality." Nonetheless, Deutsch elsewhere made clear that this could only be a pyrrhic victory, and that her own ideal was an eroticized, productive female type for whom sexually masochistic tendencies were balanced with self-protective narcissism.

Though she was 40 years old when she went to Vienna, Molly was probably a virgin. Deutsch's field of concern with respect to female sexuality was often racy—predictive of and consonant with the topics treated in women-oriented media to this day (notably the vicissitudes of erotic and reproductive fortune and related issues of female self-esteem). Her focus on prodding patients to acknowledge and work through the full roster of their inhibitions, whether to sexual freedom or sublimation, must have been a harrowing process for Molly.

Yet the troubling aspects of analysis did not hinder Molly's appreciation of life in Europe. Her letters home relay the excitement she felt at exposure to life outside of Boston and the hothouse academic centers at Berkeley and Johns Hopkins, which formed her only real experience of the world outside New England. She relished the rhythm of life overseas and the sense that she was undergoing a new, valuable form of education, both about her self and the ways of a society far more nuanced than the one she'd known as a young woman. Even two hours a day of analysis left many hours free. In her leisure time, she attended seminars, went off on excursions, and learned to loaf. "This is so typical of the cunning little towns all around Wien," she wrote in a postcard to Elizabeth showing a photograph of a picturesque hamlet. "I've taken several *good* walks with May Tayler of A. H. taking the bus out to some little town and walking the almost too well kept woods as far as we feel like, sometimes bathing in a schwimminbad, supping on one of the innumerable cafes and returning by bus. All goes well here."

A few months into her analysis, Molly began indulging a new note of irony. "On hands and knees with my face in the dust I approach you," she entreated Elizabeth. "I do not know why it is so difficult for me to establish new habits of correspondence and I profoundly hope that my analysis will reform me in that as in many other respects. So far it certainly hasn't remedied any of my defects. That isn't meant to convey any criticism or regrets re analysis. I am finding it on the whole very interesting although often a good deal like trying to make rapid progress through very deep soft mud or snow. . . . Apart from the analysis I've dabbled around with various things." Though she reported that she was attending a great deal of theater, she found "the general poverty and the gloomy outlook for Austria increasingly dispiriting."

Molly's time in Vienna coincided with increasing political unrest, and her letters show her becoming cognizant of the city's menace and the hardships being visited on the Jews. Deutsch was talking about emigrating to America and Molly wanted to help her. But Freud's refusal to contemplate emigration made the decision of his immediate circle to leave difficult.

At the end of November, so as not to interrupt their analytic sessions, Molly made plans to follow Deutsch to a spa in Czechoslovakia where Deutsch was spending the Christmas break. She informed her sisters that her treatment seemed to be going "satisfactorily" so far as she could tell, but she'd abandoned the effort to set a date for her return home, as she was now committed to thoroughly completing her analysis first. Molly gave up the notion of "accomplishing anything serious" in Europe outside of what took place on the couch with Deutsch, and began to indulge a new taste for making her way in society. "I find I am a great success at it," she wrote Louisa. "I seem to be invited to do something with somebody nearly every day. . . . I'm going to be the world's best social climber before I leave here. And around the edges are lectures, movies, theater and concerts and a good bit of reading and one new angora wool dress sort of an Indian red mixture." She reassured Louisa that rumors of Vienna having been put under martial law were false, mentioning that Dolfuss had now assumed the chancellorship and absolute power. But Austria had not stabilized, and in the summer Dolfuss was assassinated, ensuring in many people's minds the inevitability of union with Germany. Right wing gangs attacked people's homes looking for supporters of Dolfuss—including the house where Molly was staying. But she was largely unfazed.

A journal of Molly's dreams from this period hints at the degree to which the political situation was preoccupying and the limits of its relevance to her identity as a Bostonian. "I was in a house with several others," she wrote of one dream, "I think Carl [Putnam] and Jamie and perhaps Tracy, at any rate all Putnams. We were hastily preparing to resist an attack from an enemy. Presently the boys went off a little distance from the house . . . and I was commissioned to carry out some other plan downstairs in the house. As I went downstairs I looked over the railing and saw the head of one of the enemy who had got there ahead of me. I was wholly unarmed and frightened. 'The enemy' proved to be George Cabot and two or three others who then came in were also Cabots. Instead of running away or fighting I shook hands with George in very friendly fashion and said: 'I hate war, not only this war but all wars.'" The war with tiny pistols between the Cabots and the Putnams is closer to a scene from Darger than to the rumblings of brutal ethnic violence converging around Molly in central Europe.

Ruminating on her years in Vienna in an interview in 1971, Molly commented, "Well, it was a lovely life. I just have never in my life known such a carefree existence as I had there. All I did was to go to the cafes, to read every newspaper I could to get the jargon and the news, and to go to lectures in the evening wherever I could."

THE IDYLLIC CHARACTER of the time was heightened by the fact that Deutsch had grown very fond of her. A few months after Molly finally left Vienna in 1935, Deutsch emigrated to America, and for a time Molly was one of her closest companions in the new life she established in Boston. The friendship soon permeated all areas of Molly's life. Deutsch and Molly worked together on various psychoanalytic projects involving mothers and children, and when they weren't working, they vigorously socialized. Stanley Cobb, probably Boston's foremost neurologist and psychiatrist when Deutsch arrived, was related to Molly by marriage (his wife was a second cousin on the Cabot side who'd also been in analysis with Helene), and the two were good friends. The Cobbs and Molly introduced Helene to Boston's medical elite. Helene's charisma and cosmopolitanism enabled her to prosper on the local social circuit even beyond the deferential curiosity that Molly's native stature assured her.

There were strong echoes in Deutsch's reliance on Molly for a certain kind of entrée into the American social and professional scene, along with Molly's intellectual dependence on Deutsch's theoretical leadership of the Freud-Putnam relationship. But an even more acute parallel can be found in the relationship between Anna Freud and Dorothy Burlingham.

At times, Helene seemed to be consciously modeling her friendship with Molly on the "Boston marriage" between Anna and Dorothy. Just as the latter couple bought *Hochroterd*, a farm a short distance outside Vienna in 1930, ten years later, in 1940, Helene purchased a farm in New Hampshire not far from Boston and made Molly her partner in the venture. It was Molly who had the competency necessary to make pragmatic decisions about running the farm, while Helene maintained what Paul Roazen called, "something of a Marie Antoinette attitude." The demands of the garden at Cotuit and the vegetable patch at Putnam Camp had trained Molly well.

Helene named the farm "Babayaga," the name of a folktale's broomstick-riding Polish witch. The character of Babayaga is notable for her mysterious transformation from good fairy to wild woman of the underworld. Some modern interpretations have teased out the lesbian overtones of Babayaga's relationship with Vasilisa, a young woman who visited Babayaga and became enslaved by her to perform the nastier rural chores.

As the situation in Europe deteriorated, Helene wrote a series of long, nostalgic letters to her husband Felix, who'd moved to Blow's old hometown of St. Louis in search of employment. "Do you remember autumn walks in the Vienna woods? With new ideas in our heads, and with the impatience to realize them—with overflowing and the feeling that 'you don't understand me,' because everything was so happily narcissistic that one was deeply insulted when a demand for clarification came from the other party? Where is all that now?" She lamented the fact that she hadn't gone back to agricultural school to brush up on her farming skills. Meanwhile, Molly was involved with purchasing cows and naming them. Deutsch noted that Molly had fallen "in love with a highly aristocratic cow (Fanny, $300) with a long family tree," and marveled at how complex the science of breeding was.

But if Molly was stuck with more mundane chores like cow buying while Helene contemplated the intricacy of relationships that went into breeding decisions, she never expressed resentment at the arrangement. To the contrary, Molly appears to have been enamored of her role as Deutsch's companion, and took great satisfaction in the farming work just as she did in their clinical endeavors together in Boston. In the summer of 1942, even after Helene had begun to cool on the project, Molly was still writing Elizabeth about the practical intricacies of the experiment, reporting that despite the mistake they'd made planting the year's strawberries in the shade of "unusually good hay," she'd spent the whole week exuberantly haying. "My hands and arms are still stiff, but we got it in beautiful condition. The farm is really quite thriving now."

Deutsch, the urbane former colleague of Freud's, finally reached the point where she realized agriculture might not be her destiny. "To be a farmer for a hobby—all right" she wrote Felix, "but I am still too young and have too great a past to regard the hobby as filling out my life. For being *just* a farmer, I am too old." She decided that the flaw might have been in her partnership with Molly. "An intellectual Jewess and a compulsive-neurotic Yankee just aren't the right combination."

Part of what Deutsch felt she needed to disengage from was the intensity of the relationship with Molly. Where Molly sounds at times as though she viewed their pastoral retreat in the tradition of Brook Farm and Putnam Camp, as a female version of the great experiments in constructed, philosophical wilderness living that many of her forebears had engaged in, Deutsch worried that their intimacy was preventing her from doing the important work she was ordained to perform. She complained to Felix that she was not drawing on her reserves of masculinity to write the "thick books" she'd dreamt of composing by this time in her life. She noted that when her friendship with Tola Rank was at its height in Vienna she had not been able to write then either. "In one word, productive work and women's love do not go together (for me as a woman!)"

I wonder in retrospect whether Molly, who seemed to flourish on "women's love," was hurt by Helene's withdrawal from their intimacy. It may have been gentle and gradual enough that no feelings were bruised. But in her subsequent writings and the interviews she gave, Molly was notably reticent about Helene in the midst of a great deal of rumination on her early days as an analyst, a period in which Helene was far and above the dominant figure in Molly's life.

It was also in the mid-1940s that Molly began dedicating more of her time to the project that would become her primary endeavor for many years, collaborating with Beata Rank (Otto's ex-wife) on the founding of the first American clinic dedicated exclusively to treating mentally disturbed preschool children. In July of 1946, the clinic opened in Roxbury under the name the "James Jackson Putnam Children's Center."

The three-fold goal of the institution ranged from giving direct help to very young children "whose personality and behavior difficulties prevent their fitting readily into family and neighborhood life" and their parents, to studying children during the first years of life "when the foundations of personality and character are being laid, in order to discover ways in which good traits may be fostered and poor ones discouraged," to offering educational courses for co-workers in the field.

In addition to the preschool status of its patients, the Center was distinguished by the fact that it included a school designed to allow psychiatrists to "observe the children in familiar surroundings, going through all their typical daily activities and in their relationships with other children and adults." In this way, the founders hoped to create a comfortable learning environment in which play was part of the treatment as much as were the interactions with psychiatrists and social workers. Throughout the Center's existence, the economic standing of parents who applied to send children there was never a barrier to admittance.

Reading about the mission of the James Jackson Putnam Children's Center, it's apparent that Molly in many ways succeeded in marrying the three major idealistic principles to which she'd been exposed growing up: her father's theories of psychiatry and psychoanalysis, her mother's Bostonian ideals of social service, and Blow's therapeutic/philosophical Froebelian approach to early childhood education (and teacher training).

A case history recorded in the second annual report (probably written by Molly) gives a sense of how the Center's integrated approach to treatment worked in practice: "George L. was two and a half when his distracted parents brought him to the Center—a child so aggressive and destructive that the neighbors said he would grow up to be a criminal. He was regarded as a menace on the streets, hitting babies in their carriages without provocation and smashing milk bottles on door-steps." He'd cried all through infancy, and punishments did not affect the hyperactivity and destructiveness into which George's miserable infancy segued. On his arrival at the Center "George could not be tolerated at first even in our nursery school. He struck at objects and children alike so violently that it was impossible to allow him the initial freedom he needed for therapeutic purposes." For his first few weeks at the Center, he was seen only by the psychiatrist for individual sessions. Initially, "he made a shambles of the psychiatrist's room, calling anxiously for his mother when he smashed things and watching to see what the psychiatrist would do. With repeated reassurances from the latter that he would not punish him, that he liked him very much, and that he understood how afraid he felt, the little boy gradually grew quieter in his behavior and finally substituted symbolic play with clay figures for his general destructiveness." The psychiatrist realized that "George's destructiveness and hyperactivity were expressions of intense anxiety due to his conflicting feelings of dependence and antagonism toward his parents and his fear of annihilating punishment." As the child developed trust in the psychiatrist, a second effort was made to bring him into the school. "It required close attention and infinite patience on the part of the teacher to draw him into acceptable and satisfying activities and to protect him from spoiling each budding success within the group by some quick outbursts of aggression." George had never been taught to play and had to be shown how to use even rudimentary toys. It took eight months of psychotherapy before he could join the school and play with the other children. At this point, however, "he became more and more outgoing with children and adults, played constructively, took full responsibility for his own behavior, and finally assumed a place of leadership in the group. His happy face is now a joy to all who know him." The boy's mother was also given therapy to understand better how to interact with her child. "Gradually she found her reward in an increasingly tender relationship with him, and now both are radiant in their newly found capacity to give love and to receive it. A year was required to bring inner peace and happiness to this little boy and thus to free his energies for the development of constructive skills, imaginative play and, above all, successful relationships—a year of intensive effort on the part of psychiatrist, social worker and teacher."

THE IMPLICATION IS clear that what had been achieved in terms of "freeing energies" and expanding the child's ability to succeed in relationships projecting into the community was, in fact, the first phase of Putnam's sublimation process. Where none of Molly's elders had quite succeeded in making the synthesis among disciplines that all of them, on some level, believed to be essential to the nurturing of the next generation, Molly, in her own quiet, determined way, managed to create a framework in which this dream could be actively realized, among the population most vulnerable and malleable.

From the beginning, however, financing the Center was a struggle. In addition to tirelessly fundraising from private individuals, Molly and Rank fought a strenuous battle annually for grant moneys. The labor-intensive form of treatment they practiced, running against the grain of the American mental health industry as it geared toward ever quicker and easier solutions, grew harder and harder to muster support for.

As the health of Roxbury itself deteriorated in the sixties and seventies the problems of the James Jackson Putnam Children's Center proliferated. In the late sixties, in an effort to save the Center it was turned over to the local Roxbury community. Despite gifted, dedicated staff, the Center had two ineffective directors in quick succession. The budget shrank and finally was inadequate for even its stripped-down operations as a community center. A fire compounded the damage wrought by years of financial negligence. The James Jackson Putnam Children's Center closed down permanently in 1979.

And yet, though the effort to integrate the center fully into the life of the Roxbury community ultimately failed, I can't help feeling that Putnam would have approved the sense of communal obligation that was a crucial factor in the decision of the Board of Trustees to give the center to the neighborhood where it was located. An undated photograph from the *Boston Globe* shows a group of African-American children being taught by African-American teachers in a classroom of the Center. The fact that in one generation, this idealistic creation of a European Jew and a "compulsive-neurotic Yankee," the latter working in the tradition of a quintessential Boston Brahmin descended from prominent Puritans, should become the property of a community that had been still more oppressed in America than Putnam's beloved "gamins" were in Paris, carries a haunting aptness. "*Institutions*, and the evidence of the *struggles of the people*; those are what we really want to see," Putnam had written to Molly. The fate of the James Jackson Putnam Children's Center offered ample demonstration of the poignant aspirations and tragedy of both.

Although, unlike Anna, Molly wrote little, she made up for her theoretical reticence with a profoundly active clinical service, working not just at the Children's Center and in private practice, but also in New Haven at Yale's Child Study Center, where Anna Freud later spent time as both a student and teacher. She continued to work well into old age, gaining a reputation throughout New England for her powers of empathy and encouragement with respect to young patients and their families. Never concerned about her personal stature, she was a key if neglected influence on the renowned Dr. T. Berry Brazelton, who continues to play a prominent role in American popular theorizing on child development and parenting.

Both Anna and Molly lived lives of immense creative compassion that far transcended their assumed role as vestal virgins to the flame of their fathers' memory. Indeed, in a completion of the circle, in adulthood, the two women began their own correspondence, albeit one that never quite "took."

This is a shame. Despite Anna's more active participation in the political fray of the Movement, and for all the manifold differences between turn-of-the-century Boston and Vienna, one suspects they could have been friends. Their shared perspectives on psychology went well beyond the lessons of their psychoanalytic fathers. If much of Freud's theory of psychoanalysis began with the agon of the Oedipus complex, the model Anna and Molly developed of a daughter's tender and enlarging relation with the father offers a hopeful counterbalance. More balanced than Antigone (although Freud would call Anna "my Antigone"), neither so strident nor so martyristic as Electra and Griselda, the lives of Anna and Molly suggest a tender, creatively benign if still self-sacrificing female complex that may lie beyond the circumference of Greek mythology from which Freud drew his psychoanalytic lexicon. Above the two women's personal ambitions or even, in the end, their ambitions for their fathers' legacies, stands their commitment to children in need, to the responsibility of aiding a future generation out of the vulnerabilities they themselves never quite left behind.

It's fitting that one of the only pieces of correspondence to survive between Anna and Molly is a note from Anna in which she thanks Molly for "the lovely flowers from your garden, for the perfect vase and for your note." Like her father, gardening and letter writing both were passions for Molly. In the end, the gift of a beautiful blossom of nature cultivated in the garden of America to Anna in postwar Europe neatly bookends Freud's gift of a very different sort of interior wilderness, and a methodology for cultivating that unknown, across the sea to Putnam in Boston one generation before.

———

SOME TIME AFTER at last escaping or being gently exiled from the enchantments of Babayaga, Molly bought a country home on an estuary near the Cobbs in Little Compton, Rhode Island. The house itself was modern and modest, with lots of glass—vaguely Bauhaus in style. But the enormous garden that consumed the land on the other side of the house from the little lawn on which I tumbled with my siblings, and the rock we climbed to conquer our own enchanted kingdoms were unabashedly grand. As children, we greedily ate the sticky, candy red raspberries from the neat line of bushes bordering one end of the garden; for dinner we helped pick corn, squash, and lettuce. I remember how slowly Molly ate at our abundant meals together and have since learned that she alone among Putnam's children adopted her father's commitment to Fletcherizing—that arduous, ascetic dietary practice Kafka was devoted to—of chewing each bite of food so many times that it "swallows itself." We were less conscious of the extraordinary flowers Aunt Molly also grew that made for dazzling centerpieces, suggestive in their tonal range of the Old World orientals and oils from my Viennese family.

The size of the garden was far beyond what Molly could use in her very social life, even with its many opportunities for passing gifts to loved ones and colleagues. But it was only recently that I discovered how much of her garden in fact ended up on the table of the children she cared for in Roxbury. Blow opened her first educational tract by presenting what she referred to as "Twenty Gifts to help fertile young minds bud and blossom." Molly's garden fulfilled Blow's mission in both a literal and metaphorical sense. She realized the ideals of self-effacing communal service inherited from an elder generation, and revealed the values not quite malled over, media-fied, or otherwise lost in the "wild-style," wilderness-free, all-individualist, all-conforming, all-consuming, all-entitled, all-normal America we've constructed on the ashes of both Freud's psychoanalysis and Putnam's philosophical psychology.

In my memories, Molly is always laughing, a warbly delicious sound, wreathed by an infectious smile that made children know she was on their side. Her skin was ruddy in that New England seaside way, a hue I conflated with the tint of the lobsters she pulled from a great pot for our suppers. I did not realize until spending time with the photographs that with her round spectacles and the pattern of her creases beneath that silver hair, her face in later years looked identical to Putnam's. I understand now that as

Putnam's face broke through his daughter's countenance, in a pitch of hopeful pluck and excited good cheer, Molly was communicating to others Putnam's own optimism. And this happily also confirms what may be an even deeper aspect of Freud's vision than the notion of repression, or his theory of the interpretation of dreams: Freud's insights into the ways that the dead speak through us. He showed that we can learn to listen for their different, multifarious voices, and so at last become responsible for which ones we choose to single out and transmit forward in time from the stream of the past that possesses us. By lifting others' spirits with the force of Putnam's smile, Molly showed in a very simple way how Eros and Thanatos could be reconciled.

CHAPTER 36

Disinterested Love

I am sure that you do not believe, either as a scientist or as a man, that when you make some great sacrifice for the advancement of the truth (as you have done so often), or when you do some painful task in obedience to a sense of duty, you do not exert any power of free will or choice. . . . I feel sure that if anybody should threaten to take away that amount of freedom—be it never so small—which you feel yourself possessed of, you would resist the attempt with all your strength and with your life. In other words, you cherish this sense of freedom, however slight it is, and you cherish it as something which does not belong exclusively to yourself but which can be shared by other men and can constitute a bond among men in general.

Putnam to Freud, unsent letter, August 13, 1915

WHEN I FIRST read Freud as a university student, I remember feeling that, more than specific details of any one theory, I was enraptured by the sound of his written voice, a tone of cosmopolitan allure rich in literary reference, soaked in the ichor of classicism. In his analysis of the witty, wicked, wondrous, world-confecting masked ball of desire, Freud offered a language of resistance to the consumer sentimentality that glazed the surface of the violent homeland in which I'd been raised. To enter his books was to penetrate a world of more intriguing complexity—and nuanced possibility—in which the recognition of one's own fatal immurement in the labyrinth of drives was also to be enfolded in the grand history of human imagination. I read Freud as an escape of sorts, one that not even the ivy-mantled façades of my old university could quite provide, into an ideal of thought that was imbricated, yet earthy. In retrospect, I realize that part of the excitement I felt on first finding his work was that of entering a fantasy of European culture, a fantasy that my father's family had been compelled to surrender on fleeing Austria and that, indeed, my mother's Puritan forebears had abandoned hundreds of years before on leaving England. Over time, more resilient than the sense of entering a certain lost Europe on reading Freud, was the lesson he taught that this civilization was itself a dream.

As Freud arrayed the figurines from Greek and Egyptian mythology on his desk, he restored a pantheon of ancient gods and heroes in the form of names for the constellation of interior powers and compulsions strutting the stage of individual psychology. He understood that stories begot stories, that truth shifted, Emerson-style, contingent on mood, and that fixation on a single ideological vision risked obstructing the full complexity of whispered warnings from the underworld. The importance he accorded imagination and dreams reflected, beyond the apotheosis of fantasy, his devotion to dethroning humanity's sense of personal omniscience. No analysis by Freud's standards was adequate unless the patient had learned to second-guess the grounds for his conscious decision making at pivotal junctures. At its best, psychoanalysis teaches a form of radical skepticism. In his papers, Freud repeatedly insisted not only that analysts had to be psychoanalyzed themselves, but that they had to return to analysis over and over in the course of their lives, because viewpoints that were only the offshoots of earlier tangled experiences would continue to grow, like the fingernails of the dead, even after a successful analysis. The wilderness is never cleared permanently. We must go back and back with the scythe, for the biological conundrum of consciousness itself is the earth from which desire and its irrational justifications are endlessly propagated.

Near the conclusion of *Civilization and Its Discontents*, Freud wrote, "One thing only do I know for certain and that is that man's judgments of value follow directly his wishes for happiness—that, accordingly, they are an attempt to support his illusions with arguments. . . . Thus I have not the courage to rise up before my fellow-men as a prophet, and I bow to their reproach that I can offer them no consolation: for at bottom that is what they are all demanding—the wildest revolutionaries no less passionately than the most virtuous believers."

By persistently compelling people to question the consolations they staked out for themselves, Freud was making the goal of treatment a perpetual deferring of rest, a continual act of demasking. Nothing was so absent from twentieth-century politics as a methodology for detoxifying ideological solace. This side of Freud, which has continued to be drawn on by different rights movements, is not identical with that of Freud the therapist. Indeed, as Freud grew older, he increasingly dispensed with the idea of psychoanalysis as, in any traditional sense, curative, beginning a movement away from the aspiration of therapeutically determined normalcy that Lacan consummated. This latter aspect of Freudian thought suggests that self-knowledge ultimately extends only to the point of knowing that one does not know.

Freud's acceptance of the circumscription of analysis, his lack of faith in the potential for progress of humanity as such, made for what ought to have been a profoundly un-American formula of treatment. And yet his system was capacious enough that Putnam could find there nutriment for a new vision of spiritual possibility. Some of the elements in Putnam's strain of analytic thought that Freud most adamantly resisted were the same ones that made the initial generation of American psychological authorities tolerate Freud long enough for his work to be incubated in the New World. Ironically, without Putnam's differences with him, Freud would have found it far more difficult to find an audience in the United States. Not only did the infinite energies evoked in Putnam's version make it more palatable to a general American audience than a strict Freudian approach would have been, psychoanalysis in America actually helped the educated elite buttress their beliefs. Freud's idea of an unconscious filled with demonic forces along with sublime potential gave new words and fresh currency to old religious ideas. Above all, psychoanalysis, by seeming to put the last nail in the coffin of a purely physical understanding of psychology, validated the age-old New England conviction that there was something more than matter inside the skull; they called that something more the soul.

But what of Putnam's own legacy? Beyond the echoes of his thought that can be found in a spectrum of popular theorizers, where, finally, does one find more substantial correspondences?

Among subsequent generations of American psychologists and analysts, outside of Molly and her line of influence into figures like Berry Brazelton, Karl Menninger is the best known figure to explicitly credit the influence of Putnam on the formation of his theories. Menninger founded one of America's most important analytically oriented early training facilities for psychiatrists and psychologists. In books like *Man Against Himself* and *What Ever Became of Sin*, he reflected on the inveteracy of man's appetite for destruction in a manner that put him at odds with the latest breed of American optimists. The obituary of Freud that Menninger wrote for the *Nation* eulogized, above all, Freud's stature as "the most effective disturber of complacency" of the era. Writing on the eve of World War II, Menninger positioned complacency as the worst evil: "In these days when peace of mind and peace of soul are held up as desiderata of the highest order at the very moment that millions are homeless and millions are hungry and millions are in slavery and millions in fear—surely we need to fear the dreadful disease of smug complacency and illusory peace."

In "Footprints," one of Menninger's last essays, he wrote about the invaluable example Putnam's "broad-mindedness" had provided during the time Menninger himself was in training in Boston. He described the excitement he felt on being introduced to Putnam's idea of disinterested love. This notion, as Menninger saw it, was the core of Putnam's argument with Freud. Putnam argued that there were two types of love, just as there are two categories of human motives. Disinterested love is representative of the "strongly socialized, idealized forms of love" that "do not exist simply as branchings-out of anything that could be thought of as a sexual *libido*." Though informed by the larger energy wellspring that Freud refers to as libido, in fact they are "expressions of an everywhere operative, self-active, creative energy." Putnam's clearest definition of this nonsexual form of Eros appeared in the semi-mystical second case history of Susan Blow. Its existence was not intended as a disavowal of the type Freud described, but rather as a goal defining the analyst's mission: to guide love away from the "easier paths marked out by pleasure, passion and self-interest" toward a realm of disinterested Eros.

At the end of his essay, Menninger noted that despite Putnam's continued defense of Freud at a moment when Freud's unpopularity exceeded even that of our own day, "Putnam was disturbed by Freud's radical positivism." The reason, Menninger said, was Putnam's belief that "one could not dispense with value judgment." Though Freud countered that what was needed was more knowledge, Menninger sided with Putnam by suggesting that whereas in principle the effort to eliminate emotional response from the treatment process was admirable, in doing so "Freud left out of consideration aspects of the human personality not reducible to mechanical principles." Nonetheless, Menninger proposed, the indications of Freud's own developing thought are that he moved away from his "earlier radical positivism. . . . In his later years, I suspect Freud might have been more inclined to agree with the Putnam of his earlier years."

Menninger seemed to be proposing that some kind of synthesis was possible after all—opportunities for a hybrid practice that were never fully explored.

In the course of writing this book, I met a young psychiatrist whose professional situation formed an obverse complement to Putnam's early career. Where Putnam had gone to Germany to study, this doctor, a young woman, had come to America from Germany to do her residency. During a conversation in which she spoke with happy irreverence about the amalgam of therapeutic trends going into her practice, she related how, at the community hospital where she worked (foreign interns tend to be put to this service as it's viewed as less prestigious) psychopharmaceuticals and cognitive therapies were the treatment protocols of choice. This, of course, was unsurprising given their reputation for the quick results beloved of the HMOs and America's larger for-profit medical system. I asked her whether the preferred treatments were effective. She answered without hesitation that she thought they were. I wondered then about the purpose of forms of psychotherapy with affinities to psychoanalysis: Why weren't they entirely obsolete? She answered with as little hesitation that they continued to survive because of a field of troubles that cognitive therapies and psychopharmaceuticals simply could not touch. Referring to psychoanalysis and other talk therapies, she remarked, "I view them like a form of philosophy."

The patients in the community hospital where she worked, often individuals with drug problems and chronic mental illness, were supposed to be returned to the streets as swiftly as possible. But some doctors sought to countermand these policies. The director of her training program suggested that she and her colleagues should be striving for an approach that addressed the full integrity of a patient's being. In words that strikingly echoed Putnam's, he argued that the problem with these treatments of choice was that they neglected some of the most significant parts of patients' personalities. What tended to be eliminated from more expedient models was the idea that human motivation represented an instinct with history. Freud and Putnam were both, in their different ways, equally historians of motivation.

Of course it appears simply impossible today to reproduce something like Molly's Children's Clinic, with its spectacular demands on time and energy, but that does not legitimate belly-up surrender to the insurance companies.

I asked my interlocutor whether there were examples on a theoretical level of the integrative approach that her director advocated. She mentioned Louis Marinoff and the movement of philosophical counseling. Marinoff has argued that psychologists today, whatever their school, have failed because they apply inflexible, standardized models of thought to the nuanced swirl of our mental states and dilemmas. When a problem doesn't fit within one of their rigid frames, psychologists are impotent. For a philosopher, Marinoff claims, each person represents a new, individual case. Deploring the spiritual void in Western culture and the fundamentalisms that breed in this hollow, Marinoff champions a form of therapeutic dialogue that contextualizes the plight of patients with the great philosophical explorations of the past and, it is hoped, triggers new, enlarged patterns of self-reflection.

Putnam would have found aspects of this project provocative, but he would ultimately have rejected Marinoff's approach because Putnam never thought of eliminating the psychiatric dimension in favor of the philosophical. What Putnam sought was a cross-fertilization between the two disciplines, not a replacement.

After Marinoff, my doctor friend brought up the extraordinary career of Nobel Prize winner Eric Kandel. "Putnam," she said, "was the Eric Kandel of his day."

This was an intriguing analogy. Kandel, who was born in Vienna and originally trained in psychoanalysis, has done groundbreaking work synthesizing the insights of psychoanalysis with discoveries of contemporary neurobiology. One area in which this effort has borne fruit is in showing how memory receptors change in the course of psychotherapy. Kandel's work has demonstrated that talk therapy has the potential to alter brain chemistry by alternately nurturing and pruning back synapses. Going beyond what was possible for Putnam, given the state of biology in his day (despite Putnam's own deep grounding in neurology), Kandel's work has studied the organic composition and dynamics of memory.

It's more accurate in Freud's schema to speak of our being haunted by ghosts that come from the past but are not identical with it than to say that memory as a record of past experience is a dominant agent in shaping psychology. In Freud's system, by regathering the shards of memory and owning up to desire, we can better integrate our personality. We may not be happier, exactly, but we are in some way truer by being less in denial about the wellsprings of our emotions and behaviors.

Putnam's vision of memory, though less skeptical than Freud's, similarly consisted of a welter of actually remembered experience and fantasized desires of different tendencies (positive and negative). Likewise, he accepted the Freudian imperative of reintegrating shadows from the past with our present personality to make our selves whole. But in essence, the purpose of memory for him was as a springboard to elevate ourselves toward a higher destiny. By becoming conscious of the full spectrum of our intentions, we are better able to sort out the virtuous from the ignoble, thereby cultivating the former and making our behaviors more aligned with the stars.

Kandel's work has looked at ways in which the peculiar attentiveness to self that takes place in psychotherapy, when it is successful, augments the long-term memory on which all learning is dependent. In order for long-term memory to develop it must find expression at the genetic level. This idea resonates loosely with Putnam's idea of an innate potential for positive growth in the profound depths of the self, awaiting the nurturing intervention of a dedicated physician. More importantly, Kandel moves beyond the idea of the encounter with memory in psychotherapy as a revelation of the suppressed past—a classic confrontation, Oedipus-style, with primal lust—into the dynamics of memory's educative function. Memory in this schema is not only a repository of past experience and an engine of illicit fantasy, but a tool that enables future understanding and our adaptive progress as individuals. The therapeutic work involved in grappling with verbalized thought at a crossroads between recollection, desire, fear, and hope can become a step toward a biologically expanded identity, a literal transformation of personal being. In this way, memory may serve as an active instrument of positive motivation, not, as Freud sometimes seems to say, just an obstructive body of material to be exorcised on the way to catharsis.

For Kandel this recognition impels the scientist toward the molecular level of research. This, in theory, is the opposite direction from the one Putnam was pushing toward. And yet, in that atomic substrate, one has entered the space in which the stuff of humanity is literally coextensive with cosmic matter. Here all motivation originates, both the biological and something antedating even that. Putnam's self-transcendence could only transpire within Freud's interior space. The drive leading there might be Freud's Thanatos, but is equally the "creative self-active energy of the universe," the Libido, the *"Weltenergie,"*—the force pushing us at once toward personal annihilation and the sublimation of the elements of our beings into the substance of the heavens.

Yet despite provocative affinities, the thrust of Kandel's work is not, of course, intended as a defense of freedom of will. Putnam's obsession with this principle was a function of the way he saw freedom serving as the ultimate bond uniting humanity—linking the best men of Boston and Vienna—inspiring each individual to sacrifice himself for the good of the essential communal being of humanity. "It usually happens that men are moved by broader and better motives than they are consciously aware of," Putnam wrote at one point in *Human Motives*, summing up his vision, "and that to be so moved is virtually to acknowledge obligations of which the final implication can be expressed only in ideal terms." At this theoretical juncture, when Putnam broadcast a faith in the profound selflessness at the heart of every individual driving history toward the supernal, Kandel might well have tipped his hat and turned away, leaving Putnam to his own path, even if wishing him Godspeed in the climb. But Putnam was not one of the glowing self-help prophets preaching inherent human godliness and a seven-step solution to everything wrong. How could he, then, rational and intelligent as he was, embrace a philosophy that appears at times, in its wild, ingenuous idealism, hopelessly bereft of real world experience? Was he really *that* naive?

THE SOLUTION TO this puzzle may lie beyond the laboratory and the philosopher's study both, within the compass of Putnam Camp itself. There have been times, reading in the memoirs, letters, and logs, when I've come to feel that Camp guests in the early years actually did experience an intimation of that higher, liberated, socially impassioned realm that Putnam was constantly invoking in his papers. Where else might a single vacation include a synthesis of work and play that could run the gamut from creating water mills out of spider threads to climbing mountains, inventing new types of photography, talking philosophy, writing poetry, singing, engaging in theatrics, eating feasts—and falling in love?

Putnam's exuberant optimism, his faith in the creativity and good will of all humanity, found tangible form in the seasonal utopia at Putnam Camp where, at last, he felt himself "free and able to use his powers." The countless pastoral rhapsodies on Putnam Camp, many of which fill the Camp log, show scenes of untempered romanticism conjunctive with Putnam's philosophy. "And here a reminiscence holds me fast," begins one typical lyric:

> As sunrise sung along the mountain-tops
> And all the grass lay crisp in silver frost,
> A throng of beings clothed in shining robes
> Who straightway plunged them in the crystal stream,
> Then ate of milk and honey in a hall
> With stately armor decked and antique harps . . .
>
> And here my guide turned with her proudest smile:
> "They cured the body and mind of many men,
> Mended the broken life, and cleansed again
> The half polluted current of the soul."

The kind of joyful communal existence that healed the "broken life" and purified the spirit demonstrated that a form of paradise was attainable in the here and now. The secret to Putnam's idealism may have been the constituents of ideal reality he came across and helped to fashion at Putnam Camp.

PUTNAM CAMP WAS not, of course, a place or a philosophical experiment that Freud could have anticipated when he set his sights on the New World. What, then, did Freud imagine he would find in America? In truth, he was focused far more on what he himself was importing to the country than the question of what he would discover was indigenous to the United States.

When Freud stood at the railing of the *George Washington* facing Manhattan's harbor and asked his colleagues, "Don't they know we're bringing them the plague?" he was making a more enigmatic statement than might immediately be manifest. It sounds good; we know it's witty. And yet, what in God's name did Freud actually mean?

Given his focus on America's puritanical repression, the most obvious explanation for the comment would be that in some way he conceived of himself as bringing us sex. If not sex as such, at least consciousness of the sexual roots of our psychological make-up. Yet, in what way could awareness of the sexual etiology of our neuroses really be compared to a devastating epidemic? Perhaps by "plague" Freud meant something like a Midas touch. Once the psychoanalytic perspective is implanted in people, everything they finger turns to sex.

However, I wonder whether even in a moment of acid wit, Freud would ever have positioned the more probing, candid understanding of sexuality that psychoanalysis laid claim to as a malignant infectious disease. If nothing else, he was deeply skeptical as to whether Americans would actually accept the role he assigned sexuality in the mind—and aren't plagues always, whatever else, catching?

What direction should we turn, then, in trying to fathom Freud's remark? Perhaps it should be contextualized with the trans-Atlantic passage preceding its utterance. Rather than honing their shuffleboard prowess or joining a cappella choirs à la Putnam, Freud, Ferenczi, and Jung spent their sea crossing to America engaged in the world's first group analysis. From their second day at sea, the three doctors were immersed in interpreting one another's dreams. Sexual topics must have been important to their exchange; however, sex alone didn't make their conversation consuming. Rather, the hook came through the psychoanalytic process itself: the revelation that they could continue perpetually cutting deeper into one another with their self-dissecting talk without ever reaching the far side of the self. There was always another layer to uncover. Once they began peeling the onion of psychoanalytic self-consciousness, there was nowhere to stop until the self itself was gone. And here, I believe, lies the explanation for Freud's remark.

As he stood on the deck of the ship, flayed raw by Jung and exhausted by Ferenczi, Freud thought to himself, once the Americans get going, *they'll never shut up*. The operative mythological analogy was, then, not Midas and his touch, but Pandora and her box. Once the lid is opened, it can never be closed. And this partly *because* hope will always remain inside (in the case of psychoanalysis, the elusive hope of perfect self-knowledge). The talking cure is also the talking disease: logorrhea. Freud knew that once the Americans started talking the conversation they'd hold under the rubric of analysis might take them somewhere utterly alien to the founder's vision. In truth, the oracular quality of Freud's pronouncement derives from the fact that he knew such divergence was inevitable.

THE UNCANNY SADNESS of the American suburbs resembles a landscape from which a plague has receded without being reclaimed by any secondary tide of creation. Yet perhaps, if Freud had taken just a bit of Putnam's prescription to heart—absorbed the message of social responsibility without the curiously sterile spirituality—the pathogens in analysis might have been converted into their opposite. The plague might have been sublimated into an inoculation against a certain strain of New World psychology.

I traveled to Jerusalem near the end of writing this book, to Israel where, some would say, the chapter of history in which Freud was caught concluded, and where the American missionary dream of saving the world has found a new haven, far removed from Putnam's vision. While there I spoke to a Palestinian man, an ex-*maître d'* of the casino in Jericho, now hoping to be employed as a driver. He proved to be a devotee of Freud; "my dear, dear beloved Freud," he called him, praising Freud's understanding of the way the past struck back at the future like a scorpion's tail.

I explained to him the story of the debate between Putnam and Freud and he became feverishly excited, so much so that at first I thought he was enraged by the Boston doctor's charge against the Viennese master, a presumption made reasonable by the fact that much of the evening had been spent excoriating America. ("You know what hurts me *here*," he said, clutching his heart. "The Americans, who have such beautiful land, who made so much money, who could send a man to the *goddamn moon*, still have no understanding whatever of Jerusalem.") But as I started to defend my great-grandfather's position, he interrupted me. "No, no I agree with Putnam," he said. "I agree with him! We must have a goal outside of ourselves, a goal to help others. Yes, we must because we have too many devices. *The mind has too many devices. I agree with Putnam. Look what's become of us.*"

FOR ME, THE story of the extraordinary argument and friendship between Freud and Putnam ended at that moment, a few hours before dawn, in a lush Jerusalem garden twinkling with jasmine blossoms, upon the unexpected words of a lost soul for whom the essence of the old debate remained as urgent as a message in a dream.

Bibliography and Chapter Notes

The Countway Library Rare Books and Special Collections division contains the bulk of Putnam's papers, most of which were donated to Harvard by his daughter, Molly, in the 1960s. These letters were central to the composition of this book at every stage. The Blow-Putnam letters and Putnam's letters to Fanny Bowditch Katz are stored at the site, along with most of Putnam's professional correspondence. There are other family letters in the Massachusetts Historical Society and a few bits and pieces in smaller archives scattered along the East Coast. When I began writing this book I knew, also, that my family had in its possession a handful of random letters, journals, photo albums, and memoirs, several of which were largely composed of extracts from letters. The three most pertinent memoirs that redact significant family correspondence are: *A Memoir of Dr. James Jackson: With Sketches of His Father Hon. Jonathan Jackson and His Brothers Robert, Henry, Charles, and Patrick Tracy Jackson; and Some Account of Their Ancestry* by James Jackson Putnam (Cambridge: The Riverside Press, 1905), *Early Days at Putnam Camp* by Elizabeth Putnam McIver (read at the Annual Meeting of the Keene Valley Historical Society, 1941), and *Memoir of Frances Cabot Putnam, A Family Chronicle* by Marian Cabot Putnam (Cambridge: The Riverside Press, 1916). I drew on all of these sources extensively in writing this book. But it was understood that the family correspondence as such was *gone*—irreplaceably destroyed, dispersed, and rendered otherwise inaccessible. The most persistent rumor was that the letters had been sold off to an anonymous collector in the early eighties, shortly after the death of Putnam's last living daughter, by a nameless relative hard up for cash. I bridled at the thought and fumed at the relative, but what could be done?

And then, one spring day there was a kind of magic trick—a mystery and impossible conclusion to the tale of loss. I was sitting with my mother in her bedroom talking about relatives and family and history, and all at once, as though all my efforts to locate the correspondence hitherto had been but a dream, my mother told me, "Well of course I've got *tons* of family letters—you'll never be

able to get through them—but I've always told you that (she whispered a name)
didn't sell them off. She would never have done that."

"What?"

As I remember it, my mother then limped, hunched and with her shock of
silver hair shining, to a small white door in the wall opposite her bed—an inscrutable Alice in Wonderland opening into a kind of crawl space which, had
it appeared in a dream in analysis, Freud himself would have rejected as too
heavy handed. She tugged open the door with a faint grunt of effort, and then
began extracting giant black three-ply plastic lawn garbage bag after garbage
bag—three, four, five, six! More! I finally went to help her. Each bag was heavy
and bulky beyond belief. I took off the twisty tie on one and peered inside. It
was filled with huge ziplock bags, each one stuffed with crumbling letters.
Dozens, hundreds, literally thousands of letters now stood piled around me
like plunder in a pirate cave. *The letters had been inside my own childhood
home the whole time?*

I have found myself unable to ask my mother why, exactly, the letters were
never mentioned until that afternoon. My guess is that the pierce of her New
England conscience, stronger even than her New England desire to keep the
lid on the past, compelled her to confess their existence.

If the appearance of the missing letters was like the discovery of a new,
unknown room within our family home, the actual exploration of these letters
proved to be like entering a secret garden. They're so marvelously delicate and
colorful—filled, in fact, with descriptions of actual gardens, newly blossomed
plants and freshly acquired seeds, and uncultivated nature, invariably paying
loving attention to the petals and leaves of simple day-to-day being. Indeed,
the number of these epistles in which there were painstakingly pressed actual
flowers is astonishing. Not to mention the letters that include careful line drawings of geographical phenomena met with on a ramble far afield, or even a
graceful watercolor of a pastoral view, perhaps set above a quotation from Keats
or, more common still, a set of homespun verses commemorating an anniversary, an event, or just an incidence of domestic affection. The number of poems
children "wrote" to their mothers on their first, second, third, fourth, and fifth
birthdays, often including a beautifully wrapped lock of baby's hair!

What's more, even though the correspondents were not generally probing
their innermost feelings, there's a free association quality to the monologues
in these letters that on occasion does invoke thoughts of psychoanalysis. Implicit in all this correspondence is the Freudian perspective that everything
means and should be related, no matter how apparently trivial. This suggests,
again, the ways in which analysis in fact didn't only hearken forward to some

revolutionary future, but also accorded well with the patient, time-consuming practice of intimate communication that characterized the past.

The "show" that blooms from the seeds of all these myriad words, with their mixture of the diurnal and the profound, is luxuriant, intricate, and articulate. These vast, long-hidden family archives were in fact what made this book possible.

After the family archives, more than any book, drew on *James Jackson Putnam and Psychoanalysis: Letters between Putnam and Sigmund Freud, Ernest Jones, William James, Sandor Ferenczi, and Morton Prince, 1877–1917* (Cambridge: Harvard University Press, 1971). Nathan G. Hale, Jr. edited the book and Judith Bernays Heller translated German texts. Hale not only compiled almost all the extant correspondence between Putnam and the key figures responsible for the development of psychoanalysis in Europe and modern psychology in America, but has also written a rich, succinct essay on Putnam's life and involvement with the psychoanalytic movement.

In the case of Freud also, the most important sources I drew on were the various published collections of his letters, along with citations of unpublished letters in other books. Freud's brilliance, his infinitely quotable style, along with the strange blend of fatalism, romanticism, and mercurial passions that define his character come through here as nowhere else. Sources for letters included:

The Complete Correspondence of Sigmund Freud and Ernest Jones 1908–1939, edited by R. Andrew Paskauskas with an introduction by Riccardo Steiner (Cambridge: The Belknap Press of Harvard University Press, 1993).

The Freud/Jung Letters: The Correspondence between Sigmund Freud and C. G. Jung, edited by William McGuire, translated by Ralph Manheim and R. F. C. Hull (Princeton, NJ: Princeton University Press, 1979).

Complete Letters of Sigmund Freud to Wilhelm Fliess 1887–1904, translated and edited by Jeffrey Moussaieff Masson (Cambridge: The Belknap Press of Harvard University Press, 1985).

The Correspondence of Sigmund Freud and Sandor Ferenczi, Volume 1, 1908–1914, edited by Eva Brabant, Ernst Falzeder, Patrizia Giampieri-Deutsch, translated by Peter T. Hoffer, with an introduction by André Haynal (Cambridge: The Belknap Press of Harvard University Press, 1992).

The Correspondence of Sigmund Freud and Sandor Ferenczi, Volume 2, 1914–1919, edited by Ernst Falzeder and Eva Brabant with the collaboration of Patrizia Giampieri-Deutsch, translated by Peter T. Hoffer, with an introduction by Axel Hoffer (Cambridge: The Belknap Press of Harvard University Press, 1996).

Psychoanalysis and Faith: The Letters of Sigmund Freud and Oskar Pfister, edited by Ernst L. Freud and Heinrich Meng, translated by Eric Mosbacher (London: Hogarth Press and the Institute of Psycho-Analysis, 1963).

A Psycho-analytic Dialogue: The Letters of Sigmund Freud and Karl Abraham, 1907–1926 (The International Psycho-analytic Library, no. 68), edited by Hilda C. Abraham and Ernst L. Freud, translated by Bernard Marsh and Hilda C. Abraham (New York: Basic Books, 1966).

Letters of Sigmund Freud, selected and edited by Ernst L. Freud, translated by Tania and James Stern (New York: Basic Books, 1960).

The Letters of Sigmund Freud to Eduard Silberstein, 1871–1881, edited by Walter Boehlich, translated by A. Pomerans (Cambridge: The Belknap Press of Harvard University Press, 1992).

After the letters, my most important sources for this book were the essays and books published by the two men.

In the case of Putnam, I drew most frequently on:

Addresses on Psycho-analysis, by J. J. Putnam (The International Psychoanalytic Library, no. 1), edited by Ernest Jones with a preface by Sigmund Freud (New York: The International Psycho-analytic Press, 1921).

Human Motives, by J. J. Putnam (Boston: Little & Brown, 1915).

"Not the Disease Only, but also the Man," by J. J. Putnam, The Shattuck Lecture, Delivered at the Annual Meeting of the Massachusetts Medical Society, June 13, 1899.

"The Philosophy of Psychotherapy," "The Psychology of Health I," "The Psychology of Health II," "The Nervous Breakdown," in *Psychotherapy: A Course of Reading in Sound Psychology, Sound Medicine and Sound Religion*, edited by William Belmont Parker (New York: The Center Publishing Co., 1908).

I also made frequent use of the Putnam Camp Log, especially for the years 1877–1930, a facsimile of which is still on site at the Stoop (the original is in the Keene Valley Library).

With regard to Freud, I consulted the following:

The Fifteen Volume Pelican Freud Library edited by Angela Richards and Albert Dickson.

The Standard Edition of the Complete Psychological Works of Sigmund Freud under the general editorship of James Strachey.

Collected Papers of Sigmund Freud in Five Volumes, authorized translation under the supervision of Joan Riviere (London: The Hogarth Press and the Institute of Psycho-Analysis, 1956).

The Basic Writings of Sigmund Freud, edited and translated by A. A. Brill (New York: Basic Books: The Modern Library, 1938).

I referred in particular to:

Studies in Hysteria
The Interpretation of Dreams
Introductory Lectures on Psychoanalysis
New Introductory Lectures on Psychoanalysis
An Autobiographical Study
Beyond the Pleasure Principle
Civilization and Its Discontents
The Ego and the Id
Five Lectures on Psychoanalysis
The Future of an Illusion
Group Psychology and the Analysis of the Ego
Jokes and their Relation to the Unconscious
Leonardo Da Vinci and a Memory of His Childhood
On the History of the Psychoanalytic Movement
An Outline of Psychoanalysis
The Psychopathology of Everyday Life
The Question of Lay Analysis
Totem and Taboo
Moses and Monotheism
Thomas Woodrow Wilson. Twenty-eighth President of the United States — A Psychological Study

Essays

"Three Essays on the Theory of Sexuality"
"On the Sexual Theories of Children"
"Character and Anal Eroticism"
"Family Romances"
"A Special Type of Choice of Object Made by Men"
"The Dissolution of the Oedipus Complex"

"Fetishism"
"Libidinal Types"
"Female Sexuality"
"Screen Memories"
"Analysis Terminable and Interminable"
"On Narcissism: An Introduction"
"Instincts and Their Vicissitudes"
"Repression"
"The Unconscious"
"Mourning and Melancholia"
"The Ego and the Id"
"A Note Upon the 'Mystic Writing-Pad'"
"Negation"
"A Disturbance of Memory on the Acropolis"
"Delusions and Dreams in Jensen's 'Gradiva'"
"The Theme of the Three Caskets"
"The Moses of Michelangelo"
"On Transience"
"The Uncanny"

The most useful secondary sources on Putnam and his world outside of Hale's introductory essay in Putnam's collected letters was Hale's two-volume opus, an extraordinary work of scholarship, *Freud and the Americans*:

The Beginnings of Psychoanalysis in the United States, 1876–1917, by Nathan G. Hale, Jr. (New York and Oxford: Oxford University Press, 1995).

The Rise and Crisis of Psychoanalysis in the United States: Freud and the Americans, 1917–1985, by Nathan G. Hale, Jr. (New York and Oxford: Oxford University Press, 1995).

Also very useful was the short, densely researched *James Jackson Putnam: From Neurology to Psychoanalysis*, by Russell G. Vasile, M.D. (Oceanside, NY: Dabor Science Publications, 1977). In a private e-mail exchange, Dr. Vasile endorsed my suggestion that "Sketch for a Study of a New England Character" was a case study of Susan Blow.

A helpful essay contextualizing Putnam is "James Jackson Putnam and the Legacy of Liberal Protestantism in Early American Psychotherapy," a paper by Rachael Rosner (June 2000) presented at the Cheiron convention at University of Southern Maine.

In researching Freud, I drew on most of the standard biographies and critical accounts of Freud in English. The most important to my research were:

The Life and Work of Sigmund Freud in Three Volumes, by Ernest Jones (New York: Basic Books vol 1, 1953; vol. 2, 1955; vol. 3, 1957). Though the biography suffers from hagiography, Jones' personal experience of Freud and his unprecedented access to the inner sanctum of Freud's domestic existence enable Jones to exhibit a wealth of details about Freud's life and interactions with others, making this an invaluable source even when Jones' value judgments need to be taken skeptically.

Similarly lacking in critical perspective on Freud but filled with fascinating primary source material not compiled elsewhere is *The Historic Expedition to America (1909): Freud, Jung and Hall the King-maker*, by Saul Rosenzweig (St. Louis: Rana House, 1992). It includes the most comprehensive account of Freud's actual appearance at Clark and the larger scene with the appearance of Nobel Prize winners Emma Goldman and her consort, "the king of the hoboes."

Even less critical than either Jones' biography or Rosenzweig's but still a useful source for background details and occasional lively color of Freud's day-to-day life and character is the devoted yet cavalier *Sigmund Freud: Man and Father*, by Martin Freud (New York: The Vanguard Press, 1958).

A good overview to Freud and his world enlivened by a wealth of firsthand interviews is *Freud and His Followers*, by Paul Roazen (New York: The New American Library, 1976).

A Most Dangerous Method: The Story of Jung, Freud, and Sabin Spielrein, by John Kerr (New York: Knopf, 1993) provides a wealth of important background material on the relationship of Freud and Jung at the pivotal moment in their theoretical development around the time of the American expedition, as well as many useful if dispiriting examples of their Medicean approach to the politics of gaining and holding power in the germinal world of institutional psychology.

The somewhat strange and lugubrious biography written by Freud's personal physician, *Freud: Living and Dying*, by Max Schur, M.D. (New York: International Universities Press, 1972), contains intriguing primary source material on Freud not published elsewhere, including a handful of important letters.

I also drew repeatedly on the scholarship of *Freud's Women*, by Lisa Appignanesi and John Forrester (New York: Other Press, 1992), which provides useful, concise introductions both to the principal female influences in Freud's life and to his theories of female psychology.

Among the other biographies and critical analyses of Freud and his work I consulted for general background and perspective were:

Freud: Darkness in the Midst of Vision, by Louis Breger (New York: Wiley, 2000).

Freud: A Life for Our Time, by Peter Gay (New York: Norton, 1998).

Freud: the Man and the Cause, by Ronald William Clark (New York: Random House, 1980).

The Assault on Truth: Freud's Suppression of the Seduction Theory, by Jeffrey Moussaieff Masson (New York: Farrar, Straus & Giroux, 1984).

Memory Wars: Freud's Legacy in Dispute, by Frederick Crews (New York: New York Review of Books Reprint Edition, 1997).

Freud Evaluated: The Completed Arc, by Malcolm Macmillan (Cambridge: MIT Press, 1996).

Freud and the Institutionalization of Psychoanalytic Knowledge, by Sarah Winter (Stanford, CA: Stanford University Press, 1999).

Freud and Oedipus, by Peter L. Rudnytsky (New York: Columbia University Press, 1987).

A Godless Jew: Freud, Atheism, and the Making of Psychoanalysis, by Peter Gay (New Haven, CT: Yale University Press, 1987).

Reading Freud: Explorations and Entertainments, by Peter Gay (New Haven, CT: Yale University Press, 1991).

Freud in Exile: Psychoanalysis and Its Vicissitudes, edited by Naomi Segal and Edward Timms (New Haven, CT: Yale University Press, 1988).

Psychoanalysis in Its Cultural Context, edited by Edward Timms and Ritchie Robertson (Edinburgh: Edinburgh University Press, 1992).

Freud without Hindsight: Reviews of His Work, 1893–1939, edited by Norman Kiell with translations from the German by Vladimir Rus, Ph.D. and the French by Denise Boneau (Madison, CT: International Universities Press, 1988).

Fin-De-Siecle Vienna: Politics and Culture by Carl E. Schorske (New York: Vintage, 1980).

Thinking with History, by Carl E. Schorske (Princeton, NJ: Princeton University Press, 1999).

Freud Conflict and Culture: *Essays on his Life, Work and Legacy*, edited by Michael Roth (New York: Vintage, 2000).

Sigmund Freud's Mission: *An Analysis of His Personality and Influence*, by Erich Fromm (New York: Harper & Brothers, 1959).

Psychoanalysis and Feminism, by Juliet Mitchell (New York: Pantheon, 1974).

The third major figure in the book, Susan Blow, still awaits a substantive biography. I drew most on Blow's unpublished letters in the Putnam papers in the Countway. I also consulted letters in the Bentley Historical Library from the Clara Wheeler Papers and the Lucretia Treat Papers. I was also very fortunate to have access to copies of letters by Blow to Mrs. Henry Hitchcock, in particular from the collection of her descendent, Julien LeBourgeois. Mr. LeBourgeois also provided me with copies of pages from Blow's commonplace book, which were crucial in filling out a sense of her character.

Among Blow's own published works, I read:

A Study of Dante (New York: Putnam, 1886).

Symbolic Education: *A Commentary on Frobel's "Mother's Play"* (New York: Appleton, 1894).

Letters to a Mother on the Philosophy of Froebel (New York: Appleton, 1900).

Two secondary sources that were helpful for general background were:

Sketches Along Life's Road, by Elizabeth Harrison (Boston: Stratford, 1930).

The monograph: *Susan Blow: Mother of the Kindergarten*, by Joseph M. Menius (St. Clair, MO: Page One Publishing, 1993).

CHAPTER NOTES

In most cases I have not recorded where in each chapter I cite from the principal sources listed above because of the repetition this would entail. Instead, these notes are mainly a record of sources particular to each chapter beyond the ones enumerated above. Exceptions to this rule occur in certain places where I've noted the use of primary material cited in secondary sources listed in the preceding section.

Introduction

(The names of the individuals referred to on page one from the Washington, D.C. suburb where I grew up have been changed.)

The Kraus quote is taken from a collection of aphorisms compiled in *Karl Kraus and the Soul Doctors—A Pioneer Critic and his Criticism of Psychiatry and Psychoanalysis*, by Thomas Szasz (Baton Rouge: Louisiana State University Press, 1976), a book that also offers interesting, hostile thoughts on the relationship between analysis and black magic.

Chapter 1

A key source for Jung's version of major events with Freud is the chapter entitled "Sigmund Freud" in *Memories, Dreams and Reflections* by C. G. Jung, recorded and edited by Aniela Jaffé, translated by Richard and Clara Winston (New York: Pantheon Books, 1961).

C. G. Jung: Word and Image, edited by Aniela Jaffé (Princeton, NJ: Princeton University Press, 1983). This brief anthology of Jung's writing contains the whole of his longest wonderful letter home from America.

Jung: A Biography, by Deirdre Bair (Boston, MA: Little Brown, 2003). This book offers a good summary of key biographical and intellectual incidents in Jung's career.

The Assault on Truth, by Jeffrey Moussaieff Masson (see p. 432). Regardless of the controversy surrounding Masson's central thesis (that Freud mistakenly abandoned the seduction theory leading to incalculable damage among true victims of abuse), Masson's narration of the Emma Ekstein incident, along with the larger story of Freud and Jones' abandonment of Ferenczi (among others), remains compelling.

Errand into the Wilderness, by Perry Miller (Cambridge: The Belknap Press of Harvard University, 1975). This book is still one of the great treatises on American romanticism.

An invaluable source for my research into Putnan Camp, similar Adirondack retreats, and the surrounding region was the *Two Adirondack Hamlets in History: Keene and Keene Valley*, edited by Richard Plunz (Fleischmans, NY: Purple Mountain Press, and Keene Valley, NY: Keene Valley Library Association, 1999).

The Adirondacks: A History of America's First Wilderness, by Paul Schneider (New York: Owl Books, 1998) has a few notes on Adirondack camps.

Chapter 2

New York Eats Out, an exhibit on view November 8, 2002, through March 1, 2003, in the Edna Barnes Salomon Room at The New York Public Library's Humanities and Social Sciences Library. The huge array of menus in the exhibit allowed me to get a sense of what Freud would have encountered in American cuisine during his visit.

An Adirondacks Guide Cookbook, by John Gibbons (New York: North Country Books, 2001).

Genuine Reality: A Life of William James, by Linda Simons (Chicago: The University of Chicago Press, 1998). I referred to this excellent overview of James' life and career repeatedly in writing my book.

Two Adirondack Hamlets in History: Keene and Keene Valley, edited by Plunz (see p. 434).

"Freud and the Porcupine" by George F. Gifford, Jr, M.D. *Harvard Medical Alumni Bulletin* XLVI, no. 4 (Mar–Apr 1972): 28–31. This is a lovely, brief account of Freud's climb that contains remarks by Mary Lee and Anna Freud's letter to the article's author on her recollection of the porcupine.

Freud, Race and Gender, by Sandor L. Gilman (Princeton, NJ: Princeton University Press, Reprint Edition, 1995). Gilman's work is consistently fascinating and provided direction in terms of my various arguments about Freud and racial biology.

The Case of Sigmund Freud: Medicine and Identity at the Fin de Siècle, by Sandor Gilman (Baltimore: Johns Hopkins University Press, 1993).

The Games We Played: The Golden Age of Board and Table Games, by Margaret K. Hofer (Princeton, NJ: Princeton Architectural Press, 2003). The book provides a basic overview of popular American board games in different eras past, including turn-of-the century.

Nietzsche's Presence in Freud's Life and Thought: On the Origins of a Psychology of Dynamic Unconscious Mental Functioning, by Ronald Lehrer (New York: State University of New York Press, 1995). Both this book and Assoun's contain important scholarship tracing direct affinities between Freud and Nietzsche's work. Assoun glances briefly at what Nietzsche takes from Emerson, singling out in particular the Emersonian mystique regarding "eternal forces of nature," and agreeing with Charles Andler that Emerson was "'one of those beloved authors whose thought Nietzsche absorbed until he could no longer separate it from his own.'"

Freud and Nietzsche, by Paul-Laurent Assoun (New York: Athlone, 2000).

"Schopenhauer & Freud," by Christopher Young and Andrew Brook: essay from Institute of Interdisciplinary Studies, Carleton University Ottawa, Canada (http://http-server.carleton.ca/~abrook/SCHOPENY.htm). This essay succinctly outlines several of the key tropes in Schopenhauer's work that show an overwhelming kinship with major concepts in Freud, including his theory of repression and major portions of his theory of the death instinct.

Freud, Biologist of the Mind: Beyond the Psychoanalytic Legend, by Frank J. Sulloway (New York: Basic Books, 1979). One of the first major critiques on Freud to be canonized, Sulloway's book contextualizes Freud's understanding of biology with the work of his predecessors and contemporaries and shows that much of Freud's biology was obsolete even at the time.

Chapter 3

Unpublished interview between Sanford Gifford and Molly Putnam, August 11, 1971. I drew on this interview repeatedly in the book and found it particularly useful for trying to understand both the Putnam family's experience of Putnam's enthusiasm for analysis, and for tracing Molly's own initial professional involvement with analysis.

The Emmanuel Movement: The Origins of Group Treatment and the Assault on Lay Psychotherapy, by Sanford Cifford (Boston: Distributed by the Harvard University Press for The Francis Countway Library of Medicine, Boston, 1997). This is a good short history of the most influential movement offering psychotherapy outside of the professional clinic in Putnam's day. Putnam himself was an initial advocate for the movement, but he got cold feet early on and in a long letter to the founder, Reverend Elwood Worcester, tried to explain the reason for his decision to end his association with the Emmanuel Movement. The book includes Constance Worcester's observations about Putnam's domestic interior.

Boston: A Topographical History, by Walter Muir Whitehall (Cambridge: Harvard University Press, 1959). A terrific history of the city's changing landscape.

Emerson, by Lawrence Buell (Cambridge: The Belknap Press of Harvard University Press, 2003). A powerful crystallization of Emerson's thought and its reception. I found indications of the importance of Buddhism in New England in both Buell and Mishra's book.

An End to Suffering: The Buddha in the World, by Pankaj Mishra (New York: FSG, 2004).

Emerson in Concord: An Exhibition in Celebration of the 200th Anniversary of the Birth of Ralph Waldo Emerson (online exhibition catalogue, Special Collections of the Concord Free Public Library including Concord Free Press Obituary of Ralph Waldo Emerson [http://www.concordnet.org/library/scollect/Emerson_Celebration/Opening_page.html])

A visit to the Emerson Museum in Concord and to Emerson's house, along with conversations with staff at both sites, was crucial to the research for this chapter.

The Correspondence of William James: William and Henry, 1885–1896, edited by Ignas K. Skrupskelis and Elizabeth Berkeley (Charlottesville and London: University of Virginia Press, 1993).

The Correspondence of William James: Volume II (April 1905–March 1908), edited by Ignas K. Skrupskelis and Elizabeth Berkeley with the assistance of Wilma Bradbeer (Charlottesville and London: University of Virginia Press, 2003).

The Children's Judge: Frederick Pickering Cabot, by M. A. De Wolfe Howe (Boston: Houghton Mifflin, 1932). This is an often colorful history of Elizabeth's brother, their family, and their larger social world.

Psychotherapy: A Course of Reading in Sound Psychology, Sound Medicine and Sound Religion, edited by William Belmont Parker (New York: The Center Publishing Co., 1908).

"The Cover," *Massachusetts Physician,* October 1976 (contains reference to Putnam's lack of sense of humor and deathbed scene).

"James Jackson Putnam: A Life of Firsts." Anonymous article, November 17, *The M.G.H. News,* Volume 27, no. 5.

Chapter 4

The three books listed next provided background and source material on the Progressive Movement in America:

The Progressive Movement 1900–1915, edited and with an introduction by Richard Hofstadter (New York: Simon and Schuster, 1963), in particular "Theodore Roosevelt on Conservation" from Roosevelt's Seventh Annual Message to Congress.

The Age of Reform, by Richard Hofstadter (New York: Vintage, 1960).

Reform and Regulation: American Politics from Roosevelt to Wilson, by Louis L. Gould (New York: Knopf, 1986).

"Not the Disease Only but the Man," by Putnam.

Work on Myth, by Hans Blumenberg, translated by Robert M. Wallace (Cambridge: MIT Press, 1988). I found the information on Wundt's idea of energy and psychology as representative of key strands in European medical thinking of the era in Blumenberg.

"The Energies of Men," in *Memories and Studies*, by William James (New York: Longmans, Green, 1911).

Genuine Reality: A Life of William James, by Simons (p. 435). Simons' biography includes material on James' relation to Putnam Camp.

Psychotherapeutics, edited by Richard C. Badger (Boston: Gorham, 1909). This collection includes a number of essays by figures from Prince and Putnam to Boris Sidis that show the centrality of "energy thought" to the new American psychotherapy.

The Boston Transcript article is quoted in a footnote to the James-Putnam Correspondence in *James Jackson Putnam and Psychoanalysis*, edited by Nathan G. Hale (Cambridge: Harvard University Press, 1971).

Chapter 5

Boston Days, the City of Beautiful Ideals: Concord, and its Famous Authors: The Golden Age of Genius; Dawn of the Twentieth Century, by Lilian Whiting (Boston: Little Brown, 1902). A charming history of Boston in its renaissance years.

The New England Mind: The Seventeenth Century, by Perry Miller (Cambridge: Belknap Press at Harvard University Press, Reprint Edition, 1983). Miller's books offer the best introduction to American Puritan thought and original source material.

The American Puritans: Their Prose and Poetry, edited by Perry Miller (New York: Columbia University Press, 1982).

The Puritan Origins of the American Self, by Sacvan Bercovitch (New Haven, CT: Yale University Press, 1977). The Calvinist pronouncement concerning "the epitome of Christ mystical" was quoted in Bercovitch's book.

"Dansville's Castle on the Hill" by David Gilbert (http://dansville.lib.ny.us/historyo.html#/). I drew on this essay for basic information about the sanitarium where Blow stayed before consulting Putnam.

"Porn Flakes: Kellogg, Graham and the Crusade for Moral Fiber," by Carrie McLaren in *Stay Free* (http://www.stayfreemagazine.org/10/graham.htm.). McLaren's essay is a good short introduction to the subject of American concern with diet and morality.

German Culture in American Philosophical and Literary Influences 1600 to 1900, by Henry Pochmann (Madison: University of Wisconsin Press, 1957). Along with Pochmann's book on the St. Louis Hegelians and New England Transcendentalism, this was my single most important source for information on the world in which Blow grew up—filled with fantastic primary source material and an extraordinary work of scholarship.

Chapter 6

Secret Ring: Freud's Inner Circle and the Politics of Psychoanalysis, by Phyllis Grosskurth (Reading, MA: Addison-Wesley, 1991). I used this book for background information on Freud and Silberstein.

Freud—Master and Friend, by Hanns Sachs (Cambridge: Harvard University Press, 1944). Outside of Jones, Sachs provides the most complete insider account of the formation of Freud's secret ring.

In Dora's Case: Freud—Hysteria—Feminism (Gender and Culture), edited by Charles Bernheimer and Claire Kahane (New York: Columbia University Press, 1990).

The End of the Line: Essays on Psychoanalysis and the Sublime, by Neil Hertz (New York: Columbia University Press, 1988).

Pushing Time Away, by Peter Singer (New York: Ecco, 2003). Singer's book includes Freud's remarks from minutes of the fledgling psychoanalytic association on pedagogy and homosexuality.

Hitler's Vienna: A Dictator's Apprenticeship, by Brigitte Hamann (Oxford: Oxford University Press, 1999). One of the most helpful books for understanding the anti-Semitism and general political climate of Vienna in the years of Freud's friendship with Putnam. I drew on Hamann's book in this chapter for background about Hitler, Mays, and the American Wild West.

Dreaming by the Book: A History of Freud's "The Interpretation of Dreams" and the Psychoanalytic Movement, by Andreas Mayer, Lydia Marinelli, and Susan Fairfield (New York: Other Press, 2003). A book that contains important material on the neglected "extra-biographical" aspects of analytic dream interpretation.

Freud's Wishful Dream Book, by Alexander Welsh (Princeton, NJ: Princeton University Press, 1994).

Karl Kraus Apocalyptic Satirist: Culture and Catastrophe in Habsburg Vienna, by Edward Timms (New Haven, CT: Yale University Press, Reprint Edition, 1983). This major work of scholarship, in addition to providing most of my background material on Kraus, was the source for the citation from Hermann Bahr on the Ringstrasse.

Work on Myth, by Blumenberg (see p. 438) gave me direction in exploring Mesmer's context in eighteenth- and nineteenth-century European intellectual history.

The Complete Works of Oscar Wilde (London: Collins, 1948).

The Real Trial of Oscar Wilde. With an introduction and commentary by Merlin Holland. Foreword by Sir John Mortimer (London and New York: Fourth Estate/HarperCollins, 2003).

The Austrian Mind: An Intellectual and Social History 1848–1938, by William M. Johnston (Berkley: University of California Press, Reprint Edition, 1983). Johnston's analysis of the pre-war Austrian obsession with death, though it feels hypertrophied in certain places, is important for understanding the context of Freud's theoretical development.

The Austrian Enlightenment and Its Aftermath, edited by Ritchie Robertson and Edward Timms (Edinburgh: Edinburgh University Press, 1991). I found background material on Austria before the rise of Viennese modernism in these essays.

Hitler and the Power of Aesthetics, by Frederick Spotts (Woodstock, NY: Overlook Press, 2003). A fascinating lens on the ways Hitler's agenda reflected and was driven by his "artistic vision"—especially ideas of aesthetic spectacle in mass politics.

Chapter 7

Life and Confessions of a Psychologist, by G. Stanley Hall (Boston: Appleton, 1923). Hall's often dry but very useful memoir of his own coming of age as a psychologist is of necessity also a portrait of his professional American milieu.

Hitler's Vienna: A Dictator's Apprenticeship, by Hamann (see p. 440).

Bertrand Russell: 1921–1970, The Ghost of Madness, by Ray Monk (New York: Free Press, 2001). I found the remarks on Russell's experience of the American lecture circuit in this biography.

Chapter 8

I used both the translations of Freud's Clark lectures by Saul Rosenzweig in *The Historic Expedition to America* and one that was subsequently republished without a credited translator (although the translations it contains were probably by Brill) under the title *The Origin and Development of Psychoanalysis* by Sigmund Freud (New York: Henry Regnery, 1957). Rosenzweig makes a detailed argument for why the lectures may have been delivered in a different order than that in which they were finally published.

Chapter 9

The Technology of Orgasm, by Rachel Maines (Baltimore and London: Johns Hopkins University Press, 1999). This extraordinary short history continues to stand largely alone as, among other things, an overview of the history of nervous illness and sexual vibrators.

Madness in America: Cultural and Medical Perceptions of Mental Illness before 1914, by Lynn Gamwell and Nancy Tomes (New York: The State University of New York at Binghamton, 1995). I found here background material on standard psychotherapeutic treatments pre-talk therapy in America.

Unpublished interview between Paul Roazen and Molly Putnam on September 22, 1966, cited in *Freud and His Followers*, by Roazen (see p. 431). Molly told Roazen details of Putnam's determination to keep his daughters from being overstimulated.

"Neurasthenia," in Alfred Lee Loomis, M.D. and William Gilman Thompson, M.D., eds., *A System of Practical Medicine by American Authors* (New York: Lea Bros., 1898). Another important collection of essays for understanding the status of American psychotherapy pre-Freud.

Religion and Medicine: The Moral Control of Nervous Disorders, by Elwood Worcester, Samuel McComb, and Isador Coriat (New York: Moffat, Yard & Company, 1908). Probably the most succinct one-volume statement of the Emmanuel Movement's philosophy and praxis. The introduction mentions in passing that Putnam "presided at the preliminary meeting and gave the first address." This is particularly intriguing given the fact that within two years he had conceived so strong and tortured a revulsion for the movement that he had distanced himself from it as far as possible and openly criticized it in his correspondence.

Adolescence. Its Psychology and Its Relations to Physiology, Anthropology, Sociology, Sex, Crime, Religion and Education, by G. Stanley Hall (New York: D. Appleton,1905).

Classics in the History of Psychology. "Wherein Should the Education of a Woman Differ from that of a Man," by Kate Gordon (http://psychclassics. yorku.ca/Gordon/education.htm.).

Life and Confessions of a Psychologist, by Hall (see p. 441).

Chapter 10

On the Sublime by Longinus, trans. W. Rhys Roberts (http://evans-experientialism. freewebspace.com/longinus02.htm.).

Memories, Dreams, Reflections, by Jung (see p. 434). Jung goes over the incident with Freud and the supernatural in detail in the chapter of his memoir devoted to Freud and psychoanalysis.

Sigmund Freud and Art: His Personal Collection of Antiquities, edited by Lynn Gamwell (New York: Harry N. Abrams, 1989). I took information on Freud's Athena figure from Gamwell's essay in this fascinating book which, among other things, contextualizes Freud's work with the history of archaeology in the years he was developing his key theories.

Chapter 11

The Correspondence of William James, Volume II, April 1905–March 1908 (see p. 437).

The "Hodgson Report" on Madam Blavatsky, by Walter A. Carrithers, Jr. (http://www.blavatskyfoundation.org/obituary.htm.). The Blavatsky Foundation.

Studies in Spiritism, by Amy E. Tanner (New York: D. Appleton and Company, 1910).

Life and Confessions of a Psychologist, by Hall (see p. 441).

Genuine Reality: A Life of William James, by Simons (see p. 435).

The Varieties of Religious Experience, by William James (New York: Modern Library, 1994).

Chapter 12

1971 interview between Molly Putnam and Sanford Gifford (see p. 436). She mentions the disappearance of her father's side of the correspondence with Blow in this exchange.

Chapter 13

Cotton Mather sermons (*lamblion.net/Ebooks*). Source for the quotation from Mather's sermon.

Chapter 14

A Memoir of Dr. James Jackson, by James Jackson Putnam, M.D. (see p. 425). Important letters such as those between Lowell and Jackson are quoted in Putnam's memoir of his grandfather.

Robert Todd Lincoln: A Man in His Own Right, by John Goff (Norman: University of Oklahoma Press, 1969). This book cites the line about Harvard spending the war at the Parker House Bar.

Three Centuries of Harvard, 1636–1936, by Samuel Elliot Morison (Cambridge: Harvard University Press, 1936).

Both Adams' book and the essay by Goellnitz provide a general introduction to the state of American medicine at the time of the Civil War.

Doctors in Blue—Medical History of the Union, by George Adams (Baton Rouge: University of Louisiana Press, 1952).

"This Tide of Wounded . . . Civil War Battlefield Medicine: An Intro to the

Medical Middle Ages," by Jenny Goellnitz (http://www.civilwarmedicine.aphillcsa.com/).

"Terms of Pacification" college essay by James Jackson Putnam in Countway Library.

Chapter 15

Why Psychoanalysis?, by Elisabeth Roudinesco, translated by Rachel Bowlby (New York: Columbia University Press, 2001). Roudinesco's book is among other things, an astringent critique of the current approach to mental health treatment in the West.

The Sermons of Jonathan Edwards: A Reader, edited by Wilson H. Kimnach, Kenneth P. Minkema, and Douglas A. Sweeney (New Haven, CT: Yale University Press, 1999).

Chapter 16

Hitler's Vienna: A Dictator's Apprenticeship, by Hamann (see p. 440) for Lueger's funeral and Hitler's possible attendance.

Chapter 17

"William James" by James Jackson Putnan, in *The Atlantic Monthly*; December 1910; Volume 106, No. 6, pp. 835–848.

Genuine Reality: A Life of William James, by Simons (see p. 435) for more information on James' death.

The Master: 1901–1916 by Leon Edel (New York: Avon, 1972). Edel mentions Henry James' psychotherapeutic consultations with Putnam.

The James Family: A Group Biography, by F. O. Matthiessen (New York: Vintage Books, 1980). Offers wonderful primary source background matter on life in the James' home and individual psyches.

Chapter 18

American Philanthropy, by Robert H. Bremner (London and Chicago: The University of Chicago Press, 1960). A dry, standard history, which is still one of the only comprehensive overviews of the subject.

Annual Report of the Associated Charities of Salem

Annual Report of the Associated Charities of Worcester

"The Work of Volunteer Visitors of the Associated Charities Among the Poor," treatise by Robert Treat Paine.

MCP work: Friendly Visiting.

"Then and Now, A Friend in Need," Associated Charities of Boston, 1879–1921. Family Welfare Society.

"Not Alms but a Friend." The Work of Volunteer Visitors of the Associated Charities among the Poor. Its Limitations, Allies, Number of Workers, Aims, and Grand Results, by Robert Treat Paine. New York Public Library: Humanities, Ford Collection.

Protestants against Poverty. Boston's Charities, 1870–1900, by Nathan Irvin Huggins (Westport, CT: Greenwood, 1971). A valuable, well-written account of the religious roots and efflorescence of the Boston philanthropic impulse. It contains lively source material on the origins of Associated Charities, such as the account of the epic battles to determine the character of the organization in the years of its gestation.

German Culture in American Philosophical and Literary Influences 1600 to 1900, by Pochmann (see p. 439). Pochmann's book contains a valuable summary of German Pietism in America.

The Children's Judge, by De Wolfe Howe (see. p. 437). De Wolfe Howe's book gives a good sense of the limits and intentions of the Cabots' Unitarianism in Marian's generation.

Boston: A Topographical History, by Muir Whitehall (see p. 436). Describes the evolution of various neighborhoods on the arrival of the floods of new immigrants, quoting some primary source material (such as the Handlin citation).

"Bonifacus . . . an essay to do good," Cotton Mather from *Documentary History of Philanthropy and Voluntarism in America*, by Peter Dobkin Hall, 2003 (ksghome.harvard .edu/~phall/08.%20Matherpdf).

"From 'White Slave' to Labor Activist: The Agony and Triumph of a Boston Brahmin Woman in the 1910s," by Stephen H. Norwood, in *The New England Quarterly*, Vol. 65, No. 1 (March 1992). The best single account of the fascinating Rantoul trial.

Chapter 19

Art in Vienna, by Peter Vergo (London: Phaidon Press, 1994). Includes a good overview of Viennese Art in Freud's day which, like the book on Schiele, indicates the extremity of aesthetic imagery in the Austrian capital well in advance of the publication of Freud's major essays.

Egon Schiele, Art, Sexuality and Viennese Modernism, edited by Patrick Werkner (Palo Alto, CA: The Society for the Promotion of Science and Scholarship, 1994). Particularly "The 'Obscene' in Viennese Architecture of the Early Twentieth Century," by Peter Haiko.

Vienna in the Biedermeier Era 1815–1848, edited by Robert Waissenberger (London: Alpine Fine Arts Collection, 1986). Particularly the essays, "The Biedermeier Mentality," by Robert Waissenberger and "The Development of Taste in Home Decoration," by Peter Parenzan. Parenzan's essay gives an idea of "curating" home art collections that resonates with Freud's own domestic decoration arrangement.

Wonders and the Order of the Nature 1150–1750, by Lorraine Daston and Katharine Park (New York: Zone Books, 1998). One of the essays in the book is a compelling, rich history of cabinets of curiosity.

Secession—a publication of Osterreiehischer Kunst-Und Kulturverlag, particularly the essays "To the Age Its Art, to Arts Its Freedom" by Eleonora Louis, "The Beethoven Frieze by Gustav Klimt and the Vienna Secession," by Marian Bisanz-Prakken, and "The Secession Building" by Otto Kapfinger. This journal offers one of the best concise accounts of the origin of the Secession movement and its iconography. Kraus' quote on Klimt's painting of "Philosophy" and "Medicine" is cited in the publication.

Karl Kraus Apocalyptic Satirist: Culture and Catastrophe in Habsburg Vienna, by Timms (see p. 440).

Sigmund Freud and Art: His Personal Collection of Antiquities, edited by Gamwell (see p. 442), particularly the essays "The Origins of Freud's Antiquities Collection," by Lynn Gamwell and "A Mighty Metaphor: The Analogy of Archaeology and Psychoanalysis," by Donald Kuspit.

Chapter 20

German Culture in American Philosophical and Literary Influences 1600 to 1900 (see p. 439). Pochmann again offers the best introduction to the early experience and influence of Germans in America.

The New England Mind, by Perry Miller (see p. 438).

The Collected Writings of Denton J. Snider, by D. J. Snider (Saint Louis: W. H. Miner, 1921–1923).

The Biocosmos—the processes of life psychologically ordered, by D .J. Snider (St. Louis: Sigma Publishing, 1911).

Brief report of the meeting commemorative of the early Saint Louis movement in philosophy, psychology, literature, art and education, by Denton J. Snider (St. Louis: D. H. Harris, 1921).

The St. Louis Movement in Philosophy, Literature, Education, Psychology, with Chapters of Autobiography, by D. J. Snider (St. Louis: Sigma Publishing, 1920).

The American Hegelians: An Intellectual Episode in the History of Western America, edited by William H. Goetzmann (New York: Knopf, 1973). This is a source book including essays by Harris (such as the one I cite on his deepening engagement with Hegel), Brokmeyer, Blow, and Snider, among others.

New England Transcendentalism and St. Louis Hegelianism: Phases in the History of American Idealism, by Henry Pochmann (Philadelphia: Carl Schurz Memorial Foundation, 1948). Like his book on German culture in America, but in much more concise fashion, this is a fascinating and delightful work of intellectual history.

Chapter 21

Journal of Speculative Philosophy. 1867–1893.

Two Adirondack Hamlets in History: Keene and Keene Valley, edited by Plunz (see p. 434) for background material on Glenmore and Tom Davidson.

German Culture in American Philosophy and Literary Influences, by Pochmann (see p. 439).

New England Transcendentalism and St. Louis Hegelianism, by Pochmann (see above).

Chapter 22

Many of the letters describing the Putnam family's European adventures (though not the ones connected with Putnam's excursion to Weimar) were collected by Marian in *Memoir of Frances Cabot Putnam, A Family Chronicle*, by Marian Cabot Putnam (see p. 425).

Chapter 23

A version of the essay Putnam delivered at Weimar is collected in *Addresses on Psycho-analysis*, by J. J. Putnam (see p. 428). A number of the incidents surrounding Putnam's address in 1911 are described in the second volume of Jones' biography of Freud (see p. 431).

Chapter 24

The books listed below all provided important background material.

Hitler's Vienna, by Hamann (see p. 440).

Vienna and the Jews of Vienna in the Age of Franz Joseph, by Robert S. Wistrich (New York: Oxford University Press, 1989).

Vienna and the Jews, 1837–1938: A Cultural History, by Steven Beller (New York: Columbia University Press, 1991).

Vienna and Its Jews: The Tragedy of Success, 1880s–1980s, by George E. Berkley (Lanham, MD: Madison Books, 1988).

Wittgenstein's Vienna, by Allan Janik and Stephen Toulmin (New York: Simon and Schuster, 1973).

Wittgenstein's Vienna Revisited, by Allan Janik (New Brunswick, NJ and London: Transaction Publishers, 2001).

Chapter 25

The Aryan Christ: The Secret Life of Carl Jung, by Richard Noll (New York: Random House, 1997). Noll's book, which excited outrage among Jung's dogmatic defenders, presents a number of largely irrefutable case histories. I first came across Putnam and Bowditch's letters in the Countway before reading Noll's book. The letters speak for themselves with respect to the extremity of Fanny Bowditch's situation once she became caught up with Jung and his colleagues. The larger, startling circumstances of Fanny's analysis is carefully documented in this book.

Freud—Master and Friend, by Sachs (see p. 439).

C. G. Jung Speaking: Interviews and Encounters (Bollinger Series 97), edited by William McGuire and R.F.C. Hull (Princeton, NJ: Princeton University

Press, 1977). This book includes a transcript of Jung's interview with *The New York Times.*

Chapter 26

1912: Wilson, Roosevelt, Taft & Debs — The Election That Changed the Country, by James Chace (New York: Simon and Schuster, 2004). I found this book most useful for its concise background information on Debs.

Main background sources for the period surrounding Wilson's election:

The American Political Tradition and the Men Who Made It, by Richard Hofstadter (New York: Vintage Books, reprint 1989).

The Progressive Movement 1900–1915, edited by Hofstadter (see p. 438).

Woodrow Wilson and the Progressive Movement, 1910–1917, by Arthur S. Link (New York: Harper & Row, 1954).

Chapter 27

Events surrounding the fires in the Adirondacks are described in *Memoir of Frances Cabot Putnam, A Family Chronicle*, by Marian Cabot Putnam (see p. 425).

Chapter 28

The following seven books provided background on Austria in the years leading up to and including the First World War.

The Decline and Fall of the Habsburg Empire, by Alan Sked (Harlow, England and New York: Longman, 2001).

Thunder at Twilight: Vienna 1913–1914, by Frederic Morton (New York: Scribner, 1989).

A Nervous Splendor: Vienna, 1888–1889, by Frederic Morton (Boston: Little Brown, 1979).

The Habsburg: Embodying Empire, by Andrew Wheatcroft (London and New York: Viking, 1995).

The First World War, by John Keegan (New York: Knopf, 1999).

Karl Kraus Apocalyptic Satirist, by Timms (see p. 440).

Hitler's Vienna, by Hamann (see p. 440). The information on Vienna's homeless population preceding the war came from Hamann.

The Aryan Christ, by Noll (see p. 448).

Gifford interview with Molly Putnam (see p. 436), which includes Molly's speculation on Marian's experience of the Putnam-Blow friendship.

Chapter 29

The unfavorable reception accorded *Human Motives* by Putnam's peers is discussed in the introduction to *James Jackson Putnam and Psychoanalysis*, by Hale (see p. 427). Freud's response to the First World War is analyzed at some length by Jones in the second volume of his biography of Freud (see p. 431).

Chapter 30

Freud's Women, by Appignanesi and Forrester (see p. 431) includes the incident of Freud's dream of "indistinct writing" in connection with his reading of *Human Motives*.

Chapter 31

Blow's funeral at the Cathedral of St. John the Divine is described in *Susan Blow: Mother of the Kindergarten*, by Menius (see p. 433).

Chapter 32

On Duty and Off: Letters of Elizabeth Cabot Putman Written in France May, 1917–September 1918 (Cambridge: Riverside Press, 1919). Marian edited this collection of Elizabeth's letters for publication.

Chapter 33

Thomas Woodrow Wilson: A. Psychological Study by Sigmund Freud and William C. Bullitt (London: Weidenfeld and Nicolson, 1967).

The Austrian Mind, by Johnston (see p. 440) for the letter with the line "Austria-Hungary is no more. . . ."

So Close to Greatness: A Biography of William C. Bullitt, by Will Brownell (London: Macmillan: Collier Macmillan, 1987). A good overview of his life, also pointing to some of his serious character flaws.

Chapter 34

Sigmund Freud Vienna IX. Berggasse 19, Photographs and Epilogue by Edmund Engelman. I researched the later fate of Freud's apartment from the book's introductory essay, "Introduction and Legend," by Inge-Scholz-Strasser. The introduction and legends essay was translated by Lonnie R. Johnson. Vienna: Verlag Christian Brandstätter.

Chapter 35

Freud's Women, by Appignanesi and Forrester (see p. 431) for background on Deutsch.

Helene Deutsch: A Psychoanalyst's Life, by Paul Roazen (Garden City, NY: Anchor Press/Doubleday, 1985). My chief secondary source for information about Molly Putnam's relationship with Helene. Helene's letters to Felix on the farm experience are quoted in the book.

Psychoanalysis of the Sexual Functions of Women, by Helene Deutsch, edited by Paul Roazen (London: Karnac Books, 1991). Several important facets of Deutsch's theories on female sexuality emerge in this book.

JJP Children's Center Second Annual Report.

Chapter 36

A Psychiatrist's World: The Selected Papers of Karl Menninger, edited and with an introduction by Bernard H. Hall, M.D. (New York: Viking, 1959).

"A New Intellectual Framework for Psychiatry," by Eric R. Kandel in *The American Journal of Psychiatry*, 155: 457–469 (April 1998).

"Biology and the Future of Psychoanalysis: A New Intellectual Framework for Psychiatry Revisited," by Eric R. Kandel in *The American Journal of Psychiatry*, 156: 505–524 (April 1999).

Acknowledgments

—

I received inestimable help and encouragement from many quarters during the years of writing this book.

My agents, Todd Shuster and Lane Zachary both contributed tremendously to the long process of giving the book its structure and narrative trajectory. I'm thankful to Lawrence Osborne for introducing me to them, as well as for his support of the project.

Judith Feher-Gurewich graced the book with her infectious ebullience from the outset and gave me important insights on the European/American psychoanalytic divide, especially in relation to Lacan.

Rosemary Ahern was the ideal editor, bringing a patient, astute, critical eye to the manuscript in its various phases of composition—while always communicating a heartening confidence about the ultimate work that would emerge.

Judy Cohen copyedited the book with admirable thoroughness.

I owe a special debt of gratitude to Wayne Koestenbaum, who saw portions of the manuscript at an early stage and offered encouragement, along with penetrating comments on the approach I was taking to the genesis of Freud's theories.

Sanford Gifford, director of the library at the Boston Psychoanalytic Society and Institute gave generously of his time in conversation and email exchanges, pointing me to key resources in understanding the evolution of the Boston School of Psychotherapy, as well as shedding light on the latter-day history of the James Jackson Putnam Children's Center. Jack Eckert, reference librarian Rare Books and Special Collections at the Francis A. Countway Library of Medicine assisted me numerous times in gaining access to the relevant James Jackson Putnam papers in Harvard's collection, and in understanding their larger archival context. Richard Wolfe, former rare books librarian at the Francis A. Countway Library of Medicine, spoke with me about the mechanical instruments used in Putnam's pre-Freudian therapeutic approach, in addition to offering fruitful suggestions about tracking down further primary sources. Historian Nathan Hale gave helpful answers to questions I submitted about Putnam, Blow, and the subsequent fortunes of psychoanalysis in America.

Two gifted young psychologists, Nina Urban and Jada Fink, gave me important perspective on the complex, hybrid field of psychotherapy today. I also benefited from conversations with my sister, Elisabeth Prochnik, who enabled me to find my bearings in the contemporary field of psychopharmaceuticals. Natalie De Souza eloquently translated several unpublished letters by Putnam to Molly from German to English. She also did the great service of putting me in touch with Jonathan Polan, who kindly spoke with me at length about the work of Eric R. Kandel, offering a number of valuable insights. Richard Howard distilled many ideas about the lingering pleasures and discoveries readers of Freud can anticipate. I'm beholden to Fred Kaufman for my approach to the subject of Freud's colitis. Jess Taylor fluently assessed for me the place of fantasy in psychoanalytic theory.

I benefited from John Blow's thoughtfulness in putting me in contact with Susan Blow's great-nephew Julien LeBourgeois, who very generously provided me with copies of all of Blow's papers in his family collection. Tom Pearson, reference librarian at the St. Louis Public Library, gave me help both with respect to the St. Louis Public Library's archives of Blow family material and in locating other repositories of Blow's papers around the country. The Filson Historical Society in Louisville, KY gave me copies of Blow's fascinating kindergarten plans. I also profited from reading copies of Blow's correspondence archived in the Bentley Historical Society in Ann Arbor. Ron Bolte, president of the Carondelet Historical Society, provided me with the portraits of Susan Blow used in the book.

Daniel Mendelsohn offered unparalleled guidance on what to see to understand the mind, body, and spirit of Vienna. In Vienna, Christian Witt-Dörring and Michael Huey gave me a further enlightening introduction to the history and temperament of the city. At the Freud Museum in Vienna, director Ingrid Scholz-Strasser gave liberally of her time in explaining the growth of the museum and the larger story of Freud and his family in a historical Viennese context. Lydia Marinelli offered provocative thoughts on Freud's methods of scholarship. Christian Huber hunted down numerous sources for me and gave me assistance in using the museum library.

At the Freud Museum in London, both Michael Molnar and Keith Davies kindly assisted my exploration of the porcupine Putnam gave Freud.

Noga Tarnopolsky shared her thoughtful insights on many ideas I wrote about, and brought me to the scene of the book's final passage.

Conversations with Adam Cvijanovic, Jonathan Nossiter, Alexandra deSousa, Michael Greenberg. Elizabeth Berger, Arnon Grunberg, Inigo Thomas, Fernanda Eberstadt, Alfonse Borysewicz, Judy Grayson, Sara Livermore, Anne Lafond, Scott Moyers, Katherine Barrett, Benjamin Swett, Mart Greenfield, and Sima Borkovski all found their way into this book.

Barbara and Brian Mead gave me graceful sustenance in many forms throughout the book's composition. Ethan Prochnik, along with James Jodha-Prochnik and Samoa Jodha were sources of great support and helpful humor.

My parents, Marian and Martin Prochnik, in both a literal and theoretical sense gave me this story to tell. They have each in their ways shown me glimpses of the best of the worlds Putnam and Freud inhabited—and have done so with an abundance of self-effacing parental love at which I am constantly amazed and for which I am always thankful.

My older children, Yona, Tzvi, and Zach Prochnik always offer acute and sensitive responses to any speculations about psychology I indulge in. Throughout the time I was writing this book, they were a source of wit, pluck, and delight; nearing the book's completion, Rafael Prochnik added his own inimitable verve to theirs.

My wife, Rebecca Mead, helped me shape the book from the moment of its conception until it reached its final form. She tirelessly offered editorial suggestions for almost every page of the book, and my gratitude cannot convey how much I benefited from her lucid and incisive criticism. Her love and lovely spirit of good cheer sustained me through the vicissitudes of writing, and all else.

All errors in this book are entirely my own responsibility.

INDEX